D0163534

WITHDRAWN

Children
in Sport

GV
709.2
.C47
1988

Children in Sport

Third Edition

Frank L. Smoll, PhD
University of Washington

Richard A. Magill, PhD
Louisiana State University

Michael J. Ash, PhD
Texas A & M University

1744O672
MNGA

Human Kinetics Books
Champaign, Illinois

Library of Congress Cataloging-in-Publication Data

Children in sport / [edited by] Frank L. Smoll, Richard A. Magill,
   Michael J. Ash. — 3rd ed.
      p. cm.
   ISBN 0-87322-183-4
   1. Sports for children.   I. Smoll, Frank L.   II. Magill, Richard
A.   III. Ash, Michael J.
GV709.2.C47   1988
796'.01'922—dc19   88-1877
                                                                       CIP

Developmental Editor: Linda Anne Bump, PhD
Copy Editor: John Wentworth
Assistant Editor: Christine Drews
Production Director: Ernie Noa
Projects Coordinator: Lezli Harris
Text Design: Keith Blomberg
Typesetter: Sandra Meier
Text Layout: Denise Peters
Interior Art: Gretchen Walters
Cover Design: Hunter Graphics
Printed by: Braun-Brumfield

ISBN: 0-87322-183-4

Copyright © 1988 by Frank L. Smoll, Richard A. Magill, and Michael J. Ash
Copyright © 1982, 1978 by Richard A. Magill, Michael J. Ash, and
Frank L. Smoll

All rights reserved. Except for use in a review, the reproduction or utilization of this work in any form or by any electronic, mechanical, or other
means, now known or hereafter invented, including xerography, photo-
copying and recording, and in any information retrieval system, is forbidden
without the written permission of the publisher.

Printed in the United States of America

10 9 8 7 6 5 4 3 2 1

Human Kinetics Books
A Division of Human Kinetics Publishers, Inc.
Box 5076
Champaign, IL 61820

1-800-DIAL-HKP
1-800-334-3665 (In Illinois)

Contents

Preface to the Third Edition

Compiling an edited volume is a rather risky venture. A considerable amount of time is devoted to initial planning efforts, involving a multitude of decisions about what to include, how to organize, how to balance new and old, and so on. After developing a "wish list" table of contents we then hope that scholars who are invited to contribute are willing to do so. For this third edition we feel particularly fortunate in that all but one of the authors originally contacted chose to participate. Ultimately, the greatest gamble comes in presenting the completed volume to our colleagues and their students. They are, in fact, the ones who determine the success of the project. Based on response, it is gratifying to note that previous editions were well-received. Perhaps it suffices to say that the risk seemed well-taken. In any event, we are pleased and excited to present a third edition.

This volume represents a milestone for our publisher. From its energetic inception in founder Rainer Martens' basement Human Kinetics Publishers has become a thriving enterprise consisting of 70 staff members housed in a 50,000-square-foot building with the most up-to-date publishing technology and equipment. *Children in Sport* is the first Human Kinetics volume to go into a third edition.

With respect to the area of youth sport, this third edition reflects a continuing interest on the part of researchers and educators alike. The scientific study of children's athletics has generated articles that appear not only in sport science journals, but with increasing frequency in publications of traditional disciplines, such as physiology, sociology, and psychology. Moreover, the growing body of knowledge is evidenced by a proliferation of youth sport conferences and symposia. Most notably, the 1984 Olympic Scientific Congress included sport for children and youth as a major theme.

In addition to research activity, increased knowledge and understanding as well as the availability of educational resource materials has resulted in a corresponding increase in the number of college and university courses focusing on children's athletics. Concern for teaching in this area was shown at a workshop on the teaching of sport psychology. This 1-day affair was held prior to the 1985 conference of the North American Society for the Psychology of Sport and Physical Activity. The program included a presentation that examined the content of a youth sport course and various approaches utilized in its conduct.

As with the previous editions, our primary objective here is to have our collection serve as a "strong base from which much needed research will emanate." Given that chapters from the first two editions have been frequently cited in youth sport articles, it appears that these works have contributed to expanding empirical investigation. Additionally, this volume is intended to serve as a textbook for upper level undergraduate or graduate youth sport courses. To make our book more responsive to classroom needs, input was solicited from instructors who used the second edition as a text. Their evaluations and suggestions were taken into account in making the present volume interesting and enjoyable for students and other readers as well.

Profile of the Third Edition

Our third edition has been expanded to 22 chapters. Of the 20 chapters in the second edition, 14 have been retained. Six chapters were deleted not because they lacked quality, but because of considerations relative to the amount of content that can be reasonably covered in a standard academic course. Our selections were guided, in part, by our goal of developing a pedagogically sound package—that is, coverage that is comprehensive and cohesive, yet economic of space. All but 1 of the 14 chapters from the second edition have been significantly reworked and updated by the authors. With the exception of Jack W. Berryman's social-historical analysis of youth sport in the United States, none of the present chapters is an exact duplicate of an earlier effort. This is not to say that the chapters are completely changed. Although the authors have integrated into their texts significant theory and research published after our second edition, the basic format of their chapters and their discussions of works of enduring importance remain unaltered. Eight entirely new chapters have been added, six of which were written specifically for this volume. Finally, this edition has been reorganized somewhat and now includes a separate section focusing on the future of youth sport.

Section 1 has undergone extensive revision. Sport historian Jack W. Berryman's excellent analysis of the rise of highly organized sports for boys has been supplemented by two chapters examining the status of youth sport programs and research in North America. Rainer Martens' report on youth sport in the United States and Terry A. Valeriote's and Lori Hansen's paper on youth sport in Canada were previously published in the 1984 Olympic Scientific Congress Proceedings (M.R. Weiss & D. Gould [Eds.]. [1986]. *Sport for children and youths*. Champaign, IL: Human Kinetics). Because of the growing number of young women becoming involved in sport we felt that a special chapter on gender-related issues was merited. The chapter by Mary E. Duquin focuses on the problematic position of females in both gender-segregated and gender-integrated youth sport programs.

New chapters have been added to Sections 2 and 3. Section 2, Readiness for Participation, has been enhanced by a contribution from Michael W. Passer. Utilizing a psychosocial orientation, the chapter examines the controversial question of when children should begin competing in youth sports. The anatomical and physiological concerns discussed in Section 3 have been complemented by Bill Kozar's and Russell H. Lord's survey of overuse injuries in young athletes and guidelines for protecting their physical well-being.

With respect to psychological issues, Section 4 now includes a chapter on the impact of games having a cooperative rather than competitive structure. Terry D. Orlick and Anne Pitman-Davidson discuss the effects of participation in cooperative games on children's psychosocial development. Also, given the rapid increase in research on why children become involved in sport and why they drop out, a new chapter is timely. Daniel Gould and Linda Petlichkoff address these issues from both theoretical and applied perspectives.

The three chapters of Section 5, Social Processes, were retained from the second edition and have been substantially modified and updated by their authors. The new section added to the volume, Section 6, Future Directions, contains two chapters. In the first of these, Daniel Gould addresses the status, direction, and challenge in youth sport research. The final chapter is an updated version of a chapter from the second edition, in which Vern Seefeldt examines the changing image of youth sport and its future needs.

Acknowledgments

For whatever virtues are found in this volume, many people share the credit. First and foremost, the authors have diligently synthesized information in their respective areas of expertise. Our evaluation, admittedly biased, finds high-quality scholarly merit in the fruits of their efforts. We are greatly indebted to them.

We also wish to thank the instructors of youth sport courses who responded to our request for comments and suggestions. Their input provided guidance in planning this book. Finally, we wish to acknowledge the inestimable effect of the Human Kinetics staff on the present volume. In particular, the enthusiasm and creative counsel provided by developmental editor Linda Anne Bump was invaluable. We also appreciate the staff contributions to the design and copyediting of the book.

Frank L. Smoll

Richard A. Magill

Michael J. Ash

Contributors

The Editors

Frank L. Smoll, Department of Psychology, University of Washington, Seattle

Richard A. Magill, Departments of Physical Education and Psychology, Louisiana State University, Baton Rouge

Michael J. Ash, Department of Educational Psychology, Texas A & M University, College Station

The Authors

Donald A. Bailey, College of Physical Education, University of Saskatchewan, Saskatoon

Jack W. Berryman, Department of Medical History and Ethics, University of Washington, Seattle

Barbara A. Brown, Faculty of Physical Education, University of Western Ontario, London, Ontario

Mary E. Duquin, Department of Health, Physical, and Recreation Education, University of Pittsburgh

Ana M. Estrada, Department of Psychology, University of Utah, Salt Lake City

Karen E. French, Department of Physical Education, University of South Carolina, Columbia

Jere D. Gallagher, Department of Health, Physical, and Recreation Education, University of Pittsburgh

Donna M. Gelfand, Department of Psychology, University of Utah, Salt Lake City

Daniel Gould, Department of Kinesiology, University of Illinois, Urbana-Champaign

Susan L. Greendorfer, Department of Kinesiology, University of Illinois, Urbana-Champaign

Lori Hansen, Coaching Association of Canada, Ottawa, Ontario

Donald P. Hartmann, Department of Psychology, University of Utah, Salt Lake City

Bill Kozar, Department of Health, Physical Education, and Recreation, Texas Tech University, Lubbock

John H. Lewko, Centre for Child and Development Studies, Laurentian University, Sudbury, Ontario

Russell H. Lord, Department of Education, Eastern Montana College, Billings

Robert M. Malina, Department of Anthropology, University of Texas, Austin

Rainer Martens, Human Kinetics Publishers, Champaign, Illinois

Alan D. Martin, Sport and Exercise Sciences Research Institute, Max Bell Centre, University of Manitoba, Winnipeg

Barry D. McPherson, Office of Graduate Studies and Research, Wilfrid Laurier University, Waterloo, Ontario

Terry D. Orlick, Department of Kinanthropology, University of Ottawa, Ontario

Michael W. Passer, Department of Psychology, University of Washington, Seattle

Linda Petlichkoff, Department of Health, Physical Education, and Recreation, Boise State University

Anne Pitman-Davidson, Department of Kinanthropology, University of Ottawa, Ontario

Tara Kost Scanlan, Department of Kinesiology, University of California, Los Angeles

Vern Seefeldt, Youth Sports Institute, Michigan State University, East Lansing

Michael D. Smith, Departments of Physical Education and Sociology, York University, North York, Ontario

Ronald E. Smith, Department of Psychology, University of Washington, Seattle

Jerry R. Thomas, Department of Health and Physical Education, Arizona State University, Tempe

Katherine T. Thomas, Department of Health and Physical Education, Arizona State University, Tempe

Terry A. Valeriote, Coaching Association of Canada, Ottawa, Ontario

SECTION 1

Historical Perspective and Current Status

Sport has been an increasingly integral part of American culture and is regarded as a major social institution. Thus it is not surprising that more and more children participate in organized athletics each year. This is true not only for boys; the development of sport programs for girls has recently risen significantly. Moreover, the youth sport movement has demanded the involvement of increasing numbers of adults—coaches, league administrators, officials, and parents.

Growth in the scope of youth sports and in the role that they play in the lives of children is undeniable. But this expansion has generated persisting and, at times, bitter debate. Thoughtful persons have raised questions about the desirability of organized sports for children. Answers to such queries are not often simple. Just as medical doctors must have thorough histories of their patients, so must we understand the evolution of children's athletics. By analogy, this knowledge assists us in dealing effectively with both the maladies and the well-being of contemporary youth sport and in contributing to a healthy and happy future.

The opening chapter by Jack W. Berryman provides a historical overview of the growth of highly organized sport programs for young boys.

In tracing the rise of boys' sports, Berryman focuses on two separate but interrelated developments in the social and cultural milieu of U.S. society during the early 1900s. The first was the inclusion of sport in the school curriculum, which brought organized athletics closer to the children of the nation than ever before and established the rationale for their acceptance and promotion. The second factor influencing the growth of boys' sports was the recognition that childhood is an important stage in the development of an adult and that measures must be taken to ensure a happy and profitable period of growing up. As a result, an entirely new branch of social welfare, called boys' work groups, began using sports to provide wholesome leisure for young boys and to keep them out of trouble. Of particular interest are the alterations of philosophies and attitudes of professional educators and the associated shifts in sponsorship of children's athletics to community-based organizations.

In the following two chapters, the status of youth sport programs and research in the United States is examined by Rainer Martens, and youth sport in Canada is described by Terry A. Valeriote and Lori Hansen. The reports illustrate unique characteristics of youth sport within the two countries and add insight to common problems and concerns. Six major topical areas are covered: (a) the scope of youth sport participation, including sport-specific data relating to age levels and gender differences; (b) the organization of youth sport at local and national levels; (c) sources of funding; (d) the education of coaches; (e) the status of youth sport research, including major questions being studied and issues requiring future attention; and (f) major strengths and areas needing improvement.

In the final chapter of this section, Mary E. Duquin posits that the rise of female participation necessitates a renewed examination of traditional youth sport programs. Three issues having special impact on females are analyzed, showing that (a) the continued segregationist practices in sport have negative consequences for both girls and boys, (b) female growth and development are negatively affected by the sado-ascetic structures and practices of traditional sport, and (c) the socio-symbolic system of meanings in sport severely limits all children's ability to create the symbols and play structures that allow them "to sport" creatively. Based on these analyses, Duquin concludes that the necessary transformation of youth sport requires a radical restructuring of cultural thought with old fictions being laid to rest. Recommendations are presented for creating new realities and for seeking alternate paths of sport participation—paths that will allow all children to be and become caring and competent in a healthy environment.

CHAPTER 1

The Rise of Highly Organized Sports for Preadolescent Boys[1]

Jack W. Berryman

The rise of highly organized competitive sport programs[2] for boys below the age of 12 was a phenomenon of the first half of the 20th century and was indicative of the fact that sport had finally penetrated all levels of the American population. To be sure, young children played games and enjoyed a variety of sports throughout America's history, but regulated and administered sport programs by interested individuals and organizations solely for the use of small boys did not begin until after 1900. In fact, the first instances of sport teams, leagues, championships, and other examples of highly organized children's sports outside of the schools were not evident until the 1920s and early 1930s. Even then, the programs were only local affairs, usually established by communities who wanted to provide something different and special for their children. Little did they know that in another 10 to 15 years nationally organized and administered sports for children would be spreading throughout the country to eventually become one of the most pervasive forces in the lives of many American children.

Two separate but interrelated developments in the social and cultural milieu of American society during the early 20th century provided

---

[1]This is a revised and condensed version of a paper entitled "From the Cradle to the Playing Field: America's Emphasis on Highly Organized Competitive Sports for Preadolescent Boys" by J.W. Berryman, 1975, *Journal of Sport History*, **2**, 112-131. The reader is directed to the original publication for a more detailed account of the trends and factors under discussion as well as for supporting documentation. From "The Rise of Highly Organized Sports for Preadolescent Boys" by J.W. Berryman. In *Children in Sport* (2nd ed., pp. 2-15) by R.A. Magill, M.J. Ash, & F.L. Smoll (Eds.), 1982, Champaign, IL: Human Kinetics. Copyright 1982 by Richard A. Magill, Michael J. Ash, and Frank L. Smoll. Reprinted by permission.

[2]Highly organized competitive sports have been defined as: "any athletic activity which involves a considerable amount of the leisure time of the youngster in formalized practice, which encourages extensive attendance by adult spectators, which is limited to the outstanding players, and which involves the selection of winners on a state, regional, or national basis" ("Are Highly Competitive Sports," 1952, p. 423).

the most direct influence upon the rise and growth of boys' competitive sport programs. The first, of course, was the rise of sport itself in all parts of the country and the subsequent desire to participate and spectate by large numbers of the population. More specifically, though, the inclusion of sport in the school curriculum brought organized sport closer to the youth of the nation than ever before. Along with school sports came the rationale for their acceptance and promotion. This was most often provided by professional physical educators, recreation people, playground directors, and athletic coaches who were responsible for the majority of competitive sport situations during the first 3 decades of the 20th century.[3] But, when philosophies changed within this group during the 1930s, they dropped any sponsorship of children's sport they had previously provided and refused to condone high level competition for preadolescents. This change of outlook by professionally trained educators who were deeply involved with the early stages of sport competition for children was the first important development in conjunction with the overall rise of sport. Although it seemed to be antagonistic to the growth and development of children's sport, the alteration of philosophy would eventually lead to bigger, better, and more highly organized programs.

The second development influencing the growth of boys' competitive sport programs was that Americans began to realize the need and importance of protecting and providing varied opportunities for children. Childhood became recognized as an important stage in the development of an adult, and measures were taken by concerned individuals and organizations to ensure a happy and profitable period of growing up. By means of a variety of laws and policies enacted by national, state, and community organizations, children were provided with an abundance of free time, parents took a different view of their offspring, and national programs were organized to protect the child's welfare. An entirely new branch of social welfare, called boys' work, originated in the last decade of the 19th century.[4] Boys' work groups, originally composed of all voluntary members, were organized specifically to provide wholesome leisure-time pursuits for young boys and keep them out of trouble. They began using sports and other recreational activities very early in their work and realized the importance

---

[3]By the close of the 1920s, sport had become quite popular in the United States. However, with few exceptions, organized sport competition was still for the middle-aged adult population, college students, and high school students in the upper grades. Organized competitive sport had not yet developed for the elementary school aged population.

[4]One person directly associated with the movement defined boys' work as "social engineering in the field of boyhood motivation . . . supervised leisure-time education, the purpose of which is social adjustment and creative living" (Stone, 1931, p. 28).

of reaching the youthful minds and bodies of preadolescent boys. Leaders of the movement advocated the usefulness of sport for many of the same reasons that the schools turned to sport. But when the schools refused to sponsor competitive sports for the young boys, the task was left to the voluntary boys' work groups. Therefore, the linking of the overall popularity of sports and its believed values, many of which were established by school personnel in the early 20th century as well as the sport sponsorship of boys' work agencies, along with their own modifications and gradual growth, did more to promote boys' sport competition than any other factor and led directly to America's emphasis on highly organized competitive sports for preadolescent boys.

Before the 1930s, the responsibility for providing recreational activities and organized sports for small children was shared by the schools, playgrounds, and a few nationally organized youth membership agencies such as the YMCA, Boy Scouts, and Boys' Clubs. But as specific alterations of goals and purposes occurred within the physical education and recreation profession, the provision of sport competition for preadolescent boys became more and more a primary function of national voluntary boys' work agencies. Beginning in the 1930s, physical educators and professional recreation leaders denounced the overt emphasis placed on winning, the physical and emotional strain, and the attempt to organize competition into leagues for championship play which were becoming common in many children's sport programs. They also disagreed with providing competition for only the best athletes instead of allowing all children to participate. As a result, professionally trained leaders in sports and recreation retracted their support and relinquished their hold on organized competition for young children.

By allowing highly organized children's sport to leave the educational context, professional educators presented a golden opportunity to the many voluntary youth-related groups in America. These groups had no educationally imposed restrictions on their work for children and many times had the funds and support from parents and communities to provide elaborate and well-organized sport programs. The volunteer workers and members of these groups often had no educational training in child development or child psychology and operated with little or no restraints in providing the best for the children. Consequently, by giving up their support of youth sports, the school personnel could no longer enforce their rules and regulations for competition. Accordingly, the outside agencies capitalized on the child's free time from school during the evenings, weekends, and summer months, and provided numerous opportunities for competition. With very few limitations and a single goal of serving children and making them happy, boys' work groups saw no end to the sport situations they could provide.

The withdrawal of sponsorship came at a time when the values inherent to sport and its benefits to both children and society were becoming firmly established in the beliefs of most Americans. Parents, child welfare workers, and organizations established to serve youth were not easily convinced of what they believed were questionable detriments of sport competition for children. Therefore, child-related organizations, and specifically boys' work groups, stepped in to fill the void created by professional educators. The schools continued to be paramount in their sponsorship of interscholastic athletics for youth beyond the age of 12, but sport competition for preadolescent boys became the responsibility of child-oriented organizations outside of the educational framework. Their main objective was to provide wholesome character-building activities to occupy the leisure time of children in order to better enable them to make the transition from childhood to adulthood. Sport, they believed, was the one activity that was capable of providing all of the necessary conditions for this successful growth and development. Thus, it was during the 1930s, under the sponsorship of boys' work organizations outside of the educational context, that highly organized sport competition for preadolescent boys began its ascendance to present-day heights.

Professional Educators
Discourage Highly Competitive Sports

The policy statements of the professional physical education and recreation groups as well as other leading educators from the 1930s to the 1960s illustrated their discouragement of highly competitive sports for children. A steady stream of proposals, guidelines, speeches, manuals, and periodical articles containing warnings against too much competition for elementary school children flowed from the ranks of professional educators. The statements reinforced their refusal to condone and administer such programs and were released at various times during the 1930s, 1940s, 1950s, and 1960s, when children's sport in association with boys' work groups was making rapid progress.

The first formal statements by professional physical education and recreation people declaring their concern about organized competitive sports for elementary school children came during the early 1930s. The sport programs that were already in the schools came under attack because they were not in line with educational objectives and only a few of the highly skilled students were able to compete. Later in the decade, a determined effort was made to establish official policies to eliminate all interscholastic competition for elementary age children both within and outside of the school ("Mid-West District News," 1937). The American Association for Health, Physical Education and Recreation (AAHPER) was quick in approving a resolution against highly organized sports for children at their 1938 convention in Atlanta, Georgia. Their statement, like many of the ones to follow, was based on the strenuous nature of competitive sports.

> Inasmuch as pupils below tenth grade are in the midst of the period of rapid growth, with the consequent bodily weaknesses and maladjustments, partial ossification of bones, mental and emotional stresses, physiological adjustments, and the like, be it therefore resolved that the leaders in the field of physical and health education should do all in their power to discourage interscholastic competition at this age level, because of its strenuous nature. ("Two Important Resolutions," 1938, pp. 488-489)

Before the end of the decade, the Society of State Directors of Physical and Health Educators also prepared a formal statement on the subject. Their policy statement was directed to school board members and school administrators and suggested that interscholastic athletics had no place in elementary schools. They specifically discouraged postseason games and championships, extensive travel, and "all star" teams, all of which were becoming attractive aspects of organized sport programs outside of the school (Moss & Orion, 1939).

During the 1940s, educational psychologists spoke out against the emphasis placed on competition for rewards (Duncan, 1951; Skinner, 1945) and AAHPER adopted another resolution condemning interscholastic competition for the first 8 grades ("Recommendations," 1947).[5] In 1947, a Joint Statement of Policy on Interscholastic Athletics by the National Federation of High School Athletic Associations and AAHPER recommended that the competitive needs of elementary-age children be met with a balanced intramural program ("Cardinal Athletic Principles," 1947).[6] Finally, in 1949, AAHPER and its Society of State Directors of Health, Physical Education and Recreation joined with representatives from the Department of Elementary School Principals, National Education Association, and the National Council of State Consultants in Elementary School Principals to form the Joint Committee on Athletic Competition for Children of Elementary and Junior High School Age. Their recommendations were more extensive than any of the previous statements but stayed with the same overall policy of no highly organized competitive programs (AAHPER, 1952).[7] They made an attempt to influence community agencies as well as school personnel but failed to realize that the very aspects of

---

[5]For a survey of common activities in elementary schools during this time see Schmidt (1944, p. 130).

[6]Also see Lowman (1947, p. 635). A large percentage of orthopedists surveyed believed interscholastic competition should be discouraged for young boys because of its strenuous nature. They were particularly critical of swimming, tackle football, wrestling, and ice hockey.

[7]They believed elementary schools should only provide intramural playdays, sportsdays, and informal games.

competitive sport they were condemning were the interesting and unique features which were attracting the young, enthusiastic, and energetic boys. Leagues, championships, tournaments, travel, spectators, and commercial sponsors were viewed by parents, community leaders, and the boys' work agencies as examples of doing a great service for the children. In addition, the young boys wanted to play on a level as close to the "big leagues" as possible and enjoyed the new form of attention provided by sport competition.

Evidence that the formal resolutions and professional policies which were passed during the 1930s and 1940s had some impact on school-sponsored programs became noticeable by the 1950s. Specifically, surveys reflected the alteration of sponsorship for children's sport programs from the schools to independent boys' work agencies. A National Recreation Association survey in 1950 of 304 departments throughout the United States indicated only 36 approved of high level competition and championship play ("Competitive Athletics," 1951). The President's Committee on Interschool Competition in the Elementary School, representing AAHPER, found that 60% of the schools surveyed in 1950 had no competition for elementary-age children. Of the 40% that did sponsor some competitive sports, none had competition below the fourth grade level (Wayman, Hager, Hartwig, Houston, LaSalle, & McNeely, 1950). The shift of support for children's programs was finally recognized and alluded to in a professional recreation journal in 1952, whereby the author successfully captured the nature of the contemporary scene.

> Although elementary schools continue to feel pressure to adopt the characteristics of the high school and college interscholastic sports program, most of the recent developments have taken place outside of the school system.
>
> . . . As a result, the recent development of 'highly organized competitive athletics' for the elementary school age child has been sponsored largely by private independent groups not connected with the schools or the public recreation department. ("Are highly competitive sports," 1952, pp. 422-426)

Another survey (Scott, 1953) indicated the attitudes of adults toward athletic competition for young children. The results illustrated one of the major reasons why highly organized programs were growing rapidly outside of the educational realm. From a group of over 1,000 respondents from seven states, which included parents, teachers, and administrators, the majority of all three groups were in favor of intensive competition. The parents were the most favorable, and within this group, the fathers were overwhelmingly supportive.[8] With this type

---

[8]Similar results were found (Holman, 1951) in a survey of parents having boys in Little League baseball in Fresno, California, in 1951. One hundred percent of the parents regarded the program as beneficial to their sons and repudiated the claims that competition was harmful physically, psychologically, or socially.

of support from parents and even some school personnel, it was evident that professional physical education and recreation groups were competing against unfavorable odds.[9]

Boys' Work Groups Assume Leadership

While organized sport competition at the elementary school level failed to gain support and therefore faltered after its seemingly robust beginning during the first decades of the 20th century, youth sport programs outside of the school grew rapidly in the number of total participants and in the variety of sports offered. With few exceptions, the stimuli behind these programs which arose all over the United States were parents and other interested adults associated with boys' work. Organizations identifying with the boys' work movement selected the promotion, sponsorship, and organization of competitive sports as one of the best things they could do for children. To make children happy and to give them what they wanted became one of their major objectives. They progressed by paying little or no attention to the warnings from professional educators.

The boys' work movement had its beginnings in the last decade of the 19th century and resulted from efforts of concerned adults to improve the total environment for children. Citizens of the larger cities became greatly concerned with the effects of industrialization, urbanization, and immigration and, as a result of the general child study movement, were also becoming educated to realize the basic needs of children. Welfare and reform programs were therefore instituted to improve or alleviate such social problems as child labor, public health and sanitation, lack of wholesome play facilities, crime and delinquency, orphan and dependent children, and crowded housing. But the main factors which led adults to form programs and organizations to aid the plight of the child were the increased amount of leisure and delinquency and a growing population of underprivileged and neglected children.[10] Leaders of the boys' work movement during the late 19th century explored the ideas of organizing boys into clubs and groups to better carry on training programs. These early programs were designed to occupy leisure time in order to keep the boys out of trouble, keep them off the streets, and evangelize them. Most of them operated under the auspices of a religious education group or the social welfare

---

[9]It should be noted that parents were very concerned that their sons excelled and held their own among the peer group. Sport competition offered a unique setting where young boys could be compared and evaluated with reference to others of the same age.

[10]Directly related to these developments were the play movement and the child welfare movement. The combination of objectives included in each of the two distinct aspects of the overall childhood reform movement assisted the development of organized sports and additional play facilities for young children.

program of agencies.[11] But by the beginning of the 20th century, the boys' work movement developed and achieved separate status from other welfare movements. This development represented the fact that at least a portion of American society had seen the need and value of special agencies to act as conservators and curators of child life.[12]

The use and encouragement of play, games, sports, and general recreational activities began quite early in the boys' work programs. As the emphasis moved from soul saving to one of boy guidance and concern for the "whole person" during the 1920s, organized sports became more and more popular as an acceptable method of filling leisure-time hours.[13] New organizations for boys came into existence as separate enterprises. They were recreational rather than evangelical in nature, primarily because of the character-building values thought to be inherent to play, games, and sport. The concepts of clean fun as a character builder and of play as creative education rather than just something to keep boys out of trouble led to the formation of more playgrounds, gymnasiums, swimming pools, and outdoor athletic fields. Accordingly, civic groups, fraternal orders, and businesses joined the ranks of established boys' work organizations which already included religious bodies, philanthropic groups, national and state governments, and general child welfare groups in sponsoring and promoting sporting activities for the younger set. The primary objective of the new sponsors was to use sport as a preventive measure for juvenile delinquency.[14]

---

[11]It was realized early in boys' work that sport-related clubs and teams served as a better medium for organization than the earlier attempts at trying to reach large masses of boys at one time.

[12]Basically, the boys' work groups aided the overall society by protecting children through their dependency period, inducting children into the culture, and supplementing the family by providing for special needs and by sponsoring specific services. They were committed to a specific social obligation toward children not yet accepted by the whole society. Consequently, boys' work agencies began to provide services in education, health, and recreation, all of which they believed could be improved by organized sport programs. See Mangold (1924) and Wickenden (1960).

[13]Sport competition was believed to enhance personality adjustment and creative living in society. In addition, since boys' workers wanted to aid the transition from childhood to adulthood, they sponsored sport programs which combined association on a peer basis with adult leadership. See DeGraff (1933, p. 2) and Stone (1932, p. 5).

[14]The belief that a boy busy with sports had little time to get into trouble influenced many organizations in local communities to begin sponsoring boys' competitive sports. Psychological and sociological knowledge of the time indicated that problems of delinquency originated in early childhood and not during the actual time of delinquent acts. Therefore, it was deemed important to extend the age range lower for a positive delinquency prevention program. Civic clubs such as Rotary, Lions, Kiwanis, and Jaycees, fraternal orders like the Elks and Moose, and businesses such as Winchester, Curtis Publishing, General Electric, Pratt and Whitney, and John Wanamaker, all turned to sport sponsorship in the interest of protecting young children from crime and providing them with wholesome alternatives for gang life in the streets. For more information see Engle (1919), North (1931), Reckless and Smith (1932), and Shanas (1942).

During the 1920s and 1930s, highly organized competitive sport programs for young boys began to be established outside the realm of the educational system by local groups representing the fundamental boys' work beliefs. As early as 1924 the Cincinnati Community Service started city baseball tournaments for boys under 13. Likewise, Milwaukee organized its "Stars of Yesterday" baseball leagues and began sponsoring a "Kid's Baseball School" in 1936. The Los Angeles *Times* conducted its Junior Pentathlon for the first time in 1928, the Southern California Tennis Association established its junior program 2 years later, and tackle football for boys under the age of 12 began in the Denver area in 1927 and in Philadelphia 3 years later. Two further developments which occurred in 1939, however, did more for the overall development of this new trend in sport than the others.

The first development was an article entitled *"Life* Goes to a Kid's Football Game" which appeared in *Life* magazine. It concerned the Denver Young American League and included color photographs and descriptions depicting the values of such an activity. Themes such as nationalism, courage, character, the need for similar programs in other communities, and the disgrace of "turning yellow" were discussed in the article. The second major development in 1939 was the introduction of Little League Baseball in Williamsport, Pennsylvania. Formed by Carl Stotz, a local businessman, the organization grew from a few local teams at its inception to more than 300 leagues in 11 states by 1949. Part of its success can also be linked to the publication of an article entitled "Small Boy's Dream Come True" in the *Saturday Evening Post* (Paxton, 1949). This article, like the *Life* article 10 years before, included beautiful colored photographs, proclaimed the values of such a program for the small boys, and emphasized the rewards reaped by communities that had already established Little League teams. The author was correct in observing that "the Little League's chief mission in life is to give a lot of pleasure to a lot of little boys. With its realistic simulation of big-league playing conditions, with its cheering crowds, it is a small boy's baseball dream come true." From this point on, the "little league" concept spread to almost every sport on the American scene.

Interest in providing sporting competition for young children began to spread to a variety of other youth-related agencies after the 1940s. As continued emphasis was placed on providing fun and amusement for young boys and as organizations found ulterior motives for promoting sport competition, the sponsorship of children's sports began to come from previously unexpected sources. Nationally known business firms, professional sport organizations, Olympic committees, and colleges initiated particular aspects of competitive sport sponsorship for young boys. Sponsorship came in the form of funds, facilities, manpower, advertisements, and equipment. These new sponsors joined previously established sponsors such as civic groups, churches, community councils, local merchants, and some of the older youth membership organizations. They saw a chance to assist the develop-

ment of young boys but at the same time realized that boys' sport programs could help them as well. This new sidelight to sponsorship, the
idea of a "two-way street" or what could be termed a form of "ludic
symbiosis" in this context, differed radically from the earlier voluntary group support and added the aspects of big business and more
pronounced competition to sport for young boys.

By the 1960s, highly organized sport competition for preadolescents
had grown to encompass millions of American boys. Little League Baseball, Pop Warner Football, and Biddy Basketball were joined on the
national level by similar developments in other sports such as Pee Wee
Hockey and Little Britches Rodeo.[15] Most of these national sporting
bodies had member teams and leagues throughout the United States
but the youthful participants in baseball, football, basketball, and other
sports did not necessarily have to belong to one of the national controlling bodies. When this occurred, local boys' sports organizations were
oftentimes just referred to as midget leagues, the lollypop set, boys'
leagues, youth leagues, junior leagues, small-fry leagues, or tiny tot
leagues. The important factor, however, was that regardless of title,
sponsor, or organizational structure, young boys below the age of 12
were being introduced to highly organized competitive sports in just
about every community in the United States.

As indicated, radical changes occurred in the sponsorship of boys'
sports programs. By the 1960s, the most prominent sponsors could
be classified in six different categories: (a) private national sport bodies
such as Little League Baseball; (b) youth serving organizations composed of adult members such as the Jaycees; (c) youth membership
organizations composed of child membership like the YMCA; (d) youth
sport development organizations such as Junior Golf; (e) quasi-
commercial organizations like Ford's Punt, Pass and Kick; and, (f) an
individual or community like Jim's Small Fry's or Riverdale Junior
Baseball. An analysis of each of their stated objectives revealed the
same idea of sport's inherent values which had existed since the turn
of the century. Each sponsor claimed to support children's sport for
one or more of the following reasons: physical fitness, citizenship,
character, sportsmanship, leadership, fair play, good health, democratic living, and teamwork. It also was evident that a few of the sponsors took advantage of the "two-way street" concept. Boys' sports were
used as training grounds for future athletes, to prevent juvenile delinquency, as proselytizing agents, to attract new members, as methods
of advertisement, as means of identification and glory, and as methods
for direct financial gain. Parents, too, began to get more deeply involved
with the sports of their children than ever before. Eager mothers and
fathers devoted more time to sports and actually began to take part

---

[15]Some of the other popular children's sports were Midget Lacrosse, Junior Ski Jumping, Junior Nordic Skiing, National Junior Tennis League, Junior National Standard Racing, and the Junior Special Olympics for retarded children.

in the sports themselves. Many reasons could be given to explain this increased interest of parents, but it is believed that the increasing awareness of the athlete as a viable professional endeavor, overly competitive mothers and fathers, and the desire of "sure victory" for their children were the three major causes. Earlier in the history of children's sports, parents were content to be only spectators, but the decades of the 1950s and 1960s became an era of parental entrance into competition with their child. Instances of parents constructing racers for the Soap Box Derby, fine tuning engines for youthful go-kart drivers, and engineering new gear ratios for bike racers appeared as boys' sports became more and more important to the entire family. This new emphasis placed on children's competitive sport by the family unit combined with the entrance of big business and other high pressure tactics after the early 1950s caused even the most avid sponsors to begin to take a serious look at what they had developed.

The literature after 1950 concerning highly organized competitive sports for young boys was indicative of a growing concern for the welfare of the young competitors.[16] Nationally circulated journals, magazines, and newspapers carried articles emphasizing the pros and cons of children's sport in an attempt to illustrate the current status of the ever-growing youth leagues and to present the most recent findings related to the subject. Similarly, those in favor of the highly competitive situations used the mass media to advertise the goodness and need for such programs, and even went so far as to suggest new organizations in previously unchildlike sports such as yachting, motor boating, and airplane flying. Likewise, those strongly opposed to highly organized sports attacked their obvious detriments via the printed word. The issue became increasingly visible as the debate continued, but even as late as 1970 the youth sport programs were showing no signs of decline. In fact, the decade of the 1970s has ushered in a new and eager generation of youthful competitors.

Summary and Conclusions

The rise of highly organized sport competition for preadolescent boys was an important phase of the total involvement of Americans with sport and has blossomed into a new national sporting trend. Lowering the age for entrance into competitive sport indicated the faith Americans had in it and reflected a desire to provide the young with something thought to be beneficial for their overall development. Besides illustrating the breadth and depth of the nation's involvement with sport, the guided entrance of children into sporting competition also

---

[16]It is interesting to note that the *Readers' Guide to Periodical Literature* did not include a topical heading for "Sports for Children" until Volume 22 (March 1959-February 1961), p. 1564.

influenced the overall growth of sport. Young children carried their interests and desires with them into adult life which were subsequently passed along to their own children. In addition, the joy, freeness, and innocence of the youthful competitors came to be seen as desirable characteristics of sport itself. These attributes were sought as highly desired traits by the adult population. The older portion of the population attached sport to the image of youth and consequently engaged in a variety of sports beyond the time when they normally would have ceased participation.

The provision of highly organized competitive sports for boys below the age of 12 and the accompanying introduction of more sporting opportunities and facilities for all young children was one of the most significant social and cultural events of recent times. It contributed an additional dimension to the age of childhood and marked the beginning of a new era in American sport. An analysis of the origins of this trend, however, is also important outside of its contributions to the realm of sport because the history of developments in childhood is central to the study of overall social change and human behavior. The growth of sport for young boys illustrated a change in parental authority as well as an alteration in general child-rearing practices. The fact that sporting teams were usually organized by age or weight groupings indicated the increased sensitivity to the various stages of childhood and became an important step in the growth of child welfare. Children's sport organizations led to changes in the American family structure and, in many instances, added a new aspect to the socialization of children. In addition, the sponsorship and use of sport by boys' work agencies contributed to the belief that Americans should organize the life and activities of their children. Finally, the degree to which children's sports became organized mirrored an often-proclaimed American characteristic of being overly regimented, businesslike, and competitive.

References

American Association for Health, Physical Education and Recreation and Committee on Athletic Competition for Children of Elementary and Junior High School Age. (1952). *Desirable athletic competition for children*. Washington, DC: Author.

Are highly competitive sports desirable for juniors? Conclusions from the committee on highly organized sports and athletics for boys twelve and under, National Recreation Congress. (1952). *Recreation*, **46**, 422-426.

Cardinal athletic principles. (1947). Washington, DC: American Association for Health, Physical Education and Recreation and the National Education Association.

Competitive athletics for boys under twelve—Survey. (1951). *Recreation*, **45**, 489-491.

DeGraff, H.O. (1933, March). Social factors in boys' work. *Association Boys' Work Journal*, p. 2.

Duncan, R.O. (1951). The growth and development approach. *Journal of Health, Physical Education and Recreation*, **22**, 36-37.

Engle, W.L. (1919). Supervised amusement cuts juvenile crime by 96%. *American City*, **20**, 515-517.

Holman, H. (1951). *Play ball: A study of Little League baseball in operation.* Fresno, CA: Recreation Department.

Life goes to a kid's football game. (1939, October). *Life*, pp. 90-93.

Lowman, C.L. (1947). The vulnerable age. *Journal of Health and Physical Education*, **18**, 635; 693.

Mangold, G.B. (1924). *Problems of child welfare.* New York: Macmillan.

Mid-west district news. (1937). *Journal of Health and Physical Education*, **8**, 382.

Moss, B., & Orion, W.H. (1939). The public school program in health, physical education, and recreation. *Journal of Health and Physical Education*, **10**, 435-439; 494.

North, C.C. (1931). *The community and social welfare.* New York: Recreation Department.

Paxton, H.T. (1949, May). Small boy's dream come true. *Saturday Evening Post*, pp. 26-27; 137-140.

Reckless, W.C., & Smith, M. (1932). *Juvenile delinquency.* New York: Recreation Department.

Recommendations from the Seattle convention workshop. (1947). *Journal of Health and Physical Education*, **18**, 429-432; 556-557.

Schmidt, C.A. (1944). Elementary school physical education. *Journal of Health and Physical Education*, **15**, 130-131; 161.

Scott, P.M. (1953). Attitudes toward athletic competition in elementary schools. *Research Quarterly*, **24**, 352-361.

Shanas, E. (1942). *Recreation and delinquency.* Chicago: Recreation Commission.

Skinner, C.E. (1945). *Elementary educational psychology.* New York: Prentice-Hall.

Stone, W.L. (1931). *What is boys' work.* New York: Recreation Department.

Stone, W.L. (1932). *The place of activities in boys' work. Work with boys.* New York: Recreation Department.

Two important resolutions. (1938). *Journal of Health and Physical Education*, **9**, 488-489.

Wayman, F., Hager, R., Hartwig, H., Houston, L., LaSalle, D., & McNeely, S. (1950). Report of the President's Committee on Inter-school Competition in the Elementary School. *Journal of Health, Physical Education and Recreation*, **21**, 279-280; 313-314.

Wickenden, E. (1960). Frontiers in voluntary welfare services. In E. Ginzberg (Ed.), *The nation's children: Vol. 3. Problems and prospects* (pp. 124-147). New York: Columbia University Press.

CHAPTER 2

Youth Sport in the USA[1]

Rainer Martens

This report provides a brief look at the status of youth sport in the United States. The topics considered include (a) the demographics of youth sport participation, (b) the organization of youth sport, (c) coaching education, (d) the status of youth sport research, and (e) conclusions about the strengths and weaknesses of American youth sport programs.

The Scope of Youth Sport Participation

Estimates of the number of young people (ages 6-18) participating in nonschool sports are made in Table 1. These estimates were first made in 1977 (Martens, 1978) by determining the percent of youth participating in a sport for a known population and then projecting that percent to a national population of youth in this age category. Data for the estimates were obtained from a wide variety of sources and should be viewed as rough approximations. All estimates were revised and updated for this report.

Several observations from the data in Table 1 are noteworthy. Participation has increased by over 5 million. However, it is incorrect to conclude that 5 million more children are playing, because these data do not represent children participating, but rather indicate the number of participants in each sport, with many children being multiple-sport participants. About 20 million (44%) of the 45 million youth in this age range participate in nonschool youth sport. In addition, the National High School Federation estimates that 3.35 million boys and 1.78 million girls, or a total of 5.13 million young people, participate in high school sport. (No estimates of elementary and junior high school participation could be obtained.)

---

[1]From "Youth Sport in the USA" by R. Martens. In *Sport for Children and Youths* (pp. 27-33) by M.R. Weiss and D. Gould (Eds.), 1986, Champaign, IL: Human Kinetics. Copyright 1986 by Human Kinetics. Modified by permission.

Table 1 Estimate of Participation in Nonschool Sports Among Children Ages 6 to 18 (in Millions)

Sport	Boys 1977	Boys 1984	Girls 1977	Girls 1984	Combined 1977	Combined 1984
Baseball	4.20	3.91	0.79	0.62	4.99	4.53
Softball	1.97	2.10	2.41	2.62	4.38	4.72
Swimming	1.71	1.85	1.91	2.08	3.62	3.93
Bowling	2.07	2.07	1.51	1.50	3.58	3.57
Basketball	2.13	2.13	1.22	1.22	3.35	3.35
Football (tackle)	1.56	1.16	0.29	0.10	1.85	1.26
Tennis	0.88	1.35	0.95	1.24	1.83	2.59
Gymnastics	0.59	0.75	1.17	1.50	1.76	2.25
Football (flag)	1.11	1.20	0.36	0.45	1.47	1.65
Track & field	0.76	1.00	0.54	0.75	1.30	1.75
Soccer	0.72	2.20	0.52	1.70	1.24	3.90
Wrestling	—	0.25	—	0.0	—	0.25
Other	1.24	1.00	0.79	0.80	2.03	1.80
Totals	18.94	20.97	12.46	14.58	30.41	35.55
% by sex	62%	59%	38%	41%		

Gender

The pattern of participation by gender is clearly shown in Table 1. Girls' participation has increased by just over 2 million, and now represents 41% of the participants as compared to 38% in 1977. Softball, dethroning baseball, is now America's number 1 youth sport. Soccer has made the most dramatic increase, moving from 11th to 4th in popularity with an increase in total participants of 2.66 million. Gymnastics and tennis also increased significantly in the number of participants, while American football declined 600,000, and baseball ½ million.

Age

Estimates also were made of the age at which children begin participating in organized competitive sport (see Table 2). Swimming and gymnastics won honors for introducing children to sport at the ripe old age of 3 years. The mean age for the 12 sports for the "earliest" participation was 5.83 years. The mean of the mean beginning age is 11 years, which is somewhat older than might be expected.

Organization of Youth Sport

One of the few generalizations that can be made about the organization of sport in the United States is that it has not been organized by

Table 2   Age Children Begin Participation in Sports

Sport	Earliest age	Mean beginning age
Baseball	5	9
Softball	7	10
Swimming	3	11
Bowling	6	14
Basketball	7	12
Football (tackle)	8	12
Tennis	8	14
Gymnastics	3	8
Football (flag)	7	10
Track & field	5	11
Soccer	6	10
Wrestling	5	11
Average age	5.83	11.0

Table 3   Categories of Agencies Who Organize Youth Sports

Type of agency	Example of type
National youth sport organization	PONY Baseball
National youth agency	Boys Clubs of America
National governing body	U.S. Wrestling
National service organization	American Legion Baseball
National religious organization	Catholic Youth Organization
Regional youth sport organization	Soccer Association for Youth
State school activity association	Illinois High School Activity Association
Local school district	Hutchinson, KS Public School
Local service club	Champaign Optimist Club
Municipal recreation department	Champaign Park District
Private sports club	Urbana Wrestling Club

the federal government. Although sport in recent times is being influenced more by federal legislation (e.g., Title IX, Amateur Sport Act of 1978), sport, more than most elements of American life, has avoided government intervention.

The types of agencies that organize sport in the United States and an example of a specific agency are shown in Table 3. Unlike some other nations, the organization of sport in this country is diverse, without any one agency providing national coordination of all youth sport programs. Sport in America is not the prerogative of any level of government or societal institution as can be seen from Table 3. In fact, in some sports such as baseball, there are so many organizations that an organization of baseball organizations exists.

On the other hand, organizers of sport, especially Olympic sport, have recognized the value in having some centralization of sport. Through the creation of the Amateur Sport Act of 1978, a procedure was developed under the United States Olympic Committee to form National Governing Bodies (NGBs) for each Olympic sport. Thus, for at least Olympic and international competition, there is a central governing body for each sport in the United States, but these NGBs only govern a small percent of the total participants in youth sport.

Funding for Youth Sport

The funding for youth sport comes mostly from five sources. These include taxes, individual donations, participation fees, business sponsorships, and service club donations. Sport in the United States is not heavily supported by tax dollars as it is in some other countries.

Education of Youth Sport Coaches

The number of volunteer coaches in the United States is estimated at about 2.5 million, with another ½ million professional or paid coaches. Most of the volunteer coaches and many of the professional coaches have no training in sports medicine and science. The vast majority of coaching education in the United States consists of sport-specific training with emphasis on technique and strategy. The only systematic coaching education which has been offered in the United States, which combines sport-specific training with sports medicine and science training, has been through universities and colleges. However, this training has been available to only a few.

School coaches must meet minimum certification standards in only 13 states, with these standards varying from 6 to 18 semester hours of coursework in physical education. The other states assume that if a person has a teaching certificate, he or she is qualified to coach.

Because fewer and fewer teachers wish to be coaches in the public schools, it has become necessary to hire nonteacher coaches to meet the need. The qualifications of these individuals to coach tends to be based on their experience playing or coaching the sport, not on their training in sport medicine and science. In general, a belief prevails in the United States that a person is qualified to coach by having played the sport, and the better the person has played, the better coach he or she will be. This belief may be properly labeled a myth.

In the 1970s, interest grew in providing coaching education programs which emphasized sports medicine and science, especially for the 2.5 million volunteers. Several of the national youth sport organizations and the NGBs for Olympic sport began offering limited coaching education clinics. At the same time, and in some cases in cooperation with these sport organizations, several agencies emerged to help educate coaches. The three prominent programs are the Michigan Youth Sport Institute, the National Youth Sport Coaches Association, and the American Coaching Effectiveness Program.

The Michigan program is limited mostly to that state. Its primary activity is a series of workshops conducted by faculty at Michigan State University. The National Youth Sport Coaches Association has been adopted by some municipal recreation departments and United States military youth sport programs. It relies exclusively on videotapes to present very limited information to coaches about technique, strategies, and sports medicine.

The American Coaching Effectiveness Program is more comprehensive than the other programs and has now trained over 25,000 coaches. The Level 1 program has been adopted by 12 NGBs, the YMCA of the USA, the Boys Clubs of America, hundreds of local recreation and youth sport agencies, and several major national sport agencies such as PONY baseball.

Status of Youth Sport Research

This section needs to be prefaced with the statement that any research in the sports medicine and science field which increases our knowledge of how humans function or behave will be useful for youth sport. Thus, from this perspective, the research being done in sport physiology, sport biomechanics, motor learning and control, motor development, sport psychology, and sociology of sport contributes to youth sport when children are used as subjects.

During the 1970s, a substantial interest developed in studying the phenomenon of youth sport in the United States. For a period of about 5 years (1976-81), conferences abounded, publications rolled off the presses, and academicians pontificated about youth sport in America. While the topic is by no means dead today, the fashionable topic of the late 1970s has at least experienced a recession.

Most of this research has been descriptive (e.g., Martens & Gould, 1979; State of Michigan, 1976), seeking answers to such questions as how many people are involved in youth sport; players', parents', and coaches' attitudes about a variety of issues; the number and types of injuries; and the number of and reasons for children dropping out of sport programs. A major exception to the descriptive research has been the coaching behavior study by Smith, Smoll, and Curtis (1978). They developed a coaching training program, delivered it to a group of coaches, and compared the difference in coaching behaviors between trained and untrained coaches.

Some of the other topics which have been studied include anxiety in sport, motivation, perceptions of competence, aggression, attributions, moral development, self-esteem, and socialization into and through sport. Gould (1982) concluded from his review of the youth sport research that those studies contributing the most (a) asked important practical questions, (b) integrated previous research or theory into the study, and (c) employed a series of studies on the problem. More of this type of research is needed.

Major Strengths and Need for Improvement

The following are the major strengths of youth sport programs in the USA:

- Millions of children are playing and enjoying sport.
- The programs offered are diverse in types of sport, skill levels, and age groups.
- Sport is increasingly available to all children, regardless of sex, race, or economic status.
- Sport is quite safe, with remarkably low injury rates when compared to unorganized activities and the potential for injury.
- Sport is readily available because Americans donate large sums of money and time to provide children the opportunity to play through many different types of agencies.
- The facilities for many sport programs are good to excellent. It is hard to imagine, however, that many other nations have more pools, gymnasia, ice rinks, and playing fields per capita than the United States.

Although youth sport is amazingly successful in the United States, it is not difficult to find room for improvement. The following are areas which I recommend be given priority:

- Continue improving coaches' education about sport sciences and sport-specific knowledge.
- Educate parents about their role and contribution to their children's participation in youth sport.
- Modify children's sport based on biomechanical, physiological, and developmental research to make that sport appropriate for various developmental levels.
- Reduce injury rates even further.
- Eliminate boxing and contact karate as sports permitted to be played in our society.
- Increase the age children first begin to play competitively in certain sports and emphasize learning fundamental skills early.
- Increase the availability of daily physical education in the elementary schools so that children develop basic movement skills under the leadership of professional instructors.
- De-emphasize the value in our society of being a winner, and emphasize the value of pursuing personal excellence.

References

Gould, D. (1982). Sport psychology in the 1980s: Status, direction, and challenge in youth sports research. *Journal of Sport Psychology,* **4**(3), 203-218.

Martens, R. (1978). *Joy and sadness in children's sports.* Champaign, IL: Human Kinetics.

Martens, R., & Gould, D. (1979). Why do adults volunteer to coach children's sports? In G. Roberts & K.M. Newell (Eds.), *Psychology of motor behavior and sport—1978* (pp. 79-89). Champaign, IL: Human Kinetics.

Smith, R.E., Smoll, F.L., & Curtis, B. (1978). Coaching behaviors in Little League baseball. In F.L. Smoll & R.E. Smith (Eds.), *Psychological perspectives in youth sports* (pp. 173-201). Washington, DC: Hemisphere.

State of Michigan. (1976). *Joint legislative study on youth sports programs: Agency sponsored sports (Phase I report).* Lansing, MI: Author.

CHAPTER 3

Youth Sport in Canada[1]

Terry A. Valeriote
Lori Hansen

Youth sport in Canada is fairly new in terms of organization. Nevertheless, the demand by Canadian youth for additional streams of participation, improved coaching, and increased organization at all levels—local, provincial, and national—continues to increase. Accordingly, most sport associations are in the process of modifying the form of their programs.

Because very little research on Canadian youth in sport has been conducted, a questionnaire was developed and distributed to 27 major national sport associations. In Table 1 is a list of sports surveyed, categorized by team or individual sports and Olympic or non-Olympic sports.

The results support the assumption that Canadian sport still lacks consistent direction. Developmental programs leading into an established training program for elite athletes exist, but only in some sports. Associations should be more aware of their counterparts and of what else is going on in Canadian sport than they have been.

This brief report on the status of youth sport in Canada confirms what federal administrators, national and local coaches, and athletes themselves have known for a long time: Canadian youth sport needs a common base, a consistent development model, and standardized programs for both developmental/recreational and elite/competitive participants.

Participation in Youth Sports

Approximately 2.5 million Canadian youths between the ages of 6 and 18 participate in Olympic and non-Olympic team and individual sports. Team sports are more popular than individual ones. The 10 favorite sports of Canadian youth are hockey, soccer, baseball, softball, figure skating, football, basketball, lacrosse, volleyball, and swimming.

[1]From "Youth Sport in Canada" by T.A. Valeriote and L. Hansen. In *Sport for Children and Youths* (pp. 17-20) by M.R. Weiss and D. Gould (Eds.), 1986, Champaign, IL: Human Kinetics. Copyright 1986 by Human Kinetics. Reprinted by permission.

Table 1   Sports Included in National Sport Association Survey

Olympic sports		Non-Olympic sports	
Team n = 6	Individual n = 13	Team n = 6	Individual n = 2
Basketball	Alpine ski	Baseball	Rhythmic gymnastics
Field hockey	Badminton	Ringette	Tennis
Hockey	Boxing	Rugby	
Soccer	Canoe	Softball	
Volleyball	Cross-country ski	Football	
Water polo	Fencing	Lacrosse	
	Figure skating		
	Gymnastics		
	Rowing		
	Speed skating		
	Swimming		
	Track & field		
	Wrestling		

Seventy-three percent, or 1.8 million, of these youths are male. The male participation rate in team sports is twice as great as that of females, but females participate in individual sports at a rate 50% greater than males. Sixty percent of youth participation is in Olympic sports; 40% is in non-Olympic sports.

The average age of beginning competitors is 9, although the age of entry ranges from 6 to 16. The average age of entry in non-Olympic sports is 8, but it is 10½ in Olympic sports. This difference is easily accounted for: In the non-Olympic sports, instruction and skill development are the areas emphasized in programs for 8- to 10-year olds.

The age range of Canadian youth in national competition is 15 to 18. Sixty percent of the sports surveyed offer competition at the provincial and regional level for youths 11 or older; 9- and 10-year-olds are usually offered only local competition for fun. However, 12% of the sports surveyed offer 6- to 8-year olds provincial competitions, and 32% offer it to 9- and 10-years-olds.

Funding of Youth Sport

Funding for competition from the local to the national levels comes from various sources: government, private sponsorship, fund-raising, and registration fees are the major sources. The sources of funding for the three levels of sport are summarized in Table 2.

Ninety-five percent of the national associations receive 50% or more of their funding from the federal government. By contrast, at the provincial level, the provincial government accounts for 30% of financial sup-

Table 2   Percent Contribution of Local, Provincial, and National Sport Funding Sources

Source	Local	Provincial	National
Government	4.6	57.0	59.0
Sponsorship	21.6	11.7	16.6
Fund-raising	35.1	11.7	10.6
Registration fees	32.9	15.0	6.2
Other sources	5.8	4.3	6.8
Total	100.0	100.0	100.0

port. The next largest source of funding is sponsorship: 45% of the national associations and 20% of the provincial associations receive 15% or more of their total funding from this source.

At the local level, fund-raising activities and registration fees generate more than half of total monies, and government provides only minimal support.

The Status of Research on Youth Sport

Sixty-four percent of Olympic sport organizations have conducted research that has focused on equipment safety and modification, the development of Mini-Sport and skill awards programs, and physiological and psychological testing and training.

Research conducted in hockey and football has provided significant published data on injuries in contact sport as well as information on how to reduce or eliminate these injuries with safer equipment and modified rules. Volleyball, soccer, lacrosse, rugby, and basketball have implemented Mini-Sport programs in varying degrees. These programs introduce youth to the sport and develop youth within the sport. Skill awards programs accompany these Mini-Sport programs; however, most associations without a Mini-Sport program offer a skill awards program.

Considerable research is currently being done on skill awards programs, on systems for the identification of talent, on the dropout problem, on equipment modification, and on the expansion of youth programs via integration with the schools' programs. In the near future, all sports should have incorporated the results of this research into their youth programs.

Olympic sport research now focuses on the long-term effects of training and competition, whereas non-Olympic sport research emphasizes how to increase participation by the masses and, therefore, develop a broader base. Each group has indicated a desire to study the other's research interest: That is, Olympic sport leaders would like to know how to increase participation among the younger age groups, and the non-Olympic sport leaders would like to determine the long-term effect of training and competition on youth.

Safety in sport is constantly under review. All sport associations are aware of the need for safe, appropriately sized equipment for all youth. According to the vast majority of sport associations, the most effective way of eliminating injuries is by having qualified, certified coaches teach participants proper technique.

The Education of Youth Sport Coaches

Since 1974, Canada has had a coaching certification program for coaches in all sports across the country. The program has five levels, the first 3 of which have a separate theory, technical, and practical component. At Levels 4 and 5, the national and international levels, the theory and technical components are combined.

To date, 150,000 coaches have participated in the program. Furthermore, certification is more frequently expected of coaches at all levels of competition.

Strengths and Areas Needing Improvement

A wide variety of competitive and recreational programs exist across Canada. The programs, especially those in the Olympic sports, enable the youth participants of Canada to select a sport suited to their needs.

However, the involvement of all Canadian youth is far from a reality. The overemphasis at all age levels on winning contributes to the high dropout rate from competitive programs among those in their mid-to-late teens. Recognition of this fact indicates that the sport associations are becoming aware of their weaknesses and are taking steps to correct them.

Another recognized problem is violence in sport, and research on safety and equipment modification is the means of finding solutions. Also, increased parental awareness of the role of sport for youth and the continuation of the National Coaching Certification Program will help improve coaching standards and create an appropriate and positive attitude toward participation in youth sport.

However, Canada still needs a common base. Certified coaches of standardized, consistent programs will help create such a base, as will the integration of these programs into school programs. Once completed, development models should provide each sport with a set of guidelines with which to plan its programs. Organization at the base of youth sport will not only ensure enjoyable growth experiences for youth, but will also enable elite sport in Canada to move forward and achieve its goal of international success.

   The involvement of youth in sport is a compelling issue. Ongoing evaluation of the areas identified above will generate recommendations on important issues, such as the optimal age of entry into competition, the most appropriate training programs for elite athletes, the safest ways to play sport, and the most appropriate program for developmental sport at the younger age levels.

CHAPTER 4

Gender and Youth Sport: Reflections on Old and New Fictions[1]

Mary E. Duquin

"I am cherry alive," the little girl sang,
"Each morning I am something new: . . .
I am tree, I am cat, I am blossom too . . ." (Schwartz, 1958)

Girls once danced, played, and sang songs with other girls. Now daughters field balls and defend goals. But in whose field are they playing and whose goals are they defending? The cultural floodgates that once dammed female participation in sport are now open. Societal forces that shape what females *believe* they can do, what legally they *may* do, and what normatively they *should* do have united in affirming female participation in sport. Scientists have declared that the female body can, like the male body, physiologically cope with participation and competition. Laws have overturned previous restrictions and now mandate that females may participate in most male games. Moral and aesthetic approval is also evident. Our culture supports (at least in theory) the ideal of equal opportunity for girls in sport; the fashion and beauty industries have created an "athletic chic," a lean (and hungry?) look, boyishly feminine, an aesthetic standard imaging a youthful and physically active lifestyle (Banner, 1983; Freedman, 1986).

Paralleling these social forces, many communities are offering programs for girls. Many others are incorporating girls into programs once reserved for boys. As more parents are convinced of the benefits of youth sport, daughters, as well as sons, are being placed in these programs. Consequently, increasing numbers of young girls are being taught the prevailing sociosymbolic system of youth sport.

Despite traditional beliefs in natural gender differences, few modifications have been made in youth sport as a result of incorporating girls: The structure, goals, values, and norms of the American youth sport

[1]The poetry in this chapter is from "I Am Cherry Alive" by D. Schwartz. In *Summer Knowledge: New and Selected Poems (1938-1958)* by D. Schwartz, 1958, New York: Doubleday. Copyright © 1959, 1987 by the Estate of Delmore Schwartz. Reprinted by permission.

movement have generally remained intact. But although integrated programs seem blind to gender differences, segregated sport programs proceed without discussion of gender similarity. The problematic position of females in both programs is obscured by the assumed good in the growth of female opportunity in sport. The rise in female participation in sport necessitates a renewed analysis of traditional youth sport programs.

Critics using various theoretical frameworks (liberal, radical, postmodern) voice different concerns regarding female participation in sport. However, these concerns are seldom mutually exclusive. Three issues emerge that affect the health and development of all children but have special impact on females:

- Gender segregationist and integrationist practices
- Sado-ascetic structures and practices
- Systems that encourage children to generate symbols and play structures that allow them "to sport" creatively

Imaging Youth Sport

A common approach to analyzing youth sport is the enumeration of the benefits of participation in the activity. Although this may appear to be a logical starting point, history is replete with examples where the most suspect of human activities (e.g., war) has been rationalized with post hoc justification in the form of lessons learned, limits tested, or noble causes defended. Although lessons may be learned from any human enterprise, we must ask whether what is learned is worth learning and, if so, whether there is a better way to learn it. Furthermore, rationalization transformed into justification limits searching for more beneficial structures of human creation.

An alternative approach is to create images of the characteristics and quality of guidance desired in a youth sport activity and then offer activities that fulfill these images. For example, a parent may feel that a youth sport activity would nurture healthy growth and development if it: (a) is fun and enjoyable for the child, (b) provides a reasonably safe means for developing the child's movement skills, (c) fosters moral sensitivity and caring, (d) encourages taking pleasure in the body and the beauty of movement, (e) exercises a spirit of discovery and creativity, (f) prepares a path for future lifelong activity and love of movement, and (g) inspires a sense of belonging in the world.

> (And) the little girl sang, . . .
> "When I like, if I like, I can be someone new,
> Someone very old, a witch in a zoo:
> I can be someone else whenever I think who,
> And I want to be everything sometimes too." (Schwartz, 1958)

Modes and Mores of Segregation

To question the legitimacy of the *big* dichotomies (mind-body, self-other, nature-culture, thought-feeling, truth-fiction) and all reified categories of thought is to cause a crisis in the very foundation of cultural beliefs. Crucial to maintaining a dualistic structure of thinking is the constant reaffirmation of all oppositions, especially those of gender (Keller, 1985). Thus, despite the recent support of youth sport programs for girls, the imminent realization of gender integration across all youth sport is unlikely. Youth sport, like other socializing institutions, clings to an ideology of natural gender differences requiring girls and boys to be socialized and treated differently.

Exploring narratives of youth sport segregation helps us to understand the varying realities we invent for children about themselves and the world. As Jardine (1985) notes, "to recognize the ways in which we surround ourselves with our fictions is a step toward finding new ways for thinking . . . [about] sexual difference as grounded in cultural and political reality without positing that reality . . . as somehow preexisting our thought and fictions" (p. 47). The ways in which these segregation narratives are manifested have problematic consequences for children of both genders.

Sport Structures and Segregation

Various structural modalities exist for segregation in youth sport. One common choice is organizing separate teams for the same sport (e.g., girls' soccer and boys' soccer). This strategy allows a status distinction to develop and prevents girls from challenging the assumed superiority of male sport prowess by eliminating direct female-male competition. In this segregated system, males learn to feel superior to females and females are structurally prevented from presenting a reality alternative to that of gender inequality.

In another strategy, girls and boys play similar sports that warrant separate teams. Usually the girls' game is viewed as a modification of the boys' game (e.g., girls' softball and boys' baseball). This strategy also creates a status distinction that leads both girls and boys into believing that girls are incapable of playing the boys' game, again promoting a conclusion of female inferiority. Names of games and sport language are crucial in maintaining or deconstructing gender ideology. Cultural metaphors are not lost on children. *Hard* ball is somehow better than *soft* ball, *fast* pitch better than *slow* pitch. Ergo boys, who are hard and fast, are better than girls (or boys), who are soft and slow.

Gender Symbolism and Segregation

Segregation in youth sport is also accomplished by using genderized symbolism. Sport and movement expectations for children are based upon class, race, religion, ethnicity, and gender. Certain motor skills, activities, and sports are labeled *gender-inappropriate*. Children are encouraged to select those activities deemed appropriate for their gender and are either covertly or overtly discouraged from selecting inappropriate activities. Of the segregationist techniques, this is probably the most successful in keeping girls and boys in separate sport programs and in keeping an aura of masculinity around particular sport activities.

Although separately gendered teams are common in all youth sports, physical contact sports are the most likely to be exclusively male. Developmental and physiological literature, however, supports the fact that properly trained prepubescent girls could compete with boys in contact sports. Given earlier female maturation, girls at some points may even have a physiological advantage over boys in the same age group (Tanner, 1970). Yet few adults advocate female participation in contact sports. Fewer still support gender integration in these activities. While physiological rationales for female exclusion crumble, the genderized symbolism associated with contact sports remains culturally fixed.

All-male contact sports maintain and legitimize adult belief in gender ideology. Placing boys, but not girls, in these sports serves to justify adult beliefs that boys have a greater need than girls to express aggression or a greater need to learn aggression. The absence of females in contact sports in part symbolizes a desire to view females as nonviolent. At the same time, our culture expects females to be spectators and cheerleaders of male sport combat.

Through genderized symbolism of youth sport activities, adults create a world for children as they imagine it exists. As one father who is also a hockey official put it: "It's a violent society, eh? This is a tough society we're in. I put my own kid in hockey so he would learn to take his lumps . . . the day they turn hockey into a namby-pamby game for sissies is the day I get out" (Smith, this volume, p. 303). These sport practices and adult attitudes are symbolic of the structure of power in gender relations and are part of what carry these relations into future generations (Lips, 1981).

Sado-Asceticism and Segregation

Adult organization of children into sado-ascetic sport practices has resulted in severe social and moral problems (Noddings, 1984; Smith, this volume). Sado-asceticism is characterized by obsessive asceticism imposed upon others as well as oneself. The ramifications of sado-ascetic structures and practices include emotional and physical deprivation, desensitization to self and others, and the "infliction/affliction of ontological impotence which is the blockage of participation in Being" (Daly, 1984, pp. 35-36). Examples of sado-ascetic ideology in sport parlance include, No pain, no gain, If it doesn't hurt you're not doing it right, and Destroy the opposition. Sado-ascetic sports and sport practices are epitomized by, but not limited to, physical contact sports.

In physical contact sports players are involved, at least indirectly, in inflicting physical pain or injury on the opponent (e.g., boxing) or engaging in attempts to physically dominate and intimidate the opponent (e.g., wrestling, ice hockey, and football). From a health and growth perspective, contact sports for children are difficult to justify on the basis of our desired images of youth sport. From an ethical standpoint, questions must be raised regarding adult organization and encouragement of children in sport activities that require exposure to repeated physical abuse and injury. What is the meaning behind adults teaching children to coolly, instrumentally, and efficiently inflict enough physical damage or effect enough physical force to dominate or intimidate another child? The question is important. Why do adults want to teach these sado-ascetic activities to children, or, more specifically, to male children?

Boys have no innate desire to play hockey or football. In fact, considerable socialization is needed for boys to willingly expose themselves to repeated physical abuse. The majority never do. The wisdom of the body is to deny the ascetic; to affirm, No pain is sane. Generally, people try to avoid pain, injury, and unpleasant stimuli unless taught to value these experiences in pursuit of some "higher good." One higher good that boys have been socialized to pursue in the face of pain and suffering is their gender identity (Sabo & Runfola, 1980).

More recently a renewed ascetic standard has made inroads into the culture. The ascetic ideal holds that flesh should be shaped, the body disciplined, and the self controlled. Pain is redefined as discomfort. The true sport ascetic "works through" the pain—may even embrace it. Contact sports help socialize boys into this ascetic frame and teach them to value the practice of sado-ascetic rituals. As for the absence of girls in contact sports, it is not the lack of experience in asceticism that adults shield from females, but the experience of inflicting its violence on others.

Part of the reasoning behind adults trying to keep sport segregated is that boys' games and the world they imitate are violent (Daly, 1984; French, 1985). Traditional sport prepares youth for a contestable world—a closed system, heavily armored and weighted down with "truths" and "duties" that constantly demand sacrifices of bodies (eg., athletic injuries, steroid injections, pain killers, goons, intimidators). In the fiction of segregation, this world of violence should not touch females. Yet females do suffer from it, often directly, when they are physically hurt, and indirectly, as sisters, mothers, and lovers of those bodies maimed and damaged. It is a fiction that violence done to a body is not violence if we call it a fair fight, a just war, or a sport. Adults may choose to sacrifice their bodies for their perceptions of truth. In youth sport, the "truths" are those of adults, the sacrificial bodies are those of children.

And I sing . . .
The true is untrue . . .
But I don't tell the grown-ups; because it is sad,
And I want them to laugh just like I do
Because they grew up
And forgot what they knew
And they are sure
I will forget it some day too.
They are wrong. They are wrong.
When I sang my song, I knew, I knew! (Schwartz, 1958)

Stories of Integration

If segregation in youth sport programs deprecates female ability and
perpetuates a developmentally harmful gender ideology, integration
in sport elicits even more complex issues for females. Equal rights legislation is supported by physiological research that declares no biological
justification for prepubescent gender segregation in sport (Wilmore,
1977). Similarly, the social sciences enumerate the ways in which
socialization creates gender, concluding that behavioral differences
found in children are often the differences that society is ideologically
prone to foster (Pogrebin, 1980). Thus, stripped of the fiction of natural female frailty, girls are now free, and sometimes forced, to integrate
with males in sport activities. With sport integration comes the
legitimacy of overt male aggression against females. For within the
game—where a girl is now just "one of the boys" who must "learn to
take it"—can be seen a vision of a world where power, authority, and
voice are grounded in the fear and use of violence (Chafe, 1977; Scarry,
1985). It is a world where weakness is exploited, where dominance is
paramount, and where one's body not only speaks for oneself but also
silences the voices of others. In such a world, some females thrive, some
survive, many are wounded.

The risks females take in joining males in their games are not only
physical. Noddings (1984) emphasizes the moral risks that arise when
females integrate into male institutions:

[We] will have to decide whether to demand entrance into the full
world of competitive sports or to suggest a deemphasis of such
activity. Shall we insist that we can march, obey, and kill as well
as our brothers and should, therefore, hold equal places in the military? Should we show that we care so little for our bodies that we,
too, shall start knocking each other senseless in violent 'sports'?
. . . This seems the sort of madness we see again and again as the
oppressed, in wide-eyed naivete, seeing only their oppression, join
in energetically and loyally to become one with the oppressor. It

may be nothing less than the ethical ideal of caring that is at stake in our decision. (p. 119)

Girls may be as physiologically capable as boys, but the ideology of serious sport is still symbolically male. Females are expected to keep their feminine sympathies and values off the sporting field. Behavioral expectations in sport are often congruent with male socialization in other spheres. However, females must engage in amazing feats of schizophrenic rationalizations, justifying their image of themselves as caring and sensitive human beings while mastering the sado-ascetic sport rituals of physical and psychological intimidation and aggression.

Gender integration in sport requires females to reject more than their traditional values. It requires a rejection of female maturation, of physically growing. A young girl, integrated into male sport, learns that her body is most valued athletically in its prepubescent state, when it most resembles the body of a young boy. As an athlete she learns to build and shape her body. But whose body is she building? In whose image is she taught to create herself? The ascetic ethic, the boyishly feminine chic, the athletic ideal—all are at odds with her growth as a woman. She learns that her maturing female body with its accompanying growth of soft flesh is to be dreaded; some *thing* she will constantly have to monitor, master, reduce. Anorexia and bulimia are not unknown to her. Time and her body are enemies (Chernin, 1981; Williamson, 1986). She learns that with the advent of womanhood comes the demise of her period of athletic integration. A "good competitive" game, a "real" game, can no longer be played coed. She no longer numbers among the elite. Her body is not among the chosen. She may still be willing to sacrifice her body for the team, to endure the pain of training, but despite her efforts the majority of her male peers surpass her. As she becomes a woman she realizes that most of the games belong to the boys. Meanwhile, the struggle for acceptance and approval goes on and the bodies of girls (and boys) seriously hurt in the pursuit of serious sport pile up—sacrifices to those fictions of nations, states, leagues, schools, and sport teams.

This world of sport with its *natural* view of things, its continued judgments that do violence, its war with bodies, has little space for children. It is a cramped and overstructured space. In this sport/world/view there is little room to invent, too little opportunity for player creation. Most females, because of their exclusion from sport in the past, have avoided total internalization of male sport mores. Integration, however, holds for females the risk of losing alternative visions of what sport might be, of regressing to an outmoded and physically destructive system of reality, identity, and meanings. It isn't simply that integration jeopardizes the advantageous position of female perspective, or that females might forget to laugh and sing, to play and dance, but that female integration could silence what has been hidden, denied articulation, left out, de-emphasized—what we need to hear now if we are to live in a world of nonmastery (Jardine, 1985).

And I sing: *It is true; It is untrue;* . . .
The peach has a pit,
The pit has a peach:
And both may be wrong
When I sing my song, . . . (Schwartz, 1958)

Imaging Youth Sporting

Adults can create alternative images of the world for children. Return-ing to our desired images of youth activities, we seek symbols and sport-ing structures that allow children to be creative, caring, and sensuous; that develop physical competence in a healthy environment; and that let children experience joy in their bodies and in their being in the world. What then are the alternatives for females to segregation and integration into traditional youth sport? Some other paths of sportive participation can be imagined.

Segregation is an enforced separation. Female separatism is a chosen ideological and structural separation from traditional male systems (Birrell, 1984). A long history of female athletic separatism came to an end with the implementation of integrationist policies in schools. Ironi-cally, it is this same female sport ideology that is invoked in writings about the moral reform needed in youth sport. Separatism could replace segregation in youth sport. Rather than trying to approximate male sport, an alternative ideology and structure would characterize female youth sport teams. With an alternative symbolic system and structure and care-filled guidance, females may be able to realize the afore-mentioned images of sportive participation. What is still needed, how-ever, is an analysis of how even these alternative female frameworks of sport may be attached to traditional categories and dichotomies of thought (Griffin, 1982).

Our desired images of youth sport may be even easier to realize if we relinquish our professional definitions of sport and envision *sport-ive* activities (i.e., activities that allow children "to sport"). This term connotes activities that are spirited, exuberant, joyful, playful, and lively, that let children display, put forward, and flourish. Outdoor activities such as hiking, rock scrambling, caving, canoeing, rafting, snorkeling, horseback riding, skating, sledding, skiing, and biking are lifetime activities that children can learn and participate in with their families as well as their peers.

Sportive activities yet to be imagined could be combinations of art, circus, dance, innovative movement, drama, and aquapark/playground activities. These views of sport might picture huge indoor or outdoor arena-size sportgrounds with gravity-free rooms, cycles and ropes, trampolines and slides, sand and water, bridges and balls, trees, costumes, and musical instruments. Activities for children would in-clude solo sports as well as pairs, triples, and group sport activities requiring children of different ages. Choices to play, perform, compete, or achieve criteria might characterize these new sport activities.

"I am cherry alive," the little girl sang,
"Each morning I am something new:
I am apple, I am plum, I am just as excited
As the boys who made the Hallowe'en bang . . ." (Schwartz, 1958)

Conclusion

Much of present-day youth sport structure and symbolism is anachronistic, tied to a destructive ontology of oppositions, boundaries, and domination. This situation often leads to a less than hospitable world for children. Thus the history of youth sport is one of repeated attempts to improve the image, to idealize the representation, to conceptually repair a structural system based upon a morally and physically repressive symbolic system. The result is the repeated failure of meaningful change to be realized; yet the talking and writing about the necessity of change continues (Martens, 1978; Seefeldt, this volume).

The necessary transformation of youth sport requires a radical restructuring of cultural thought. What then is beyond truth, the absolute, the body in pain? We know that when principles are held over the body, some *body* is inevitably sacrificed to those principles. What if we ceased to harm bodies? Would the demise of sado-ascetic practices in sport be enough to achieve a transformation? Maybe it would be a starting point.

How are we to understand youth sport in relation to cultural creation and moral consciousness? Let us imagine ourselves back at a time long ago when a knife loomed over a sacrificial child on an altar. Just before the knife falls we see the substitution of a lamb for the child. History will record this as a significant leap in moral consciousness. If, however, we now imagine not two but three pictures—the knife over the child, the child giving way to the lamb, and, finally, the lamb giving way to a piece of wood, the transition in consciousness is so great as to require a total reperception of the knife. It is no longer a weapon for wounding, but a tool for creating (Scarry, 1985). The challenge for adults is to imagine and structure a sporting world where our children learn to be instruments for creation, not weapons for destruction.

For many females, traditional youth sport programs do not offer a sociosymbolic system or structure conducive to creative development. In exploring the fictions of segregation and integration, we found that with integration our differences were not lost, nor with segregation our worlds separated. Both practices act as modalities of foreclosure in that females, as subjects, have little chance of inventing new configurations within the traditional system of youth sport (Kristeva, 1982). Our visions of the future should not be limited by the past, but informed by it. We need to move to create; we need to create space to move. Remembering this and remembering our past, females may choose to sport—but should be cautious about joining games already in progress. For to join in a game is to enter the circle of society; to make up a game is to widen the circle; but "to sport" is to erupt the shape—creating space.

"I am cherry alive," the little girl sang,
"Each morning I am something new: . . .
"I am red, I am gold,
I am green, I am blue,
I will always be me,
I will always be new!" (Schwartz, 1958)

References

Banner, L.W. (1983). *American beauty*. Chicago: The University of Chicago Press.

Birrell, S. (1984). Separatism as an issue in women's sport. *Arena Review*, **2**, 21-30.

Chafe, W.H. (1977). *Women and equality*. Oxford: Oxford University Press.

Chernin, K. (1981). *The obsession: Reflections on the tyranny of slenderness*. New York: Harper & Row.

Daly, M. (1984). *Pure lust*. Boston: Beacon.

Freedman, R. (1986). *Beauty bound*. Lexington, MA: D.C. Heath.

French, M. (1985). *Beyond power: On women, men and morals*. New York: Summit.

Griffin, S. (1982). The way of all ideology. In N.O. Keohane, M.Z. Rosaldo, & B.C. Gelpi (Eds.), *Feminist theory: A critique of ideology* (pp. 273-292). Chicago: The University of Chicago Press.

Jardine, A.A. (1985). *Reflections on gender and science*. New Haven, CT: Yale University Press.

Keller, E.F. (1985). *Reflections on gender and science*. New Haven, CT: Yale University Press.

Kristeva, J. (1982). Women's time. In N.O. Keohane, M.Z. Rosaldo, & B.C. Gelpi (Eds.), *Feminist theory: A critique of ideology* (pp. 31-54). Chicago: The University of Chicago Press.

Lips, H.M. (1981). *Women, men and the psychology of power*. Englewood Cliffs, NJ: Prentice-Hall.

Martens, R. (Ed.). (1978). *Joy and sadness in children's sport*. Champaign, IL: Human Kinetics.

Noddings, N. (1984). *Caring: A feminine approach to ethics and moral education*. Berkeley: University of California Press.

Pogrebin, L. (1980). *Growing up free: Raising your child in the eighties*. New York: McGraw-Hill.

Sabo, D., & Runfola, R. (1980). *Jock: Sport and male identity*. New Jersey: Prentice-Hall.

Scarry, E. (1985). *The body in pain: The making and unmaking of the world*. New York: Oxford University Press.

Schwartz, D. (1958). *Summer knowledge: New and selected poems (1938-1958)*. New York: Doubleday.

Seefeldt, V. (1988). The future of youth sport in America. In F.L. Smoll, R.A. Magill, & M.J. Ash (Eds.), *Children in sport* (3rd ed., pp. 335-348). Champaign, IL: Human Kinetics.

Smith, M.D. (1988). Interpersonal sources of violence in hockey: The influence of parents, coaches, and teammates. In F.L. Smoll, R.A. Magill, & M.J. Ash (Eds.), *Children in sport* (3rd ed., pp. 301-316). Champaign, IL: Human Kinetics.

Tanner, J.M. (1970). Physical growth. In P. Mussen (Ed.), *Carmichael's manual of child psychology* (pp. 77-155). New York: Wiley.

Williamson, J. (1986). *Consuming passions: The dynamics of popular culture*. London: Marion Boyars.

Wilmore, J.H. (1977). *Athletic training and physical fitness*. Boston: Allyn & Bacon.

SECTION 2

Readiness for Participation

Perhaps one of the most common questions asked by parents about youth sport is "At what age should my child get involved in a youth sport program?" The significance of this question is that it reflects a genuine concern for the welfare of the child. Given that the overall objective of youth sport is to provide a positive developmental experience, it follows that the issue of readiness is paramount in the study of youth sport. In this section, three chapters provide different, yet complementary perspectives on the readiness issue.

Chapter 5, by Vern Seefeldt, considers the mechanisms of development that relate to children's readiness to learn motor skills. He provides a concise background of what is meant by the construct that we typically label "readiness." He then discusses information that can provide us with appropriate cues to recognizing the behaviors that foretell readiness to learn specific skills in specific skill learning situations. The thrust of Seefeldt's approach is to provide a much needed base for developing guidelines for suggesting when a particular sport skill should be introduced to a child. In a treatise that extends Seefeldt's chapter, Richard A. Magill provides a working model of the essential components involved in determining readiness to learn skills or to become involved in youth sport. Basing this model on views related to critical learning periods, Magill focuses on identifying when a child is optimally ready to learn a skill, a process that can occur only when the child's maturation level, past experiences, and motivation to learn are taken into account.

In the final chapter of this section, Michael W. Passer deals directly with the age-based question about readiness for participation in youth sport. Approaching this question from a psychosocial perspective, Passer first discusses the key issues of motivational and cognitive readiness for competition. Motivational readiness for competition is seen as being related to the child's development of an orientation toward social comparison with peers. Cognitive readiness for competition is examined by focusing on the development of children's role-taking and attributional capacities. After highlighting several potential hazards of children being involved in youth sport too early, Passer proposes some general age-related guidelines for youth sport participation.

CHAPTER 5

The Concept of Readiness Applied to Motor Skill Acquisition

Vern Seefeldt

The word *readiness* implies that an organism has reached a certain point in an ongoing process. In learning, readiness implies that an accumulation of events or experiences has occurred that places the learner in a position to acquire additional information, skills, or values. The past half-century has provided abundant information that gives us clear indications about when children are ready to learn many of the fine and gross motor skills of infancy and early childhood (Branta, Haubenstricker, & Seefeldt, 1984; Seefeldt & Haubenstricker, 1982). This information has allowed us to become much more confident about identifying the period of readiness for learning than we are about defining the sequence of events that must precede every instance of readiness.

Teachers of movement and physical education are making decisions daily about the readiness of children to learn skills, but available materials indicate that most activity programs are based on tradition, rather than on a well-defined sequence of developmental progressions. This situation exists because most definitions of readiness depend upon an overt attempt on the part of the child to perform a certain task to indicate readiness. In other words, we depend on the observable behavior of the performer to tell us when the state of readiness exists. If our predictive information was adequate, however, we would have at our disposal a series of signs that convey readiness; these signs would be recognizable by the teacher as the learner moves from rudimentary to mature performance levels. It is feasible that children may be biologically or mentally ready and yet not make any attempt at performing specific tasks because some of the components necessary for successful completion are not available in the present environment. Clearly, if we are to assist individuals in achieving their motor potential, we must be able to (a) identify the antecedent variables that provide the state of readiness for specific tasks, and (b) recognize the behavior that foretells the readiness of the learner for specific skill-learning situations.

The construct of readiness has undergone some changes in its interpretation during the past several decades. During the first half of the 20th century it was commonly believed that the biological maturation of children was the primary influence in their ability to perform fine and gross motor skills. However, subsequent research has produced abundant evidence concerning the significant contribution that the environment makes to children's learning. An indication of a transition in the definition of readiness for learning motor skills can be drawn from Bruner's (1965) statement regarding the ability to deal with cognitive material. His chapter "Readiness for Learning" is introduced with the statement, "We begin with the hypothesis that any subject can be taught effectively in some intellectually honest form to any child at any state of development" (p. 33). This more recent interpretation of readiness removes the burden of prerequisite biological maturation from the learner. It places the responsibility for the assessment of developmental status and the provision of antecedent experiences on the teacher. Bruner's definition suggests that the child is always ready for some type of experience, but the selection and provision of the stimuli that elicit the desired responses are the responsibility of the teachers in charge of the child's activity program. The implication is that the ability to learn motor skills is no longer solely attributable to the maturational level that the learner brings to the task. Rather, it is a combination of previous proficiency and a series of appropriate experiences that lead to motor skill acquisition.

Interrelationship Between Cognitive and Motor Functions

The teaching of motor skills has traditionally ignored the importance of learning styles and cognitive functions that may influence the rate of learning. Recent attempts to identify and incorporate the hierarchy of cognitive structures into situations that involve motor skill learning are a welcome addition to the literature. For example, Piaget's developmental sequence, originally presented in 1952, has only received attention in the United States during the last two decades. Hebb's (1949) hypothesis of how all experiences affect subsequent learning is an earlier attempt to explain readiness to learn. He hypothesized that movements, if repeated often enough, are incorporated into cell assemblies and phase assemblies within the central nervous system. The control of similar movements in the future is thereby transferred from a series of stimuli to central processes, thus freeing the performer from the need to concentrate on numerous stimuli. As a result, attention can be focused on the important elements in complex tasks. Additional experiences add to the pool of cell and phase assemblies, which increases the possibility of transferring identical components from task to task. Meanwhile, the larger motor repertoire decreases the likelihood of inappropriate responses. Hebb's model suggests that experience in a variety of tasks aids the performer in (a) selecting more appropriate stimuli, (b) making finer discriminations concerning the accuracy of the response, (c) attending to a task for a longer period of time, (d) being able to depend more on transfer of elements, (e) being able to retain more of what was learned by integrating it with previous experience, and (f) eliminating faulty responses from the alternatives available.

The concurrent and inseparable development of cognitive and motor processes in early life was emphasized by Bruner (1969), who affirmed this relationship as a result of extensive research with children below 6 months of age. He noted that the ability to solve problems that require a motor response is a process that begins soon after birth. According to Bruner, the infant's initial movements are not random responses, but represent the answers to hypotheses that are formed by the problems unique to early development. Out of these early movements the infant develops a hierarchy of functions that provides the basis for future learning. The reflexes and reactions that are present at birth provide the repertoire from which the infant learns to *differentiate* the actions that are effective and efficient in completing a specific task. The second mechanism, which Bruner termed *modularization*, permits the infant to partition and recombine the movements into additional patterns. *Substitution* is a means whereby one action is used in place of another, thus adding variety to the responses available. *Sequential integration* permits the selection of a variant order, in lieu of solving the same problems with a rigid sequence of movements. *Place-holding* permits the infant to carry on two motor skills while devoting alternate degrees of attention to both of them. *Internalization of action* is the ability to carry out behavior symbolically. The ability to perform complex motor operations and the transferability of these mechanisms to many motor tasks during the first 2 years of life underscore the importance of abundant stimulation in early infancy. It also illustrates the need for the concurrent study of cognitive and motor development during the periods of childhood and adolescence.

The onset of locomotion increases the opportunities for sensory stimulation available to the child. The motor repertoire is expanded when responses are made to an incessant desire for sensory stimulation. A cyclic process is initiated whereby an increase in sensory experiences contributes to the variety and frequency of motor responses. An enlarged repertoire of motor patterns provides more options to the performer, while a greater proportion of successful responses contributes to a desire for additional stimulation. This cycle is self-sustaining, with the provision that the environment contains appropriate stimuli and the child has the opportunity to formulate the motor responses. On the basis of this proposed sequence, it is evident that an abundance of experiences that culminate in successful motor responses early in life is an efficient way to establish the readiness necessary for subsequent learning.

Generality Versus Specificity of Motor Skills

The controversy concerning the generality versus specificity of motor skills has waxed and waned through the decades. Although research favors those who contend that skills are specific, we lack conclusive evidence that the fundamental motor skills of infancy and childhood are unrelated one to another. The evidence most often cited in support of specificity is based on correlational studies in which the data were derived via quantitative measures, with little regard for the neurological patterns of development used by the performers. Yet, there is sound evidence that the substrate of the basic movements and fundamental motor skills of infancy and childhood is comprised of reflexes and reactions that are common to all human beings.

The role of reflexes and reactions that are associated with future skill acquisition has been the focus of several investigations. The reports of Knott and Voss (1968) and Shambes and Campbell (1973), based on the theory of proprioceptive neuromuscular facilitation, suggest the existence of four diagonal patterns that form the basis of all movement, whether reflexive, developmental, or ontogenetic. The authors contend that once the basic diagonal patterns are perfected, all future skills are acquired through a variation of these patterns in temporal-spatial relationships. Examples of other reports that trace the transition from reflexes and reactions to voluntary movement include such tasks as grasping and prehension (Twitchell, 1965), the use of the tonic neck reflex in writing (Waterland, 1967), and righting reactions in the achievement of erect posture (Milani-Comparetti & Gidoni, 1967). The sequential description of the reflexes and reactions that must be suppressed or built upon for normal motor development to occur during the first year of life—given by Milani-Comparetti and Gidoni—is an excellent example of the high level of prediction that can accompany motor function when qualitative assessment is used.

Order and Sequence in Motor Skill Acquisition

The orderly nature of early motor behavior has frequently led to the erroneous impression that infants or young children acquire their motor repertoire at approximately the same chronological age. However, because genetic endowment determines the boundaries within which the skills are expressed, there is a wide range in the ages at which children learn basic motor skills. Consequently, classification by age has little utility for teachers of movement. Also of little use are the scales available to assess motor performance for the purposes of compensatory or remedial motor education. These scales were developed primarily by psychologists and physicians and have basic problems in their definition of developmental patterns common to children beyond one year of age.

The Motor Performance Study at Michigan State University, now in its 20th year, was designed to determine the manner in which children learn some of the fundamental motor skills. The pioneer work in this area was done by Gesell and his associates (1946) and at the University of Wisconsin by Wild (1938) and Hellebrandt, Rarick, and Carns (1961). To date, the developmental sequences in walking, running, hopping, jumping, skipping, throwing, catching, kicking, galloping, punting, and striking have been identified. Preliminary evidence is available in sliding and rope jumping. The most significant information concerning this phase of the study (Seefeldt & Haubenstricker, 1982) is that almost all children display clearly definable sequences when moving from the rudimentary to the mature levels of performance in these skills. This is true of children who function within the normal range, those who have learning disabilities, the mentally retarded, and those who are blind. The evidence obtained from the motor functions of blind children, who have not had the benefit of watching others perform specific motor skills, suggests to us that the rudimentary patterns that are the basis of these skills are ingrained in the central nervous system and are expressed when an appropriate combination of biological maturation and the opportunity for practice is available.

The identification of this orderly sequence of development in various skills has provided us with practical guides concerning the readiness of children to move on to the next level of a particular skill. However, we do not yet have sufficient evidence to suggest when the introduction to specific skills should occur; nor do we know which antecedent conditions are essential or helpful in moving the child into a position of readiness for specific skills. Apparently, these movements have their origins in the reflexes and reactions displayed during the first year of life.

Predicting the Rate of Motor Skill Acquisition

The concept of maturation and the use of skeletal age and body size as criteria for readiness to engage in certain activities is discussed by Malina (this volume). Despite the fact that research evidence suggests that the selection and classification of performers for subsequent competition in sports and dance be determined by variables such as maturity, skill, body size, and expertise, the grouping of young athletes has been primarily a season-by-season procedure based on chronological age. Virtually all of the investigators whose work was reviewed for this topic reported the retrospective prediction of success, often through the use of regression equations that were obtained from cross-sectional studies or computed at the termination of longitudinal studies. None of the investigators attempted to predict the success of individuals in motor performance prior to their involvement in activity programs, nor did they conduct a longitudinal follow-up to determine the accuracy of the original predictions. In no case were the predictive equations applied to other samples as a test of their validity. This neglect is unfortunate in light of the national interest currently focused on organized sports and dance for young children, the well-defined objectives for success that are commonly associated with these programs, and the desire on the part of most coaches and teachers to foretell the success of their clients at the earliest possible age.

The relationship between the various indicators of maturity, commonly classified under the phrase *primary* and *secondary sex characteristics*, is modest to high, depending on whether the individual matures early or late. As might be expected, the relationship between skeletal age and the primary and secondary sex characteristics is also in the modest-to-high range. Thus, if skeletal age has a high positive relationship with height, weight, breadth, and circumference measures, and also with the primary and secondary sex characteristics, it seems ironic that some form of predictive equation is not used more frequently as a means of predicting the readiness of children to engage in various sports.

Part of the reluctance to use skeletal age as a predictor of motor performance is that teachers and coaches cannot easily obtain such an assessment. The determination of skeletal age requires special competencies in its procurement and assessment that are not required when obtaining other growth data. Additional deterrents may result from a reluctance to expose children to X-irradiation except for diagnostic purposes. However, the most logical reason for its exclusion from predictive equations involving motor performance is its high positive relationship to parameters that are considerably easier to assess. If it can be demonstrated that height, weight, or other bodily dimensions account for most or all of the variance in performance attributable to physical growth, there is no need to include an estimate of biological maturity. This is precisely what research reports have indicated. Espenschade in 1940, Rarick and Oyster in 1964, and our own longitudinal data (Howell, 1979; Seefeldt, Haubenstricker, & Milne, 1976) confirm that skeletal age adds little to the prediction of motor performance if chronological age, height, and weight are already part of the equation.

Summary

In conclusion, there is little evidence to suggest that the readiness to learn specific motor skills can be identified through chronological age, body size, or the various assessments of biological maturation. The most feasible procedure for ensuring that young performers will be ready to learn motor skills involves a task analysis of the skills to be learned, accompanied by an opportunity for the learner to acquire the requisite antecedent skills. Although the order in which children learn the sequence in fundamental motor skills is invariant, there is great variation in the rate at which they move through the sequences to maturity.

References

Branta, C., Haubenstricker, J., & Seefeldt, V. (1984). Age changes in motor skills during childhood and adolescence. *Exercise and Sport Sciences Reviews*, **12**, 467-520.

Bruner, J. (1965). *The process of education*. Cambridge, MA: Harvard University Press.

Bruner, J. (1969). Processes of growth in infancy. In A. Ambrose (Ed.), *Stimulation in early infancy* (pp. 205-225). New York: Academic Press.

Espenschade, A. (1940). Motor performance in adolescence. *Monographs of the Society for Research in Child Development*, **5**, 1-127.

Gesell, A. (1946). The ontogenesis of infant behavior. In L. Carmichael (Ed.), *Manual of child psychology* (pp. 295-331). New York: Wiley.

Hebb, D. (1949). *The organization of behavior*. New York: Wiley.

Hellebrandt, F., Rarick, G., & Carns, M. (1961). Physiological analysis of basic motor skills. *American Journal of Physical Medicine*, **40**, 14-25.

Howell, R. (1979). *The relationship between motor performance, physical growth, and skeletal maturity in boys nine to twelve years of age*. Unpublished master's thesis, Michigan State University, East Lansing.

Knott, M., & Voss D. (1968). *Proprioceptive neuromuscular facilitation*. New York: Harper & Row.

Malina, R.M. (1988). Growth and maturation of young athletes: Biological and social considerations. In F.L. Smoll, R.A. Magill, & M.J. Ash (Eds.), *Children in sport* (3rd ed., pp. 83-101). Champaign, IL: Human Kinetics.

Milani-Comparetti, A., & Gidoni, E. (1967). Routine developmental examination in normal and retarded children. *Developmental Medicine and Child Neurology*, **13**, 631-638.

Piaget, J. (1952). *The origins of intelligence in children*. New York: International Universities Press.

Rarick, G., & Oyster, N. (1964). Physical maturity, muscular strength and motor performance of young school-age boys. *Research Quarterly*, **35**, 523-531.

Seefeldt, V., & Haubenstricker, J. (1982). Patterns, phases and stages: An analytical model for the study of developmental movement. In J. Kelso & J. Clark (Eds.), *The development of movement control and coordination* (pp. 309-318). New York: Wiley.

Seefeldt, V., Haubenstricker, J., & Milne, C. (1976, March). *Skeletal age and body size as variables in motor performance.* Paper presented at the Third Symposium on Child Growth and Motor Development, University of Western Ontario, London.

Shambes, G., & Campbell, S. (1973). Inherent movement patterns in man. In C. Widule (Ed.), *Kinesiology* (Vol. 3, pp. 50-58). Washington, DC: American Association for Health, Physical Education and Recreation.

Twitchell, T. (1965). Attitudinal reflexes. *Physical Therapy,* **45**, 411-418.

Waterland, J. (1967). The supportive framework for willed movement. *American Journal of Physical Medicine,* **46**, 266-278.

Wild, M. (1938). The behavior pattern of throwing and some observations concerning its course of development in children. *Research Quarterly,* **9**, 20-24.

CHAPTER 6

Critical Periods as Optimal Readiness for Learning Sport Skills

Richard A. Magill

A question commonly asked by parents of young children is, If I want my child to be successful in a sport, is it important that he or she get involved in that sport as early in life as possible? This is a reasonable question given the frequent media stories about how young a particular champion athlete was when he or she began competing in that sport. The problem is, however, we do not know if that athlete is an exception or a typical champion athlete. We do not know what percentage of champion athletes started in their sports at a very young age. For the present, then, we can put aside this issue of how common early sport involvement is for champion athletes and focus on a related aspect of the early involvement question. That is, what do we know about characteristics of children that would give us some insight into determining how early they should be involved in sport?

The answers to two questions about the characteristics of children will help us better understand this early-involvement issue. First, because sport involves competition, what do we know about children's attitudes about competition and what that means in terms of their involvement in competitive sport? This important question is the focus of the next chapter by Michael W. Passer, so it will not be dealt with here. The second question, however, will provide the basis for the present discussion. That is, because an important element of sport is knowing how to perform the skills of that sport successfully, what do we know about when the child is ready to learn those skills? Taken together, information about readiness for competition and readiness to learn can provide us with a base of information from which to operate in determining whether or not it is important to involve children in sport as early in life as possible.

You have already been introduced to the readiness-to-learn issue in the preceding chapter by Vern Seefeldt. The approach in this chapter will be to amplify some of Seefeldt's points, as well as to add some different perspectives. Specifically, this approach will be to look at the readiness question by considering two related questions. First, do certain *critical periods* exist for learning sport skills that if not taken advantage of will lead to less success than would have been possible if these skills had been introduced during these critical periods? Second, how essential are early experiences for later success? Or, what do we know from research concerned with *early intervention* of experiences with motor skills that will shed light on the readiness or early-development question?

Critical Periods for Learning

Critical period is a phrase often seen in behavioral science literature that is concerned with growth and development. Unfortunately, this phrase is often misunderstood, misused, and even overused. Some of the confusion results from the lack of a consistent definition in addition to a lack of understanding about what determines the onset and duration of a critical period. What is known, however, is that there are at least three types of critical periods related to human behavior. Each type seems to have its own meaning, means of determination, and implications. An excellent review of these three types of critical periods is included in an article by Scott (1962) as well as in any number of child development textbooks.

Briefly, the three types of critical periods that have been identified are those that have their effects on emotional development, social development, and learning. The bulk of the research concerned with critical periods has focused on the formation of basic social relationships and has been primarily animal research, beginning with the classic imprinting studies by Lorenz in 1935. For the present discussion, however, the focus will be on critical periods for learning, with special attention given to implications for youth sport involvement.

Determinants of Critical Periods

The person generally credited with first noticing the phenomenon of critical periods in children was Myrtle McGraw (1935). Her studies of the twins named Jimmy and Johnny are well known to all who have studied motor development. McGraw pointed out that for certain activities, such as walking and tricycling, early practice was not beneficial to learning. For example, Johnny was given considerable practice and instruction for tricycle riding beginning when he was 11 months old. Jimmy, on the other hand, was not exposed to a tricycle until he was 22 months old. Despite the later exposure, Jimmy actually learned to ride much faster than his brother had. However, for other skills, such as roller-skating, early exposure proved beneficial to learning. Johnny was taught to roller-skate at about 1 year old while Jimmy did not begin until he was almost 2 years old. Johnny became quite skilled at skating while Jimmy never achieved the same level. From situations such as these, McGraw concluded that critical periods for learning vary from activity to activity and that there is an optimal period for rapid and skillful learning of each motor skill.

Maturation as the Primary Determinant.   An obvious question that arises from McGraw's conclusion is, What determines the critical period for learning? McGraw (1939) was confident that the primary determinant of critical periods was *maturation*. Her recounting of the original Jimmy and Johnny study led her to conclude that the early practice of tricycling by Johnny proved ineffective because the "activity was initiated before his neuro-muscular mechanisms were ready for such a performance" (p. 3). Later, McGraw (1945) stated rather definitively that it is simply wasted effort to begin training before adequate "neural readiness."

This maturation viewpoint was actually an extension of a developmental theory commonly accepted in McGraw's time. Influential child development theorists such as G. Stanley Hall (1921) and Arnold Gesell (1928) helped promote what was known as the *growth-readiness model* of development. This model proposed that certain organized patterns of growth must occur before learning can effectively contribute to development. In support of this approach, Gesell and Thompson (1929) provided evidence from a motor skill learning study involving a pair of identical twins. At the age of 46 weeks, one twin was given special training in stair climbing while the other received no training. Seven weeks later, the untrained twin did not climb the stairs as well as the trained twin. However, following only 2 weeks of training, which was 5 weeks less than the other twin received, the originally untrained twin surpassed her sister in climbing the stairs. Gesell and Thompson concluded that better learning with less training will result when the child's maturation level is adequate for the skill to be learned. Keep in mind here, however, that it is uncertain what the originally untrained twin was doing and learning during those 7 weeks of no special training.

Maturation Plus Environment as Determinants.   Since the time of the Jimmy and Johnny studies, other viewpoints have been proposed to explain the onset of critical periods. Piaget promoted one influential viewpoint that credits maturation as being a major contributor to development but gives additional consideration to the child's interaction with the environment and to learning, although learning is given a relatively minor role. With regard to cognitive development, Flavell (1963) has pointed out that this model might properly be labeled an *adaptive* model, meaning that development occurs as a result of the child adapting to the demands of the environment and intellectualizing that adjustment.

The intellectualizing process is critical to cognitive development, which Piaget (see Flavell, 1963) saw as strongly dependent on acquired movement capabilities, which, conversely, were strongly dependent on intellectual capabilities. The process was seen to occur through two stages Piaget called assimilation and accommodation. *Assimilation* involves the child attempting to interpret new experiences in view of that child's present stage of development. The child attempts to assimilate new experiences into what he or she currently perceives the world to be. *Accommodation* involves adjusting thought processes to deal with these new experiences; the child attempts to accommodate the new in his or her way of viewing the world. How the child perceives the world at any given time depends on his or her developmental stage. These well-known stages, sensorimotor (birth to 2 years), pre-operational (2 to 8 years), concrete operational (8 to 11 years), and formal operational (11 to 12 years), relate to the cognitive capabilities of the child during his or her preadolescent life. As a result, children will perform tasks consistent with their stages of development; however, new experiences will constantly challenge the child to make appropriate adaptations to the environment.

While the Piaget view is closely tied to maturation as a determinant of the critical periods, it is not as extreme in its view of the role of maturation as the Gesell view. Piaget held that the appearance of a new developmental stage could be facilitated by appropriate environmental interactions. The role of learning in development is seen as a factor involved in adaptation.

Another point of view depicting the interaction of maturation and environment as primary determinants of critical periods gives learning a more important role than the Piaget view. This *cumulative* model, proposed by Robert Gagné (1968, 1970), suggests that the "child progresses from one point to the next in his development . . . because he learns an ordered set of capabilities which build upon each other in progressive fashion through the process of differentiation, recall, and transfer of learning" (1968, p. 181). In effect, this model classifies what is to be learned into a particular category of learning, such as stimulus-response connections, multiple discriminations, concepts, and rules. These classifications are hierarchically organized. This means that if a "rule" is to be learned, all the categories in the hierarchy that underlie the category "rule" are prerequisite skills and must be learned before effective rule learning can occur.

While Gagné developed his model primarily to represent learning cognitive skills, the basic principles appear applicable to motor skills as well. For example, a major tenet of this model is the role of transfer of learning. Gagné (1968) stated that "any learned capability, at any stage of a learning sequence, may operate to mediate other learning which was not deliberately taught" (p. 168). What this means in terms of our present discussion is that if we look again at the Gesell and Thompson (1929) stair-climbing study, a different conclusion than the one they offered can explain the results. According to Gagné's model, it would be possible to argue that the originally trained twin did not have the appropriate prerequisite skills to successfully climb stairs at the time the training took place. On the other hand, during the 7 weeks of training of that twin, the untrained twin was gaining these prerequisite skills. Although the expected result of this study would be the same for the Gagné view and the Gesell view, the explanation of the result would be markedly different. According to the Gagné view, the first twin had to learn prerequisite skills during the training period that her sister did not have to learn during her training because the skills were developed through her own play activity before the formal training began.

An Interactive Viewpoint.   The views of determinants of critical periods just discussed can be considered as falling on a continuum with maturation at one end and learning at the other. The view expressed by Gesell and McGraw should be seen as being much closer to the maturation end of the continuum. The Piaget view would be somewhere nearer the center but still on the maturation end. We can place the Gagné view on the learning end of the continuum. Unfortunately, no conclusive evidence exists to support which one of these approaches is correct. An example demonstrating the state of affairs concerning evidence establishing what the determinants of critical periods are comes from Bruner (1960). He argued that no evidence existed to contradict his hypothesis that falls closer to the learning side of our continuum, while considerable evidence existed to support it.

The best way to resolve the question of what determines a critical period is to look at a view promoted years ago by Scott (1962) in his discussion of critical periods. His conclusion, based on a synthesis of many studies on animal and human learning, was that "the critical period for any specific sort of learning is that time when maximum capacities—sensory, motor, and motivational, as well as psychological ones—are first present" (p. 955). Thus, *no one factor* can be considered as the primary determinant of a critical period. Maturation, environmental interactions, and learning all interact to establish the onset of a critical period.

Critical Periods as Optimal Readiness Periods

According to an interactive view of critical periods in which the child's maturation level, environment, and learning experiences must be taken into account, there is no one critical period for learning a skill. Rather, there are undoubtedly *many* critical periods for skill learning. Therefore, a critical period for learning cannot be viewed as a time during which initiating the learning of a new skill *must* take place if that skill is to be learned at all. Neither will this interactive view accommodate the belief that a skill introduced during the initial critical period will be learned better than if introduced at some other time.

An interactive viewpoint of critical periods also indicates that even when instruction and practice time are sufficient the maturation level of the individual must also be taken into account. And, conversely, even when the child is of the appropriate maturation level for the skill being taught, he or she must also have the appropriate prerequisite skills for successful performance of that skill or instruction and practice will be inefficient.

The interactive view of critical periods, then, suggests it is best to look at critical periods as *optimal readiness periods* for learning. That is, periods of time exist in a person's life when he or she is optimally ready to learn a given skill. When undertaken during an optimal readiness period, learning occurs with greater effectiveness and efficiency than it would at some other time in the person's life. Thus the key is to determine *when* a person is optimally ready to learn.

An Optimal Readiness Model. What factors should be considered in determining when a person is optimally ready to learn a particular skill? I would like to argue that three factors are absolutely critical to include in any list or model of optimal readiness. These factors are the maturation level of the individual, the prior experiences of the individual in relation to those required for the skill being learned, and the motivation of the individual to learn the skill (see Figure 1).

The weighting of any one factor in determining the onset of an optimal period will vary from skill to skill for the same individual as well as from individual to individual for the same skill. For example, suppose the skill to be learned by a child is pitching a baseball to a batter. Two children may be the same age, yet one may not be ready to learn this skill. Why? First of all, one child's physical maturation requirements may not have been met. As you will see in other chapters in this book, chronological age does not equal maturational age. It is possible that the two children in this example could differ by years in their maturational ages, giving credence to the possibility that one of these children is maturationally ready to learn to pitch while the other is not.

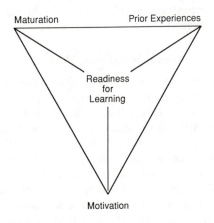

Figure 1. Optimal readiness to learn occurs when a person's maturation level, prior experiences, and motivation are appropriate for the skill to be learned.

Now, suppose both children are maturationally ready to learn the skill of pitching a baseball. The critical factor now becomes the role of previous experiences related to pitching. If only one of these two children has had previous experience with throwing as a movement skill, he or she will be more ready to learn to pitch than the other.

Before discussing the motivation factor in this model it will be instructive to stop and look at an earlier part of this discussion in light of the current readiness model. Recall the Jimmy and Johnny study by McGraw (1935) and the stair-climbing twins study by Gesell and Thompson (1929). Both studies had been used to support the maturational view of readiness. If we consider those studies in view of the interactive readiness model proposed here, the explanation for the results found in those studies will look quite different.

For Jimmy and Johnny, early training in tricycle riding was not beneficial, while early training in roller-skating was. It is easy to apply the interactive readiness model to explain these apparently conflicting results. While the maturation level of the twins played a role undoubtedly in the outcome of the study, it could also be said that neither of the twins had the necessary prerequisite skills needed for tricycle riding. Early training did not benefit either child because appropriate training would have had to include an opportunity to acquire these skills. On the other hand, the twins may not have been equal in their levels of prerequisite experiences necessary to successfully learn to roller-skate. Based on the information available about these twins, it is impossible to determine if such a hypothesis is correct.

Regarding the stair-climbing study by Gesell and Thompson, the possibility was proposed earlier that at the time of initial training of one twin neither had acquired the prerequisite skills for successful stair climbing. However, over the course of the 7-week training session for one twin, the prerequisite skills were part of what was learned and what contributed to the lengthy training period. The other twin could have gained the prerequisite skills as a result of her own exploring activities during the first twin's training period, therefore requiring much less time to learn stair climbing when she was given instruction. Again, this view does not negate the importance of maturation but adds another dimension—previous experience with prerequisite skills—to the explanation of the skill-learning differences observed in the twins.

At this point, then, the interrelationship between maturation and prior experiences should be evident: Neither can stand alone to explain the onset of optimal readiness. For certain skills, there is ample evidence to show that maturation is more important as the determining factor. For other skills, however, especially for the more complex skills, the evidence points to prior experience with prerequisite skills as the more powerful determining factor. The relative importance of maturation and prior experience on the learning of a complex motor skill is an issue worthy of much debate and further research. However, for this discussion it is sufficient to indicate that for initial learning, the acquisition of prerequisite skills is a critical factor in determining the period of optimal readiness to learn.

The Role of Motivation.   Thus far in this discussion the one element of the optimal readiness model that has been ignored is *motivation*. Although this term is difficult to categorically define, we can, for purposes here, define motivation as a state of being energized to engage in an activity. Just as a battery-driven toy needs a battery to operate, a human needs to be energized to be able to perform in a situation where learning must occur. However, unlike the battery-driven toy, the energizing does not always originate within the individual. Adequate motivation to learn may exist in an individual for a given skill, but for a different skill the motivation to learn must be induced from some external source, such as social approval.

The source of adequate motivation to learn has been debated for many years. However, in line with the view being presented here, a statement by Ausubel (1968) is pertinent. He stated that "the causal relationship between motivation and learning is typically reciprocal rather than unidirectional" (p. 365). According to such a view, it could be argued that instruction should not necessarily be postponed until the child is adequately motivated to learn the skill to be taught. On the contrary, Ausubel's position indicates that by simply introducing the skill to the child, he or she may become sufficiently motivated to learn it. Many children resist getting involved in learning a particular skill because of preconceived notions about the skill, which may be unfounded. For example, I have taught college badminton to men who took the class only because they were required to. They had resisted because of a lack of knowledge about the game that resulted in an incorrect perception. However, as a result of being introduced to badminton, they developed a tremendous motivation to learn the game and became avid players long after the class was over.

The Influence of Early Experiences

In the preceding section, the role of prior skill-related experiences was seen as essential for determining when a child is optimally ready to learn a particular skill. If the prerequisite skills that should have been acquired as a result of those experiences have not been acquired, then instruction in the skill of interest will have to provide them. The question then arises, Will exposure to those prerequisite experiences as early in life as possible be beneficial? For example, if my goal is to develop a child into a champion swimmer, would it be beneficial to expose the child to the basic fundamentals of swimming as early in life as possible? Would it be an *advantage* over not having the early exposure?

While the benefit, or the lack of benefit, of exposure to sport skills as early in life as possible has not been heavily researched some evidence exists that could shed light on the question of early exposure.

You have already seen some conflicting evidence in the discussion of the Jimmy and Johnny study. Recall that for some skills early training did little to create an advantage in later performance, while in other skills early exposure seemed beneficial. But, is what happened with Jimmy and Johnny common, or was it unique to these two twins? The best way to answer this question is to look at the results of early training in other situations.

An excellent discussion of the effects of early exposure and early deprivation is in a motor development text by Payne and Isaacs (1987). They discuss, among other early-exposure programs, infant swim programs and the Suzuki violin program. These two programs offer interesting examples, as they deal with two quite different skills—one a sport skill and the other a music skill—both of which require a high degree of motor skill learning.

Swimming is a sport well-known for early involvement. Teaching infants to swim (without emphasis on competition) has become very popular. Since a successful swimmer on any competitive team must first learn how to swim, it seems to make good sense to teach a child the basics of swimming as early as possible. If a child is maturationally capable of learning the rudiments of swimming as an infant, shouldn't early training be an advantage for the child who has aspirations of being a successful competitor? While this logic may have intuitive appeal, the evidence supporting it is negligible. While there have been children who were involved in infant swim programs that became champion swimmers, there also have been other children who were involved in these programs that did not achieve any level of competitive success. In fact, there are some who made either no improvement in their swimming skill or, worse, developed a fear of the water that was greater than when they began the program.

Similar results are found with the Suzuki program, in which children begin learning to play the violin as early as 2 years old. The process of preparing the child for learning, however, is a carefully planned approach that appears to take into account all three factors in the readiness model described earlier. Children are introduced to the sound of the violin as early as birth. Parents are instructed to provide well-played, tonal violin music to establish an interest as well as a base of understanding from which to operate at a later time. Using this approach, both the motivation to learn and some of the prerequisite skills are developed before the child begins to learn the mechanics of playing violin. When the child begins lessons, a violin of appropriate size is provided, rather than the usual larger instruments. Given these factors, it would appear the early violin learning experience of the young child should put him or her at an advantage over a child that begins violin lessons later in life. But, again, while this expectation has intuitive appeal, the evidence is equivocal. Some world-class violinists began by using the Suzuki method. However, there are many who did not begin by using this method, nor did they begin at such a young age. Also, many who began in the Suzuki program failed to develop any success, while others lost interest in playing the violin altogether.

These two examples support the view that it is impossible to predict who will benefit from early exposure to sport skills and who will not. There are too many factors that must be taken into account. These factors include those related to the characteristics of the individual child as well as factors related to the characteristics of the skill to be learned. With regard to the child, the model that has been discussed in this chapter indicates that an important first consideration is the physical, cognitive, and emotional maturation level of the child. If the maturation level is appropriate for the skill to be learned, then it is necessary to consider whether or not the child has the prerequisite skills to learn a sport skill. Finally, there is the need to consider the motivation level of the child. Does the motivation level merit the time and energy required to learn the skill? If not, is it likely that involvement in the activity will develop the motivation level necessary for learning to occur? Each of these child-related issues must be addressed before we can determine if a child is ready to learn the skills required of a particular sport. If deficiencies are seen in any of these factors, appropriate measures should be taken to provide compensation.

Application to Youth Sport

If we go back to the question asked at the beginning of this chapter about the importance of a child's early involvement in sport, what answer has emerged from the discussion so far? To answer the question, it will be helpful to recap what has been concluded from the information presented in this chapter. First, there are certain critical periods in which the child is optimally ready to learn a skill. The onset of these periods is characterized by levels of maturation, past experiences, and motivation that are appropriate for the skill to be learned. Second, after considering some examples of involving young children in motor skill training programs as early as possible, it became clear that it was impossible to predict the potential benefits of involving children in these programs. Although many successful athletes began their sport experience in these types of programs, many did not.

The evidence, then, indicates that the key to success in sport does *not* lie in how early a child gets involved in sport. Rather, the key lies in the child getting involved in sport when he or she is optimally ready to get involved. Since there appear to be several periods in a child's life when optimal readiness occurs, it is not essential to involve the child as early as possible. However, there are benefits to involvement in organized youth sport programs if the child has the appropriate maturation level to perform the skills required in that sport.

As has been discussed, an important need for learning any sport skill is having the prerequisite skills for successful participation in that sport. If a child is to be a successful baseball player, basic baseball skills must be learned first. This is where involvement in youth sport programs is beneficial. The programs provide instruction in these skills. Also, involvement in youth sport programs can provide the type of exposure to a sport that will establish motivation in the child to stay involved in the sport and develop his or her capabilities.

While the points made thus far have been directed to concerns related to the child, there are several implications from this chapter for youth sport programs. If these programs are to provide the types of experiences that will accommodate a child's needs, especially in terms of what is required to foster learning during optimal readiness periods, then certain features must be characteristic. *First*, youth sport programs must regard the teaching of skills necessary to play a specific sport successfully as a priority of the program. If a child has the physical maturation level and the desire necessary to play baseball but lacks the necessary skills to play the game, where will he or she learn them? For the youth sport program, competing to win games must be subservient to the goal of teaching children the skills of the game. This means the coaches of teams must be capable of providing adequate instruction in the basic or fundamental skills of the game. If the sport is baseball, then all coaches should be able to teach a child how to hit properly, throw from the outfield, throw from the infield, throw as a catcher, run the bases, and so forth. Eventual success in any sport depends on having learned the skills of that sport. Consequently, it is critical that youth sport programs emphasize instruction in basic sport skills.

Second, children should be encouraged to get involved in a variety of sport activities. While the question of early specialization in one sport has not been discussed here, there is no question that early specialization, especially before puberty, has little benefit for later success. In fact, sociologists of sport have found that Olympic-class athletes have typically competed in a variety of sports as children rather than specializing in the one they competed in at the Olympics (see McPherson and Brown, this volume). If you consider variety in experiences in light of the discussion of the factors determining the onset of optimal readiness to learn periods, even further support for involvement in a variety of activities is provided. Let's consider the simpler case of variety within one sport. Suppose a boy who is large for his age, an early maturer, decides to play on a youth football team. Early on, the coach tells the boy he will be a lineman because of his size. Then, suppose that as this boy gets older his growth rate slows, so that he is no longer bigger than other kids and consequently not a good lineman. Now, again because of his size, the boy decides he wants to be a running back. Consider the disadvantage he faces—he has never had the opportunity to learn the skills necessary to be a running back. For example, he has never handled the football before. If the coaches do not provide the necessary training for this boy, he will likely drop out of football due to his lack of success. The lack of success may have been avoided had there been an adequate variety of skill experiences provided when the boy was younger.

Third, youth sport programs should provide an environment in which children want to participate. This point is important based on the earlier discussion about motivation and learning, where it was evident that the motivation necessary to learn a skill can be established by providing experiences for the child that give him or her a desire to learn more and participate more in the activity. A successful way to accomplish this goal is to provide a range of opportunities in which children can experience success. Children continually confronted with activities they are incapable of performing will likely develop a lack of interest in those activities. In some cases, the realization of a lack of capability to compete is beneficial to the developing child. In other cases the lack of success is due to being in situations that do not take the child's present capabilities into account. A child provided with situations in which he or she can successfully compete will be able to develop his or her skill level and may eventually be capable of competing at higher levels of competition.

Fourth, youth sport programs should *not* have policies that allow the "cutting" of players. Because there are several optimal readiness periods in a child's life, it is possible that what is judged by a coach as poor skill or a lack of future potential for success may actually be the lack of being ready to learn the skills necessary to perform the sport. All three factors that determine optimal readiness periods are important here. If a child is late to mature, he or she may not show the level of skill others his or her age show. There are accounts of many successful world-class and professional athletes who were cut or almost cut from teams when they were young. One wonders how many potentially great athletes never became great because they did not return to sport participation after being cut. The lack of prerequisite skills and/or motivation can also be a factor if a child shows poor skill at a young age. It is essential that youth sport programs accommodate the young child who cannot compete successfully with the best athletes of his or her age. Programs developed on the basis of comparable skill levels or maturation age levels (rather than on chronological age) accomplish the goal of providing an opportunity for all children to participate.

These few implications for youth sport programs are just some of the many that could be developed from the readiness model presented in this chapter. Youth sport programs need to be closely tied to the concept of readiness to learn. Individuals responsible for organizing and supervising these programs have a responsibility to run programs that take into account each child's maturation status, prior skill experiences, and motivation to participate.

References

Ausubel, D.P. (1968). *Educational psychology: A cognitive view*. New York: Holt, Rinehart, & Winston.

Bruner, J.D. (1960). *The process of education*. Cambridge, MA: Harvard University Press.

Flavell, J.H. (1963). *The developmental psychology of Jean Piaget*. Princeton, NJ: Van Nostrand.

Gagné, R.M. (1968). Contributions of learning to human development. *Psychological Review*, **75**, 177-191.

Gagné, R.M. (1970). *The conditions of learning* (2nd ed.). New York: Holt, Rinehart, & Winston.

Gesell, A. (1928). *Infancy and human growth*. New York: Macmillan.

Gesell, A., & Thompson, H. (1929). Learning and growth in identical twin infants. *Genetic Psychology Monographs*, **6**, 1-124.

Hall, G.S. (1921). *Aspects of child life and education*. New York: Appleton.

McGraw, M.B. (1935). *Growth: A study of Johnny and Jimmy*. New York: Appleton-Century.

McGraw, M.B. (1939). Later developments of children specifically trained during infancy: Johnny and Jimmy at school age. *Child Development*, **10**, 1-19.

McGraw, M.B. (1945). *The neuromuscular maturation of the human infant*. New York: Hafner.

McPherson, B.D., & Brown, B.A. (1988). The structure, processes, and consequences of sport for children. In F.L. Smoll, R.A. Magill, & M.J. Ash (Eds.), *Children in sport* (3rd ed., pp. 265-286). Champaign, IL: Human Kinetics.

Payne, V.G., & Isaacs, L.D. (1987). *Human motor development: A lifespan approach*. Mountain View, CA: Mayfield.

Scott, J.P. (1962). Critical periods in behavioral development. *Science*, **138**, 949-958.

CHAPTER 7

Psychological Issues in Determining Children's Age-Readiness for Competition

Michael W. Passer

A local evening news broadcast several years ago provided some film coverage of a children's competition held in a suburb of Seattle. As memory serves, it was a short foot race—perhaps only 10 or 15 yards long—but even so it took the competitors quite a while to finish. Then again, not all of them *did* finish. Some merely stood still, some wandered in circles, and others made their way toward the crowd on the sidelines; some smiled, some cried, and others simply looked confused. I guess you can't expect much more of 1-year-olds; at least the parents who organized the competition seemed to be having a good time.

The very young age of these track stars did not come as a total surprise to me, for some time earlier I had heard of a "baby decathlon" competition held in the Midwest. Still, the news footage of the race was disconcerting because it suggested that such events might be more common than I had thought and reaffirmed just how far some parents will go to give their children an early thrust into the world of competition. I was left wondering whether neonatal or prenatal competitions might not be too far behind.

Although these "contests" for toddlers do not (yet) represent formal youth sports, they vividly highlight one of the most basic questions that researchers, educators, coaches, and parents ask about children's involvement in adult-organized athletics: At what age are children ready to compete? This issue takes on added significance in light of recent information detailing the earliest age at which children in various countries begin participation in organized competitive sports. In Brazil, for example, 6-year-olds compete in swimming, soccer, and gymnastics (Ferreira, 1986). In Canada, competition for 6- to 8-year-olds is offered in some sports at the provincial level (Valeriote & Hansen, this volume). Some 4-year-old Australian children are involved in organized sports (Robertson, 1986), and in the United States the earliest age of participation is 3 years for swimming and gymnastics, 5 years for track and field, wrestling, and baseball, and 6 years for soccer and bowling (Martens, this volume).

While most children join the ranks of youth sport at a later age (to be discussed shortly), the preceding figures suggest that participation by 3- to 6-year-olds has become increasingly common. Should children be competing in organized sport at such a young age? Whether viewed at the level of the individual child or in terms of general age guidelines, the concept of readiness for competitive sport is extremely complex; it involves issues of physical, motor skill, psychological, and social development, along with considerations of the task demands of the particular sport, parental readiness, and broader socialization factors (see reviews by Coakley, 1986; Malina, 1986; Seefeldt, this volume; Sharkey, 1986). Focusing here on psychological evidence for developing general age guidelines for participation in youth sport, three issues will be addressed: motivational readiness, cognitive readiness, and potential harmful consequences of participation at too early an age.

Motivational Readiness for Competition

Competition is a social comparison process. Whether in music, academics, or sport, competition gives children the direct opportunity to test and evaluate their abilities against those of other youngsters. This is important to children because it is a primary means by which they assess their competence (Horn & Hasbrook, 1986; Scanlan, this volume). From a motivational standpoint, readiness for competition occurs when children become attracted to and seek out opportunities for comparing themselves with peers. In fact, several investigators have emphasized that very young children cannot and do not compete because they are incapable of or uninterested in social comparison (Roberts, 1980; Scanlan, this volume; Sherif, 1976).

At what age do children become oriented toward social comparison? When they are about 1½ to 2½ years old, children develop a well-organized, autonomous achievement orientation that evolves from a more basic mastery or competence motivation (Veroff, 1969; White, 1959). The child masters new skills via exploration and play and readily evaluates mastery attempt outcomes. Competence is judged based on autonomous standards, and satisfaction is derived from successful mastery attempts. From 3½ to 5½ years of age children increasingly act to maximize their self-gain at the expense of others when placed in conflict-of-interest situations (see Pepitone, 1980). To adults, it often appears that these children are competing rather than cooperating because they vie with peers for desired objects or limited rewards. But this is not competition in a social comparison sense. Rather, these children simply act to acquire more of something they value (Pepitone, 1980). In essence, they are still pursuing autonomous achievement goals.

According to Veroff (1969), it is not until the age of 5 or 6 that children begin to spontaneously compare their performance with that of other children for the purpose of evaluating their own competence. He also notes that this social comparison orientation strengthens during the elementary school years. Research not only supports Veroff's contentions (see Pepitone, 1980; Veroff, 1969; Weiner & Kun, 1978), but also provides evidence that children's interest in competition stems directly from this burgeoning desire for social comparison. Naturalistic observation studies (e.g., Rowen, 1973), for example, indicate that around the ages of 6 or 7 children begin to transform all sorts of situations into competitive ones to determine who is "the best." Similarly, gaming research reveals that competition becomes an independent social motive around the age of 7, and also indicates that children from various countries will increase their competitive behavior when social comparison information is made available (Toda, Shinotsuka, McClintock, & Stech, 1978). In sum, findings from diverse lines of research suggest that the early elementary school years are when most children develop an interest in social comparison and seek out competitive situations specifically for their social comparison value.

Although numerous qualities serve as focal points for youngsters' social comparison and competition, physical and athletic ability are particularly valued attributes among children of elementary and secondary school age (Buchanan, Blankenbaker, & Cotten, 1976; Coleman, 1961; Duda, 1981). Therefore, as social comparison motivation strengthens during the elementary school years, it would be expected that an increasing number of youngsters would seek out sport opportunities to develop and assess their athletic skills relative to their peers. This is, in fact, what happens. Depending on the sport, the average beginning age of participation in nonschool (i.e., nonmandatory) youth sport programs typically ranges from 8 to 12 years (Martens, this volume; Valeriote & Hansen, this volume), and the total number of participants across most sports grows steadily until peaking at around the ages of 11 to 13 (State of Michigan, 1976).

This analysis suggests two conclusions. First, if motivational readiness for competition is the main criterion upon which general age guidelines in youth sport are to be based, then participation should not begin until children are about 7 years old. At this age the desire for and ability to use social comparison information should be reasonably well developed in most children. Second, for the vast majority of children, their age of initial involvement in youth sport currently falls well within this guideline.

As noted earlier, however, some 3- to 6-year-olds do compete in youth sport. Is this not evidence that even preschoolers are able to compete? Indeed, the issue of motivational readiness is complex, and several arguments could be given for involving such young children. Perhaps the social comparison function of competition has been overemphasized. After all, children who developmentally are not in a social comparison stage surely can participate in sport, have fun, learn skills, attempt goals, and gain feedback about their abilities that would feed into their autonomous achievement orientation. This stance is reasonable but fails to take into account one important fact: Every one of these benefits can be obtained from noncompetitive instructional or play settings. If the activity is truly being conducted for the child's benefit and enjoyment, rather than for the satisfaction of parents or other adults, then there is absolutely no need to formalize and structure physical activities into highly organized competitive games for children to whom social comparison is meaningless or unimportant.

But what if preschoolers can engage in social comparison? A second counterpoint to the age guideline proposed above stems from the social comparison literature itself. In a clever study by Pascuzzi (1981), second graders and preschoolers ran in races with two other children of the same sex and age group. After each race, Pascuzzi measured the children's emotional responses, self-concept of ability, and expectancy of future success. All of these psychological variables had been shown in earlier research to be influenced by perceptions of success and failure. Thus, Pascuzzi reasoned that if the children's psychological responses after the race differed according to whether they finished first, second, or third, this would indicate that they judged their own performance relative to how well their peers did. If the children did not engage in social comparison, then the order of finish would have no bearing on their postrace responses. As predicted, second graders' responses varied according to their place of finish; surprisingly, so did the responses of the preschool boys. Only the preschool girls showed similar psychological responses regardless of their order of finish.

It is essential to keep in mind that the children in Pascuzzi's study (1981) were *placed* in races; her results do not imply that preschoolers spontaneously seek out opportunities to socially compare or compete. Nevertheless, her findings suggest that preschool age boys do engage in social comparison when they find themselves in a competitive situation. This supports Veroff's (1969) contention that even 4-year-olds can learn social comparison standards and are capable of comparing themselves to others if asked to. Veroff also proposes that children may become intrinsically socially comparative if their environment (e.g., attending preschool) orients them toward this. Therefore, it could be argued that some preschoolers may be intrinsically oriented to compare and compete with others, that others are capable of social comparison when externally prompted, and that for the remainder, involvement in competitive sport will accelerate their capacity for and interest in social comparison and competition. Whether this is a desirable developmental goal can be answered only in relation to one's personal values about childhood.

Cognitive Readiness for Competition

It is all too easy for adults to take for granted the numerous cognitive abilities and reasoning skills that come into play during competition and which help make competition a maximally rewarding experience. Even though children may be motivationally ready to compete once they become oriented toward social comparison, their perception of competition will differ significantly from that of adults. Both Coakley (1986) and Roberts (1980), for example, propose that children's cognitive abilities are such that they do not develop a mature understanding of the competition process until they are about 12 years old.

Coakley (1986) notes that regardless of whether coactive (e.g., swimming, running) or counteractive (e.g., wrestling, football) sports are involved, full comprehension of what it means to compete against an opponent cannot occur until children possess the ability to put themselves into the point of view or role of other participants. Citing developmental work by Selman (1971, 1976), Coakley argues that such perspective- and role-taking abilities do not begin to develop until 8 to 10 years of age. Between the ages of 10 and 12, children develop the capacity to comprehend more than just one other viewpoint; after age 12 they can readily adopt a group perspective. An implication of this developmental sequence is that in team sports children under the age of 10, and even many 10- to 12-year-olds, will have difficulty understanding that a team is comprised of interdependent positions that must simultaneously respond to each others' and the opposing players' movements (Coakley, 1986). Overall, Coakley proposes that organized sport programs for children younger than 8 should focus almost entirely on developing individual physical skills, that a competitive emphasis should be gradually introduced during the ages of 10 to 12, and that competition should take on a primary emphasis in youth sport only after children attain the age of 12.

The capacity to perceive complex causal relationships also is essential to a mature understanding of the competition process. As noted earlier, children seek out competition because it provides social comparison information that helps them assess their competence. Yet, competence cannot be judged accurately until one becomes aware that success-failure and other performance outcomes in sport are the product of interactive causal factors such as physical skill, strategy, and effort in relation to task (opponent) difficulty. In turn, the operation of these causes cannot be fully assessed until the individual has learned to be sensitive to numerous antecedent cues (e.g., own and opponent's past success-failure history, the pattern of current performance). It is not until the late elementary and early secondary school years that these cognitive capabilities become well developed (Nicholls, 1978; Roberts, 1980, 1986; Weiner & Kun, 1978). For example, research by Ewing, Roberts, and Pemberton (cited in Roberts, 1986) with 9- to 14-year-old youth sport participants found that children younger than 12 were not able to differentiate between the relative contributions of effort and ability as determinants of success and failure.

These developmental shifts in causal reasoning influence not only how children of different ages will assess their competence based on performance outcomes, but also how they will respond emotionally to those outcomes, what their future performance aspirations and success expectancies will be, and how they will approve or disapprove of other children based on those children's outcomes. For example, whereas at age 6 children's expectancies of future success begin to be influenced by their past success-failure outcomes, it may not be until 10 to 12 years of age that their success expectancies become influenced by the attributions they make for these outcomes (Weiner & Kun, 1978). As Weiner and Kun note, in order to develop realistic performance expectancies and achievement goals, children may first need to understand that how well one does in the future depends on the *cause* of having done well or poorly in the past. Similarly, Roberts (1986) suggests that children's attributional capacities influence their general achievement goals in sport.

As was the case in discussing children's motivational readiness for competition, the present analysis of cognitive readiness must be qualified by research indicating that children's cognitive abilities develop more quickly than previously believed. Even preschoolers, for example, have been shown in numerous studies (see Gelman, 1979; Modgil & Modgil, 1982) to have rudimentary perspective-taking abilities and some other basic cognitive capacities (e.g., the belief that causes occur before their effects, sensitivity to temporal order) that are needed to understand the competition process. Nevertheless, these formative cognitive skills are a long step from the more sophisticated role-taking and attributional abilities described above.

Potential Harmful Consequences

Parents often ask about age guidelines for youth sport because they are concerned that participation at too early an age might produce harmful physical or psychological consequences. From a psychological perspective, the most important point is that youth sport competition *at any age* can have negative effects if the setting is aversive. For example, psychological stress brought about by an overemphasis on competition and winning can adversely affect children's and young adolescents' health, enjoyment of sport, and performance (see Passer, this volume). There simply is no magic age beyond which participation in youth sport can be delayed so as to guarantee that such outcomes will not occur. Still, there are some special hazards that must be considered prior to involving young children in organized sport.

Several negative consequences can arise when children who are not motivationally ready are placed in competitive events. At best, the physical activity will be enjoyed, but the competitive component simply will be meaningless or irrelevant to children who are not oriented toward social comparison; they will focus instead on autonomous individual achievement goals. At worst, the children will not enjoy the activity for intrinsic reasons and may find themselves involved in youth sport, not because they want to be, but because others—such as their parents—have decided they ought to be. In turn, research suggests that children who feel it is not their own decision to participate in youth sport are less likely to be satisfied with their sport experience and more likely to discontinue their involvement (McGuire & Cook, 1983). Children who report participating in youth sport to please their parents have also been found to have higher competitive stress (Scanlan & Lewthwaite, 1984).

As noted earlier, young children do not understand complex causal relationships and may be especially likely to form inaccurate assessments of their physical competence based on success-failure outcomes in sport. Indeed, the correlation between perceived and actual competence is weaker among younger children (see Roberts, 1986). Inaccurate perceptions of ability subsequently may cause children to develop unrealistic achievement goals. This difficulty in assessing competence also increases young children's dependence on performance-related feedback from adults. Thus, young children are especially sensitive to comments and reactions by adults, sometimes in ways that adults do not realize. For example, when 7- to 9-year-olds perform well or do something positive and coaches ignore it (i.e., they fail to offer praise), the children may interpret the lack of reaction as punishment or criticism (Smith, Smoll, & Curtis, 1978). Similarly, constructive mild criticism from adults may be perceived by young children as evidence of failure rather than as helpful advice, the result being that the children experience stress (Roberts, 1986).

Another potential hazard of participation at an early age is that young children, limited by language capacity and other undeveloped cognitive skills, cannot understand the directions or instructions of adults as well as older children can. This inability may cause frustration and stress not only for the child, but also for parents and coaches who feel they are communicating clearly and become annoyed when their instructions are not obeyed. In some cases these adults may have unrealistic expectations of children's cognitive abilities and speak to them as if they are miniature adults (a tendency facilitated, perhaps, by the stylish uniforms and other adult trappings of many youth sport programs). In other cases, well-meaning parents and coaches may do a good job of adjusting task demands and their level of speech to the age of the child, but may not be fully aware of the sometimes subtle limitations in children's cognitive abilities (e.g., very young children find it much more difficult to understand negative instructions [Don't do X] than positive instructions [Do Y]). Thus, the readiness of parents and coaches to work within the level of youngsters' cognitive abilities becomes another important consideration in determining the age at which children should become involved in youth sport (Malina, 1986).

Age Guidelines and Conclusions

Given the necessary motor development, children of virtually any age— even toddlers—can be placed in athletic events or physical contests that are organized and labeled by adults as *competition*. But it is not until the early elementary school years that most children will have a fairly well-developed orientation to respond to these contests as competition in the social comparison sense that adults do, much less spontaneously seek out competitive sport situations for their social comparison value. Psychological arguments can be given for involving younger children and, alternatively, for delaying their involvement. Specifically, while some of the research on children's capacity for social comparison could be used to justify the involvement of preschoolers in competitive sport, research on children's cognitive abilities suggests that they are not fully ready to participate in organized competitive sport until the late elementary school years.

In sum, although psychological research pertaining to children's age-readiness is suggestive, it does not provide clear-cut answers. The issue of readiness is further complicated by the considerable differences that exist in the rate of children's psychological development and in the kinds of competitive sport environments to which they are exposed. Nevertheless, based on the present analyses, it is recommended that children younger than 7 or 8 be discouraged from participating in organized youth sport. By this age most children should have a general motivational readiness for competition and cognitive abilities sufficient for a basic understanding of the competition process. In agreement with Coakley (1986), however, the competitive emphasis of sport should be phased in gradually as children get older. Certainly the age of initial involvement should be delayed in specific sports if concerns about physiological capacity, anatomical development, or other physical growth matters exist. Additionally, because children's understanding of competition will not be well developed until they are about 12, it is essential that the parents and coaches of preteens competing in youth sport be made aware of the ways in which children's cognitive capacities differ from those of adults. This educational goal should be a central component of coach and parent training programs.

Some adults might argue that involving preschoolers in sport competition is necessary if the children are to become highly skilled performers or possibly champions when they grow older. In response, I would ask them first for data to support this argument, since I know of none. Second, I would note that if very young children are to be involved in adult-supervised physical activity or sport, their time would be better spent on skill development than on competition. Third, I would point out that even in countries such as the Soviet Union, where elite training programs in some sports begin as early as age 4 or 5, many sport specialists have begun to doubt whether the final level of skill achieved by athletes is proportional to the number of years spent in training (Jefferies, 1986). Lastly, to those few parents desirous of entering their toddlers in physical contests, I have one simple suggestion: Ask your child, "What does competition mean?" The response should prove illuminating.

References

Buchanan, H.T., Blankenbaker, J., & Cotten, D. (1976). Academic and athletic ability as popularity factors in elementary school children. *Research Quarterly*, **3**, 320-325.

Coakley, J. (1986). When should children begin competing? A sociological perspective. In M.R. Weiss & D. Gould (Eds.), *Sport for children and youths* (pp. 59-63). Champaign, IL: Human Kinetics.

Coleman, J.S. (1961). Athletics in high school. *Annals of the American Academy of Political and Social Science*, **338**, 33-43.

Duda, J.L. (1981). *A cross-cultural analysis of achievement motivation in sport and the classroom*. Unpublished doctoral dissertation, University of Illinois, Urbana-Champaign.

Ferreira, M.B.R. (1986). Youth sport in Brazil. In M.R. Weiss & D. Gould (Eds.), *Sport for children and youths* (pp. 11-15). Champaign, IL: Human Kinetics.

Gelman, R. (1979). Preschool thought. *American Psychologist*, **34**, 900-905.

Horn, T.S., & Hasbrook, C. (1986). Informational components influencing children's perception of their physical competence. In M.R. Weiss & D. Gould (Eds.), *Sport for children and youths* (pp. 81-88). Champaign, IL: Human Kinetics.

Jefferies, S.C. (1986). Youth sport in the Soviet Union. In M.R. Weiss & D. Gould (Eds.), *Sport for children and youths* (pp. 35-40). Champaign, IL: Human Kinetics.

Malina, R.M. (1986). Readiness for competitive youth sport. In M.R. Weiss & D. Gould (Eds.), *Sport for children and youths* (pp. 45-50). Champaign, IL: Human Kinetics.

Martens, R. (1988). Youth sport in the USA. In F.L. Smoll, R.A. Magill, & M .J. Ash (Eds.), *Children in sport* (3rd ed., pp. 17-23). Champaign, IL: Human Kinetics.

McGuire, R.T., & Cook, D.L. (1983). The influence of others and the decision to participate in youth sports. *Journal of Sport Behavior*, **6**, 9-16.

Modgil, S., & Modgil, C. (Eds.). (1982). *Jean Piaget: Consensus and controversy*. New York: Praeger.

Nicholls, J.G. (1978). The development of the concepts of effort and ability, perception of own attainment, and the understanding that difficult tasks require more ability. *Child Development*, **49**, 800-814.

Pascuzzi, D.L. (1981). Young children's perception of success and failure [Abstract]. *Psychology of Motor Behavior & Sport—1981*, p. 97.

Passer, M.W. (1988). Determinants and consequences of children's competitive stress. In F.L. Smoll, R.A. Magill, & M.J. Ash (Eds.), *Children in sport* (3rd ed., pp. 203-227). Champaign, IL: Human Kinetics.

Pepitone, E.A. (1980). *Children in cooperation and competition*. Lexington, MA: D.C. Heath.

Roberts, G.C. (1980). Children in competition: A theoretical perspective and recommendations for practice. *Motor Skills: Theory Into Practice*, **4**, 37-50.

Roberts, G.C. (1986). The perception of stress: A potential source and its development. In M.R. Weiss & D. Gould (Eds.), *Sport for children and youths* (pp. 119-126). Champaign, IL: Human Kinetics.

Robertson, I. (1986). Youth sport in Australia. In M.R. Weiss & D. Gould (Eds.), *Sport for children and youths* (pp. 5-10). Champaign, IL: Human Kinetics.

Rowen, B. (1973). *The children we see: An observational approach to child study*. New York: Holt, Rinehart, & Winston.

Scanlan, T.K. (1988). Social evaluation and the competition process: A developmental perspective. In F.L. Smoll, R.A. Magill, & M.J. Ash (Eds.), *Children in sport* (3rd. ed., pp. 135-148). Champaign, IL: Human Kinetics.

Scanlan, T.K., & Lewthwaite, R. (1984). Social psychological aspects of competition for male youth sport participants: I. Predictors of competitive stress. *Journal of Sport Psychology*, **6**, 208-226.

Seefeldt, V. (1988). The concept of readiness applied to motor skill acquisition. In F.L. Smoll, R.A. Magill, & M.J. Ash (Eds.), *Children in sport* (3rd ed., pp. 45-52). Champaign, IL: Human Kinetics.

Selman, R.L. (1971). Taking another's perspective: Role-taking development in early childhood. *Child Development*, **42**, 1721-1734.

Selman, R.L. (1976). Social-cognitive understanding: A guide to educational and clinical practice. In T. Lickona (Ed.), *Moral development and behavior* (pp. 299-316). New York: Holt, Rinehart, & Winston.

Sharkey, B.J. (1986). When should children begin competing? A physiological perspective. In M.R. Weiss & D. Gould (Eds.), *Sport for children and youths* (pp. 51-54). Champaign, IL: Human Kinetics.

Sherif, C. (1976). The social context of competition. In D. Landers (Ed.), *Social problems in athletics* (pp. 18-36). Urbana: University of Illinois Press.

Smith, R.E., Smoll, F.L., & Curtis, B. (1978). Coaching behaviors in Little League baseball. In F.L. Smoll & R.E. Smith (Eds.), *Psychological perspectives in youth sports* (pp. 173-201). Washington, DC: Hemisphere.

State of Michigan (1976). *Joint legislative study on youth sports programs: Phase I*. East Lansing, MI: Author.

Toda, M., Shinotsuka, H., McClintock, C.G., & Stech, F.J. (1978). Development of competitive behavior as a function of culture, age, and social comparison. *Journal of Personality and Social Psychology*, **36**, 825-839.

Valeriote, T.A., & Hansen, L. (1988). Youth sport in Canada. In F.L. Smoll, R.A. Magill, & M.J. Ash (Eds.), *Children in sport* (3rd ed., pp. 25-29). Champaign, IL: Human Kinetics.

Veroff, J. (1969). Social comparison and the development of achievement motivation. In C.P. Smith (Ed.), *Achievement-related motives in children* (pp. 46-101). New York: Russell Sage Foundation.

Weiner, B., & Kun, A. (1978). *The development of causal attributions and the growth of achievement and social motivation*. Unpublished manuscript, University of California, Los Angeles.

White, R.W. (1959). Motivation reconsidered: The concept of competence. *Psychological Review*, **66**, 297-334.

SECTION 3

Anatomical and Physiological Concerns

The issue of physical harm to young athletes is one of the most frequently cited concerns pertaining to the desirability of youth sport. Does participation in youth sport constitute a danger to the anatomical and physiological well-being of children and youth? There is little question that physical activity is necessary for normal growth and that vigorous activity is essential for promoting optimal physical fitness. However, some physicians, educators, community leaders, and parents have opposed youth sport on the grounds that sport may cause excessive physical stress and might be hazardous for youngsters. More specifically, they have expressed concern about (a) whether stresses of competition are sufficiently great to endanger normal growth, (b) whether sports requiring endurance training have a deleterious effect on the cardiovascular system of young athletes, (c) whether sport participation causes menstrual dysfunction, and (d) whether the injury risks of youth sport are worth the potential benefits of participation. The chapters that follow are directed to these concerns as well as other salient issues.

In chapter 8, Robert M. Malina presents a comprehensive survey of the physical growth and maturation of young male and female athletes. A preliminary topic focuses on the complex interrelationships among maturity status, body size, physique, and body composition in children and adolescents. This information is vital in understanding associations between biological maturity and athletic performance. Malina then reviews evidence indicating that (a) size differences between young athletes and nonathletes are primarily the result of maturity-associated variation in growth and, in some instances, selection for body size in certain sports; (b) male athletes tend to be advanced in biological maturation compared to nonathletes, while female athletes tend to be delayed; and (c) although regular training has no effect on stature, skeletal maturation, or sexual maturation, it is a significant factor in the growth of bone, muscle, and fat, and in the development and maintenance of aerobic capacity. Thus, in summarizing the influence of regular physical activity, Malina concludes that the experience of training for sport does not have harmful effects on the physical growth and maturation of youngsters. In the final part of the chapter, emphasis is given to the importance of biosocial factors in selection for and success in sport.

Cardiovascular functioning is a major concern within the domain of exercise physiology. In chapter 9, Donald A. Bailey and Alan D. Martin approach this topic by considering the cardiorespiratory differences between children and adults. Emphasizing that children are not simply scaled-down models of adults, the authors cite important adult-child differences in aerobic and anaerobic responses to strenuous physical exercise. The question of whether or not functional changes resulting from early sport training persist into adult years is addressed, along with an examination of problems inherent in investigating training effects in children. Next, Bailey and Martin explain why children are less efficient than adults with respect to temperature regulation. They point out that such differences have precautionary implications for children's sport programs conducted in climatic extremes of heat or cold. Concern is then given to the topic of exercise-induced amenorrhea and its harmful effect on skeletal integrity in extremely active young women. Finally, both physiological and philosophical perspectives are included in a discussion of factors contributing to the early identification and development of athletic potential.

In the last chapter of this section, Bill Kozar and Russell H. Lord present information pertaining to overuse injuries in young athletes. In describing the nature of this condition, the authors indicate that an overuse injury occurs when a movement is repeated with an intensity level greater than the musculoskeletal structure involved can withstand. Because of the growth the child is experiencing, the epiphysis, a delicate structure, is most susceptible to injury. Several factors that contribute to the occurrence of overuse injuries are identified, including (a) the fact that taller, heavier, and in many cases less physically fit youngsters are entering intensive training programs at a time when they are most vulnerable to overuse injuries; (b) the role of social facilitation effects; and (c) the limited knowledge and/or training possessed by youth coaches regarding prevention, recognition, and treatment of sport injuries. The chapter concludes with a series of recommendations and guidelines to make the sport environment a safer place for children to play.

CHAPTER 8

Growth and Maturation of Young Athletes: Biological and Social Considerations

Robert M. Malina

The social sanction given to childhood athletics, and the necessary skills for successful participation in athletics, gives sport awesome power not only in the child's world, but also in the broader sociocultural complex within which the child lives. Interscholastic athletic competition for boys at the high school level has been an established feature of the American way of life and is rapidly attaining salience for many high school girls as well. While interscholastic athletic competition at the elementary school level, particularly for boys, has increased, so has agency-sponsored athletic competition. Many communities provide some form of agency-sponsored athletic competition for both young boys and girls, at times in a coeducational setting.

In addition, the frequency with which young participants compete in international sporting events is increasing. It is not uncommon to see in international competitions female swimmers and gymnasts who are 12 and 13 years of age, or male swimmers and track athletes who are 15 and 16 years of age.

Hence, a consideration of the effects of sport participation on growth and development is in order, as is an overview of the growth and maturity characteristics of youngsters successful in sport. Numerous discussions exist on the role of competitive sport in childhood and adolescence, and it is not within the scope of this review to consider the pros and cons of the situation; suffice it to note that most discussions are based on opinion rather than objective data. This report considers the physical growth and maturity characteristics of young athletes (especially those between 9 and 16 years of age), the effects of regular physical activity on growth and biological maturation, and the need for a biocultural or biosocial perspective in youth sport.

General Considerations: Who Is the Young Athlete?

The young athlete is different from his or her peers in that he or she is successful in sport. Differences in size, physique, and behavior are often noted. However, it is necessary to consider whether the differences are attributable to physical training, to variability in maturation rate, and/or to specific selection criteria for some sports. The age range comprising childhood athletics usually encompasses years 9 through 16, a period of significant biological maturity-associated variation in boys and girls (Malina, 1974, 1978, 1988b; Tanner, 1962) that may affect performance and behavior. Comparisons of athletes and non-athletes in the late teens are complicated by late-maturing children catching up with early maturers. While some early-maturing children have decelerated in growth or have already attained adult height at 15 or 16 years of age, the late-maturing children continue to grow, so that the size differences so apparent during early and midadolescence are reduced considerably or even eliminated.

Young athletes are usually defined in terms of success on interscholastic or agency teams (especially football, ice hockey, baseball, basketball, and track), in national and international competitions (especially swimming, track, and gymnastics), and in selected athletic club and age-group competitions (especially swimming, gymnastics, tennis, and figure skating). Young athletes tend to be a highly selected group. Selection is ordinarily based on skill, but sometimes size and physique may also be criteria. Large body size is an advantage in some sports (e.g., American football), but can be a limiting factor in others (e.g., gymnastics). Physique might also be a limiting factor, especially at the somatotype extremes. Endomorphy tends to be negatively related to performance on a variety of motor tasks, while ectomorphy tends to be negatively related to strength. Mesomorphy generally correlates well with strength and performance. Note, however, that correlations between somatotype components and performance are generally low to moderate, and are limited in predictive utility (Malina, 1975).

Relationships between physique and activity pursuits should also be considered. Are individuals with certain physiques predisposed or socialized (including selection) toward certain kinds of physical activities? Studies of outstanding athletes often indicate that they began regular participation and/or competition in sport by 5 or 6 years of age. Many such athletes came from families in which one or both parents had been active in sport. The selection process for athletic ability in many sports apparently begins early in life, and familial influences are significant. The interrelationships of these factors and genetic factors (e.g., heritability of body size and aerobic capacity) must also be considered.

Before evaluating the growth and maturity characteristics of young athletes, the interrelationships of maturity status, body size, physique, and body composition in children must be considered. In many analyses of these relationships, early- and late-maturing children are compared. Note, however, that biological maturity is a continuum upon which these categories are superimposed. Early-maturing boys and girls (i.e., those advanced in skeletal and sexual maturation for their chronological ages) are generally heavier and taller age for age and have more weight for height than their slower maturing peers (i.e., those delayed in skeletal and sexual maturation for their chronological ages). Extreme mesomorphy tends to be related to early maturation in boys, while endomorphy tends to be related to early maturation in girls. On the other hand, extreme ectomorphy or linearity in physique is associated with lateness in maturity in both sexes. Children advanced in maturity generally have larger amounts of fat, muscle and bone tissues, and a larger lean body mass, reflecting larger body size than late-maturing children.

Thus, any evaluation of the relationship between maturity status and athletic performance must consider the relationships among size, build, composition, and maturity status. In their classic studies of strength and performance during adolescence, Jones (1949b) and Espenschade (1940) reported positive maturity relationships for boys. Early-maturing boys are stronger age for age than their average- and late-maturing peers, with the difference between the early- and late-maturing boys being most marked between 13 and 16 years of age. These extreme differences are in part a function of the size differences between the early- and late-maturing groups. The strength differences so evident during the peak of male adolescence are considerably reduced in later adolescence, when late-maturing boys begin to catch up. Early-maturing girls are stronger than late maturers early in adolescence, but they do not maintain this superiority as the adolescent period approaches its termination (Jones, 1949b).

Motor performance of adolescent boys is also positively and significantly related to biological maturity status. Early-maturing boys generally perform better than late maturers (Clarke, 1971; Ellis, Carron, & Bailey, 1975; Espenschade, 1940). Motor performance of adolescent girls, on the other hand, is poorly related to maturity status. However, better performance levels are generally reported for late-maturing girls (Beunen, de Beul, Ostyn, Renson, Simons, & Van Gerven, 1978; Espenschade, 1940), and the differences between contrasting maturity groups are more apparent in later adolescence (16-18 years).

Growth and Maturity Characteristics of Young Athletes

The systematic study of the growth and maturation of youngsters who regularly train for and participate in competitive sport is relatively recent. Except for the early study of Rowe (1933; see following paragraphs), the growth and maturation of young athletes was not a common focus of study. However, with the popularity of Little League baseball, which began in 1939, interest in and perhaps concern for the effects of competitive sport on growth and maturation gradually emerged. Initially, interest focused on boys, but more recently, and with the development of sport programs for women, interest now also focuses on girls who train and compete regularly. The subsequent sections summarize information on the growth and maturity characteristics of young male and female athletes.

Males

Data considering maturity status and relationships to size, physique, and body composition in young male athletes are not extensive, and most information comes from participants in several sports. Much of the data is limited to height and weight, and, more recently, body-composition estimates. Young male athletes (approximately 9 to 16 years of age) are generally taller and heavier, more mesomorphic, stronger, and further advanced in sexual and skeletal maturity than their nonathletic peers. The data, however, are not entirely consistent within and across sports.

At times, young athletes from several sports are combined and treated as a single group. In this regard, the early and occasionally misquoted study of Rowe (1933) must be considered. Comparing growth in height and weight of junior high school athletes and nonathletes (matched on age, height, and weight) over a 2 year period from 13.75 to 15.75 years, Rowe noted that the athletes were larger but grew at a slower rate than nonathletes. This observation is occasionally taken at face value without heeding Rowe's comments (Pařizkova, 1974; Rarick, 1973). Because biological maturity status of the sample was not controlled, Rowe (1933) stressed that the observed differences probably reflected differential timing of the adolescent spurt: ". . . since the athletic group is composed of boys who have matured earlier, age considered, than the group of non-athletic boys the athletic boy is not going to grow as much as the non-athletic boy over the period studied" (p. 115). On the other hand, in a similar study of male junior high school athletes and nonathletes, Shuck (1962) reported no marked alterations in height and weight that could be related to athletic participation.

Growth and maturity characteristics of young male and female athletes in specific sports have been reviewed in more detail elsewhere (Malina, 1982, 1983b, 1986b, 1988a; Malina, Meleski, & Shoup, 1982). For young male athletes, the evidence indicates that advanced maturity in early adolescence (about 10-13 years), with its concomitant size and strength advantages, constitutes an asset positively associated with success in several sports: American football, baseball, swimming, cycling, and track and field. Given the concern for distance running in children, observations of successful long-distance runners between 10 and 12 years of age suggest growth and maturity characteristics consistent with reference data for children of the same age. Participants in ice hockey present an exception. Boys average or delayed in skeletal maturity are more commonly successful at young ages. Data for soccer are not extensive; some evidence at the local club level indicates no clear size and maturity relationships.

As adolescence approaches its termination, the size and maturity status of young male athletes is of less significance in many sports. Clearly, football and basketball, two sports that place a premium on large body size, are exceptions. Many young males are often selected for body size in these sports. Nevertheless, the deceleration in the growth and maturation of early-maturing boys and the catch-up of late-maturing boys reduce the size differences that were so apparent in early adolescence, although physique differences remain.

Hence, a question that merits consideration is, Who are the successful athletes in early and late adolescence? There is no guarantee that success in sport at the elementary or junior high school levels transfers to success at the senior high school level. Many youngsters drop out as the level of competition becomes more difficult and specialization is required. Thus, the sample comprising young male athletes at the pre- and early-adolescent ages may be different from that in late adolescence. For example, in small samples of all-star ice hockey players and nonathletes matched for chronological age, Hamilton and Andrew (1976) noted that the prepubertal all-star hockey players (about 10 years of age) were slightly shorter and lighter on the average, though the differences were not significant. However, at a postpubertal age (about 16 years), the all-star hockey players were significantly taller and heavier and had more weight for height than nonathletes of the same age. These observations, though limited to small samples, suggest that the population of successful ice hockey players in late adolescence may be quite different from that during pre- or early adolescence.

Data on the skeletal maturity of young hockey players are consistent with this suggestion. At the Pee Wee level (11-12 years), the majority of players are average or delayed in skeletal maturity (Malina et al., 1982), but at older levels (Bantam, 13-14 years; Midget, 15-16 years), elite ice hockey players are advanced in maturity status (Larivière & Lafond, 1986).

Females

Among girls, the data indicate delayed biological maturity in athletes compared to nonathletes, with the possible exception of young swimmers. By and large, however, the majority of data for young female athletes is limited to individual sports, specifically gymnastics, figure skating, and swimming. Young female swimmers tend to be average or slightly advanced in maturity status and larger in body size, while young gymnasts and figure skaters are delayed in maturation and are smaller. Limited data for track athletes indicate a delay in maturation not as great as that observed in young gymnasts. Longitudinal data on the heights and weights of young swimmers and gymnasts show size variation at the preschool and elementary school ages (Åstrand,

Engström, Eriksson, Karlberg, Nylander, Saltin, & Thoren, 1963; Peltenburg, Erich, Bernink, Zonderland, & Huisveld, 1984). In the latter study of Dutch swimmers and gymnasts, the swimmers were taller and heavier than Dutch reference data since 3 years of age, while the gymnasts were shorter and lighter than the reference data since 3 years of age. Further, midparent heights and weights (mother's height plus father's height divided by two; the same for weight) were also greater in the swimmers than in the gymnasts (Peltenburg et al., 1984).

These observations would suggest that early in the selection process, the size of the child is a factor affecting the parents' decision to enroll a child in a gymnastics or a swimming program. Further, because height is a characteristic that is under strong genetic control, it is reasonably clear that the size difference between the young gymnasts and swimmers, which is consistent with the size differences between their respective parents, represents genetic differences and is not related to training at an early age.

Clearly, the data for young girls are derived primarily from individual sports. These, however, are the sports most often accessible to young girls, in contrast to team sports, which are ordinarily more available for boys. Individual sports have a smaller number of participants and often have more rigorous selection criteria at the more elite competitive levels. It is of interest that growth and maturation information on elite young tennis players is not extensively reported.

Data on the growth and maturation of young female athletes in team sports are quite limited. Nevertheless, casual observations of participants in volleyball or softball at the local level would seem to indicate somewhat similar trends to those evident in team sports for boys. In little league softball or interschool volleyball competition at the elementary school level, for example, the more successful girls are often larger and more advanced in maturity. The size and, in turn, strength advantage is especially evident in batting, throwing, and serving. There is thus a need to study young athletes of both sexes in different sports, at different competition levels, and at different ages.

Retrospective Studies of Menarche

Maturity status of female athletes can be inferred from retrospective studies of the age at menarche, or the first menstrual period. The age at menarche is perhaps the most commonly reported developmental milestone in female adolescence. It is, however, a rather late maturational event. Menarche occurs, on the average, about 1.2 to 1.3 years after the age of maximum growth (peak height velocity) during the adolescent growth spurt (Malina, 1988b).

The retrospective study of menarche relies on the memory of the individual and thus has the limitation of error of recall. Nevertheless, the studies dealing with age at menarche in athletes, especially the more elite athletes, use the retrospective method. A comprehensive review of such studies has been previously reported (Malina, 1983b). The evidence suggests that with few exceptions menarche is attained later in athletes than in nonathletes and that there is an association between delay in menarche and more advanced competitive levels.

Menarche data for swimmers are somewhat at variance to the preceding. The data for elite young swimmers of 10 to 20 years of age indicate attainment of menarche at an age that approximates the average for nonathletes—about 13.0 years (Malina, 1983b). However, recent estimates of the age at menarche in elite university level swimmers are considerably later, occurring at about 14.3 and 14.4 years (Malina, 1986a; Stager, Robertshaw, & Miescher, 1984). This trend probably reflects the changing makeup of elite women's swimming teams and is related to the issue raised in the discussion of young male athletes— that is, those training for sport, and those who are perhaps successful at sport, at prepubertal or early adolescent ages are not necessarily representative of those who are successful at later ages, who are the athletes that comprise the samples upon which most menarcheal data are based. This is directly relevant for swimming. In the not-too-distant past, many elite swimmers stopped training and competing at 16 or 17 years of age. The opportunity provided by Title IX legislation in the United States has permitted many female athletes to train and compete through their college years. This is especially true for swimming, which was not a common college sport for women 10 to 15 years ago.

Training, Growth, and Maturation

Because participation in sport is concerned to a large extent with intensive physical activity in the form of training for a specific sport or event within a sport, the effects of regular training on the growing child and adolescent also need to be considered. A synopsis of the influences of regular physical activity on physical growth and biological maturation follows. More detailed reviews have been reported previously (Malina, 1979, 1983a, 1986b).

At the outset, physical activity is not necessarily the same thing as regular physical training. Physical activities are obviously a part of training programs, but not all physical activities qualify as training. *Training* refers to the regular, systematic practice of specific physical activities, for example, calisthenics, weight lifting, isometric exercises, running, games or sport activities, and other activities performed at specific intensities and for specific durations. Training programs vary in type, including endurance running or swimming, strength training, sprint training, and skill training. The effects of such programs are generally specific to the type of training stimulus, although training effects induced by one kind of program may be more general. Running, for example, apparently has more general effects than cycling. Thus, training is not a single entity, but varies in kind, intensity, and duration. It can be viewed as a continuum, ranging from relatively mild work to severely stressful activity.

In studies of training during growth, programs vary in type, intensity, and duration, and are often described as mild, moderate, or severe, without more specific definition. At times, youngsters are simply defined as *active* or *inactive*. These labels are often based on teacher and/or coach assessment of frequency and duration of sport participation and on self-reported activity levels, which may or may not be accurate. There is thus a need to qualify and quantify training programs (e.g., how many sessions per week, duration of workouts, how many meters swum during a workout and at what intensity, how many miles run per workout and at what time or pace, and so on). Consider the differences in training of active children in the following example. Swimmers 9 through 12 years of age in some programs may swim about 4,500 meters per session at varying intervals 6 days per week, while in other programs they may swim only 2,500 meters per session. In either instance, such a training load is quite different from that in a competitive gymnastics training program.

Data from a variety of study designs have been used to make inferences about the effects of regular physical activity on growth and maturation. These include, for example, short-term experimental studies of humans and animals, comparisons of athletes and nonathletes both young and adult, studies of extreme unilateral activity such as tennis, and clinical observations such as the effects of immobilization. The most common with children is the comparison of young athletes with nonathletes of the same chronological age. In such comparisons, it is assumed that the athletes had been training regularly, and the differences in growth and maturation relative to nonathletes are attributed to the training programs required for the specific sports. Problems with such an approach are the definition of an athlete at a young age and subject selection. As noted earlier, youngsters proficient in sport are undoubtedly selected for skill and, in some sports, for size. Size, physique, strength, and motor skill proficiency are generally related, and an individual's strength and motor ability may in turn influence his or her level of habitual activity and sport pursuits. Maturity differences also characterize youngsters who excel in sport and these differences are especially apparent circumpuberally. Males who are successful in sport competition are more often than not somewhat advanced in biological maturity status, which reflects the size, strength, and performance advantages associated with earlier maturation. In contrast, females who excel in sport tend to be average or late in biological maturity status. Late-maturing girls tend to be more linear in physique and leaner, both factors that may be more suitable for sport performance.

Given the nature of the data and study designs, the following generalizations on physical activity and growth seem warranted (Malina,

1986c). Physical activity has no apparent effect on stature in growing individuals, but is, however, an important factor in the regulation and maintenance of body weight. Regular activity generally results in an increase in lean tissue and a corresponding decrease in body fat, quite frequently without any appreciable change in body weight. However, most of the changes with training are associated with fat tissue.

Regular physical activity is a significant factor influencing the growth and integrity of bone and muscle tissue. Activity functions to enhance skeletal mineralization and density and to stimulate bone growth in width. Activity can result in muscular hypertrophy, an increase in contractile proteins, and enhanced oxidative enzyme activity in muscle tissue. However, such changes are specific to the type of training program (e.g., endurance versus strength training).

The preceding generalizations on changes in body composition and specific tissues in association with regular physical activity are a function of the intensity and duration of training and of continued activity. Individuals who are more active generally show greater changes in association with training programs than those who are less active. Nevertheless, responses to regular activity tend to be highly individualized.

Changes in response to short-term training programs are generally not permanent and vary with the quantity and type of training. This is especially clear in fluctuating levels of fatness commonly observed with regular activity. During the active training period, fat levels generally decrease; however, as activity levels begin to decline, fat levels may slowly increase.

Because studies of young athletes are often considered in the context of the effects of activity on growth and maturation, the available data indicate that young athletes of both sexes grow as well as nonathletes. The experience of athletic training and competition does not apparently have a negative influence on physical growth.

The effects of regular activity on biological maturation as ordinarily measured in growth studies (i.e., sexual and skeletal maturation) are less studied, but the limited evidence suggests little, if any, effect. More emphasis is placed on sexual maturation of girls because menarche tends to occur later in athletes than in nonathletes. And, because athletes who begin training before menarche tend to have later ages at menarche than those who begin training after menarche, intensive training has been suggested as a factor that *may* delay menarche (Malina, 1983b, 1988a). The data that deal with the inferred relationship between training and delayed menarche are, however, associational, generally based on small samples, and limited to observations of postmenarcheal samples.

Frisch, Gotz-Welbergen, McArthur, Albright, Witschi, Bullen, Birnholz, Reed, & Herman (1981), though not the first to suggest that training may delay menarche, concluded that for every year a girl trains before menarche, her menarche will be delayed by up to 5 months.

This conclusion was based upon a correlation of +0.53 between years of training before menarche and age of menarche in 12 swimmers and six runners. A correlation of this magnitude is moderate at best and accounts for only about 28% of the sample variance. Further, correlation does not imply a cause-effect sequence; rather, the association is likely an artifact. The older a girl is at menarche, the more likely she would have begun training prior to menarche; conversely, the younger a girl is at menarche, the more likely she would have begun training after menarche or would have a shorter period of training prior to menarche (Stager et al., 1984). Also, delayed maturation may be a factor in a girl's decision to take up sport rather than the training causing the lateness (Malina, 1983b). Other factors known to influence menarche (e.g., family size) must also be considered. The influence of family size on an athlete's age at menarche is similar to that observed in samples of nonathletes (Malina, 1988b).

The suggested mechanism for the association between training and delayed menarche is hormonal. It is suggested that intensive training, and perhaps associated energy drain, influences circulating levels of gonadotrophic and ovarian hormones, which, in turn, affect menarche. Exercise is an effective means of stressing the hypothalamic-pituitary-gonadal axis, producing short-term, exercise-related increases in serum levels of almost all gonadotrophic and sex steroid hormones. Other factors, such as diurnal variation, state of feeding or fasting, emotional states, and so on also influence hormonal levels. Further, virtually all hormones are episodically secreted, so that studies of hormonal responses based on single serum samples may not reflect the overall pattern. What is needed are studies in which 24-hour levels of hormones are monitored or in which actual pulses are sampled every 20 minutes or so in response to exercise. Otherwise, the evidence from the available studies of the hormonal response to exercise is inconclusive.

It should perhaps be emphasized that the data upon which the suggestion that training delays menarche is based are derived from samples of postmenarcheal women, both athletes and nonathletes, who are physiologically quite different from the developing girl. Specifically relevant for the prepubertal or pubertal girl are the possible cumulative effects of hormonal responses to regular training. The hormonal responses are apparently essential to meet the stress that intensive activity imposes on the body. Whether or not hormonal responses have an effect on the hypothalamic center, which apparently triggers the changes that initiate sexual maturation and eventually menarche, remains uncertain. Such data are presently lacking. Hormonal data for prepubertal or pubertal girls involved in regular training for sport are limited and the results are variable among studies and inconclusive (Malina, 1988b).

A corollary of the suggestion that training delays menarche is that the weight or body composition changes associated with training may function to delay menarche—by keeping bodies lean, for example. This corollary is, in turn, related to the critical weight or fatness hypothesis that a certain level of weight (about 48 kg) or fatness (about 17%) must be attained for menarche to occur (Frisch, 1976). Accordingly, intensive regular training apparently serves to reduce and maintain fatness below the hypothesized minimal level, thus delaying menarche. The critical weight and fatness hypothesis has been discussed at length by many, with the conclusion that the data do not support the specificity of weight or fatness as the critical variable for menarche (see, for example, Johnston, Roche, Schell, & Wettenhall, 1975; Malina, 1978; Scott & Johnston, 1982; Trussell, 1980).

In contrast to the concern for training and menarche, little is said about the effects of training on the sexual maturation of boys. Given the logic used by Frisch and others (1981) and given the generally advanced maturity status of young male athletes, should it be concluded that regular training accelerates their maturation? Definitely not! Before any conclusions can be drawn, the stress of training and competition as factors that influence sexual maturation needs more systematic and controlled study. Prospective studies in which youngsters are followed from the prepubertal state through puberty, in which several indicators of growth and maturity are monitored, and in which training as well as other factors known to influence growth and maturation are considered are obviously needed. Active youngsters of both sexes should be followed, as it is somewhat puzzling why one would expect training to delay the maturation of girls and not boys, since the underlying neuroendocrine processes are quite similar. Moreover, some evidence (e.g., Bielicki & Charzewski, 1977; Malina, Little, Buschang, DeMoss, & Selby, 1985; Stinson, 1985) suggests that males are more susceptible to various environmental stresses, while females are better buffered against such stresses.

Sexual maturation is related to skeletal maturation in boys and girls, and there is reduced variation in skeletal age at the time of menarche (Malina, 1986b). Hence, the effects of training on skeletal maturation merit consideration. The process of skeletal maturation, which is most often monitored in the bones of the hand and wrist, is influenced by growth hormones during the prepubertal years and the gonadal hormones and others during puberty. Thus, if the hormonal responses to regular training are viewed as important influences on sexual maturation, one might also expect them to influence skeletal maturation, as epiphyseal capping and union are influenced by gonadal hormones (among others). However, regular training for sport does not accelerate or delay skeletal maturation of the hand and wrist in athletes of either sex (Kotulán, Reznickova, & Placheta, 1980; Novotny, 1981).

Biosocial Considerations in Youth Sport

Although the physical growth and maturation of youth athletes is the focus of this chapter, the role of social or cultural factors has been mentioned throughout. Sport at any level cannot be approached purely socially or purely biologically. Rather, a biosocial or biocultural perspective is necessary. Sport may be a social phenomenon, but the biological organism performs and competes within a particular cultural context. And, both biological and social factors contribute to the development of athletes beginning early in life.

Social circumstances may either interact with or vary with a youngster's growth and maturation, in turn influencing his or her opportunities and pursuits in sport. Many individuals have the potential to be good athletes, but not all have the opportunity or the environment in which to realize this potential. Outstanding young athletes are not, therefore, a random sample and are probably not representative of the general population of children and youth.

Biological and social factors are clearly apparent at relatively young ages. Parental encouragement and support often influence the youngster's first experience in competitive sport. In some sports, such as gymnastics, figure skating, swimming, and tennis, economic factors are probably a significant consideration. Those most suited to the demands of a sport, or perhaps most capable of adapting to them physically, physiologically, psychologically, and emotionally, presumably are successful and may eventually comprise the elite competitors. Numerous factors, however, intervene. Selection is an important factor in any consideration of successful young athletes. Selection for sport may be made by the child, the parents, the coaches, or a combination of the three. Self-selection is a critical factor; the child is the one who must train, perform, and compete. The motivation of the child to train and be receptive to coaching is important for success in sport. Selection also occurs, to some extent, by default. Some individuals choose not to participate for reasons unrelated to sport, although they may have the skill and physical characteristics conducive to success.

The skill and physical characteristics of a young athlete are probably important factors in providing early competitive advantages. Success associated with skill and size in turn may facilitate the acquisition of expert coaching and teaching that build upon the young athlete's talent. This process is a good example of an individual's physical characteristics (i.e., size and skill) interacting with social circumstances to secure expert coaching and, in turn, further success, heightened motivation, and so on, all of which may lead to persistence in sport. However, not all talented young athletes benefit from such biosocial interactions. Often, the lack of economic resources may be a limiting factor in securing expert coaching and related requisites for success.

Changing relationships with peers, parents, and coaches often accompany the adolescent growth spurt and sexual maturation. The growth and maturation of children do not occur in a social vacuum. Individual variation in the timing of biological maturation and the associated changes in size, body composition, performance, and behavior are the backdrop against which youth evaluate and interpret their own growth, maturation, and social status among peers. Participation in sport is an important component of this evaluative process. As the late-maturing boy begins to catch up to the early maturer in size and strength, the disadvantage faced previously by the former may be considerably reduced and success in sport may become a reality.

Similar interactions between biological maturation and social circumstances occur among adolescent girls. In contrast to boys, among whom the early maturer's size and strength advantage more often leads to success in sport, it is the late-maturing girl who more often experiences success in sport and persists in sport through adolescence into young adulthood. A two-part hypothesis, a biosocial interpretation, for the later menarche commonly observed in talented athletes has been suggested (Malina, 1983b). First, the physique characteristics associated with later maturation in girls (i.e., linearity) are generally more suitable for successful athletic performance. There is, of course, variation by sport or according to event/position within a given sport. The late-maturing girl has, on the average, characteristically long legs for her stature, relatively narrow hips, and a generally linear physique; she also has less weight for height and less fatness than peers who matured at an earlier age (Tanner, 1962). Late maturers tend to perform better on many motor tasks and the differences between contrasting maturity groups of girls are more apparent in later adolescence—between 16 and 18 years of age. In contrast, the physique characteristics of early-maturing girls (i.e., relatively broad hips, short legs, and excessive fatness) have a negative effect on physical performance, especially in those events in which the body must be projected.

The preceding does not preclude the possibility that some early- and average-maturing girls will have a physique suitable for athletic performance and will perform well in motor tasks. However, on average, late-maturing girls more often have such characteristics.

The association between physique and success in sport is reasonably well established (Carter, 1981), and selection for physique implies that regular training does not significantly alter an individual's physique. Physique is a composite concept, referring to the conformation of the entire body as opposed to emphasis on specific features. The available evidence, based primarily on studies of boys, indicates little, if any, significant changes in physique associated with regular training during childhood and adolescence (Malina, 1983a).

The second part of the hypothesis relates to the socialization process. Early-maturing girls are perhaps socialized away from sport participation, while late-maturing girls tend to be socialized into sport participation. Among females, advancement in maturity may represent a performance advantage early in adolescence (i.e., 9 to 12 years of age). During this period, the larger size of early maturers may be an advantage in sports that place a premium on size and strength. However, with the attainment of menarche, the early-maturing girl is socialized away from sport participation through a number of social- and status-related motives, including new social roles and changing interests, and perhaps through the structure of the sport system. The status of the young teenager in her social group is linked to her femininity, and sport is not ordinarily considered feminine. However, with the increased acceptance of women as athletes, and with more opportunities for young girls to participate and train for sport competition, this perception is changing.

Early-maturing girls are often at a disadvantage socially compared to their late-maturing peers (Jones, 1949a). The latter are more in phase in a developmental sense with early- and average-maturing boys of the same chronological age and may thus have a more favored position in the adolescent social setting. A late-maturing girl who attains menarche at 14 years of age is biologically (developmentally) closer to early- and average-maturing boys, who are more often the good athletes. Early-maturing girls, on the other hand, are out of phase with their female and male chronological age peers. An early-maturing girl, who is advanced in biological maturity by a year or two compared to her late-maturing female peers, is 3 to 4 years advanced biologically relative to most of her male chronological age peers. Such a difference in developmental status is a considerable maturity distance and influences social interaction. Early-maturing girls thus commonly seek out associations with older age groups, who are closer to their physiological developmental level. In this way, biological earliness may influence socialization away from physical activity and sport within a given chronological age group.

Hence, if early-maturing girls are socialized *away* from sport, late-maturing girls are perhaps socialized *into* sport, partly through their biological lateness. Late maturers have the opportunity to continue in athletic activities and thus more time to learn and experience athletic skills before reaching a given maturational event in adolescence. Because late-maturing girls are older chronologically when they attain menarche (and different in physique), they have not experienced the social pressures regarding competitive athletics for girls and/or are more able to cope with the social pressures. Late-maturing girls may have heightened motivational levels because of success in athletic competition; this success may carry over into their social interactions.

Summary

Young athletes of both sexes grow as well as nonathletes—the experience of athletic training and competition does not have harmful effects on the physical growth and development of the youngster. The young trained athlete is also generally leaner, having a lesser percentage of body weight as fat. Young athletes, especially those who participate in endurance sports, show higher functional measures, particularly maximal oxygen consumption. Maturity relationships are not entirely consistent across sports. Male athletes more often than not tend to be advanced maturationally compared to nonathletes. These differences seem more apparent in sports or positions within sports where size is a factor. On the other hand, female athletes tend to be delayed in maturity status, except for age-group swimmers.

Numerous opinions suggest that the larger size and/or optimal growth of the young athlete is due to training. However, regular training has no effect on stature, skeletal maturity, or sexual maturity. Training is a significant factor in influencing the growth and integrity of specific tissues as bone, muscle, and fat and in the development and maintenance of aerobic capacity. However, few studies have really considered the complex interrelationships of chronological age, biological age (skeletal age, age at menarche), body size, and body composition. For example, some data indicate that the capacity to perform near or at optimal intensity for prolonged work is related to skeletal age during growth (see Krahenbuhl, Skinner, & Kohrt, 1985 for a comprehensive review). These relationships, however, tend to be low to moderate and can be translated into common variance estimates ranging from 0% to 50%. The estimates vary according to the age and nature of the physical work capacity criteria used. Some data also suggest that the relationship between skeletal age and submaximal work capacity is somewhat higher during male adolescence. However, work capacity is also related to chronological age, height, and weight; at the same time, skeletal age, chronological age, height, and weight are themselves highly related during adolescence (Bouchard, Malina, Hollmann, & Leblanc, 1976).

The relationships between growth, maturity, and athletic performance are indeed complex. Further, most of the data are derived from small cross-sectional samples, and the limited amount of longitudinal data available is treated in a cross-sectional manner. This fact emphasizes the need for longitudinal studies of young athletes and appropriate controls.

A need exists for follow-up studies of young athletes relating to the persistence of training-associated changes. A number of changes in response to short-term training are generally not permanent and vary with the quantity of training. This is especially clear in the fluctuating levels of fatness in young athletes. Fatness varies inversely with the quantity of training.

The need for continued activity is strikingly evident in a follow-up study (Eriksson, Engström, Karlberg, Saltin, & Thoren, 1971) of the young female swimmers studied by Åstrand and others (1963). The 30 young swimmers were restudied at about 22 years of age, 7 to 8 years after their initial examination, and, on the average, about 5 years after they had stopped regularly swimming. Changes were marked in the functional measures relative to age and body size. In the original study, the young swimmers had maximal oxygen uptakes that were 20% higher than untrained girls; at the follow-up, this functional measure was 15% below the average for Swedish females 20 to 30 years of age. The former young swimmers' average maximal oxygen uptake per kilogram of body weight decreased by almost 29%, from 52 to 37 ml/kg/min. Total hemoglobin decreased by 13%. Their larger heart and lung volumes, on the other hand, did not change appreciably since regular training stopped. The implications of these results are obvious. Continued training is necessary to maintain the high level of functional efficiency attained during the adolescent years.

Related to the persistence of activity-related changes are clinical reports on young athletes in certain sports. Epiphyseal injuries and epiphysitis in the adolescent athlete, for example, in baseball, tennis, and football, though not extremely common, do represent a potential growth-influencing factor and might cause an unevenness of growth. Fortunately, most of the epiphyseal injuries that occur in young athletes are amenable to medical treatment or correction.

More recently, a relatively high incidence of lower back problems has been reported in young gymnasts (Jackson, Wiltse, & Cirincione, 1976; Micheli, 1985). This is a different kind of injury situation that includes back pain associated with a variety of conditions from hyperlordosis, problems with intervertebral discs, stress fractures of the vertebrae, and spondylolysis. Nevertheless, injuries to the growing individual always present the possibility of permanent damage. The data reported, however, are largely clinical cases, and growth of the skeletal element involved or of the young athlete is usually not considered or followed after recuperation or repair. In spite of best medical care, injuries to developing bones of young athletes may result in problems that do not surface until later in life. Such "residual handicaps" (Larson, 1973) associated with childhood athletic injuries might influence the young athlete's subsequent activities in adulthood.

References

Åstrand, P.-O., Engström, L., Eriksson, B.O., Karlberg, P., Nylander, I., Saltin, B., & Thoren, C. (1963). Girl swimmers. *Acta Paediatrica Scandinavica*, **147** (Suppl.), 1-75.

Beunen, G., de Beul, G., Ostyn, M., Renson, R., Simons, J., & Van Gerven, D. (1978). Age of menarche and motor performance in girls aged 11 through 18. In J. Borms & M. Hebbelinck (Eds.), *Pediatric work physiology* (pp. 118-123). Basel: Karger.

Bielicki, T., & Charzewski, J. (1977). Sex differences in the magnitude of statural gains of offspring over parents. *Human Biology*, **49**, 265-277.

Bouchard, C., Malina, R.M., Hollmann, W., & Leblanc, C. (1976). Relationships between skeletal maturity and submaximal working capacity in boys 8 to 18 years. *Medicine and Science in Sports,* **8**, 186-190.

Carter, J.E.L. (1981). Somatotypes of female athletes. In J. Borms, M. Hebbelinck, & A. Venerando (Eds.), *The female athlete* (pp. 85-116). Basel: Karger.

Clarke, H.H. (1971). *Physical and motor tests in the Medford Boys' Growth Study.* Englewood Cliffs, NJ: Prentice-Hall.

Ellis, J.D., Carron, A.V., & Bailey, D.A. (1975). Physical performance in boys from 10 through 16 years. *Human Biology,* **47**, 163-281.

Eriksson, B.O., Engström, I., Karlberg, P., Saltin, B., & Thoren, C. (1971). A physiological analysis of former girl swimmers. *Acta Paediatrica Scandinavica,* **217** (Suppl.), 68-72.

Espenschade, A. (1940). Motor performance in adolescence. *Monographs of the Society for Research in Child Development,* **5** (Serial No. 24), 1-126.

Frisch, R.E. (1976). Fatness of girls from menarche to age 18 years, with a nomogram. *Human Biology,* **48**, 353-359.

Frisch, R.E., Gotz-Welbergen, A.V., McArthur, J.W., Albright, T., Witschi, J., Bullen, B., Birnholz, J., Reed, R.B., & Herman, H. (1981). Delayed menarche and amenorrhea of college athletes in relation to age of onset of training. *Journal of the American Medical Association,* **246**, 1559-1563.

Hamilton, P., & Andrew, G.M. (1976). Influence of growth and athletic training on heart and lung functions. *European Journal of Applied Physiology,* **36**, 27-38.

Jackson, D.W., Wiltse, L.L., Cirincione, R.L. (1976). Spondylolysis in the female gymnast. *Clinical Orthopaedics and Related Research,* **117**, 68-73.

Johnston, F.E., Roche, A.F., Schell, L.M., & Wettenhall, N.B. (1975). Critical weight at menarche: Critique of a hypothesis. *American Journal of Diseases of Children,* **129**, 19-23.

Jones, H.E. (1949a). Adolescence in our society. In Community Service Society of New York (Ed.), *The family in a democratic society* (pp. 70-84). New York: Columbia University Press.

Jones, H.E. (1949b). *Motor performance and growth.* Berkeley: University of California Press.

Kotulán, J., Rezničkova, M., & Placheta, Z. (1980). Exercise and growth. In Z. Placheta (Ed.), *Youth and physical activity* (pp. 61-117). Brno, Czechoslovakia: J.E. Purkyne University Medical Faculty.

Krahenbuhl, G.S., Skinner, J.S., & Kohrt, W.M. (1985). Developmental aspects of maximal aerobic power in children. *Exercise and Sport Sciences Reviews,* **13**, 503-538.

Larivière, G., & Lafond, A. (1986). Physical maturity in young elite ice hockey players [Abstract]. *Canadian Journal of Applied Sport Sciences*, **11**, 24P.

Larson, R.L. (1973). Physical activity and the growth and development of bone and joint structures. In G.L. Rarick (Ed.), *Physical activity: Human growth and development* (pp. 32-59). New York: Academic Press.

Malina, R.M. (1974). Adolescent changes in size, build, composition and performance. *Human Biology*, **46**, 117-131.

Malina, R.M. (1975). Anthropometric correlates of strength and motor performance. *Exercise and Sport Sciences Reviews*, **3**, 249-274.

Malina, R.M. (1978). Adolescent growth and maturation: Selected aspects of current research. *Yearbook of Physical Anthropology*, **21**, 63-94.

Malina, R.M. (1979). The effects of exercise on specific tissues, dimensions and functions during growth. *Studies in Physical Anthropology*, **5**, 21-52.

Malina, R.M. (1982). Physical growth and maturity characteristics of young athletes. In R.A. Magill, M.J. Ash, & F.L. Smoll (Eds.), *Children in sport* (2nd ed., pp. 73-96). Champaign, IL: Human Kinetics.

Malina, R.M. (1983a). Human growth, maturation, and regular physical activity. *Acta Medica Auxologica*, **15**, 5-27.

Malina, R.M. (1983b). Menarche in athletes: A synthesis and hypothesis. *Annals of Human Biology*, **10**, 1-24.

Malina, R.M. (1986a). Age at menarche in university athletes: Pre- and post-Title IX comparisons [Abstract]. *Medicine and Science in Sports and Exercise*, **18** (Suppl.), S50.

Malina, R.M. (1986b). Maturational considerations in elite young athletes. In J.A.P. Day (Ed.), *Perspectives in kinanthropometry* (pp. 29-43). Champaign, IL: Human Kinetics.

Malina, R.M. (1986c). Physical growth and maturation. In V. Seefeldt (Ed.), *Physical activity and well-being* (pp. 3-38). Reston, VA: American Alliance for Health, Physical Education, Recreation and Dance.

Malina, R.M. (1988a). Biological maturity status of young athletes. In R.M. Malina (Ed.), *Young athletes: Biological, psychological and educational perspectives* (pp. 117-136). Champaign, IL: Human Kinetics.

Malina, R.M. (1988b). Growth, performance, activity, and training during adolescence. In M. Shangold & G. Mirkin (Eds.), *Women, exercise and sports medicine* (pp. 120-128). Philadelphia: F.A. Davis.

Malina, R.M., Little, B.B., Buschang, P.H., DeMoss, J., & Selby, H.A. (1985). Socioeconomic variation in the growth status of children in a subsistence agricultural community. *American Journal of Physical Anthropology,* **68**, 385-391.

Malina, R.M., Meleski, B.W., & Shoup, R.F. (1982). Anthropometric, body composition, and maturity characteristics of selected school-age athletes. *Pediatric Clinics of North America,* **29**, 1305-1323.

Micheli, L.J. (1985). Back injuries in gymnastics. *Clinics in Sports Medicine,* **4**, 85-93.

Novotny, V. (1981). Veränderungen des Knochenalters im Verlauf einer mehrjährigen sportlichen Belastung. *Medizin und Sport,* **21**, 44-47.

Pařizkova, J. (1974). Particularities of lean body mass and fat development in growing boys as related to their motor activity. *Acta Paediatrica Belgica,* **28** (Suppl.), 233-243.

Peltenburg, A.L., Erich, W.B.M., Bernink, M.J.E., Zonderland, M.L., & Huisveld, I.A. (1984). Biological maturation, body composition, and growth of female gymnasts and control groups of schoolgirls and girl swimmers, aged 8 to 14 years: A cross-sectional survey of 1064 girls. *International Journal of Sports Medicine,* **5**, 36-42.

Rarick, G.L. (1973). Competitive sports in childhood and early adolescence. In G.L. Rarick (Ed.), *Physical activity: Human growth and development* (pp. 364-386). New York: Academic Press.

Rowe, F.A. (1933). Growth comparisons of athletes and non-athletes. *Research Quarterly,* **4**, 108-116.

Scott, E.C., & Johnston, F.E. (1982). Critical fatness, menarche, and the maintenance of menstrual cycles. *Journal of Adolescent Health Care,* **2**, 249-260.

Shuck, G.R. (1962). Effects of athletic competition on the growth and development of junior high school boys. *Research Quarterly,* **33**, 288-298.

Stager, J.M., Robertshaw, D., & Miescher, E. (1984). Delayed menarche in swimmers in relation to age at onset of training and athletic performance. *Medicine and Science in Sports and Exercise,* **16**, 550-555.

Stinson, S. (1985). Sex differences in environmental sensitivity during growth and development. *Yearbook of Physical Anthropology,* **28**, 123-147.

Tanner, J.M. (1962). *Growth at adolescence* (2nd ed.). Oxford: Blackwell.

Trussell, J. (1980). Statistical flaws in evidence for the Frisch hypothesis that fatness triggers menarche. *Human Biology,* **52**, 711-720.

CHAPTER 9

The Growing Child and Sport: Physiological Considerations

Donald A. Bailey
Alan D. Martin

Physical activity is an important consideration during the growing years if normal growth and development of children are to be maintained and encouraged. This fact has long been recognized. In recent years a new phenomenon has emerged in many countries. With the national and international prestige presently attached to athletic success, we are seeing more and more training and sport programs being developed for progressively younger children. Some of these programs are of extreme intensity and duration. Indeed, some young children today are involved in training programs that are more intensive than would have been believed possible even for adults 25 years ago. Do these programs have an effect on the dynamics of human growth? When are children ready for the rigors of intense sport training and competition? Are there critical times during which a training stimulus may be more important in terms of functional capacity? These and many more questions are waiting for answers. But answers are not easy to come by for a variety of reasons, including the difficulty in isolating the training stimulus from the multiplicity of other factors that affect the growing organism. There are, however, certain things we do know about the effects of sport training on physiological function in growing children. This chapter will touch on some of these.

Overview

From a physiological point of view, concern has been voiced from some quarters that the stresses imposed by certain competitive sport-training regimes, particularily those of an endurance nature, may make excessive demands on the cardiovascular systems of children or early adolescents. In healthy children there is little evidence to substantiate this concern. Under certain circumstances heavy exercise can have deleterious effects on a child's health, but these can usually be categorized into sport injuries or overuse syndromes, conditions that are covered elsewhere in this book (Kozar & Lord, this volume). It is true that there have been cases of sudden death or cardiac arrest in young athletes during or immediately following games or practices, but, invariably, underlying pathology has been identified as the cause of death. Even in young cardiac patients sudden death during exertion is not as high as might be expected. Lambert, Menon, Wagner, and Vlad (1974) examined pooled data from nine countries on cardiac deaths in girls under age 21. Only 10% died while engaged in sport, 32% while playing, and 58% during sleep or at rest. The investigators concluded that catastrophe was not prevented by the avoidance of physical exertion in young cardiac patients. For this age group at least, Jokl's contention that exercise never caused death in a normal heart is probably correct (Jokl & McClellan, 1971).

Similarly, there is little reason to believe that the physical demands of sport have any deleterious effects on growth and development of physiological function in the young athlete. Numerous studies have verified that in the absence of injury or disease, the dynamics of growth do not seem to be adversely affected by athletic participation. A comprehensive review of the growth and maturity characteristics of young athletes is beyond the scope of this chapter but appears elsewhere in this book (Malina, this volume). In general, it can be said that young athletes of both sexes grow as well as nonathletes. The experience of athletic training and competition does not harm the growth and development of the youngster.

There is one area of concern that is currently receiving considerable attention: the skeletal integrity in extremely active young women experiencing menstrual dysfunction. Chronic exercise can result in delayed menarche and amenorrhea in some young women (Cumming & Belcastro, 1982). The situation has led to a concern that bone loss, secondary to an estrogen deficit, is a potential cause of stress fractures in the short term and osteoporosis in later years. The topic of exercise-induced amenorrhea and bone density will be discussed later in this chapter.

For the present, it can be said that healthy children have few adverse physiological responses to exercise; on those rare occasions when they do occur they are usually reversible and can be minimized with proper precautions. The body of a youngster is a wonderful machine with sophisticated built-in controls and instinctive limit-defining sensors. In the absence of externally created pressure or stress, a young body functions very effectively. However, children are not scaled-down adults and there are fundamental physiological differences between children and adults that affect the ability to perform. Recognition and consideration of this fact are basic to any acceptable sport program involving growing children.

Children Are Not Miniature Adults

The ability to sustain physical performance while competing in or training for a sport activity depends to a large degree on the ability of the
organism to transfer oxygen from the atmosphere to the working
tissues. Maximal aerobic power represents the greatest volume of oxygen that can be utilized per unit of time under conditions of maximal
exertion. To this end, maximal aerobic power is considered to be the
best measure of cardiorespiratory efficiency because it is dependent
on the interrelationships of all the body systems concerned with oxygen transport and is independent of motivation.

Compared to adults, values for relative maximal aerobic power are
high in children. However, if one looks at metabolic reserve—that is,
the difference between maximal oxygen uptake and oxygen uptake
needed for a given task—children are shown to be at a disadvantage.
The higher oxygen cost in young children in performing a given task
is probably the result of mechanical inefficiency (Daniels, Oldridge,
Nagle, & White, 1978). The relative oxygen cost of walking or running
is higher among children (Åstrand, 1952; Krahenbuhl, Pangrazi, &
Chomokos, 1979; MacDougall, Roche, Bar-Or, & Moroz, 1979; Skinner,
Bar-Or, & Bergsteinova, 1971). MacDougall and others (1979) found
that an 8-year-old child running at a pace of 180 meters per minute
is operating at 90% of maximal aerobic power, while a 16-year-old running at the same speed is operating at only 75% of maximum. Thus,
in comparison to an adult, the child is not as aerobically efficient as
might be expected from looking at the high relative maximal aerobic
power values.

Curiously, in spite of the above consideration, children grade physical effort lower than adolescents, and adolescents perceive the same
effort as being less strenuous than adults do. Bar-Or (1977) conducted
a study on over 1,000 male subjects, ranging in age from 7 to 68 years,
who performed an identical cycle ergometry test. The younger the individual, the lower the subjective perceived effort, although the relative intensity of effort demonstrated by heart and circulatory reactions
was equally great. These data suggest that a given physiologic strain
is perceived to be less stressful by children than by older individuals,
which raises a disturbing question: Is it possible that young children
under external pressure may be pushed too far?

There are also differences between children and adults with respect
to the anaerobic energy system. This system can be employed by the
working muscles in the absence of oxygen. Work that results from
anaerobic reactions can only be sustained for short periods of time, in
contrast to aerobic work, which can be carried on for many minutes,
even hours. Accumulating evidence supports the contention that the
ability to derive energy from the anaerobic lactate pathway is not as

developed in the preadolescent child as it is in the adult (Eriksson, 1980; Eriksson & Saltin, 1974; Inbar & Bar-Or, 1986; Karlsson, 1971).

A detailed discussion of child-adult differences with respect to the individual components of the aerobic and anaerobic systems has been provided elsewhere (Bailey, Malina, & Mirwald, 1986; Bar-Or, 1983; Cunningham, Paterson, Blimkie, & Donner, 1984). It is sufficient here to refer to a statement by Åstrand and Rodahl (1986):

> It may be concluded that children are physically handicapped compared with adults (and fully grown animals of similar size). When related to the child's dimensions, its muscular strength is low and so are its maximal oxygen uptake and other parameters of importance for the oxygen transport. Furthermore, the mechanical efficiency of children is often inferior to that of adults. The introduction of dimensions in the discussion of children's performance clearly indicates that they are not mature as working machines. (pp. 401-402)

Adaptation of Children to Sport Training

Sport competition and training subjects the developing organism to a variety of stresses that may give rise to any number of significant responses. Whether adapting to repeated training sessions or to a single game situation, the growing child undergoes changes. The magnitude of these changes varies with the timing, duration, and intensity of the training stimulus. It should be noted that the physical exertion associated with sport training is only one of many factors that may affect the growing child. Thus, our knowledge of children's adaptation to exercise is difficult to define and not completely understood. Notwithstanding, when the literature is critically analyzed, some facts are apparent.

It is clear that regular sport training has no apparent effect on stature in growing youngsters. Also, skeletal maturity as assessed in growth studies does not appear to be influenced by physical training in young adolescent boys and girls (Bailey, Martin, Houston, & Howie, 1986). The regulation and maintenance of body weight, however, are affected by regular physical activity. Youngsters regularly engaged in sport programs, be they formal in nature or recreational, have proportionally more lean body mass and less fat than those who are not regularly involved (Malina, Meleski, & Shoup, 1982; Ruffer, 1965). One question remains open: Do these training-associated changes in body composition persist into adult years?

In studying the physiological response of the oxygen transport system to sport training, another dimension is added beyond simple quantitative change. Qualitative changes may occur in children during growth and/or training with or without quantitative alteration. Qualitative changes at the cellular level are not easily observed or measured; therefore major gaps exist in our understanding of the processes involved in the physiological response to exercise. The traditional approach to studying the influence of sport training and physical activity on functional growth of the oxygen transport system has been to compare athletes with nonathletes or trained subjects with untrained subjects. Most of these studies have been of short duration involving pretest and posttest measurement and many have failed to control for maturational differences. Taking into consideration all the constraints and limitations inherent in studying training-mediated responses in growing children, what conclusions can be drawn?

A consistent finding is that sport training has a small or limited effect on maximal aerobic power prior to adolescence. The preponderance of evidence suggests that the trainability of aerobic power in young preadolescents is lower than expected in spite of improved athletic performance (Bar-Or, Zwiren, & Ruskin, 1974; Gilliam & Freedson, 1980; Mocellin & Wasmund, 1973; Schmucker & Hollmann, 1974; Stewart & Gutin, 1976; Yoshida, Ishiko, & Muraoka, 1980). Because most sporting tasks at this age are performed at less than maximal work rates, it has been suggested that the use of maximal aerobic power as a measure for evaluating the efficiency of the oxygen transport system in prepubescent children may be misleading (Stewart & Gutin, 1976). Sport training or a high level of physical activity has been shown to lead to improvements in submaximal efficiency that are independent of changes at maximal effort (Lussier & Buskirk, 1977; Mirwald & Bailey, 1984; Stewart & Gutin, 1976).

In adolescence, the effect of sport training on aerobic power is less clear, and it is difficult to draw any firm conclusions. Some studies report expected improvements following training during the adolescent years (Ekblom, 1969; Sprynarova, Pařizkova, & Irinova, 1978; Weber, Kartodihardjo, & Klissouras, 1976) and other studies do not (Cumming, Goodwin, & Baggley, 1967; Daniels et al., 1978; Hamilton & Andrew, 1976). It has been suggested that the effectiveness of aerobic training may be greatest at or around the time of peak height velocity in boys (Kobayashi, Kitamura, & Miura, 1978; Mirwald, Bailey, Cameron, & Rasmussen, 1981). Biologically, this would seem reasonable in view of the marked changes taking place in endocrine function during this state of development, but further investigations are needed to confirm this hypothesis.

What happens when training ceases in growing children? Here again there are no clear answers, although it appears that, as in adults, adaptations to short-term training are not permanent (Michael, Evert, & Jeffers, 1972). Similarly, the aerobic response to long-term training in children appears to be lost in adult years with the cessation of training (Eriksson, 1976).

A major consideration in studies looking at the effects of sport training in children is the role of heredity. Early data from twin studies suggested that the principal determinant of variability in maximal aerobic power among individuals who lived under similar environmental conditions was genetic (Howald, 1976; Klissouras, Pirnay, & Petit, 1972; Komi, Klissouras, & Karvinen, 1973; Weber et al., 1976).

However, recent studies are more cautious in the interpretation of the environment-heredity interaction (Bouchard, 1978). Details of the genetics of aerobic power and adaptations to work have been provided elsewhere (Bouchard & Malina, 1983; Malina & Bouchard, 1986).

Why is it our understanding of the growing child's response to sport training is still so fragmentary in spite of the surge of interest in the child as a sportsperson? The gaps in our understanding are primarily attributable to an inherent methodological constraint that has been and continues to be a major challenge for investigators working in this area. As Bar-Or (1983) states:

> In adults, changes in function between pre- and post-intervention can be attributed with fair certainty to the conditioning program. Not so with children or adolescents. Here, changes due to growth, development, and maturation often outweigh and mask those induced by the intervention. It is intriguing that many of the physiologic changes that result from conditioning and training also take place in the natural process of growth and maturation. (p. 38)

Thermoregulation in Children

Not all sporting events or training sessions are held under ideal climatic conditions. In many regions of the world, climate can play a crucial role in terms of an individual's ability to perform. Climate is an especially important consideration in regard to sport programs for children where many activities are performed outside in sometimes quite hostile weather. In general, it can be said that children are not as efficient as adults in terms of temperature regulation, especially under conditions of extreme heat or cold.

A child has a smaller absolute surface area than an adult. However when surface area is expressed per unit of body mass, the situation is reversed. Because heat loss is related to surface area and heat production to body mass, children should, theoretically, be at a disadvantage in a cold climate and favored in a warm one. However, there are other considerations that place children at a disadvantage in a hot climate as well, in spite of their relatively large surface area. Children have a lower sweating rate than adults; consequently, their evaporative capacity is deficient (Davies, 1981; Inbar, Bar-Or, Dotan, & Gutin, 1981). The effect of a deficient evaporative capacity is to raise skin temperature and create a less favorable temperature gradient between the body core and the periphery, which, in turn, inhibits heat transfer by convection. The lower sweating rate in children is apparent both in absolute terms and when normalized per unit of body surface area (Bar-Or, 1983), and results from a lower output per sweat gland rather than a reduced number of glands. Sweat excretion per gland is 2.5 times greater in the adult compared to the child (Bar-Or, 1980). In summary, although low sweat production conserves water in the exercising child, it inhibits heat transfer in a hot climate.

Another age-related difference in adaptation to exercise in heat is the rate of acclimatization. The process of adaptation to heat takes considerably longer in children than in adults (Inbar et al., 1981). Further, children do not instinctively drink enough fluids to replenish fluid loss. Bar-Or (1983) reports that children exercising in dry heat will voluntarily become dehydrated even if allowed to drink ad libitum.

The American Academy of Pediatrics, Committee on Sports Medicine (1982) has published a position paper on "Climatic Heat Stress and the Exercising Child" that reflects the importance attached to this topic. All leaders involved in sport programs for children should be made aware of the fact that in climatic extremes of heat or cold children are less efficient in terms of temperature regulation than adults and that precautions are warranted.

Menstrual Dysfunction and Skeletal Integrity

Disturbances of the menstrual cycle have long been associated with high levels of physical activity, both in growing girls and mature women (Cumming & Belcastro, 1982). Until recently, these disturbances have generally been regarded as benign because the dysfunction is readily reversible with a reduction in training intensity (Baker, 1981). However, it is now clear that athletic amenorrhea is associated with a significantly reduced trabecular bone density, thus increasing the probability of stress fractures in the short term and osteoporotic fractures in the long term (Martin & Bailey, 1987). This problem is of direct relevance to those concerned with growing girls because the incidence of athletic amenorrhea is closely linked to activity patterns during growth. In particular, the factors predisposing to athletic amenorrhea are (a) delayed menarche, (b) onset of training close to menarche, (c) menstrual dysfunction before training, (d) high training intensity, and (e) low body weight and fat (Martin & Bailey, 1987). The high incidence of eating disorders in teenage girls further aggravates the problem, as very low caloric intakes, even without athletic activity, can induce amenorrhea (Wentz, 1980), leading to the general hypothesis that amenorrhea is a "functional adaptation to a negative energy balance, whether it is induced by low energy intake alone or increased energy expenditure together with low energy intake" (Nelson, Fisher, & Catsos, 1986, p. 914).

It is likely that, as in postmenopausal women, most of the bone loss resulting from estrogen deprivation occurs in the 5 to 10 years immediately following loss of menses. If this is so, athletic amenorrhea in teenage girls should be viewed with serious concern for three reasons. It may reduce the peak bone mass attained in early adulthood and therefore lower the age at which the osteoporotic fracture threshold is reached (Bailey, Martin, Houston, & Howie, 1986). It significantly increases the incidence of stress fractures (Marcus, Cann, & Madvig, 1985; Lloyd, Triantafyllou, & Baker, 1986). And, perhaps most important of all, it may affect skeletal development in a qualitative fashion. This hitherto unexamined possibility should be given high priority by researchers.

With continuing amenorrhea, bone loss is difficult to reverse. Despite claims to the contrary, calcium supplementation has not proved effective in middle-aged women and has not been tested in young women (Martin & Houston, 1987). Fortunately, those girls at risk can be readily identified by their late menarche, high training intensity, and low body fat level. They should be advised of the skeletal hazard and encouraged to induce normal menses through appropriate lifestyle changes and to seek medical advice when necessary.

Is Earlier Better?

On the theory that if some training is good, vast amounts must be better, we are seeing youngsters at increasingly earlier ages being subjected to intensive training regimes in the hopes of developing world champions. In some countries of the world, exceptional talent is identified at an early age, and children are put through intensive programs in hopes that they will eventually arrive at the top. We are not told what happens to the youngsters who do not make it.

The theory that the younger we start a child, the better the chances of his or her becoming an adult champion deserves close scrutiny. Some studies have suggested that early success offers no promise of the same later on. Clarke (1971) found that outstanding elementary school athletes may not be outstanding in junior or senior high school and vice versa. Could it be that intensive participation and competition in the under-11 age group is not the great spawning ground it is purported to be? True, there are examples of child athletes who later set world records, but the examples are not nearly as numerous as we have been led to believe.

Many world-class runners, for instance, were not outstanding internationally as juniors—names like Doubell, Wottle, Viren come to mind. Before discovering the gift of running, Keino, Temu, and Gammoudi primarily played soccer until their late teens. It is abundantly clear that future champions and world record holders do not have to be outstanding childhood athletes. In fact, it can be argued that success too early makes future success more doubtful. As in all human endeavor, there are exceptions to this observation, but the exceptions are rare enough not to discredit the hypothesis.

Sweeney (1973) documents the case of a New Jersey junior high school track team called the "4:47 team"—a team with seven boys who ran the mile in under 5 minutes, with an average time of 4:47. Surely, here was a team that would create a dynasty in their new high school. Three years later only one member of the 4:47 team was still participating for that school. In the ninth grade he had run 4:27.7 and as a high school senior his best time was still only 4:23. What happened? The reasons run the gamut from too much early success to not enough later on, or from an overly active, highly concerned coach to a rather remote one. The point to be made is that all that can safely be said about fast young runners is that they are fast young runners. Early success has only a distant relationship to future stardom.

Dr. Gabe Mirkin, medical editor for *Runner's World* magazine and co-author of *The Complete Sportsmedicine Book for Women* has documented the case of his young running son. As a 9-year-old, the boy ran the mile in under 5 minutes. He held 12 age-class world records before he was 10. He is now 25 and has not run since he was 10 years old. Mirkin's observations (1984) as a sports medicine physician and as a former advocate of running training at an early age are pertinent to this discussion:

> Kids burn out. They don't get injured. Of the hundreds of kids who came through, I didn't see a single long term injury. Some of these kids were running 70 or 80 miles a week, hard. You'd see a few injuries then—but, boy, the drop-out rate was frightening. Too much too soon. (p. 24)

Swimming is often cited as an example of what can be accomplished if training is started at an early age. Shane Gould of Australia, for example, was only 15 when she held every world freestyle record from 100 to 1500 meters, an unparalleled achievement. But swimmers not only start early, they also tend to quit early—as young as 18 or 19 in the case of top women performers. The assistant United States swimming coach at the Montreal Olympics is quoted as saying, "In some ways, the age-group program is backfiring. Sure it gets young kids into swimming, but it also burns them out before they're even close to their potential peak" (Kirshenbaum, 1977, p. 49). It is certainly reasonable to hypothesize that more success would be achieved if the people involved in the sport stayed with it longer.

Even granting the opposite point of view—that is, to get a world-beater of tomorrow we must train and crown young champions at an early age (an unverified premise)—and further assuming that it is possible to identify and select potential champions at an early age (a dubious assumption), the primary mandate of people working in children's sport programs should still be to respond to the longer-term activity needs of all children. If athletic potential can be identified at an early age, it is logical to assume that a lack of potential should be just as easy to identify. If this is the case, should we not devote more time to the unskilled youngsters who have no motivation or encouragement toward physical activity? Perhaps what is needed in programs for the very young is to pay less attention to the selection of athletes and provide more encouragement to all youngsters to take an active interest in sports, games, and activities. If this occurs, every child has a chance to realize his or her potential, and the talent pool will be enlarged.

In North America a significant number of children who are late maturing and following a slower-than-average developmental timetable are denied a chance to even try to participate in sport because most competitions for youngsters and adolescents are based on chronological age. Because size is an important determinant in many activities, youngsters who are small for their age are often discriminated against or discouraged, though they may have potential and may eventually be of average or even above-average adult size. Somehow we need to organize physical activity and sport programs so that more children can experience the feeling of success that comes from someone saying, "Well done!".

Conclusion

Only selected aspects of the physiological response of the child to the rigors imposed by sport training and competition have been considered in this chapter. Other areas of research are undoubtedly relevant and important. For instance, there is a need for a more detailed examination of hormonal responses to sport training, especially as they relate to bone mineral content in young female endurance athletes. Further studies are obviously necessary as there are still many gaps in our knowledge of the underlying biological processes involved in the response of the growing child to sport participation. From a physiological perspective, the following quotation, drawn from a position statement on Children in Competitive Sports prepared by the Canadian Association of Sports Sciences, summarizes material presented in this chapter and represents an appropriate guideline for adults involved in sport programming for children (Hughson, 1986).

> From a physiological and medical point of view, it should be recognized that each child is different in his/her response and tolerance to exercise due to a great range of variability in growth rates, anthropometric indices, gender and state of health, even in children of a similar chronological age. Younger pre-pubertal children should be encouraged to participate in a wide variety of motor skills, whereas older post-pubertal children can become more specialized in their training and sport participation. A child's performance and adaptation to training should not be directly compared to an adult's as significant differences exist, especially during the years of accel-

erated growth. Environmental exercise tolerance is also more limited in children than adults. (p. 162)

Are young children ready for sport? Perhaps the question should be rephrased. Are adults, represented by parents, coaches, teachers, and spectators, ready to be involved in children's sport? While sport participation can be healthy for children, it is unfortunately not always the case. Adults involved in sport situations for children, be they local recreational leagues or elite championship venues, have a responsibility to ensure that a child's happy participation is not jeopardized by unrealistic adult expectations. It is imperative that adults make the distinction between encouraging children to gain satisfaction from doing their best, and pushing children beyond their capabilities and levels of interest. At this age, the burden is on the leadership. Adults should have a thorough understanding of structural and functional differences that exist between children and adults. Sport programs for children should be designed accordingly.

References

American Academy of Pediatrics, Committee on Sports Medicine. (1982). Climatic heat stress and the exercising child. *Pediatrics*, **69**, 808-809.

Åstrand, P.-O. (1952). *Experimental studies of physical working capacity in relation to sex and age*. Copenhagen: Munksgaard.

Åstrand, P.-O., & Rodahl, K. (1986). *Textbook of work physiology* (3rd ed.). New York: McGraw-Hill.

Bailey, D.A., Malina, R.M., & Mirwald, R.L. (1986). Physical activity and growth of the child. In F. Falkner & J.M. Tanner (Eds.), *Human growth—Postnatal growth neurobiology* (Vol. 2, pp. 147-170). New York: Plenum Press.

Bailey, D.A., Martin, A.D., Houston, C.S., & Howie, J.L. (1986). Physical activity, nutrition, bone density and osteoporosis. *Australian Journal of Science and Medicine in Sport*, **18**, 3-8.

Baker, E.R. (1981). Menstrual dysfunction and hormonal status in athletic women: A review. *Fertility and Sterility*, **36**, 691-696.

Bar-Or, O. (1977). Age-related changes in exercise perception. In G. Berg (Ed.), *Physical work and effort* (pp. 255-266). Oxford: Pergamon Press.

Bar-Or, O. (1980). Climate and the exercising child—A review. *International Journal of Sports Medicine*, **1**, 53-65.

Bar-Or, O. (1983). *Pediatric sports medicine for the practitioner*. New York: Springer-Verlag.

Bar-Or, O., Zwiren, L.D., & Ruskin, H. (1974). Anthropometric and developmental measurements of 11- to 12-year-old boys, as predictors of performance 2 years later. *Acta Paediatrica Belgica*, **28**(Suppl.), 214-220.

Bouchard, C. (1978). Genetics, growth and physical activity. In F. Landry & W.A.R. Organ (Eds.), *Physical activity and human well being* (pp. 29-45). Miami: Symposia Specialists.

Bouchard, C., & Malina, R.M. (1983). Genetics of physiological fitness and motor performance. *Exercise and Sport Sciences Reviews*, **11**, 306-339.

Clarke, H.H. (1971). *Physical and motor tests in the Medford Boys' Growth Study*. Englewood Cliffs, NJ: Prentice-Hall.

Cumming, D.C., & Belcastro, A.N. (1982). The reproductive effects of exertion. *Current Problems in Obstetrics and Gynecology*, **5**, 3-41.

Cumming, G.R., Goodwin, A., & Baggley, G. (1967). Repeated measurements of aerobic capacity during a week of intensive training at a youth's track camp. *Canadian Journal of Physiology and Pharmacology*, **45**, 805-811.

Cunningham, D.A., Paterson, D.H., Blimkie, C.J., & Donner, A.P. (1984). Development of cardiorespiratory function in circumpubertal boys: A longitudinal study. *Journal of Applied Physiology*, **56**, 302-307.

Daniels, J., Oldridge, N., Nagle, F., & White, B. (1978). Differences and changes in VO_2 among young runners 10 to 18 years of age. *Medicine and Science in Sports*, **10**, 200-203.

Davies, C.T.M. (1981). Thermal responses to exercise in children. *Ergonomics*, **24**, 55-61.

Ekblom, B. (1969). Effect of physical training in adolescent boys. *Journal of Applied Physiology*, **27**, 350-355.

Eriksson, B.O. (1976). The child in sport and physical activity—Medical aspects. In J.G. Albinson & G.M. Andrews (Eds.), *Child in sport and physical activity* (pp. 43-65). Baltimore: University Park Press.

Eriksson, B.O. (1980). Muscle metabolism in children—A review. *Acta Paediatrica Scandinavica*, **283**(Suppl.), 20-27.

Eriksson, B.O., & Saltin, B. (1974). Muscle metabolism during exercise in boys aged 11 to 16 years compared to adults. *Acta Paediatrica Belgica*, **28**(Suppl.), 257-265.

Gilliam, T.B., & Freedson, P.S. (1980). Effects of a 12-week school physical fitness program on peak VO_2, body composition and blood lipids in 7 to 9 year old children. *International Journal of Sports Medicine*, **1**, 73-75.

Hamilton, P., & Andrew, G.M. (1976). Influence of growth and athletic training on heart and lung functions. *European Journal of Applied Physiology*, **36**, 27-38.

Howald, H. (1976). Ultrastructure and biochemical function of skeletal muscle in twins. *Annals of Human Biology*, **3**, 80.

Hughson, R. (1986). Children in competitive sports—A multidisciplinary approach. *Canadian Journal of Applied Sport Sciences*, **11**, 162-172.

Inbar, O., & Bar-Or, O. (1986). Anaerobic characteristics in male children and adolescents. *Medicine and Science in Sports and Exercise*, **18**, 264-269.

Inbar, O., Bar-Or, O., Dotan, R., & Gutin, B. (1981). Conditioning versus exercise in heat as methods for acclimatizing 8- to 10-year-old boys to dry heat. *Journal of Applied Physiology: Respiratory, Environmental and Exercise Physiology*, **50**, 406-411.

Jokl, E., & McClellan, J. (1971). *Exercise and cardiac death*. Baltimore: University Park Press.

Karlsson, J. (1971). Muscle ATP, CP and lactate in submaximal and maximal exercise. In B. Pernow & B. Saltin (Eds.), *Muscle metabolism during exercise* (pp. 383-393). New York: Plenum Press.

Kirshenbaum, J. (1977, April 25). Gimmicks, gadgets, goodby records. *Sports Illustrated*, pp. 40-49.

Klissouras, V., Pirnay, F., & Petit, J.M. (1972). Adaptation to maximal effort: Genetics and age. *Journal of Applied Physiology*, **35**, 288-293.

Kobayashi, K., Kitamura, K., & Miura, M. (1978). Aerobic power as related to body growth and training in Japanese boys: A longitudinal study. *Journal of Applied Physiology: Respiratory, Environmental and Exercise Physiology*, **44**, 666-672.

Komi, P.V., Klissouras, V., Karvinen, E. (1973). Genetic variation in neuromuscular performance. *Internationale Zeitschrift fur Angewandte Physiologie*, **31**, 289-304.

Kozar, B., & Lord, R.H. (1988). Overuse injuries in young athletes: A "growing" problem. In F.L. Smoll, R.A. Magill, & M.J. Ash (Eds.), *Children in sport* (3rd ed., pp. 119-129). Champaign, IL: Human Kinetics.

Krahenbuhl, G.S., Pangrazi, R.P., & Chomokos, E.A. (1979). Aerobic responses of young boys to submaximal running. *Research Quarterly*, **50**, 413-421.

Lambert, E.C., Menon, V.A., Wagner, H.A., & Vlad, P. (1974). Sudden unexpected death from cardiovascular disease in children. *American Journal of Cardiology*, **34**, 89-96.

Lloyd, T., Triantafyllou, S.J., & Baker, E.R. (1986). Women athletes with menstrual irregularity have increased musculoskeletal injuries. *Medicine and Science in Sports and Exercise*, **18**, 374-379.

Lussier, L., & Buskirk, E.R. (1977). Effects of an endurance training regimen on assessment of work capacity in pre-pubertal children. *Annals of the New York Academy of Sciences*, **301**, 734-747.

MacDougall, J.D., Roche, P.D., Bar-Or, O., & Moroz, J.R. (1979). Oxygen cost of running in children of different ages; maximal aerobic power of Canadian school-children [Abstract]. *Canadian Journal of Applied Sport Sciences*, **4**, 237.

Malina, R.M. (1988). Growth and maturation of young athletes: Biological and social considerations. In F.L. Smoll, R.A. Magill, & M.J. Ash (Eds.), *Children in sport* (3rd ed., pp. 83-101). Champaign, IL: Human Kinetics.

Malina, R.M., & Bouchard, C. (Eds.). (1986). *Sport and human genetics*. Champaign, IL: Human Kinetics.

Malina, R.M., Meleski, B.W., & Shoup, R.F. (1982). Anthropometric, body composition and maturity characteristics of selected school-aged athletes. *Pediatric Clinics of North America*, **29**, 1305-1323.

Marcus, R., Cann, C.E., & Madvig, P. (1985). Menstrual function and bone mass in elite women distance runners. *Annals of Internal Medicine*, **102**, 158-163.

Martin, A.D., & Bailey, D.A. (1987). Athletic amenorrhea and skeletal integrity. *Australian Journal of Science and Medicine in Sport*, **19**, 3-7.

Martin, A.D., & Houston, C.S. (1987). Osteoporosis, calcium and physical activity: A review. *Canadian Medical Association Journal*, **136**, 587-593.

Michael, E., Evert, J., & Jeffers, K. (1972). Physiological changes of teenage girls during 5 months of detraining. *Medicine and Science in Sports*, **4**, 214-218.

Mirkin, G. (1984, December). A conversation with Gabe Mirkin. *Runner's World*, p. 24.

Mirwald, R.L., & Bailey, D.A. (1984). Longitudinal comparison of aerobic power and heart rate responses at submaximal and maximal workloads in active and inactive boys aged 8 to 16 years. In J. Borms, R. Hauspie, A. Sand, C. Susanne, & M. Hebbelinck (Eds.), *III International congress of auxology: Human growth and development* (pp. 561-570). New York: Plenum Press.

Mirwald, R.L., Bailey, D.A., Cameron, N. & Rasmussen, R.L. (1981). Longitudinal comparison of aerobic power on active and inactive boys aged 7.0 to 17.0 years. *Annals of Human Biology*, **8**, 405-414.

Mocellin, R., & Wasmund, U. (1973). Investigations on the influence of a running-training programme on the cardiovascular and motor performance capacity in 53 boys and girls of a second and third primary school class. In O. Bar-Or (Ed.), *Pediatric work physiology* (pp. 279-285). Natanya, Israel: Wingate Institute.

Nelson, M.E., Fisher, E.C., & Catsos, P.D. (1986). Diet and bone status in amenorrheic runners. *American Journal of Clinical Nutrition*, **43**, 910-916.

Ruffer, W.A. (1965). A study of extreme physical activity groups of young men. *Research Quarterly*, **36**, 183-196.

Schmucker, B., & Hollmann, W. (1974). The aerobic capacity of trained athletes from 6 to 7 years of age on. *Acta Paediatrica Belgica*, **28**(Suppl.), 92-101.

Skinner, J.S., Bar-Or, O., & Bergsteinova, V. (1971). Comparison of continuous and intermittent tests for determining maximal oxygen intake in children. *Acta Paediatrica Scandinavica*, **217**(Suppl.), 24-28.

Sprynarova, S., Pařizkova, J., & Irinova, I. (1978). Development of the functional capacity and body composition of boy and girl swimmers aged 12-15 years. In J. Borms & M. Hebbelinck (Eds.), *Pediatric work physiology* (pp. 32-38). Basel: Karger.

Stewart, K.J., & Gutin, B. (1976). Effects of physical training on cardio-respiratory fitness in children. *Research Quarterly*, **47**, 110-120.

Sweeney, H. (1973). When interest dies. In J. Henderson (Ed.), *The young runner* (p. 24). Mountain View, CA: World Publications.

Weber, G., Kartodihardjo, W., & Klissouras, V. (1976). Growth and physical training with reference to heredity. *Journal of Applied Physiology*, **40**, 211-215.

Wentz, A.C. (1980). Body weight and amenorrhea. *Obstetrics and Gynecology*, **56**, 482-487.

Yoshida, T., Ishiko, I., & Muraoka, I. (1980). Effect of endurance training on cardiorespiratory functions of 5-year-old children. *International Journal of Sports Medicine*, **1**, 91-94.

CHAPTER 10

Overuse Injuries in Young Athletes: A "Growing" Problem

Bill Kozar
Russell H. Lord

Since the formation of Little League baseball in 1939, there has been a tremendous increase in the number of children participating in sport. The number of youngsters involved in youth sport programs in the United States has been estimated at well over 20 million (Martens, this volume). Further, the recently completed National Children and Youth Fitness Study reports that over 80% of a child's physical exercise takes place outside of the school (McGinnis, 1985). Much of this exercise involves participation in youth sport programs conducted by volunteers, many of whom have limited knowledge or training in working with youngsters in sport. As more children become active participants in a greater variety of sports at an earlier age, both laypersons and professionals have expressed concern about the impact such programs have on young participants (American Academy of Pediatrics, 1981; Rarick, 1978).

While a variety of concerns have been expressed, ranging from moral and social development to physiological and psychological development of the child during the formative years, a new concern has surfaced in the last few years in the form of the overuse injury. Sport scientists and sports medicine practitioners have recently begun to report increased incidences of overuse injuries in youngsters. These injuries are not surprising in light of reports that (a) children as young as 6 years of age are running up to 80 miles per week and completing full marathons (Lopez & Pruett, 1982), (b) young gymnasts in elite programs spend hours perfecting routines (Walsh, Huurman, & Shelton, 1985), (c) ballet dancers work for hours practicing "en pointe" position and jumps (Micheli, Sohn, & Solomon, 1985), and (d) young swimmers churn 20,000 meters per day (Dominguez, 1980). There is little question that a greater number of youngsters are becoming intensely involved in highly competitive programs. This degree of involvement usually results in the young athlete specializing in one sport at a much earlier age—specialization that often entails virtual year-round conditioning, practice, and competition.

Camps for aspiring athletes in tennis, hockey, basketball, gymnastics, and every other sport abound—evidence for the increasing emphasis placed upon earlier sport specialization. These specific sport camps where, according to Stanish (1984), the youngster is on a 6- to 8-hour training schedule are a significant departure from traditional camp experiences where children participate for several weeks in a variety of activities, ranging from crafts to strenuous sport. These camps are also a long way from the free-play situation that prevailed in children's physical activity before the advent of organized youth sport programs. Micheli (1983) has concluded that specialized sport camps are one of the main causes for the dramatic increase in overuse injuries in youngsters.

As the number of nonschool sponsored programs directing local, regional, national, and even international competition increases, the number of children making early commitments to extensive and intensive training in a single sport can be expected to increase. This, combined with the pressure from parents, community, peers, and society in general to practice long hours, compete, and win, can and is leading, according to Micheli (1983), to an epidemic in overuse injuries in young athletes, causing temporary and perhaps permanent injury.

Nature and Incidence of Overuse Injuries

Boland (1982) defines overuse injury as a "chronic inflammatory condition caused by repeated microtrauma from a repetitive activity" (p. 116). Harvey (1986) describes several overuse injuries:

> Performing the same activity time and time again may cause one structure to rub against another (chondromalacia), repetitive traction on a ligament or tendon (plantar fascutis, Osgood-Schlatter disease), or cyclic loading of impact forces (lower extremity stress fractures). The result of these frictional, tractional, or cyclic loading forces is inflammation of the involved structure. This produces the clinical complaints of pain, tenderness, swelling, and disability. (p. 152)

These are the types of injuries that Micheli (1983) believes result not simply from overuse but from improper training techniques and anatomical malalignment. Stanish (1984) calls the overuse injury "the most troublesome problem of the musculoskeletal system" (p. 1).

While children respond in basically the same way as adults to intense training (Seefeldt & Steig, 1986), it must be kept in mind that a growing child is not simply a scaled-down adult. Teeple (1978) notes that while an adult's leg length represents almost half of the overall height, in a child it is considerably less. Consequently, for a young athlete to run the same distance as an adult places greater stress upon the young-ster. Further, growth rates in children are basically nonlinear (Hay-wood, 1986; Teeple, 1978); therefore, a training load, which during a nongrowth period is acceptable, may prove excessive during a growth spurt. Because of the presence of growth cartilage and the process of growth, the child, unlike the adult, is putting energy into growth as well as training (Wilkerson, 1981). According to Micheli (1983), this makes the youngster more susceptible than adults to certain mechani-cal injuries.

As youngsters mature, the ratio of muscle and tendon strength to bone length is constantly changing. Caine and Lindner (1984) point out that a youngster is more susceptible to overuse injury than an adult "because of the difference in the ratio of contractile muscle strength and static tendon strength to bone length" (p. 120). In children this ratio is lower and unidirectional because muscular strength lags be-hind bone length throughout the prepubertal years. Tabin, Gregg, and Bonci (1985) support this contention by reporting that during pre-pubescence, quadriceps strength is equal to 70% of lean body weight in both sexes. This increases to 80% for girls and 90% for boys in the postpubescent period.

Weight training for the prepubescent does not appear to provide a solution. While recent evidence by Micheli (cited in Legwold, 1983) sug-gests that strength gains do occur, it is important to remember that making the muscular system stronger results in an increase in stress that the biological structures must withstand. At this point in the child's development, the weak link in the musculoskeletal system is the epiphysis (Singer, 1986). Bone growth that outdistances muscle and tendon growth can also lead to tightness about the joint. This loss of flexibility can lead to a further risk of overuse injury.

Ligamentous tissue in children is often as much as 3 times stronger than the cartilage and bone of the growth plate (Micheli, Santore, & Stanitski, 1980), which makes epiphyseal fractures much more likely than an injury to the ligament. Wilkerson (1981) claims that overtrain-ing a youngster can in fact cause premature closure of the epiphyseal plate and, depending on the athlete's mechanics of movement, the long bones may stop growing at different times. A study by Kato (cited in Micheli, 1983) suggests that excessive physical work can cause growth plate injury and lead to permanent changes in bones. It appears that in order to maintain function under heavy and continuous work, the growth plate undergoes permanent change (Larson, Singer, Bergstrom, & Thomas, 1976). Rarick and Seefeldt (1977) warn that the overload-ing of immature and growing joints is the primary cause of epiphyseal damage in young sportspersons.

While the reporting of overuse injuries in young athletes has in-creased in the sports medicine literature over the last several years, the epidemiological procedures to study the cause and prevention of these injuries have not been well developed. This lack is not surprising, as the concentrated commitment to a sport by youngsters is a fairly recent phenomenon. The few studies that are available deal primarily with highly successful national level participants (Bailey & Martin, this volume). The fact that a limited number of genetically exceptional individuals are capable of withstanding strenuous long-term training loads (Sharkey, 1986) does not mean that less-endowed youngsters will not suffer from overuse injuries that may prevent further participation for an extensive time. Additionally, aversion to a specific sport is becoming more frequently observed in young athletes who burn out long before reaching their physical, emotional, psychological, or competitive peaks.

Even the exceptional young athlete may not escape overuse injury. Bill Masucci, the winning pitcher in the 1954 Little League World Series, has stated that because he threw so often as a Little Leaguer he can hardly throw a ball today (Michener, 1976). In addition, it is likely that excessive pitching at a young age prematurely ended the career of Sandy Koufax (Singer, 1986). Micheli (1983) suggests that repeated microtrauma to the proximal humerus in the growing skeleton is the etiology of Little League shoulder.

Lipscomb (1975) maintains that the most serious injury incurred by young pitchers is osteochondritis of the capitellum. The end result according to Lipscomb is "varying degrees of traumatic arthritis and permanent joint impairment" (p. 31). X rays taken of young pitchers by Mike Marshall, former Los Angeles Dodger pitcher, showed that excessive pitching could cause permanent damage to the elbow (cited in Michener, 1976). Mcmanama, Micheli, Berry, and Sohn (1985) report elbow surgery was deemed necessary to correct osteochondritis of the capitellum due to repetitive microtrauma in seven patients, six of whom reported considerable involvement in Little League and Pony League baseball.

Adams (1965), who was one of the first to report Little League shoulder problems, found that virtually all pitchers he studied had suffered some degree of injury to the medial epicondyler epiphysis. His findings contributed significantly to the decision by Little League officials to restrict the number of innings a youngster could pitch. However, despite the rule changes, the problem of overuse injuries still seems to be present.

A retrospective questionnaire given to 389 students (Kujala, Kvist, & Heinonen, 1985) found that of 49.6% who had been active in sport, 21.2% had suffered from Osgood-Schlatter's disease, compared to only 4.5% of those who had not participated in sport. Walsh and others (1985), while presenting no specific data, indicate that the majority of injuries they treat in girls' gymnastics deal with overuse of the knee and spine. Additional reports of runners (Caine & Lindner, 1984; Godshall, Hansen, & Rising, 1981), ballet dancers (Micheli et al., 1985), tennis players (Rettig & Beltz, 1985), and swimmers (Dominguez, 1980) attest to the prevalence of overuse injury in children's sport.

Contributing Factors

Besides the increased population of serious young athletes, other factors may contribute to the rise in overuse injuries in young athletes. Those factors include diminished fitness levels of America's youth, social facilitation effects encouraging participation in the face of injury, and a general lack of well-trained adult leadership.

Diminished Physical Fitness

Hamill, Johnson, and Grams (1970) cite evidence that over the last century the average height of the American child has increased 10% while average weight has increased 10% to 30%. This evidence is supported by the recently completed National Children and Youth Fitness Study (Pate, Ross, Dotson, & Gilbert, 1985), which found that youngsters have become fatter since the 1960s. Like others before it, this study reports that the physical fitness level of children has remained the same or decreased over the last 20 years, despite the advent of fitness and sport programs that have become so popular with the adult sector. These statistics indicate that taller, heavier, and, in many cases, less-fit youngsters are beginning strenuous repetitive training at a time when they are most susceptible to overuse (or, as Micheli [1983] terms them— "over growth") injuries.

Social Facilitation Effects

Another factor involved in overuse injuries in young athletes appears to be the well-documented phenomenon of social facilitation (Geen & Gange, 1977). Youngsters experiencing pain alone, or with a few friends in the backyard or playground, may respond in a manner quite different than in the presence of their coach, parents, fellow competitors, and spectators. While we know that the presence of coactors, competitors, and evaluators exerts a tremendous influence on motor performance, similar effects on the perception and reporting of pain are not well documented. However, because pain is a perceptual rather than a purely sensory phenomenon, effects similar to those found for motor performance seem reasonable. Lord and Kozar (1986) found that second and third grade children tolerated significantly more cold pressor pain in the presence of peers than when alone, in contrast to college students, who did not differ under observed or unobserved conditions. Do young athletes, because of their natural enthusiasm for sport, systematically tolerate greater levels of pain because of the social facilitation effects often present in the youth sport environment? The answer to that question is of considerable importance to youth sport.

Lack of Trained Adult Supervision

A final factor that may be significant in overuse injuries is that the typical volunteer coach of a community-based sport program must meet minimal, if any, requirements to assume his or her position as the main role model of young athletes. While excellent training workshops, such as the American Coaching Effectiveness Program, exist, they have yet to reach but a small number of the 2-million-plus volunteers responsible for youth sport programs. The typical training clinic generally concentrates on the teaching of the fundamental skills and strategy of the sport. Most youth sport coaches, in fact, have very limited knowledge of and receive little or no training in prevention, recognition, and treatment of any sport injuries—least of all those subtle and at times ambiguous overuse injuries that are difficult for even professionals to diagnose. This trend is ongoing despite the fact that, historically, a prime reason for introducing adult supervision into children's sport was supposedly to reduce the chances of injury.

While the entire area of sports medicine is relatively new, research on the training and physiology of the young athlete has even less history behind it. Consequently, research-based information to guide those who must deal directly with overuse injuries in young athletes is rather limited. It can even be argued that many family physicians are ill prepared to diagnose, properly treat, and recommend appropriate preventive measures for dealing with young athletes and their special problems. Wilkins (1980) notes that "usually, there is preliminary pain but very little swelling and clinical symptomatology" (p. 379) accompanying overuse injuries. Roberts (1982) cautions that because the young athlete has "open epiphysis, more cartilage, and greater flexibility of the bone" (p. 126), an initial X ray may not show the extent of the injury. The stage may well be set for coaches, parents, and even physicians to encourage the young athlete to work through the "growing pains," because obvious symptoms denoting injury are absent. To reduce the danger, Harvey (1986) indicates that the use of xerography rather than conventional X ray results in a much higher percentage of correct diagnoses, while Micheli (1983) recommends the use of bone scans where absolute certainty of diagnosis is necessary.

Recommendations

Presently there are far more questions than answers concerning the dangers of the overuse injury in children's sport. The long-term effects cannot be examined until the athlete is mature—years after the competition and injury. In the interim, as youth sport programs continue to grow and until pediatric and adolescent sports medicine practitioners and scientists can provide more definitive answers, the following recommendations can perhaps provide some reasonable guidelines for those directing youth sport programs.

- Clinics and workshops to increase the competencies of those responsible for youth sports should become an integral part of all programs. The clinics need to teach the latest in basic applied sport sciences information relative to such areas as growth and development, exercise physiology, biomechanics, pedagogy, prevention and care of injuries, and social and psychological guidelines. These training clinics and workshops will help coaches make informed decisions regarding the training load that young athletes can safely tolerate.

- Keep accurate and extensive records of each athlete's injury and fitness history. It is imperative that longitudinal research, similar to that ongoing at the Youth Sports Institute at Michigan State University, continues and expands to include the study of both short- and long-term effects of injuries to youngsters involved in sport. Steps need to be taken to institute an effective and systematic injury data system in youth sport programs. Such a system operating within the scope of the National Athletic Injury Reporting System (NAIRS) could establish endemic levels of overuse and other types of sport-related injuries in children and be an important step in a preventive program.

- Treat young athletes as children or adolescents first and as athletes second. Do not assume that youngsters (through puberty at least) are capable of as much exertion as adults. It is crucial that those involved realize that children and adolescents are, as Åstrand (1976) has stated, "physically handicapped compared to adults" (p. 25). Factors such as muscular strength, skeletal stability, maximal oxygen uptake, and cardiac output are all proportionately lower. The ratio of skin surface to body volume in children may also make them more susceptible to heat stress.

- Reject the adult model of sport preparation and performance demands and adopt a model appropriate for young athletes who are not only physically but socially and psychologically immature. Martens, Christina, Harvey, and Sharkey (1981) recommend the following stages of training and competition: For the 6- to 10-year-old the emphasis should be on awakening interest in sport, having fun, and learning basic skills; the 11- to 14-year-old needs to be given the opportunity to develop versatility, proper techniques, and tolerance for increased training; the 15- to 18-year-old is ready for more extensive and intensive competition. This model will not only reduce the risk of overuse injury but will also reduce the dropout rate of young athletes.

- Respect the young athlete's limits. Wilkerson (1981) states that children have more intelligence regarding their limitations than adults. They will not drive themselves to the point of injury. However, well-meaning yet uninformed coaches and parents sometimes place unreasonable training and performance demands on youngsters. Especially for young children, coaches need to determine limits in basically noncompetitive situations and resist the temptation to expect significantly greater effort or performance in competition.

• Allow for the wide range of developmental rates existing in youngsters. Programs often categorize participants into competitive groups solely on the basis of age (age-group competition). This type of grouping ignores the fact that at age 6 maturity level can vary as much as 4 years. At age 12 it is not unusual to find some children with the maturity level of a 9-year-old, while others have a maturity level of a 15-year-old (Rarick & Seefeldt, 1977). One 12-year-old may be ready for increased training and competition, while a second should still be concentrating on developing basic skills. Gilliam (1982) recommends that when using age categories, athletes should be no more than 2 years apart and coaches should be allowed flexibility to move players based on maturity and skill. This approach will reduce the risk of overstressing the less mature individuals who, despite their chronological age, are not ready for a particular work load.

• Adhere to a game, practice, and season length appropriate for the developmental level of the athlete. Because of developmental differences, some youngsters will be able to practice and participate more frequently and for longer periods than others without risking an overuse injury. The Little League rule restricting pitchers to six innings per week certainly demonstrates awareness of the developmental state of the athlete. The increased emphasis on early specialization in some sports, however, has resulted in 8- and 9-year-olds practicing and participating 10 to 11 months a year. This type of early commitment certainly increases the possibility not only of overuse injury, but of sport burnout as well. According to Gilliam (1982), 8- and 9-year-olds should be restricted to sessions 6 to 8 weeks long with two to three practices and one game per week. This restriction does not prevent the children from practicing on their own, but, as indicated earlier, children seldom overload their systems to the point of injury in nonadult-organized practices.

References

Adams, J.E. (1965). Injury to the throwing arm: A study of traumatic changes in the elbow joints of boy baseball players. *California Medicine*, **102**, 127-132.

American Academy of Pediatrics. (1981). Committee on pediatric aspects of physical fitness, recreation, and sports: Competitive athletics for children of elementary school age. *Pediatrics*, **67**, 927-928.

Åstrand, P.-O. (1976). The child in sport and physical activity-physiology. In J.G. Albinson, & G.M. Andrew (Eds.), *Child in sport and physical activity* (pp. 19-33). Baltimore: University Park Press.

Bailey, D.A., & Martin, A.D. (1988). The growing child and sport: Physiological considerations. In F.L. Smoll, R.A. Magill, & M.J. Ash (Eds.), *Children in sport* (3rd ed., pp. 103-117). Champaign, IL: Human Kinetics.

Boland, A.L. (1982). Upper-extremity injuries: Overuse syndromes of the shoulder. In R.C. Cantu (Ed.), *The exercising adult* (pp. 115-120). Lexington, MA: Collamore Press.

Caine, D.J., & Lindner, K.J. (1984). Growth plate injury: A threat to young distance runners? *The Physician and Sportsmedicine*, **12**, 118-124.

Dominguez, R.H. (1980). Shoulder pain in swimmers. *The Physician and Sportsmedicine*, **8**, 37-42.

Geen, R.G., & Gange, J.J. (1977). Drive theory of social facilitation: Twelve years of theory and research. *Psychological Bulletin*, **84**, 1267-1288.

Gilliam, T. (1982). Answers to the most frequently asked questions about youth sports. In R.H. Cox (Ed.), *Educating youth sports coaches: Solutions to a national dilemma* (pp. 26-33), Reston, VA: American Alliance for Health, Physical Education, Recreation and Dance.

Godshall, R.W., Hansen, C.A., & Rising, D.C. (1981). Stress fractures through the distal femoral epiphysis in athletes: A previously un-reported entity. *American Journal of Sports Medicine*, **9**, 114-116.

Hamill, P.V.V., Johnson, F.E., & Grams, W. (1970). Height and weight of children. *United States Vital and Health Statistics*, **104**(11), 1-46. Rockville, MD: U.S. Dept. of Health, Education and Welfare, National Center for Health Statistics.

Harvey, J.S., Jr. (1986). Overuse syndromes in young athletes. In M.R. Weiss & D. Gould (Eds.), *Sport for children and youths* (pp. 151-163). Champaign, IL: Human Kinetics.

Haywood, K.M. (1986). Modification in youth sport: A rationale and some examples in youth basketball. In M.R. Weiss & D. Gould (Eds.), *Sport for children and youths* (pp. 179-185). Champaign, IL: Human Kinetics.

Kujala, U.M., Kvist, M., & Heinonen, O. (1985). Osgood-Schlatter's disease in adolescent athletes. *American Journal of Sports Medicine*, **13**, 236-240.

Larson, R.L., Singer, K.M., Bergstrom, R., & Thomas, S. (1976). Little League survey: The Eugene study. *American Journal of Sports Medicine*, **4**, 201-209. [Editorial comment on article]

Legwold, G. (1983). Preadolescents show "dramatic" strength gains. *The Physician and Sportsmedicine*, **11**, 25.

Lipscomb, A.B. (1975). Baseball pitching injuries in growing athletes. *The Journal of Sports Medicine*, **3**, 25-34.

Lopez, R., & Pruett, D.M. (1982). The child runner. *Journal of Physical Education, Recreation and Dance*, **53**, 78-81.

Lord, R.H., & Kozar, B. (1986, April). *Social facilitation and pain attenuation: Implications for youth sports.* Paper presented at the conference of the American Alliance for Health, Physical Education, Recreation and Dance, Cincinnati, OH.

Martens, R. (1988). Youth sport in the USA. In F.L. Smoll, R.A. Magill, & M.J. Ash (Eds.), *Children in sport* (3rd ed., pp. 17-23). Champaign, IL: Human Kinetics.

Martens, R., Christina, R.W., Harvey, J.S., & Sharkey, B.J. (1981). *Coaching young athletes.* Champaign, IL: Human Kinetics.

McGinnis, J.M. (1985). The national children and youth fitness study: Introduction. *Journal of Physical Education, Recreation and Dance*, **56**, 44.

Mcmanama, G.B., Micheli, L.J., Berry, M.V., & Sohn, R.S. (1985). The surgical treatment of osteochondritis of the capitellum. *American Journal of Sports Medicine*, **13**, 11-19.

Micheli, L.J. (1983). Overuse injuries in children: The growth factor. In M.W. Korn (Ed.), Symposium on special considerations in sports medicine. *The Orthopedic Clinics of North America*, **14**, 337-360.

Micheli, L.J., Santore, R., & Stanitski, C.L. (1980). Epiphyseal fractures of the elbow in children. *American Family Physician*, **22**, 107-116.

Micheli, L.J., Sohn, R.S., & Solomon, R. (1985). Stress fractures of the second metatarsal involving lisfranc's joint in ballet dancers. *The Journal of Bone and Joint Surgery*, **67**(A), 1372-1375.

Michener, J.A. (1976). *Sport in America.* Greenwich, CT: Fawcett.

Pate, R.R., Ross, J.G., Dotson, C.O., & Gilbert, G.G. (1985). The new norms: A comparison with the 1980 AAHPERD norms. *Journal of Physical Education, Recreation and Dance*, **56**, 70-72.

Rarick, G.L. (1978). Competitive sports in childhood and early adolescence. In R.A. Magill, M.J. Ash, & F.L. Smoll (Eds.), *Children in sport: A contemporary anthology* (1st ed., pp. 113-128). Champaign, IL: Human Kinetics.

Rarick, G.L., & Seefeldt, V. (1977). Characteristics of the young athlete. In J.R. Thomas (Ed.), *Youth sports guide for coaches and parents* (pp. 24-44). Washington, DC: Manufacturers Life Insurance Company and The National Association for Sport and Physical Education.

Rettig, A.C., & Beltz, H.F. (1985). Stress fracture in the humerus in an adolescent tennis tournament player. *American Journal of Sports Medicine*, **13**, 55-58.

Roberts, J. (1982). Diagnosis and management of children's injuries discussion: Meeting notes. *The Physician and Sportsmedicine*, **10**, 126-127.

Seefeldt, V., & Steig, P. (1986). Introduction to an interdisciplinary assessment of competition on elite young distance runners. In M.R. Weiss & D. Gould (Eds.), *Sport for children and youths* (pp. 213-217). Champaign, IL: Human Kinetics.

Sharkey, B.J. (1986). When should children begin competing?: A physiological perspective. In M.R. Weiss & D. Gould (Eds.), *Sport for children and youths* (pp. 51-54). Champaign, IL: Human Kinetics.

Singer, K. (1986). Injuries and disorders of the epiphysis in young athletes. In M.R. Weiss & D. Gould (Eds.), *Sport for children and youths* (pp. 141-150). Champaign, IL: Human Kinetics.

Stanish, W.D. (1984). Overuse injuries in athletes: A perspective. *Medicine and Science in Sports and Exercise*, **16**, 1-7.

Tabin, G.C., Gregg, J.R., & Bonci, T. (1985). Predictive leg strength values in immediately prepubescent and postpubescent athletes. *American Journal of Sports Medicine*, **13**, 387-389.

Teeple, J. (1978). Physical growth and maturation. In M.V. Ridenour (Ed.), *Motor development: Issues and applications* (pp. 3-27). Princeton, NJ: Princeton Book Co.

Walsh, W.M., Huurman, W.W., & Shelton, G.L. (1985). Overuse injuries of the knee and spine in girls' gymnastics. *The Orthopedic Clinics of North America*, **16**, 329-350.

Wilkerson, J. (1981). Strength and endurance training of the youthful performer. In C.H. Strong & D.D. Ludwig (Eds.), *Directions in Health, Physical Education, and Recreation: Proceedings of the National Olympic Academy IV, The Olympic Ideal: 776 B.C. to the 21st Century, 2,* (2, pp. 589-609). Bloomington: School of Health, Physical Education, and Recreation, Indiana University.

Wilkins, K.E. (1980). The uniqueness of the young athlete: Musculoskeletal injuries. *American Journal of Sports Medicine*, **8**, 377-382.

SECTION 4

Psychological Issues

As emphasized earlier in this volume, children's participation in sport has become an important part of the fabric of North American society. In ever-increasing numbers, boys and girls spend part of their days practicing or competing in athletics. How does this involvement affect the psychological makeup of the participant? Many parents, educators, and other interested parties have become acutely concerned about the psychological effects of youth sport. In response to this concern psychologists and physical educators have joined forces to delineate and investigate the psychological issues associated with children's sport participation.

To begin this section, Tara Kost Scanlan establishes the significance of the sport experience for children. Focusing on youngsters between 4 and 12 years of age, Scanlan presents a four-stage model of the competition process typically encountered by children in sport. In order to understand the consequences of sport participation, the author cautions that competition must be placed within the larger context of children's socialization. Social evaluation is thus highlighted as a key developmental element in the competition process. In addition to conceptualizing the elements of the competition process, consideration is given to the long-term developmental consequences of the child's sport experience.

The next chapter presents a provocative counterpoint to the competitive nature of sport. Terry D. Orlick and Anne Pitman-Davidson make a strong case for the development and use of children's games that emphasize mutual acceptance, cooperation, and positive outcomes. Like Scanlan in her chapter, Orlick and Pitman-Davidson place the experience of sport within the larger context of social development. They profess that if this expanded perspective provides a variety of desirable experiences, then children will develop positive social values. If, however, children have an overabundance of experiences that place a premium on competition, their social development may be distorted.

A critical youth sport issue is the question of why so many children drop out of participation. In chapter 13, Daniel Gould and Linda Petlichkoff seek to explain why an estimated 35% of children who have become involved in sport withdraw each year. After reviewing research relating to attrition in youth sport, Gould and Petlichkoff present a conceptual model of youth sport withdrawal that integrates both the descriptive and theoretical research in the area. Next, the model is modified to explain motives for youth sport participation. The chapter concludes with a section on practical implications for maintaining and enhancing participation motivation in young athletes.

An important theme of chapter 14 is that professionals interested in motor skill development have failed to study children as they perform in sport settings. Jerry R. Thomas, Karen E. French, Katherine T. Thomas, and Jere D. Gallagher feel quite strongly that in order to have an accurate idea of how sport proficiency is acquired, improved, and maintained, children must be studied in the actual sport situation. Furthermore, Thomas and his associates assert that we need to know how children's developing cognitive and memory capabilities interact with sport performance. Specifically, they feel that such studies need to (a) adopt a sport-specific research model, and (b) use the expert-novice paradigm for conducting the research.

The next pair of chapters examines the role of stress in youth sport. In chapter 15, Michael W. Passer describes stress as a process involving situational demands, appraisal processes, aversive emotional responses, and consequences. Research on children's stress in sport is then reviewed within this framework. Passer first discusses the demands inherent in the athletic setting and children's appraisal of these demands. Next, he presents empirical findings on the cognitive and physiological components of children's emotional responses to competition. Passer then examines the behavioral and health-related consequences of children's competitive stress, including decreased enjoyment and dropping out, performance impairment, and sleep loss. To conclude the chapter, Passer discusses the controversial issue of whether sport is too stressful for children and offers several recommendations for future research.

In a sequel to the Passer chapter, Frank L. Smoll and Ronald E. Smith present a conceptual model of stress and its implications for stress reduction in children's sport. The model emphasizes relationships between the situation, cognitive appraisal processes, physiological arousal, and behavioral responses to the situation. After describing their model, the authors consider a number of points at which intervention strategies might be employed. Specifically, they offer readers guidelines and procedures that have proven effective in decreasing situational sources of stress associated with the nature of the sport, coaching roles and relationships, and parent roles and responsibilities. Next, Smoll and Smith describe their stress management training program, which has been used to help child athletes acquire cognitive and physiologic coping skills. Finally, stress reduction at the behavioral level is explored with respect to increasing young athletes' level of physical skill.

In chapter 17, Ana M. Estrada, Donna M. Gelfand, and Donald P. Hartmann use a different approach to look at some of the same issues analyzed by Scanlan in the opening chapter of this section of psychological issues. Using Albert Bandura's cognitive social learning model, the authors examine the socialization process and agents that shape the behaviors of children involved in sport programs. Coaches, parents, peers, and even the media are scrutinized for their influence on competitiveness, modeling, and competence. Finally, a specific set of recommendations are made to reduce the detrimental effects of competition.

CHAPTER 11

Social Evaluation and the Competition Process: A Developmental Perspective

Tara Kost Scanlan

Almost half of our nation's youth spend a large amount of their time participating in an achievement arena of considerable importance to them—competitive sport. The significance of this achievement experience to the developing child needs to be determined, and the complex relationship between competition and social-psychological development requires understanding. The present chapter takes a necessary first step in this regard by presenting a conceptualization of the competition process typically encountered by youth in the naturalistic competitive sport environment. Of primary interest are children between the ages of 4 and 12 years. The focus is on the examination of *social evaluation* as a key element of the competition process because of its centrality, pervasiveness, and developmental importance. Related discussion concerns whether the social evaluation is actually perceived by participants and, if so, whether the evaluative information is actively sought. Finally, potential long-term, developmental consequences of the socially evaluative sport experience are considered.

Selection of a Viable Approach to Study Competition

To understand the complex competition process, it is necessary to determine a viable basic approach to serve as a starting point for its study. Two major approaches to the study of competition are the traditional reward approach and a more recent formulation by Martens (1975, 1976). The reward approach defines competition as a situation in which rewards are distributed unequally among participants based on their performance in an activity (Church, 1968). The many problems with the reward approach that have limited its scientific viability have been enumerated extensively by Martens (1975, 1976) and will be reviewed only briefly.

The major limitation of the reward approach is that the competitive situation defined on a reward basis cannot be clearly operationalized. It is difficult to achieve "consensus on the criteria for the distribution of rewards, on the subjective value of the rewards, and on the goal to be achieved" (Martens, 1975, p. 70). It is quite possible that the goals strived for and the rewards sought might be entirely different for each competitor involved in the competition. Therefore, use of the reward definition forces the experimenter to make critical assumptions and inferences about the individual's perceptions, responses, and response consequences regarding the competitive situation.

The more viable approach to the study of competition, conceptualized by Martens (1975, 1976), has overcome the major deficiencies of the reward definition and provides a more workable alternative for scientific inquiry. Hence, this approach will be used to provide the underlying framework for the ensuing discussion. Martens provides clear operational definitions and makes no assumptions regarding how the individual perceives the competitive situation, the response made to it, or the consequences of the response. Instead, these factors have been divided into stages to be examined systematically.

Martens (1975) has depicted competition as a process consisting of four interrelated stages that filter through the individual. The stages include the objective competitive situation, subjective competitive situation, response, and consequences.

The *objective competitive situation* (OCS) refers to those "real factors in the physical or social environment that are arbitrarily defined as constituting a competitive situation" (Martens, 1975, p. 69). OCS is based on social evaluation rather than on reward and is defined as a situation in which the comparison of an individual's performance is made with some standard in the presence of at least one other person who is aware of the criterion for comparison and can evaluate the comparison process (p. 71). The comparison standard can be an individual's past performance level, an idealized performance level, or another individual's performance.

The second stage of the competition process is the *subjective competitive situation* (SCS) and involves how the individual perceives, appraises, and accepts the OCS. The SCS is very important, as it is the manner in which the individual perceives reality. Therefore, it is from this base that the individual operates. The resultant *response* emitted in Stage 3 is a direct function of the SCS. Responses can be made on a psychological, physiological, or behavioral level. Possible responses include the decision to compete or to avoid competition, attempts to modify the objective competitive situation, and overt competitive behavior.

The fourth stage of the competition process involves the short- or long-term *consequences* arising from the comparison process, which can be perceived as positive, negative, or neutral. The perceived consequences provide important information that updates the SCS and affects future competitive responses.

Beginning with this framework, which identifies social evaluation as a key component of the competition process, it is now possible to detail the social evaluation potential in the naturalistic objective competitive situation encountered by children engaged in competitive youth sport. The subjective competitive situation and response stages will be examined to determine if children perceive the social evaluation potential in the OCS and, if it is perceived, how children then respond in terms of information-seeking and self-protective behavior. The potential long-term consequences of the competition process will then briefly be discussed in terms of implications for social psychological development. Figure 1 provides a schematic overview of the ensuing discussion.

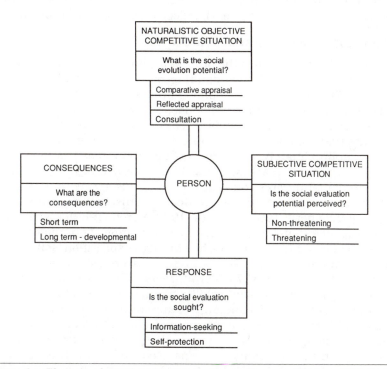

Figure 1.   The role of social evaluation in the sport competition process. *Note.* From "Social Evaluation: A Key Developmental Element in the Competition Process" by T.K. Scanlan. In *Children in Sport* (2nd ed., p. 140) by R.A. Magill, M.J. Ash, and F.L. Smoll (Eds.), 1982, Champaign, IL: Human Kinetics. Copyright 1982 by Richard A. Magill, Michael J. Ash, and Frank L. Smoll. Reprinted by permission.

The Nature of Social Evaluation as It Occurs in the Naturalistic Objective Competitive Situation (OCS)

The naturalistic OCS typically encountered by children encompasses considerable social evaluation potential. *Social evaluation* is the appraisal of one's ability based on information received from other persons (Jones & Gerard, 1967). Children have been found to be active information seekers who derive information from both social and nonsocial sources, with most of their information coming from social sources (Jones & Gerard, 1967; White 1959). The developing child has little past experience upon which to draw and, consequently, is very dependent on significant peers and adults for information about reality and the adequacy of his or her abilities for dealing with this reality (Horn & Hasbrook, 1986; Jones & Gerard, 1967). As depicted in Figure 1, the typical OCS includes at least three separate social evaluation processes, including comparative appraisal, reflected appraisal, and consultation.

The Comparative Appraisal Process

Comparative appraisal is the process of comparing with others to determine one's own relative standing on a specific ability (Jones & Gerard, 1967). Comparative appraisal occurs in the OCS when the comparison standard is another individual's performance rather than a past or idealized performance standard. The developmental findings clearly indicate that comparative appraisal becomes very important to children at approximately 4 to 5 years of age and intensifies through the elementary school years (Masters, 1972; Veroff, 1969). The following developmental progression indicates why this seems to occur.

Very young children do not compare themselves or compete with others (Greenberg, 1932; Masters, 1972; Veroff, 1969). Instead, their time is spent autonomously accruing information about their own personal abilities. This is accomplished through exploration, solitary play, mastery attempts, and striving to attain autonomous achievement goals (Cook & Stingle, 1974; Veroff, 1969; White, 1959). Eventually, however, personal or absolute ability has to be placed into a larger relative framework through comparative appraisal to achieve an accurate, meaningful, and complete assessment of ability. Developmentally, the child appears to be ready to engage in this process around 4 or 5 years of age, when the first signs of comparative and competitive behavior are evidenced (Cook & Stingle, 1974; Greenberg, 1932; Leuba, 1933; Masters, 1972; Ruble, Boggiano, Feldman, & Loebl, 1980; Veroff, 1969). Further, there is an increase in comparative and competitive behavior with age throughout the elementary school period, with the greatest intensity occurring around Grades 4, 5, and 6 (Cook & Stingle, 1974; Kagan & Madsen, 1972; McClintock & Nuttin, 1969; Nelson, 1970; Nelson & Kagan, 1972; Veroff, 1969). It is during this important age span that many children are engaged in competitive youth sport activities, where much of the comparative appraisal occurs. Further, the focus of the appraisal is on motor ability. To excel motorically is one of the most prized and esteemed abilities of children, particularly boys, of this age level. Therefore, the comparative appraisal process involves a central ability, making the outcomes potentially very important.

The Reflected Appraisal Process

Reflected appraisal is the second social evaluation process that can occur in the OCS. This is the process by which the child "derives an impression of his position on some attribute through the behavior of another person toward him" (Jones & Gerard, 1967, p. 321). Children can obtain extensive information about their motor abilities by attending to the overt or covert cues emitted by one who is in the position to evaluate their abilities. Comparative and reflected appraisal are similar in that evaluative ability information is derived from a social source. However, the two processes differ in certain ways. First, in comparative appraisal, children evaluate their relative abilities by comparing with another person's ability, but do not make any reference to the other person's direct behavior toward them (Jones & Gerard, 1967). Reflected appraisal involves the evaluation being "mediated by the behavior of the other person toward the person himself" (Jones & Gerard, 1967, p. 324). In this sense, the evaluation is inferred from the emitted behavior. Second, comparative appraisal involves evaluation through comparison with social standards, whereas reflected appraisal includes comparison with either social or objective standards. For example, a coach might unintentionally transmit reflected appraisal cues to a child after the child has won or lost a wrestling match where the comparison standard was social, or after the child has caught or missed a fly ball where the comparison standard was objective rather than social.

A considerable amount of reflected appraisal exists in the OCS. First, most competitive situations are public, so there are numerous persons from whom to extract cues, including coaches, parents, teammates, opponents, and spectators. Second, evaluation from these significant others—particularly parents, coaches, and peers—is more important and creates a greater impression on children than evaluation from persons of lesser status (Jones & Gerard, 1967). Third, numerous evaluative cues may be unintentionally emitted, yet obvious to the child, as exemplified by parental cues of pride and approval after a touchdown, and embarrassment and disapproval after a fumble. Other examples include the nonverbal indicants of elation by coaches, teammates, and supporting fans when a player of superior ability steps up to bat with the bases loaded, or the chagrin revealed by these same individuals when an inferior player is placed in a similar situation. These latter examples also illustrate how reflected appraisal frequently represents an evaluation that is based on many observations rather than on a one-time occurrence—which only tends to increase the potency of reflected appraisal. Fourth, evaluative cues in the OCS are often overtly manifested. Spectators often cheer or jeer, teammates frequently offer praise or reproof, and opponents sometimes congratulate or ridicule.

The Consultation Process

Consultation, the third social evaluation process, involves children asking another person for an ability appraisal or receiving an evaluation without explicitly requesting one (Jones & Gerard, 1967). The evaluation is direct rather than inferred and, again, is typically received from significant others. For example, parents are often very concerned about their child's motor ability; consequently they have much to say about his or her performance. It is the coach's job to evaluate ability, and players receive extensive information during practices that indicates their strengths, weaknesses, progress, and areas requiring improvement. Frequently, coaches make overt evaluations that indicate their appraisal of a player's ability compared to other players. Selecting a team, choosing the starters, and picking all-star candidates are all examples of evaluations coaches make that reinforce important comparative appraisal information for the youth.

In sum, the OCS encompasses extensive potential social evaluation through the processes of comparative appraisal, reflected appraisal, and direct consultation. Therefore, much information is available to participants from which to establish accurate and complete ability assessments. Involvement in the competition process occurs during the age period when the social evaluation process is particularly intense and important. Furthermore, the specific ability being appraised—motor ability—is of central importance to the developing youth. Therefore, it is contended that the social evaluation potential in the OCS is high.

The Subjective Competitive Situation

The subjective competitive situation (SCS) requires examination to determine if the social evaluation in the OCS is actually perceived by the competitors (see Figure 1). Evidence of this perception would establish that social evaluation is a real and salient factor to the competition process.

The SCS is difficult to assess because it is a cognitive variable, requiring inference. One indicant used to assess the social evaluation potential in the SCS has been the perception of threat to self, evidenced by state anxiety. Potential threat to self generally increases when social evaluation potential is high, when success and failure are clearly defined, and when negative outcomes and evaluation can be incurred. This perceived threat can induce psychological stress as manifested by state anxiety. *State anxiety* is defined by Spielberger (1966) as "subjective consciously perceived feelings of apprehension and tension, accompanied by or associated with activation or arousal of the autonomic nervous system" (p. 17). State anxiety is a *right-now* reaction to the immediate situation and can be assessed by physiological measures of autonomic arousal, by observation, and by psychological inventories. Two of the most commonly used and psychometrically sound psychological inventories currently available to study youth are Spielberger's (1973) State Anxiety Inventory for Children (SAIC) and the Competitive State Anxiety Inventory for Children (CSAI-C) developed by Martens and his associates (Martens, Burton, Rivkin, & Simon, 1980). Studies from three related lines of research that provide insight into the SCS and the perception of threat are reviewed next.

The first line of research was initiated by the author with a laboratory experiment designed to assess threat in the SCS and to determine the factors that induce it (Scanlan, 1975, 1977). Specifically, the effects of competitive trait anxiety (A-trait) and success-failure on state anxiety (A-state) manifested prior to and after a highly socially evaluative competition were investigated. An overview of this experiment is provided because it was the first study to assess perceived threat resulting from high social evaluation potential in the OCS.

Competitive A-trait, assessed by the Sport Competition Anxiety Test (SCAT; Martens, 1977), is an important intrapersonal factor related to perceived threat. It is a "relatively stable personality disposition that describes a person's tendency to perceive competitive situations as threatening or non-threatening" and to respond with varying A-state levels (Martens & Gill, 1976, p. 699). Findings in the general and test anxiety literatures have shown consistently that high A-trait individuals exhibit greater A-state than low A-trait individuals when in evaluative or psychologically stressful situations (Hodges & Durham, 1972; Lamb, 1972; Phillips, Pitcher, Worsham, & Miller, 1980; Sarason, 1968; Wine, 1982). Therefore, it was hypothesized in this study that high competitive A-trait children would evidence higher A-state than low competitive A-trait children when facing a socially evaluative competitive situation.

The degree of success or failure experienced during competition, defined in terms of win-loss outcomes, is an important situational determinant of perceived threat to self. Individuals achieving successful outcomes should be less threatened by the information about their ability, should expect greater positive evaluation from others, and should be more confident in their ability to effect positive outcomes in similar future encounters than individuals incurring failure. Individuals attaining moderately successful outcomes receive little definitive evaluative information and should approximate their precompetitive perceptions. Results from the general anxiety literature have indicated consistently that A-state decreases with success and increases with failure (Hodges & Durham, 1972; Ishiguro, 1965). Therefore, it was hypothesized that children experiencing more successful competition outcomes would evidence lower postcompetition A-state than children experiencing fewer successful outcomes.

The experimental design was a Competitive A-trait X Success-Failure (2 X 3) factorial. The two levels of the first factor were high and low competitive A-trait. The Sport Competition Anxiety Test (SCAT) was administered to 306 boys between 10 and 12 years of age several weeks prior to the experimental phase of the study. The 41 high competitive A-trait boys and the 42 low competitive A-trait boys, representing the respective upper and lower quartiles on SCAT, were selected as participants. The three levels of success-failure were induced by manipulating win percentage. The success group won 80% (W80), the moderate-success group won 50% (W50), and the failure group won only 20% (W20) of the 20 contests. Both high and low A-trait subjects were randomly assigned to success-failure conditions.

A-state was assessed by Spielberger's State Anxiety Inventory for Children (SAIC) at four different time periods. An initial basal measure was taken after a lengthy rest period. Assessments were also made just prior to competition, immediately after competition, and after a final debriefing session.

The findings demonstrated that competitive A-trait and success-failure are important factors in the perception of threat and, thereby, provided support for the two hypotheses. Competitive A-trait was found to be a significant predictor of precompetitive A-state, with high competitive A-trait individuals indicating greater A-state than low competitive A-trait individuals when anticipating the pending competition. The results also indicated that postcompetition A-state levels significantly increased between successful (W80), moderately successful (W50), and failure (W20) outcome groups.

The results of this study have been shown to be internally and externally valid. They have been successfully replicated under similar laboratory conditions (Martens & Gill, 1976) and in the natural field setting of competitive youth sport (Scanlan & Lewthwaite, 1984; Scanlan & Passer, 1978, 1979). Extensive social evaluation potential existed in the objective competitive situation of each study. Evidence suggests that this social evaluation is actually perceived. Moreover, it is perceived by participants of both genders in both individual and team sports.

Further evidence that the social evaluation in the OCS is perceived by young competitors has been supported by two additional lines of research. First, studies have indicated that even greater precompetition state anxiety is manifested in the particularly evaluative individual sport context than in the team sport domain (Griffin, 1972; Johnson, 1949; Simon & Martens, 1979; see Scanlan, 1984 for an elaboration of this issue). Second, it has been demonstrated that participants evidence concern about performance failure and negative social evaluation. These cognitions have been shown to be predictors of higher competitive trait anxiety (Gould, Horn, & Spreemann, 1983; Passer, 1983) and precompetition state anxiety levels (Scanlan & Lewthwaite, 1984).

In sum, the findings of the three lines of research reviewed provide insight into threat in the subjective competitive situation. The evidence indicates that the social evaluation potential in the OCS is actually perceived and, therefore, is a salient factor in the competition process. The manner in which the subjective competitive situation is responded to in terms of seeking the available ability information and subsequent evaluation is examined next.

Response

It has been shown that children are very aware of and can feel threatened by the social evaluation potential in the objective competitive situation. Referring again to Figure 1, the next point of interest is determining how children respond to this social evaluation. Do they actively seek the ability information that emanates from evaluation, or do they avoid this information, when possible, to protect themselves? Answers to these questions are needed to further establish the importance and pervasiveness of social evaluation information.

A matter of particular relevance to this discussion is determining how children, under different levels of perceived threat, structure the competitive situation when given the opportunity to select their own future opponents. Do they structure the situation to maximize or minimize information about their abilities? Festinger's social comparison theory provides some insight into the issue.

Festinger (1954) developed a theory of social comparison based on the premise that human beings are motivated to obtain evaluative information about their abilities and, in the absence of objective standards, seek comparative appraisal. Further, comparison is made with similar-ability others to maximize information gain. The paradigm usually used to assess this hypothesis has been structured in the following way. Subjects are told that their score, representing performance on a positively or negatively valued attribute, has fallen at the median of a list of scores ordered by rank. Subjects are then asked which score in the ranked list they would like to see. Typically, if the extreme scores have been established and the trait is positive, subjects choose to see the score of a similar or slightly superior other in the rank order (Gruder, 1971; Hakmiller, 1966; Radloff, 1966; Singer & Shockley, 1965). This consistent finding indicates support for Festinger's information-seeking hypothesis.

However, several findings have demonstrated that when threat to self exists in social evaluation situations, self-protective behavior occurs. Further, such behavior increases as the probability of incurring threatening ability information increases. Results indicate that individuals reduce the probability of receiving this threatening information by comparing with individuals of lesser relative ability, thereby assuring successful comparative appraisal (Dreyer, 1954; Friend & Gilbert, 1973; Hakmiller, 1966).

The following hypotheses can be derived from the social comparison findings. First, successful, unthreatened subjects structure the situation to maximize information gain by selecting opponents of equal or slightly greater relative ability. Conversely, unsuccessful, threatened subjects minimize information gain by selecting opponents of lesser relative ability. In this way, they protect themselves from incurring further negative appraisal information.

Scanlan (1977) tested these two hypotheses in the competition laboratory experiment presented earlier. Opponent preference questions were administered during the postcompetition period immediately after postcompetition A-state was assessed. The results supported the first hypothesis but not the second. Children in all three success-failure groups (W80, W50, W20) indicated a strong preference for opponents who equaled their abilities. These findings indicate that children engage in maximum information-seeking behavior during competition, regardless of their level of perceived threat.

Consequences

The final stage of the competition process involves the short- and long-term consequences, which may be positive, negative, or neutral (see Figure 1). Whenever social evaluation of ability occurs, positive or negative consequences can result during any given competition. The child might receive successful comparative appraisal information and positive reflected and/or consultation evaluation from significant others. Conversely, unsuccessful comparative appraisal and negative social evaluation might be incurred. It is probable that the consequences of any one *isolated* competitive experience will have minimal effect on social psychological development—unless, perhaps, the consequences are particularly aversive. The important point is that many children engage in intense competition over extended periods of time with similar consequences potentially being repeated over and over again. This repetition makes developmental considerations, such as self-esteem development, relevant. Through this repetition the potential accrual of primarily successful or primarily unsuccessful experiences, as perceived by the participant, can result. Also through this repetition, success-failure experiences might somewhat balance out, leading to relatively neutral long-term consequences.

The second important point is that the consequences of the competition process must be kept within the perspective of the total socialization process. The extensive evaluative information available in the objective competitive situation can result in children establishing an accurate assessment of an ability that is very important to them. Whether or not this information, be it positive or negative, results in perceived favorable, neutral, or adverse consequences is probably largely dependent upon the manner in which significant others evaluate and interpret the information and the perspective they provide. For example, children who continually receive negative comparative appraisal but gain support and guidance from their parents and coaches might benefit considerably from the competitive experience. The potential negative consequences might be neutralized or even supplanted with more positive outcomes. The children might learn to put comparative appraisal outcomes in perspective, learn to accept their capabilities and limitations within this particular achievement arena, and learn to define success and failure in terms of accomplishing realistic personal performance and effort goals. The potential negative impact of the consequences might further be reduced if the children can demonstrate other abilities, function competently in other evaluative achievement settings, and receive positive evaluation from significant others.

In sum, the competition process must be placed within the larger socialization process to be adequately understood. Although competition is an important process, it cannot be isolated from the child's greater social context. The role of significant others and competence in other situations must be considered as they influence the positive, negative, or neutral long-term consequences of competition.

References

Church, R.M. (1968). Applications of behavior theory to social psychology: Imitation and competition. In E.C. Simmel, R.H. Hoppe, & G.A. Milton (Eds.), *Social facilitation and imitative behavior*, (pp. 135-168). Boston: Allyn & Bacon.

Cook, H., & Stingle, S. (1974). Cooperative behavior in children. *Psychological Bulletin*, **81**, 918-933.

Dreyer, H.S. (1954). Aspiration behavior as influenced by expectation and group comparison. *Human Relations*, **7**, 175-190.

Festinger, L.A. (1954). A theory of social comparison processes. *Human Relations*, **7**, 117-140.

Friend, R.M., & Gilbert, J. (1973). Threat and fear of negative evaluation as determinants of locus of social comparison. *Journal of Personality*, **41**, 328-340.

Gould, D., Horn, T., & Spreemann, J. (1983). Sources of stress in junior elite wrestlers. *Journal of Sport Psychology*, **5**, 159-171.

Greenberg, P.J. (1932). Competition in children: An experimental study. *American Journal of Psychology*, **44**, 221-248.

Griffin, M.R. (1972). An analysis of state and trait anxiety experienced in sports competition at different age levels. *Foil* (Spring), 58-64.

Gruder, C.L. (1971). Determinants of social comparison. *Journal of Experimental Social Psychology*, **7**, 473-489.

Hakmiller, K.L. (1966). Threat as a determinant of downward comparison. *Journal of Experimental Social Psychology Supplement*, **2** (1), 32-39.

Hodges, W.F., & Durham, R.L. (1972). Anxiety, ability and digit span performance. *Journal of Personality and Social Psychology*, **24**, 401-406.

Horn, T.S., & Hasbrook, C. (1986). Informational components influencing children's perceptions of their physical competence. In M.R. Weiss & D. Gould (Eds.), *Sport for children and youths* (pp. 81-88). Champaign, IL: Human Kinetics.

Ishiguro, S. (1965). Motivational instructions and GSR on memory, especially as related to manifest anxiety. *Psychological Reports*, **16**, 786.

Johnson, W.R. (1949). A study of emotion revealed in two types of athletic contests. *Research Quarterly*, **20**, 72-79.

Jones, E.E., & Gerard, H.B. (1967). *Foundations of social psychology*. New York: Wiley.

Kagan, S., & Madsen, M.C. (1972). Rivalry in Anglo-American and Mexican children of two ages. *Journal of Personality and Social Psychology*, **24**, 214-220.

Lamb, D.H. (1972). Speech anxiety: Towards a theoretical conceptualization and preliminary scale development. *Speech Monographs*, **39**, 62-67.

Leuba, C. (1933). An experimental study of rivalry in children. *Journal of Comparative Psychology*, **16**, 367-378.

Martens, R. (1975). *Social psychology and physical activity*. New York: Harper & Row.

Martens, R. (1976). Competition: In need of a theory. In D.M. Landers (Ed.), *Social problems in athletics* (pp. 9-17). Urbana: University of Illinois Press.

Martens, R. (1977). *Sport competition anxiety test*. Champaign, IL: Human Kinetics.

Martens, R., Burton, D., Rivkin, F., & Simon, J. (1980). Reliability and validity of the Competitive State Anxiety Inventory (CSAI). In C.H. Nadeau, W.R. Halliwell, K.M. Newell, & G.C. Roberts (Eds.),

Psychology of motor behavior and sport—1979 (pp. 91-99). Champaign, IL: Human Kinetics.

Martens, R., & Gill, D. (1976). State anxiety among successful and unsuccessful competitors who differ in competitive trait anxiety. *Research Quarterly*, **47**, 698-708.

Masters, J.C. (1972). Social comparison by young children. In W.W. Hartup (Ed.), *The young child* (pp. 320-339). Washington, DC: National Association for Education of Young Children.

McClintock, C., & Nuttin, J. (1969). Development of competitive game behavior in children across two cultures. *Journal of Experimental Social Psychology*, **5**, 203-218.

Nelson, L.L. (1970). *The development of cooperation and competition in children from ages five to ten years old: Effects of sex, situational determinants, and prior experiences.* Unpublished doctoral dissertation, University of California, Los Angeles.

Nelson, L.L., & Kagan, S. (1972). The star-spangled scramble. *Psychology Today*, **6**, 53.

Passer, M.W. (1983). Fear of failure, fear of evaluation, perceived competence, and self-esteem in competitive trait anxious children. *Journal of Sport Psychology*, **5**, 172-188.

Phillips, B.N., Pitcher, G.D., Worsham, M.E., & Miller, S.C. (1980). Test anxiety and the school environment. In I.G. Sarason (Ed.), *Test anxiety: Theory, research, and applications* (pp. 327-346). Hillsdale, NJ: Lawrence Erlbaum.

Radloff, R. (1966). Social comparison and ability evaluation. *Journal of Experimental Social Psychology Supplement*, **2** (1), 6-26.

Ruble, D., Boggiano, A., Feldman, N., & Loebl, J. (1980). Developmental analysis of the role of social comparison in self-evaluation. *Developmental Psychology*, **16**, 105-115.

Sarason, I.G. (1968). Verbal learning, modeling, and juvenile delinquency. *American Psychologist*, **23**, 254-266.

Scanlan, T.K. (1975). *The effects of competition trait anxiety and success-failure on the perception of threat in a competitive situation.* Unpublished doctoral dissertation, University of Illinois, Urbana-Champaign.

Scanlan, T.K. (1977). The effects of success-failure on the perception of threat in a competitive situation. *Research Quarterly*, **48**, 144-153.

Scanlan, T.K. (1984). Competitive stress and the child athlete. In J.M. Silva, III & R.S. Weinberg (Eds.), *Psychological foundations of sport* (pp. 118-129). Champaign, IL: Human Kinetics.

Scanlan, T.K., & Lewthwaite, R. (1984). Social psychological aspects of competition for male youth sport participants: I. Predictors of competitive stress. *Journal of Sport Psychology*, **6**, 208-226.

Scanlan, T.K., & Passer, M.W. (1978). Factors related to competitive stress among male youth sports participants. *Medicine and Science in Sports*, **10**, 103-108.

Scanlan, T.K., & Passer, M.W. (1979). Sources of competitive stress in young female athletes. *Journal of Sport Psychology*, **1**, 151-159.

Simon, J., & Martens, R. (1979). Children's anxiety in sport and non-sport evaluative activities. *Journal of Sport Psychology*, 160-169.

Singer, J.E., & Shockley, V.L. (1965). Ability and affiliation. *Journal of Personality and Social Psychology*, **1**, 95-100.

Spielberger, C.D. (1966). *Anxiety and behavior*. New York: Academic Press.

Spielberger, C.D. (1973). *Preliminary test manual for the state-trait anxiety inventory for children ("How I Feel Questionnaire")*. Palo Alto, CA: Consulting Psychologists Press.

Veroff, J. (1969). Social comparison and the development of achievement motivation. In C.P. Smith (Ed.), *Achievement-related motives in children* (pp. 46-101). New York: Russell Sage Foundation.

White, R.W. (1959). Motivation reconsidered: The concept of competence. *Psychological Review*, **66**, 297-334.

Wine, J.D. (1982). Evaluation anxiety. In H.W. Krohne & L. Laux (Eds.), *Achievement, stress and anxiety* (pp. 207-219). Washington, DC: Hemisphere.

CHAPTER 12

Enhancing Cooperative Skills in Games and Life

Terry D. Orlick
Anne Pitman-Davidson

We live in an increasingly complex and sometimes frightening world in which the quality and harmony of our lives is becoming more and more dependent on our ability to be cooperative and empathic. In searching for a better tomorrow, the learning and refinement of cooperative interaction is perhaps the most important and valuable lesson of all.

Cooperation During Competition

In many present-day games and sports, a basic structural problem exists where two or more people or teams want what only one of them can have—the ball, the space, the victory, and so on. In such situations the question becomes, How far will each go in order to achieve these goals? The issue of reactions, by and toward the "losers," also becomes a problem. One way to alleviate such problems is to work within a competitive structure in an attempt to bring competition into perspective.

At its best, competition can be a forum for the positive pursuit of personal excellence—a way for athletes to explore their potential. At its worst, competition pits person against person in a destructive rivalry, resulting in high levels of anxiety, self-depreciation, insensitivity toward others, cheating, and destructive aggression.

Problems surface when children's recreational time is monopolized by competitive activities with no playtime to balance their lives and values. By turning everything into a competition or a quest for mastery, we rob children of an important life perspective. As much as we can gain from mastery, we can lose by not having a place free from the need for mastery. Even as adults, we need in our lives some space free from evaluation and from having to perform or live up to the expectations of others. Children tunneled through a high-achievement system often learn to live only for the future, to evaluate their overall worth by numbers, to accept that there is no place or play free from evaluation. They learn that they are always being judged and must always do their best or suffer the consequences of being a failure. When a high level of evaluation is stressed, children lose their playfulness at a very early age and carry the void with them for life (Orlick, 1986).

To create a more positive learning experience, competitive games can be played in a more cooperative and humanistic fashion by showing children how to control them. Within competitive structures are countless opportunities for teaching important social values. What better place than in the midst of a game to discuss the true meaning of such values as winning, losing, success, failure, anxiety, rejection, fair play, acceptance, friendship, cooperation, and healthy competition? What better place to help children become aware of their own feelings and become more sensitive to the feelings of others? What better place to encourage children to help one another learn how to cope constructively with some of these problems and concerns? A time-out can be called to take advantage of a meaningful learning opportunity. The value (or devaluation) can be discussed quickly, the behavior can be reinforced or a change in behavior recommended, and play can resume. Then, if another positive value (e.g., helping) or troublesome value (e.g., hurting) surfaces, another quick time-out can be taken for a few constructive comments. With little direction, the children can decide for themselves what they want to get out of the game. They can discuss what other children do that makes them feel good or bad, how they think children should treat one another, how to help one another, and how to help one another follow the value or behavior guidelines they feel are important. Orlick (1979a; 1979b; 1979c; 1980a; 1980b; 1981b), Orlick and Botterill (1975), Botterill (1978), Glashagel, Johnson, Laundry, and Orozco (1976) and Halas (1987) have some good practical suggestions on how to carry out activities that promote discussion and cooperation.

Cooperative Sports and Games

One way to eliminate the problems children experience in intense competitive experiences is to simply alter the basic competitive structure— for example, by removing the need to compete and the rewards for demonstrating mastery over others. Many of you have probably had an opportunity to experience cooperatively structured games or have witnessed games where freedom, fun, joy, and playfulness are exhibited by children playing free from competition.

The distinctive feature of cooperative games, which separates them from all other games, old and new, is their structural makeup. For example, in the game "King of the Mountain," the rules dictate that one person be king while all others are shoved down the mountain. The game has a competitive structure in that players act against one another and only one attains the object of the game.

In the cooperative version, "People of the Mountain," the structural demands of the game are completely reversed. Children play together in getting as many people as possible to the top of the mountain. This version frees the players from the pressure to compete, eliminates the need for destructive behavior, and by design encourages helpful and fun-filled interaction (Orlick, 1982).

The concept is simple: People play with one another rather than against one another; they play to overcome challenges, not to overcome other people; and they are freed by the very structure of the games to enjoy the play itself. No player need find himself or herself a bench warmer nursing a bruised self-image. Because the games are designed so that cooperation among players is necessary to achieve the objective(s), children play together for common ends rather than against one another for mutually exclusive ends. In the process, they learn in a fun way how to become more considerate of one another, more aware of how other people are feeling, and more willing to operate in one another's best interests.

Designing Cooperative Games

If you want to design a cooperative game or counsel a player about how to treat others within the game structure, try to integrate some of the qualities that help meaningful working and loving relationships grow. It is best to structure time-outs within, between, or after activities, so that participants can practice and subsequently perfect some of the following life- and love-enhancing skills:

- *Empathic responses*—Try to develop the skills necessary to climb inside another person's feelings, to know how he or she feels, and to act on the basis of this knowledge.
- *Appreciative responses*—Try to develop the skills necessary for one person to recognize, appreciate, and express appreciation for another person's perceptions, contributions, and personal growth needs.
- *Cooperative responses*—Try to develop the skills necessary to share the daily work load, whether in the game or at home, to share experiences, good times and bad times, and to promote the idea of solving problems or seeking solutions together with others.
- *Communicative responses*—Try to develop the skills necessary for individuals to express their own feelings, knowledge, appreciation, problems, concerns, and perspectives.
- *Balanced responses*—Try to develop the skills necessary for participants to respect the various phases of their lives so that one area (e.g., sport or work) does not result in the exclusion of important others (e.g., family, relationships, relaxation) (Orlick, 1983, p. 155).

Over the past 15 years we have developed hundreds of cooperative games for various age groups. Some are active, some quiet, some in between, but *all* are cooperative. Most of the games are outlined in *The Cooperative Sports and Games Book* (Orlick, 1978a) and *The Second Cooperative Sports and Games Book* (Orlick, 1982). People of every size, shape, age, and ability—from infants to the aged—can enjoy these games, which can be played virtually anywhere with almost no equipment. When these games are appropriately selected or adapted for a specific age group, they almost always result in total involvement, feelings of acceptance, cooperative contribution by all players, and lots of smiling faces (Orlick, 1979a). Several other books have addressed the competition issue and have presented practical alternatives that most children really enjoy (Michaelis & Michaelis, 1977; Morris, 1980; Orlick, 1978a, 1978b; Weinstein & Goodman, 1980).

Cooperative Game Studies

Almost all young children agree that cooperative games are fun to play. But, do they really affect a child's learning of prosocial values?

One major goal of cooperative learning experiences is to enable children of the future to become more receptive to sharing both human and material resources (e.g., ideas, talents, concerns, feelings, respect, possessions, equipment, turns, time, space, responsibility, and the betterment of each other's lives). With this in mind, a series of games was created and several studies conducted to assess the social impact of well-designed cooperative game programs.

The results have consistently shown an increase in cooperative behavior not only in games, but also in free play and in classroom situations for children involved in these programs. The cooperative change does not occur overnight, but within a period of several months most children seem to become more considerate and caring (Fritsch, 1981; Jensen, 1979; Orlick, 1981a; Orlick & Foley, 1976; Orlick, McNally, & O'Hara, 1978; Provost, 1981; Slack, 1978; Witt, 1980).

Based on these studies and on our systematic observations to date, the following conclusions can be drawn (Orlick, 1983, p. 156):

- Cooperatively designed play and games are an effective medium for introducing children to the concepts and skills involved in cooperation and sharing (Orlick, 1978b).
- Very young children of both sexes (even 1- and 2-year-olds) are fully capable of cooperating and sharing and will do so with some regularity if their natural gestures of giving are encouraged and reinforced (Orlick, 1982; Pines, 1979).
- Team harmony and mutual helping among players on competitive teams can be developed and enhanced through the use of group-awareness sessions and on-site reminders for positive action (e.g., cue cards) (Orlick, 1980a).
- Television can be an effective medium for introducing young children to cooperative games and cooperative values (Provost, 1981).

- Less sex-segregated play has been observed when the play was physical and cooperative, for example, a team working cooperatively together while in competition with another team (Orlick, 1982; Richer, 1984).

The most recent studies indicate that after an exposure to a cooperative game program of several months' duration, preschool children cooperate more during recess activities (Orlick, 1981a) and share more with their peers when given the option to keep goodies (candy) for themselves or share with others (Orlick, 1981b). Overall prosocial effects appear to be sped up with the use of cooperative games viewed on television (Provost, 1981).

Perhaps the most significant finding emerging from the cooperative game studies is that one can design games and game intervention techniques with prosocial objectives in mind, and actually influence behavior in a positive direction as a result. Through thoughtfully designed play and sport experiences, one can provide valuable opportunities for children to act out, experience, and acquire important humanistic life skills. Learning to cooperate and share is only one area of potential impact. Others include learning stress-control strategies, improving nonverbal communication skills, enhancing self-acceptance, and increasing enjoyment (Orlick, 1980a; Orlick & Botterill, 1975).

Cooperative Values in Day-to-Day Living

Although the cooperative game studies show significant positive effects and suggest that physically active learning has great potential for humanistic development, there are some pervasive problems that may negate potential long-term impact. First, the number of children currently exposed to active cooperative learning opportunities is relatively low, their time involvement is minimal, and programs are usually not continued from one age group to the next (or from year to year).

Second, those children who do experience cooperative learning opportunities live in a system (or world) that often supports contrary models of behavior (e.g., violent heroes in television programming, in professional sport, and in films; highly competitive structures in school and sport programming). The mediums of television, school, and sport (especially if supported by either peers or parents) provide a powerful yet largely insensitive model to overcome (Orlick, 1983). To illustrate, suppose children have positive experiences with cooperative games at school. They learn that everyone involved is important, no one sits on the sidelines, and the cooperation of all participants is necessary to meet the highest goal of the playing. They learn that in this structure everyone has a right to be heard. Through their play, then, these children learn that they are important and worthwhile; they learn also to listen and to respect others.

Suppose at home, though, the message is different. The parents may not ask the child's opinion on matters that concern him or her, or undervalue that opinion when it is given, or simply not take the time to listen at all. Sometimes even parents with the best intentions do not give their children the respect equal to that received in cooperative play. The result is confusion for the child and a devaluation of his or her importance and self-worth.

Clearly, many positive skills can be learned within a cooperative structure—but how does one foster life- and love-enhancing skills in everyday life? The way we react to and with children from the very beginning can embellish the qualities encouraged by the structure of cooperative play—shared empathy, flexibility of thought, and the search for humor and fun. These qualities surface naturally in young children. The only reason they fade as children grow is that they are not nurtured.

Traditionally, developmental psychologists describe young children as egocentric, slow to take another's point of view, and troubled by taking turns in games and/or developing a concern over other people's feelings. Essentially, they deem children as *precooperative* until about 7 years of age. Nothing could be farther from the truth.

The traditional view of children does not stand up in the light of cross-cultural analysis. Clearly, very young children share and cooperate with great regularity among Inuit, Australian aborigines, Siwai from Papua New Guinea, Chinese from the People's Republic of China, Israelis living on kibbutzim, Tasaday, Zuni Indians, Mountain Arapesh, and others. Cooperation becomes a natural way of living together when modeled as natural, common, and desirable. To practice and perfect positive social interaction skills, children need the opportunity to interact with other children in constructive ways through their play. The earlier this begins, the better. By age 3, children in cooperative cultures share and help one another with some regularity. The high value placed on loving and caring for one another comes from a variety of sources, including stories, songs, dance, play, games, and people. By providing collective play areas and cooperative playthings, and by fostering all of these values in and out of play, these children begin a history of living and sharing with other children.

Young children in North America share these inherent qualities and retain them when they are encouraged to let their natural tendencies grow.

My daughter began food sharing when she was three months old. I accepted her offers and shared in return. We played simple sharing games by passing blocks, balls, sticks, earth, flowers, and other things back and forth.

At eight months old she was sharing her food with some regularity, taking some off her plate while she was eating and feeding it to me. It didn't always reach my mouth (more often my beard, shirt, or eye), but her aim improved over time; her intent, not her skill, was the point.

By ten months old she was pressing her cup to my lips and raising the bottom so that I could drink. At this age she also quite clearly shared her playthings by taking turns. One of the first times this happened was with a small container with seeds inside, which made a noise when shaken. We sat on the floor one morning, and after she rattled it, I put my hand out in a receiving manner. She gave me the toy; I rattled it and handed it back. This was actually a very early form of cooperative play, and it went on for some time, holding both our interests.

Sometimes, of course, your child's idea of a gift may not be the same as yours; but think before you react! The other day after a steak cookout, Anouk ended up parading around with a large greasy T-bone in her hand. She looked like she had walked right out of a cave as she waddled over to me offering the new toy. The last thing I wanted was that greasy old bone, but I accepted it, and gratefully returned it to her, and she waddled off on her merry way. If I had responded "No—dirty!" and had thrown the bone in the garbage, I would have been rejecting her sharing gesture rather than the bone itself. It's too simple to reject without thinking. We have to make a special effort to accept.

Moving from sharing with parents to sharing with others seems to occur naturally. Anouk had been sharing her bottle with us for several weeks when, just after her first birthday, she began to share it with her cousin Alex. She sat next to him on the floor, drank a little herself, then stuck the bottle in his mouth for about an equal length of time, then took a sip herself . . . back and forth for several minutes.

If you share some of your own activities and interests with very young children, you can enhance their social development. For example, if I read the newspaper when Anouk is around, I sit on the floor with her and give her a section to "read" (that is, to play with or tear up). Often it is a section of yesterday's paper, but she hasn't complained yet.

When an infant is giving, accept her offerings, show appreciation, demonstrate your affection, and give again in return. Give her hugs, accept her hugs, and give them in return. Play her game of give and take and give—whether it be with a teddy bear, a book, or a bone. If you make the effort to accept your baby's offerings and then return those same offerings, you may lose a little time in the short run, but you will certainly both gain in the long run. (Orlick, 1982, pp. 22-25)[1]

---

[1]From *The Second Cooperative Sports and Games Book* (pp. 22-25) by T. Orlick, 1982, New York: Pantheon. Copyright 1982 by Terry Orlick. Reprinted by permission.

The more human we are, the more human our children become. The more we show our appreciation for humanistic actions, the more common they become.

Cooperative games teach people a more humanistic and relaxed approach to each other and to the goal at hand. They insist on a non-judgmental approach of all participants—this is okay; everybody has a right to be heard and even to make mistakes. Everyone helps everyone else. They listen and help. Children and adults learn through these games to be more tolerant of others. The structure of the games allows for more flexible thought; thus the experience is not rigid or stressful.

The same values may be introduced to everyday life. In the following example it is demonstrated that children, as a result of daily cooperative living, can be flexible, tolerant, and helpful to each other. In addition, they can be taught to deal with the stresses that may be inevitable in their lives.

> I discussed the concept of not worrying about what is beyond our control with my daughter and her 5-year-old cousin. I attempted to communicate the idea that if something is already past, we cannot control it, so it does not help us to worry about it. One day my daughter, my nephew and I were out walking next to a lake. My nephew slipped off a log and his foot fell into the water, soaking his shoe and sock. Looking up with that sheepish look hanging on terror, he glanced over to see if I had noticed. I had glanced away as if I had not seen in order to spare him unnecessary anguish. My daughter, however, said quite clearly "Alex got his feet wet" and immediately followed up by providing him with a comforting coping strategy. "But it doesn't matter. It's already did, we can't do anything, we can't do magic." Alluding to the concept of "magic" was all hers. She was telling him in her own words that we cannot do magic and control the past, so we should not worry, for we cannot do anything about it. Her comments seemed to calm him as he breathed a sigh of relief.

> I have thought of her "can't do magic" coping strategy in other situations. For example when a child's game is over and done, we also "can't do magic" and control the past so we are best to set it aside . . . and move on without unnecessary anguish. (Orlick, 1986, p. 176)

These are only a few examples. The ways of helping children's warm and loving qualities grow are endless. Here are some further suggestions for parents or parent substitutes, like teachers and coaches (Orlick, 1983, p. 158).

- Freely demonstrate your affection toward your children (and other children) so that children experience people as kind and loving.

- Through example, play, games, role-playing, and discussion, repeatedly teach cooperation and empathy. Conversely, teach that children must not hurt others.
- Repeatedly acknowledge and encourage children's responsiveness and sharing gestures toward others (whether "others" are real or imaginary).
- Play with children for the sheer joy of play.
- Clearly demonstrate concern for the distresses faced by your own children as well as others (even strangers).
- Emphatically demonstrate dissatisfaction with your child's behavior if he or she hits or hurts another person (Pines, 1979).
- Explain why he or she should not hurt others either physically or psychologically and have him or her practice a more appropriate response.
- Promote children's natural tendencies toward sharing and empathy (catch them being good!).
- Have children practice sharing behaviors after disruptive acts (Barton & Osborne, 1978) and before anticipated problems.
- Learn to make better use of play experiences to promote altruistic behavior (Orlick, 1982).

Parent and parent substitutes (including other children) can be especially influential because infants are first exposed to these people. Other important lines of intervention come from professionals who work and play with preschool children; from those who design children's toys, games, play equipment, school curriculums, and television programs; and from those who are in a position to influence the parents and teachers of young children. Programs designed with a social conscience in mind, and people who support this type of programming, will lead us to the kind of social development that is most needed today—which will enable us to live peacefully together on this planet.

Cooperation is essential for the survival of our species. A sense of self-worth is essential to the survival of each individual. Fun is essential to the human spirit, adding joy and meaning to life. In games and living, the value of cooperating with others and the significance of fun becomes increasingly important as our society becomes increasingly competitive and technical in makeup. In play, children and adults alike can become immersed in joy, at the same time extracting valuable lessons and experiences. In addition to attempting to positively influence children's play and games, we must ensure that we act upon our own humanistic beliefs in day-to-day living and interaction with others. The most important consideration is not how we write or preach, or what kind of research we do, or even what we believe; rather, how we *live* should be our primary concern. Those of us concerned with the overall quality of life and, more specifically, with the quality of children's lives must work together so that confident, cooperative, carefree, and jubilant children do not become an endangered species.

References

Barton, E., & Osborne, J. (1978). The development of classroom sharing by a teacher using positive practices. *Behavior Modification*, **2**, 231-250.

Botterill, C. (1978, July). Psychology of coaching. *Coaching Review*, pp. 45-57.

Fritsch, H. (1981). *It's gotta be we—Towards a humanistic physical education*. Unpublished master's thesis, Merrill-Palmer Institute, Detroit.

Glashagel, J., Johnson, M., Laundry, B., & Orozco, B. (1976). *Coaching, a new look: Strategies for values education in youth sports programs*. LaGrange, IL: National YMCA Values Education Center.

Halas, J. (1987). *The effect of a social learning intervention program on a grade seven physical education program*. Unpublished master's thesis, University of Ottawa, Ontario.

Jensen, P.K. (1979). *The effect of a cooperative games programme on subsequent free play of kindergarten children*. Unpublished doctoral dissertation, University of Alberta, Edmonton.

Michaelis, B., & Michaelis, D. (1977). *Learning through noncompetitive activities and play*. Palo Alto, CA: Learning Handbooks.

Morris, G.S. (1980). *How to change the games children play* (2nd ed.). Minneapolis: Burgess.

Orlick, T.D. (1978a). *The cooperative sports and games book*. New York: Pantheon.

Orlick, T.D. (1978b). *Winning through cooperation: Competitive insanity, cooperative alternatives*. Washington, DC: Acropolis Press.

Orlick, T.D. (1979a). Children's games: Following the path that has heart. *Elementary School Guidance and Counseling*, **14**, 156-161.

Orlick, T.D. (1979b). Cooperative games: Cooperative lives. *Recreation Research Review*, **6**, 9-12.

Orlick, T.D. (1979c, January). What do parents want for their kids, coach? *Coaching Review*, pp. 19-21.

Orlick, T.D. (1980a). Cooperative play and games. In J. Knight (Ed.), *All about play: A handbook of resources on children's play* (pp. 46-59). Ottawa, Ontario: Canadian Council on Children and Youth.

Orlick, T.D. (1980b). *In pursuit of excellence*. Champaign, IL: Human Kinetics.

Orlick, T.D. (1981a). Cooperative play socialization among preschool children. *Journal of Individual Psychology*, **37**, 54-64.

Orlick, T.D. (1981b). Positive socialization via cooperative games. *Developmental Psychology*, **17**, 426-429.

Orlick, T.D. (1982). *The second cooperative sports and games book.* New York: Pantheon.

Orlick, T.D. (1983, June). Enhancing love and life mostly through play and games. *Humanistic Education and Development,* pp. 153-164.

Orlick, T.D. (1986). Evolution in children's sport. In M.R. Weiss & D. Gould (Eds.), *Sport for children and youths* (pp. 169-178). Champaign, IL: Human Kinetics.

Orlick, T.D., & Botterill, C. (1975). *Every kid can win.* Chicago: Nelson-Hall.

Orlick, T.D., & Foley, C. (1976). Pre-school cooperative games: A preliminary perspective. In A. Yiannakis, T.D. McIntyre, M.J. Melnick, & D.P. Hart (Eds.), *Sport sociology: Contemporary themes* (2nd ed., pp. 266-273). Dubuque, IA: Kendall/Hunt.

Orlick, T.D., McNally, J., & O'Hara, T. (1978). Cooperative games: Systematic analysis and cooperative impact. In F.L. Smoll & R.E. Smith (Eds.), *Psychological perspectives in youth sports* (pp. 203-225). Washington, DC: Hemisphere.

Pines, M. (1979, January). Good samaritans at age two. *Psychology Today,* pp. 66-77.

Provost, P. (1981). *Immediate effects of film-mediated cooperative games on children's prosocial behavior.* Unpublished master's thesis, University of Ottawa, Ontario.

Richer, S. (1984). Sexual inequality and children's play. *Canadian Review of Sociology and Anthropology,* **21**, 167-180.

Slack, J. (1978). *The effects of a cooperative perceptual-motor program in the learning disabled child.* Unpublished master's thesis, University of Ottawa, Ontario.

Weinstein, M., & Goodman, J. (1980). *Play fair: Everybody's guide to non-competitive play.* San Luis Obispo, CA: Impact.

Witt, W.M. (1980). *Comparison of a traditional program of physical education and a cooperative games program on the cooperative classroom behavior of kindergarten children.* Unpublished master's thesis, Temple University, Philadelphia.

CHAPTER 13

Participation Motivation and Attrition in Young Athletes

Daniel Gould
Linda Petlichkoff

Understanding the major motives young athletes have for sport participation and withdrawal has been a topic of concern for youth sport leaders, coaches, and sport psychologists for well over a decade. This concern has prompted some researchers in the area of youth sport to concentrate their efforts on determining the reasons that millions of American children have for becoming involved in sport and, once involved, what motivates an estimated 35% of them to withdraw from these activities each year (Gould, 1987). Such efforts have advanced our knowledge and understanding of the participants and dropouts of youth sport and have provided insight into a number of important questions: What motivates young athletes to participate in sport? What motivates children to discontinue their sport involvement? Do children of differing ages, sex, and levels of experience have similar motives for participating in and withdrawing from sport? How do coaches and parents influence participation motivation?

In an attempt to help answer these questions, Gould and Horn (1984) reviewed the descriptive research conducted to determine major motives children cite for participating in and discontinuing participation in youth sport. Typical of the studies reviewed were an ice hockey participation motivation investigation conducted by Fry, McClements, and Sefton (1981) and a swimming attrition investigation conducted by Gould, Feltz, Horn, and Weiss (1982). In the investigation made by Fry and others (1981), male ice hockey participants, ages 8 to 16 years, were asked to rate a number of motives for participating in hockey. Results revealed that 98% of the boys participated to have fun, 87% to become good players, 68% to make friends, 61% to win a trophy, and 54% to get exercise. The attrition investigation by Gould and others (1982) examined the motives that 50 former male and female competitive swimmers, ages 10 to 18 years, cited for discontinuing their involvement. Findings revealed that 42% of those polled discontinued involvement because there were other things to do, 28% because they were not having fun, 24% because they wanted to play another sport,

24% because they were not as good as they wanted to be, 20% because they disliked the coach, 16% because of the pressure involved, 16% because of boredom, and, finally, 16% because training was too difficult.

Based on their review, Gould and Horn (1984) concluded that children cite multiple motives for sport involvement, focusing primarily on such reasons as improving skills, having fun, being with friends, enjoying excitement, experiencing success, and developing physical fitness. Similarly, dropouts cited multiple motives for sport withdrawal, including conflicts of interest, lack of play time, lack of success or skill improvement, competitive stress, lack of fun, dislike of the coach, boredom, and injury.

The descriptive research identifying motives for youth sport participation and withdrawal has been important in providing an empirical base to assist investigators in understanding children's participation motivation. The research has also served as a catalyst in generating further research interest on this important topic, as well as providing a foundation on which guidelines for enhancing motivation can be based. Despite these benefits, however, the descriptive research has not provided a complete understanding of the participation motivation process. A theoretical framework must be developed that not only describes the reasons young athletes cite for sport participation and withdrawal, but also explains the cognitive processes underlying these decisions.

The purpose of this chapter is threefold: First, a model of youth sport withdrawal will be presented in an effort to integrate the descriptive and theoretical literature into a conceptual framework to guide further discussion and research. Second, the model will be modified to demonstrate its utility in explaining motives for youth sport participation. Third, the original and adapted models will be integrated and utilized to derive practical guidelines for maintaining and enhancing motivation in young athletes.

A Motivational Model of Youth Sport Withdrawal

In an effort to synthesize the existing literature on the attrition process, a motivational model of youth sport withdrawal has recently been proposed (Gould, 1987). The model, contained in Figure 1, depicts a microanalysis of youth sport withdrawal and is composed of three interrelated components that represent different aspects in the attrition process. Of particular importance in the model is the emphasis placed on defining the underlying process of withdrawal, rather than solely examining the end result (dropping out of sport).

Component 1—Sport Withdrawal

The attrition process ends when a child stops participating in an orga-

Component 1

Component 2

Component 3

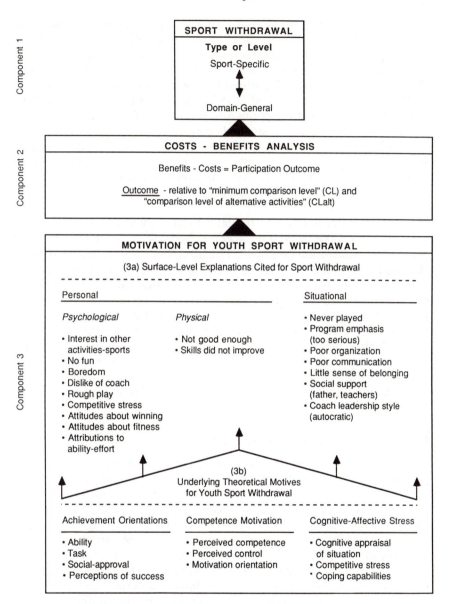

Figure 1.   A motivational model of youth sport withdrawal.

nized sport program. However, it is a mistake to assume that young athletes who discontinue participation in one sport will never participate again. Recent research (Gould et al., 1982; Klint & Weiss, 1986) indicates that young athletes may experience several *types* or levels of withdrawal. Many children, for example, will withdraw from one sport to join or stay involved in another sport (sport-specific withdrawal). Gould and others (1982) found that 80% of the competitive youth swimming dropouts interviewed reentered or planned to reenter sport, while Klint and Weiss (1986) found that 35 of 37 of the dropouts they surveyed reentered gymnastics or another sport. In contrast to these findings, Petlichkoff (1982) interviewed junior high school and high school sport dropouts and found that 59% had not participated in organized sport since discontinuing involvement in their respective sports, nor did they plan to participate in the future. Thus, sport withdrawal must be viewed on a continuum that ranges from *sport-specific* (e.g., dropping out of basketball or a specific basketball program) to *domain-general* (e.g., dropping out of all competitive sport permanently).

The first component of the model is extremely important from both a practical and theoretical perspective because it defines sport withdrawal in a continuous manner. The imprecision of the previous misleading label, "sport dropout," is recognized, and the importance of operationally defining types or levels of withdrawal is emphasized. For example, a young athlete may drop out of basketball, citing limited playing time, a nonstarting role, and a negative coaching style as reasons for withdrawing. This same athlete may then become involved in swimming, where everyone is given an opportunity to participate if they practice and commit their time to swimming after school. Contrary to being a sport dropout, this athlete has discontinued basketball to become involved in swimming and should be considered a sport transfer.

Component 2—Costs-Benefits Analysis

Component 2 is an intuitively appealing aspect of the model. This component suggests that the athlete's decision to maintain involvement in or to withdraw from sport is based on the perceived benefits and costs he or she experiences in the situation. Smith's (1986) application of Thibaut's and Kelley's (1959) social exchange theory suggests that an individual weighs the perceived benefits and costs of participation. The decision to withdraw, however, is not determined by a simple rewards-minus-costs analysis. The decision to withdraw is mediated by the athlete's minimum comparison level (the lowest criteria the child uses to judge something as satisfying or unsatisfying) and the comparison level of alternative activities. As Gould (1987) suggests, a youngster will withdraw from a sport if the perceived costs of participating outweigh the perceived benefits and if alternative activities (e.g., band, schoolwork, another sport, etc.) are evaluated as more attractive. However, even if rewards are exceeded by costs, a young athlete may choose to continue involvement in a sport simply because more desirable alternatives are not available. Thus, it is not simply a rewards-minus-costs analysis but rather a decision-making process that an athlete utilizes.

The decision-making process is employed in an effort to determine whether the athlete should remain involved in sport at that level, withdraw from that level and enter sport at another level, or withdraw completely from sport and become involved in a nonsport activity.

Component 3—Motivation for Sport Withdrawal

Component 3 of the model is subdivided into two highly interrelated subcomponents that represent the motivational explanations for sport withdrawal. Specifically, Subcomponent 3a represents the findings of the descriptive research on sport withdrawal, while Subcomponent 3b represents the newly emerging theoretical constructs that are thought to underlie these surface level explanations for withdrawal. As can be seen in Subcomponent 3a, surface level explanations focus on both personal (psychological and physical) and situational explanations cited by young athletes for sport withdrawal.

The theoretical motives that underlie and affect the surface-level reasons for sport withdrawal are contained in Subcomponent 3b and focus on achievement orientations, competence motivation, and cognitive-affective stress. Specifically, three theoretical orientations have been advanced to explain children's motivation for withdrawing from sport. These include Maehr's and Nicholls's (1980) cognitive interpretation of achievement goals, Harter's (1978, 1981) competence motivation theory, and Smith's (1986) cognitive affective model of stress. While these theoretical frameworks will be discussed in depth in a subsequent section of this chapter, it is important to recognize their major contentions.

Maehr and Nicholls (1980) contend that a young athlete's decision to withdraw from sport is determined by his or her achievement goals and by the perception of success in achieving these goals. Similarly, proponents of Harter's (1978, 1981) competence motivation model contend that the perceived competence of the child will affect the attrition process, with dropouts being characterized by lower levels of competence than participants. Moreover, competence motivation is influenced by the child's perception of his or her control over the environment (perceived control) and his or her motivational orientation or the domain-specific nature of perceived competence (physical, social, or cognitive competence). Finally, Smith (1986) contends that burnout occurs in a specific subgroup of youth sport dropouts who discontinue involvement because of stress resulting from a perceived imbalance between performance demands and their ability to meet those demands and/or because they lack the coping capabilities to alleviate this chronic stress.

Summary

In summary, this model integrates both the descriptive and theoretical findings on attrition in children's sport. It dispels the notion that most children who withdraw from a sport withdraw from all sports and never again participate. In contrast, it is emphasized that attrition must be viewed on a continuum from sport- or program-specific to domain-general withdrawal. Second, it is recognized that the child's decision to withdraw from sport does not occur in a vacuum, but is dependent on the young athlete's perceptions of the costs and benefits of involvement relative to other activity options available. Finally, an analysis of the model suggests that for the youth sport dropout to be fully understood investigators must recognize the important psychological, physical, and situational reasons cited for discontinuing involvement as well as the motivational systems that influence and underlie these descriptive responses.

A Motivational Model of Youth Sport Participation

Although researchers have learned a great deal about the possible underlying reasons for young athletes dropping out of sport, these findings have been retrospective and, at times, inconclusive. To further understand attrition in young athletes, sport scientists must examine the motives of young athletes for becoming involved in sport. Moreover, the attrition model outlined by Gould (1987) can be easily adapted to explain motives for participation in sport.

Figure 2 contains a model of sport participation that begins with the major motives for involvement cited by young athletes as well as the theoretical constructs thought to underlie these motives (see Component 1). An ongoing costs-benefits analysis occurs (Component 2) that may result in continued involvement (Component 3).

Component 1—Motivation for Participation

Subcomponent 1a of the model depicts the surface-level reasons children cite for participating in sport. Inspection of this subcomponent reveals that young athletes identify a wide variety of personal (psychological and physical) and situational motives for participation. And, although considerable variation exists in the motives cited, those consistently rated as most important include improving skills, having fun, being with friends, making new friends, experiencing thrills and excitement, achieving success or winning, and developing fitness (Gould & Horn, 1984).

As discussed earlier, several theoretical frameworks have been identified as possible explanations of the underlying causes of attrition in children's sport. These same theoretical frameworks can also be used to explain participation motivation in young athletes. Hence, they are contained in Subcomponent 1b.

The first framework contained in this subcomponent is based on Maehr's and Nicholls's (1980) cognitive interpretation of achievement motivation, which suggests that for achievement behavior to be under-

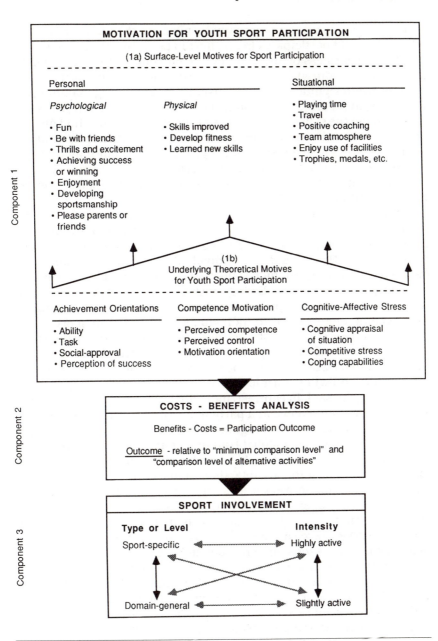

Figure 2. A motivational model of youth sport participation.

stood the child's perception of success and failure, as well as his or her achievement orientation, must be identified. While athletes may have many different achievement orientations, the three general orientations said to exist are (a) an ability orientation where a child participates in an activity in an effort to demonstrate high ability and minimize demonstrating low ability—usually by winning, (b) a task orientation where the child participates in an effort to perform the task as well as possible—regardless of any competitive outcome, and (c) a social approval orientation where the child participates in an effort to seek approval from significant others—usually by exhibiting maximum effort. Thus, to predict sport involvement and withdrawal, it is necessary to determine the salient achievement orientations of the child and the degree to which he or she perceives these achievement orientations are fulfilled in any given sport setting. This fulfillment may be manifested in such surface-level explanations (Component 1a) as achieving success, winning, pleasing parents or friends, improving skills, or enjoying the team atmosphere.

While extensive testing of the achievement orientation framework has not taken place, some evidence has shown support for the different achievement orientations being related to sport persistence. Specifically, Ewing (1981) found that individuals who are social-approval-oriented persist longer in high school sport than those individuals who are ability- or task-oriented. Ewing concluded that sport provides opportunities to seek social approval and that this achievement orientation may become more salient to individuals who persist in sport.

A second theoretical framework used to explain sport participation is Harter's (1978, 1981) competence motivation. Harter (1978) suggests that individuals who perceive themselves to be highly competent at a particular skill will persist longer at that skill and maintain interest in mastering the skill. In contrast, individuals who perceive themselves as having low competence at a particular skill will withdraw from the activity. It is important to recognize, however, that perceived competence is defined not as a global trait or unitary construct, but rather as having specific domains in the areas for physical, social, and cognitive concerns. It is quite possible, then, that a child could show variations in motivation across these competence domains depending on his or her history of experiences and socialization. Thus, a child who has been reinforced on the social aspects of sport participation may cite such surface-level motives as being with friends or team atmosphere as major reasons for continued involvement in sport; whereas a child who has been socialized into demonstrating competence in the physical domain may cite such motives as improved skills or learning new skills as major motives for continued involvement.

Several investigators have found support for the relationship between sport participation and perceived competence. Specifically, Roberts, Kleiber, and Duda (1981) found that male and female fourth and fifth graders involved in youth sport, when compared to their peers who were not involved in sport, were not only higher on perceived physical competence, but rated higher in social competence and general self-worth as well. Two additional studies (Feltz, Gould, Horn, & Weiss, 1982; Feltz & Petlichkoff, 1983) have reported similar results. In both investigations, significant but lower correlations were reported to exist between perceived competence and sport participation where active athletes or athletes with a greater number of years experience had higher levels of perceived competence than dropouts or athletes with fewer years of experience. Several questions remain unanswered, however. Are children with higher levels of perceived competence drawn to sport? Are these children's levels of perceived competence higher as a result of their participation in sport? Or, do children with lower perceived competence drop out of sport?

Finally, although Smith's (1986) cognitive-affective model of stress may be more appropriate as an underlying theoretical framework to explain major motives cited by sport burnouts, it may provide us with implications on how to prevent this particular class of sport dropout. Basically, Smith suggests that when caught in an imbalance between situational demands (e.g., the need to demonstrate ability) and resources (e.g., lack of ability), children may perceive sport participation as too stressful and consequently withdraw from the activity. If, however, the situational demands focus on skill improvement and having fun and the child perceives that these surface-level motives are fulfilled, then he or she will become more actively involved.

Smith's (1986) cognitive-affective model also suggests that individual differences exist in children's coping capabilities and perceptions of stress. Thus, children may react differently to the same situational factors: One might persist while the other drops out. Although no empirical evidence exists, individual differences appear to be the major factor in some athletes' rising to the occasion (e.g., two out, two on, the bottom of the ninth) whereas others prefer to be taken out of the game.

Component 2—Costs-Benefits Analysis

The general findings generated from Component 1 of the model of youth sport participation motivation certainly lead into Component 2 of the model—the costs-benefits analysis. The basic premise is that children are motivated primarily to maximize rewards and to minimize costs. The initial involvement in a situation depends on anticipated rewards and costs, whereas the decision to continue to participate depends on the rewards (costs) received and the rewards (costs) anticipated and is not simply a rewards-minus-costs outcome. As suggested earlier, a child dissatisfied with his or her present situation, but with no alternatives available that are more satisfying, may remain involved in his or her current activity or sport. For example, a sophomore in high school who had been a starter in basketball in junior high finds that a senior holds the position he or she would like to play. The coach places the sophomore on the specialty or scouting team for practices, and he or she never gets a chance to play during a game. During the season, the team develops a supportive attitude and compiles an outstanding record. For the sophomore, the season was fun although he or she did not play in a game. Did the athlete adjust motives to meet the situation? Or were all the other outcomes more satisfying than any alternatives? In this case, the rewards (e.g., fourth in the state, having fun, learning new skills) outweighed the costs (not starting), and the athlete remained involved in basketball.

Component 3—Sport Involvement

Component 3 of the model focuses on examining the type and intensity of participation characterizing sport involvement in young athletes. In particular, participation can range from sport-specific involvement (e.g., participation in baseball or one particular baseball program) to domain-general involvement (e.g., participation in all available programs—baseball, football, basketball, soccer, etc.). Inspection of Component 3 also shows that sport involvement is comprised of an intensity dimension, where a young athlete can be highly active (e.g., an Olympic caliber youth gymnast training 3 to 6 hours a day, 7 days a week) to slightly active (e.g., a young novice gymnast who attends one 90-minute practice once a week). Thus, sport involvement must be viewed on two interacting continuums that define participation in terms of type as well as intensity of involvement.

As was the case with the attrition model, it is imperative that those interested in studying participation motivation in young athletes precisely define sport involvement relative to the type and intensity dimensions. Simply labeling a child a participant or nonparticipant is not enough. As Robinson and Carron (1982) have shown, significant differences in participation motivation exist between active high school football players who started the majority of their games, football survivors who participated for the entire season but received little playing time, and football dropouts who started the season but did not complete it. Similarly, Klint and Weiss (1986) found that competitive gymnasts, recreational gymnasts, and former gymnasts had different motives for participation. The competitive gymnasts most often cited fitness and challenge as their motives for participation; the recreational gymnasts cited fun and situational factors as important motives; and the former gymnasts cited fun, challenge, and action as their main motives. In essence, this evidence clearly shows that sport involvement must be more precisely defined if the young athlete's motives for participation are to be more fully understood.

Summary

Adapting Gould's (1987) motivational model of youth sport withdrawal to explain the youth sport participation motivation literature is very useful. Gould's model clearly integrates the descriptive and theoretical findings in the area, emphasizes the need to consider the child's perception of program costs and rewards relative to alternative activities, and demonstrates the importance of precisely defining sport involvement by considering both the type and intensity of participation.

Practical Implications for Enhancing and Maintaining Participation Motivation in Young Athletes

An examination of the youth sport attrition and participation motivation models presented in this chapter reveals that young athletes' motives for participation and withdrawal can be explained by the same processes and are influenced by a common set of factors. In fact, it has recently been argued that investigators cannot study attrition in children's sport without understanding motivation for participation (Klint & Weiss, 1986). It is imperative, then, that those interested in enhancing and maintaining motivation in young athletes understand and link these two models.

Figure 3 contains an integrated model of participation motivation and withdrawal in youth sport. The model is comprised of the same

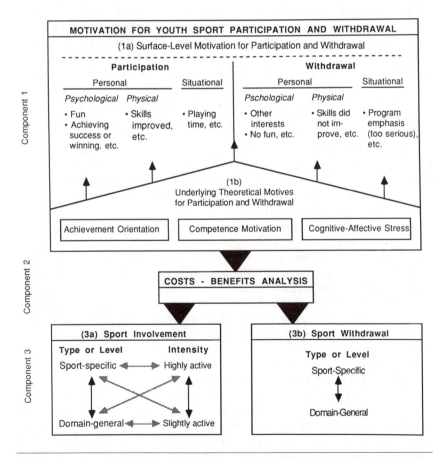

Figure 3.   An integrated motivational model of youth sport participation and withdrawal.

components used in the separate sport withdrawal and participation motivation models presented previously. In particular, Component 1a of the model summarizes the surface-level motives young athletes cite for participation and withdrawal; Component 1b summarizes those theoretical motives that underlie the surface-level responses cited for participation and withdrawal; Component 2 depicts the costs-benefits decision process that occurs in the young athlete; and Component 3 reflects the type and intensity of involvement or withdrawal that can occur. The importance of each of these components and practical implications derived from them are now outlined.

Component 1—Motivation for Youth Sport Participation and Withdrawal

Component 1 of the integrated model depicts the varied surface-level motives young athletes cite for sport participation and withdrawal, as well as those theoretical motives that underlie and influence these surface-level responses. Subcomponent 1a of the model clearly reflects the findings that children have multiple motives for participating in and for dropping out of sport. The major surface level motives for participation include improving skills, having fun, being with friends, experiencing thrills and excitement, achieving success, and developing fitness. When these motives are not achieved, children weigh the costs against the benefits of being involved (Component 2) and often withdraw, citing other things to do. In addition, the theoretical literature (Subcomponent 1b) suggests that children have varying achievement orientations for sport, differing perceived competence levels, and varying amounts of stress. These constructs have a major influence on motivation and often influence the surface-level responses cited for participation or withdrawal.

A major implication derived from this component is that children cite a number of varied motives for participation and withdrawal. To enhance motivation, then, the youth sport leader must recognize individual differences in motivational patterns. He or she must determine (a) which young athletes are affiliation-oriented, (b) which are primarily success- or outcome-oriented, and (c) which are motivated to improve their skills. Moreover, because most young athletes cite multiple motives for participation and withdrawal, efforts must be made to determine which individual motives seem most salient to each youngster.

In addition to recognizing the surface-level motives children cite for participation (or withdrawal), adult leaders must also make efforts to recognize the less visible theoretical motives characterizing the psychological makeup of young athletes. In particular, efforts must be made to recognize the children's dominant achievement orientation (task or self-improvement, ability or outcome, and social approval), their level of perceived competence or confidence, their trait anxiety level or tendency to perceive evaluative environments as threatening, and their ability to cope with stress.

Excellent methods of discovering individual motives in young athletes involve individual discussions, the development of good listening skills, and observation. Every youth sport coach should try to talk individually with the children on his or her team. Ask them what they like about the sport, what they dislike, and why they came out for the team. Be sure to keep these discussions low-key and informal. Coaches should also employ good listening skills. Listen carefully to the young athlete, search for the meaning in his or her message, and be particularly sensitive to nonverbal behavioral patterns. For example, a youngster may tell the coach that he or she is not feeling well and cannot go in the game. A careful analysis of the child's nonverbal behavior, however, reveals that he or she has low perceived competence and is experiencing a great deal of stress—these are the real reasons he or she does not want to play. Lastly, coaches should carefully observe their young athletes. Observe how they react to stressful situations, assess the degree to which they enjoy participating in social activities with their teammates, watch how they react when their parents attend games and how much effort they expend in drill situations. Observing the children will help determine the salience of particular motives for each child.

Once the young athletes' motives for participation are identified, coaches and adult leaders should structure the athletic environment so that these motives are fulfilled. Special emphasis, for example, should be placed on skill development because improved skills is one of the most frequently cited reasons young athletes give for participating in sport. Unfortunately, skill development is often neglected. Many coaches feel that participation alone will improve skills and that practice makes perfect. However, it is planned, purposeful practice that makes perfect (Martens, Christina, Harvey, & Sharkey, 1981). Effective instruction requires that practices be planned and well organized and that all athletes, regardless of their ability, receive appropriate instruction. Equally important is the method of instruction. Smith, Smoll, Hunt, Curtis, and Coppel (1979) have provided convincing evidence that a positive approach is most effective when coaching young athletes. The important components of a positive approach are sincerity, realistic expectations, frequent rewarding and encouraging statements, rewarding effort rather than just outcome, and utilizing a constructive approach when mistakes occur.

Fulfilling the *fun* objective that children have for sport participation is also essential. Treating young athletes like miniature adults can stifle their motivation and creativity by not allowing them to have fun. The youth sport coach must develop realistic expectations and remember that children's attention spans are shorter, their self-concepts more fragile, and their abilities not as fully developed as an adult's. Coaches must also remember that most young athletes have fun when they are active and participating, not when they are sitting on the bench or standing in line. Finally, research by Griffin (1978) has shown that most young athletes would rather be on a losing team and play than sit on the bench of a winning team!

Everyone wants to be a winner; the young athlete is no different. In fact, Subcomponent 1a of the model shows that it is incorrect to think that young athletes do not value winning, especially as they grow and mature. But winning should not be the sole objective for sport participation. As Component 1 of the model shows, young athletes have multiple reasons for participating in sport—winning or demonstrating ability is only one. Thus, coaches and adult leaders should keep winning in perspective and not neglect the other needs of the young athletes (e.g., affiliation need, improving skills, etc.)

Efforts should also be made to define the success motive of young athletes more broadly by viewing success in terms of personal improvement rather than competitive outcome. By defining success in this manner, more children will see their skills improve and view themselves as successful.

Lastly, meeting the affiliation motives of young athletes is also an important responsibility of youth sport leaders and coaches. An excellent way to accomplish affiliation is by scheduling social functions at various times throughout the season (e.g., ice cream socials, pizza parties, etc.). In addition, coaches must remember to provide time for kids to be kids and have fun with their friends during practices.

While making efforts to structure the athletic environment to meet the individual needs of the young athlete, it is also important for adult leaders to facilitate the development of various motives or orientations. For example, a major implication generated by the model contained in Figure 3 is that perceived competence and ability play important roles in sport participation and sport withdrawal (see Component 1b). The development of perceived competence is influenced by the child's history of successes and failures at the activity. It is essential, then, that efforts be made to develop realistic but positive perceptions of competence in young athletes. As Gould (1987) suggests, such efforts can be accomplished by (a) equalizing competitive settings so that all children will experience some success, (b) providing positive but contingent evaluative feedback, (c) enhancing skill development, and (d) emphasizing the attainment of individual performance goals. Similarly, many young athletes are too ability- or outcome-oriented and do not place enough emphasis on task or self-improvement goals. Instead, they base their self-worth on their win-loss record alone and not on personal improvements. By stressing performance (self-improvement) as opposed to outcome goals, however, coaches can enhance the child's self-worth and motivation (Martens et al., 1981).

Finally, youth sport leaders can help children successfully cope with the stress of competition by reducing the importance placed on athletic events and by reducing children's uncertainty about their relationships with leaders by creating positive, supportive atmospheres, regardless of the game score (Martens, 1978). Children who have especially difficult times coping with stress can also be taught any number of stress-reduction strategies (see Smoll, 1986).

Component 2—Costs-Benefits Analysis

Component 2 of the model shows that to understand participation motivation and withdrawal in youth sport the complex decision-making process of the child must be understood. Children do not simply participate in rewarding activities and withdraw from activities when all the benefits they desire are not available. In contrast, the young athlete weighs the costs and the benefits of participation relative both to his or her own criterion for what costs and benefits are acceptable and to the costs and benefits that exist for other activities.

It is imperative that youth sport leaders learn to recognize which aspects of their program are perceived by children to be most beneficial and which incur the greatest costs. Periodically survey young athletes; ask them to indicate what they like most and least about their sport. In a study of youth swimming dropouts, Gould, Feltz, Horn, and Weiss (1982) found that the children most liked competing, winning, getting ribbons, and improving new skills and least liked distance workouts, repetitions, and time demands. While all costs of participation cannot be eliminated or controlled by coaches (e.g., one must swim distances to increase fitness), coaches can insure that during organized practice activities the perceived costs (e.g., distance workouts) are outweighed by the perceived benefits (e.g., make distance training workouts more exciting by inducing competition and/or set practice goals when doing repetitions to reflect skill improvement).

Coaches should always discuss program costs and benefits with their current participants; also, whenever possible, exit interviews should be conducted by league administrators with those children who discontinue involvement. In particular, efforts should be made to determine why the child is discontinuing participation in the program and what he or she liked best and least about the program. In this way, adult leaders can develop realistic impressions of the child's perception of the benefits and the costs of participation.

Component 3—Sport Involvement and Withdrawal Implications

The third component of the model shown in Figure 3 represents the type and intensity of sport involvement (3a) and the type of sport withdrawal (3b). This component is extremely important because it reflects the need to assess the level of involvement of young athletes (sport-specific to domain-general), as well as the intensity of involvement (highly active to slightly active). In addition, it suggests that sport withdrawal must be viewed on a continuum ranging from sport- or program-specific (e.g., drop out of a basketball program) to domain-general (e.g., drop out of all sport).

The sport involvement and withdrawal component of the model is important because it identifies the need for those involved in youth sport to more precisely define terms such as *participant* and *dropout*. For example, the child who drops out of a particular softball program because practice time conflicts with another sport may be markedly different in his or her motivational orientation than the child who drops out of softball and never again participates in any organized sport. In the first case, the young athlete may be engaged in trial-and-error sport sampling. That is, the child is sampling different sport situations in an effort to meet his or her psychological needs by weighing the costs-benefits (Component 2) of each situation and selecting the most beneficial activity in which to invest time. In the second instance, the young athlete discontinues all involvement and shows no motivation for participation in any type of sport. Perhaps this child has low perceived competence that was constantly reinforced through negative feedback from the coach. Or the child could have possessed a task goal orientation, which focuses on self-improvement, but found that the sport environment focuses predominantly on the fulfillment of ability or outcome goal orientations.

The research has not yet determined the frequency in which sport sampling and domain-general dropping out occurs; nor have the major explanations for these decisions been determined. However, by closely examining and identifying the type and intensity of participation and withdrawal, youth sport leaders will be better able to identify if attrition occurs in their programs as a result of normal trial-and-error sport sampling or if it results from the failure of the sport program to meet the psychological needs of the child.

In addition to precisely defining sport participation and withdrawal, it would be fruitful for league organizers to keep yearly statistics on the number of children who originally participate in the program, the number who discontinue and transfer to other sports, and the number who discontinue participation in all sport. These statistics could be used to set goals for lowering attrition rates and, when combined with information about program costs and benefits, could provide valuable information on the reasons participation and attrition increase or decrease. League organizers could use this information to restructure programs to increase participation and decrease attrition.

Finally, the sport involvement-withdrawal component of the model is based on the findings that individual differences exist in the type and intensity of children's sport participation. Not every child is motivated to participate in a highly competitive sport program that involves large commitments of time. That does not mean the children do not want to participate, however. As Klint and Weiss (1986) found in their study of gymnasts, some athletes decide to discontinue participation in high-intensity competitive programs, but do not want to discontinue involvement in the sport altogether. Instead of dropping out, these athletes transfer to less intense recreational programs. This type of sport transferring can only occur, however, if children have the opportunity to participate in programs of different levels and intensities. Hence, whenever possible, youth sport administrators should provide programs that vary in their competitive intensities and in the time demands placed on the athletes. In this way, more children can become involved and stay involved in programs that fulfill their needs.

Conclusion

Participation motivation and attrition are complex phenomena of tremendous importance to those adults involved in children's sport. This chapter summarized both the descriptive and theoretical research in the area by presenting separate models for understanding and explaining participation motivation and attrition in young athletes. An integrated model was presented and used to derive practical implications for maintaining and enhancing motivation in young athletes. Neither this model nor its implications are of value, however, unless those involved in youth sport programs employ the model. It is imperative, then, that youth sport coaches, parents, and leaders implement the model and the guidelines derived from it on a day-to-day basis in their programs. Use of the model will help maximize participation and insure that the psychological needs of young athletes are fulfilled.

References

Ewing, M.E. (1981). *Achievement orientations and sport behavior of males and females.* Unpublished doctoral dissertation, University of Illinois, Urbana-Champaign.

Feltz, D.L., Gould, D., Horn, T.S., & Weiss, M.R. (1982, June). *Perceived competence among youth swimmers and dropouts.* Paper presented at the meeting of the North American Society for the Psychology of Sport and Physical Activity, College Park, MD.

Feltz, D.L., & Petlichkoff, L. (1983). Perceived competence among interscholastic sport participants and dropouts. *Canadian Journal of Applied Sport Sciences, 8*(4), 231-235.

Fry, D.A.P., McClements, J.D., & Sefton, J.M. (1981). *A report on participation in the Saskatoon Hockey Association.* Saskatoon, Canada: SASK Sport.

Gould, D. (1987). Understanding attrition in children's sport. In D. Gould & M. Weiss (Eds.), *Advances in pediatric sport sciences— Behavioral issues* (pp. 61-85). Champaign, IL: Human Kinetics.

Gould, D., Feltz, D., Horn, T., & Weiss, M.R. (1982). Reasons for discontinuing involvement in competitive youth swimming. *Journal of Sport Behavior, 5*, 155-165.

Gould, D., & Horn, T. (1984). Participation motivation in young athletes. In J.M. Silva, III & R.S. Weinberg (Eds.), *Psychological foundations of sport* (pp. 359-370). Champaign, IL: Human Kinetics.

Griffin, L.E. (1978, April). *Why children participate in youth sports.* Paper presented at the American Alliance for Health, Physical Education, Recreation and Dance National Convention, Kansas City, MO.

Harter, S. (1978). Effectance motivation reconsidered: Toward a developmental model. *Human Development,* **21**, 34-64.

Harter, S. (1981). The development of competence motivation in the mastery of cognitive and physical skills: Is there still a place for joy? In G.C. Roberts & D.M. Landers (Eds.), *Psychology of motor behavior and sport—1980* (pp. 3-29). Champaign, IL: Human Kinetics.

Klint, K., & Weiss, M.R. (1986). Dropping in and dropping out: Participation motives of current and former youth gymnasts. *Canadian Journal of Applied Sport Sciences,* **11**(2), 106-114.

Maehr, M.L., & Nicholls, J.G. (1980). Culture and achievement motivation: A second look. In N. Warren (Ed.), *Studies in cross-cultural psychology* (pp. 221-267). New York: Academic Press.

Martens, R. (1978). *Joy and sadness in children's sport.* Champaign, IL: Human Kinetics.

Martens, R., Christina, R., Harvey, J., & Sharkey, B. (1981). *Coaching young athletes.* Champaign, IL: Human Kinetics.

Petlichkoff, L.M. (1982). *Motives interscholastic athletes have for participation and reasons for discontinued involvement in school sponsored sport.* Unpublished master's thesis, Michigan State University, East Lansing.

Roberts, G.C., Kleiber, D.A., & Duda, J.L. (1981). An analysis of motivation in children's sport: The role of perceived competence in participation. *Journal of Sport Psychology,* **3**, 201-211.

Robinson, T., & Carron, A. (1982). Personal and situational factors associated with dropping out versus maintaining participation in competitive sport. *Journal of Sport Psychology,* **4**, 364-378.

Smith, R.E. (1986). Toward a cognitive-affective model of athletic burnout. *Journal of Sport Psychology,* **8**, 36-50.

Smith, R.E., Smoll, F.L., Hunt, E., Curtis, B., & Coppel, D.B. (1979). Psychology and the bad news bears. In G.C. Roberts & K.M. Newell (Eds.), *Psychology of motor behavior and sport—1978* (pp. 109-130). Champaign, IL: Human Kinetics.

Smoll, F.L. (1986). Stress reduction strategies in youth sport. In M.R. Weiss and D. Gould (Eds.), *Sport for children and youths* (pp. 127-136). Champaign, IL: Human Kinetics.

Thibaut, J.W., & Kelley, H.H. (1959). *The social psychology of groups.* New York: Wiley.

CHAPTER 14

Children's Knowledge Development and Sport Performance

Jerry R. Thomas
Karen E. French
Katherine T. Thomas
Jere D. Gallagher

Because individuals interested in children's motor skill development have not studied children as they perform skills in sport settings (French & Thomas, 1987; Thomas, French, & Humphries, 1986), little information exists concerning how children acquire the sport skills that play prominent roles in our culture. The purpose of this chapter is to provide some insight into how children learn and perform sport skills.

Sport skills are complex movements that are used in various ways depending on the situation. Sometimes considerable time for planning the movement is available (e.g., golf), whereas in other instances the performer must make a rapid decision about how and when to move (e.g., basketball). The performance environment may be relatively stable (e.g., gymnastics) or very unstable (e.g., soccer). To understand how children learn and perform skills in these complex and varying environments requires evaluation of cognitive and motor skills and their interaction during sport performance. Unfortunately, the study of skill acquisition processes has generally occurred in constrained laboratory settings, an unlikely place to produce a parsimonious theory with adequate power to describe, predict, and explain children's sport performance.

Shortcomings in Skill Acquisition Research

Since the late 1960s, the focus of motor skill research has been on understanding the processes that lead to the performance, learning, and control of skilled behavior. This emphasis on process resulted in the development of several theories (e.g., closed-loop theory, Adams, 1971; schema theory, Schmidt, 1975) explaining cognitive factors in movement learning and memory. However, considerably less emphasis was given to the control of movement—memory representations such as motor programs were simply assumed to transmit signals for movement action, but how this occurred was not considered. In more recent years, the study of the control of action has received increased attention (e.g., Kelso, Holt, Kugler, & Turvey, 1980; Saltzman & Kelso, 1983). However, researchers studying memory processes and action control have tended to use rather simple and trivial tasks to represent movement. (This is understandable, as simple tasks tend to be unidimensional and involve few muscle groups over which control must be assessed.) Consequently, the question remains as to whether the underlying memory processes and control mechanisms are adequately explained for more complex actions in real-world sport settings.

A second shortcoming of skill acquisition research is that the tasks selected were novel in nature so that the subjects' previous experience could be controlled. This resulted in studying tasks during only the very early stages of skilled performance. It is questionable whether direct application to performing and learning sport skills can be made from studying simple skills performed for few trials where performance peaks quickly. At best, knowledge gained from such situations is unlikely to be useful when applied to sport skills where practice is spread over thousands of trials and years of experience. However, knowledge gained from studying early learning can be used to help us plan effective experiences for beginners or young children. Understanding how initial learning occurs is important, but we must also understand how long-term, permanent changes in performance occur. In nearly all sport settings, performers have previous experience with the skills and make many attempts at skilled performance. Because sport skills are complex and may be used in various ways depending on the situation, *previous experience becomes the single most important characteristic of performance.*

The situation in the motor development area has been no better, with some researchers studying the development of underlying memory and learning processes (e.g., Thomas, 1980), the development of motor control (e.g., Kelso & Clark, 1982), or the development of fundamental movement patterns (e.g., Roberton, 1984). The study of memory, learning, and control factors in children's movements suffers from the same problem as the study of these issues in more mature subjects: a lack of ecological validity of the movements, calling into question the answers obtained about underlying processes and motor control. The study of fundamental motor patterns has involved more real-world movements. Unfortunately, these movements have been studied in constrained settings (e.g., in front of a camera) and there is no compelling evidence (other than intuitive) that fundamental movements are precursors of similar movements as used in a specific sport setting. For example, does learning the fundamental pattern of overhand throwing using balls of various sizes and weights lead to more effective learning of throwing a baseball in a game? Or might children invest their time more wisely by practicing throwing a baseball?

A more useful approach would be to study children in sport settings as they increase their competence in sport skills. While studying real-world sport behaviors involves problems—it is difficult to adequately control and manipulate independent variables in the traditions of true research design—the potential to gain knowledge about how children learn and perform sport skills is substantial.

If children are to be studied in real-world sport settings, several issues must be addressed. First, each sport has its own unique set of skills, strategies, and knowledge. Thus, each sport is the unit of study. Trying to investigate the knowledge, strategies, and skills of a sport apart from their use in practice and games will provide limited information. By the same token, sports with different sets of knowledge, skills, and strategies cannot be combined for study. However, coherent theories about the development of processes that underlie skills, knowledge, and strategies can emerge from sport-by-sport research. For example, when studying experts and novices from many different areas (e.g., computer programmers, chess players, airplane pilots, basketball players, baseball players, teachers), consistent findings have emerged concerning how knowledge is represented and how underlying processes develop (e.g., Berliner, 1986; Murphy & Wright, 1984; Thomas, French, & Humphries, 1986).

Memory Development

Knowledge has been represented in memory frameworks as an interaction of processes in short-term and long-term memory. *Short-term memory*, or working memory, is conceptualized as a temporary storage area for information necessary to perform a given task and is limited in capacity. *Long-term memory* is conceptualized as permanent memory (knowledge base) and is unlimited in capacity. *Control processes* used in working memory (encoding, labeling, rehearsal, grouping, recoding, retrieval) maintain information and assist in the storage and retrieval of information in long-term memory. Thus, the knowledge base involves the effective use of working memory processes to store and retrieve information from long-term memory as well as the actual contents of long-term memory.

Many studies (see Thomas, 1984 for a review) have shown that children either fail to use control processes in working memory (production deficiency) or fail to use control processes efficiently (mediation deficiency). Many performance deficits commonly seen in the motor performance of young children can be attributed, in part, to ineffective use of control processes. Recently, researchers have begun to examine the influence of lack of sufficient knowledge on children's performance (Chi, 1978; Lindberg, 1980).

In most situations, young children, due to their limited experience and exposure to a wide variety of knowledge domains, can be considered universal novices. However, comparisons of novice adults with children who possess a greater amount of knowledge in a given domain have shown that knowledge plays a salient role in performance of domain-related tasks. Chi (1978) compared the recall of chess positions by child expert chess players and adult novice chess players. Child experts in chess recalled significantly more chess positions than adult novices. Similar findings were reported by Lindberg (1980). These results clearly suggest that children can perform as well or better than adults when children possess greater amounts of task-related knowledge.

Other research suggests that domain-specific knowledge may reduce the capacity limitations of working memory (Chase & Simon, 1973), reduce the attentional demands of certain tasks (Leavitt, 1979), and facilitate more effective use of control processes, especially organizational processes (Ornstein & Naus, 1984). These processes have been documented as areas in which children typically exhibit deficits. Thus, lack of knowledge may play a major role in the deficits of children's performance.

How Knowledge May Be Represented

Chi (1981) defined three types of knowledge. *Declarative knowledge* is the knowledge of factual information. *Procedural knowledge* is the knowledge of "how to do something." Both declarative knowledge and procedural knowledge are task specific within a given knowledge domain. *Strategic knowledge* is knowledge of general rules (i.e., control processes, such as rehearsal) that may be generalized across all knowledge domains.

Many studies have shown that experts possess greater declarative knowledge than novices in a variety of knowledge domains—for example, dinosaurs, (Chi & Koeske, 1983), chess, (Chase & Simon, 1973; Chi, 1978), and baseball (Chiesi, Spilich, & Voss, 1979; Spilich, Vesonder, Chiesi, & Voss, 1979). The results of these studies substantiate that experts have more concepts with more defining features within each concept. Murphy and Wright (1984) and Chiesi, Spilich, and Voss (1979, Experiment 4) have also shown that experts report a high degree of consensus concerning the features generated for each concept, which suggests that information is organized similarly within a given domain.

Chi, Feltovich, and Glaser (1981) and Adelson (1984) have shown that experts also possess greater procedural knowledge than novices. Both studies suggest that experts possess more productions and order these productions in such a way that the solution to a given problem is apparent.

Ways in Which Experts and Novices Differ

Research comparing the performance of experts and novices in problem-solving activities has also been conducted. Berliner (1986) listed several ways in which experts and novices differ in problem-solving activities. In this section we have used Berliner's categories to organize the ways experts and novices differ. First, the general differences are presented. These are followed with differences between experts and novices that have been reported in sport. In addition, we speculate about the reason differences should exist in certain categories (note that categories 4 and 5 lack studies related to sport—possible directions for research—and category 10 is sport-specific and not included in Berliner). We have included references pertinent to the sport situation, although many examples exist in other domains.

1. *Novices hold literal views of objects and events, whereas experts make inferences about these objects and events.* Several studies suggest that expert sport participants make inferences about objects and events. Studies from tennis (Fluery, Goulet, & Bard, 1986; Jones & Miles, 1978) and field hockey (Starkes, 1985; Starkes & Deakin, 1984) found that experts were more able to predict upcoming events prior to completion of the present movement.

   Expert sport participants may use their greater knowledge to make predictions in other ways as well. We speculate that expert players select the relevant cues from the situation and attach probabilities to possible game actions. For example, a right-handed basketball player is likely to drive to the right more often. A left-handed batter is likely to hit the ball to the right side of the baseball field. This type of anticipation can be developed from preliminary information about the players and the team or during the course of the game by observing and remembering the actions that are likely to be repeated. Before these anticipations can be developed, players must understand the relation of the specific cues and the probability that certain actions are related to these cues.

2. *Experts categorize problems to be solved at a higher level, whereas novices characterize problems by the surface characteristics given in the problem.* Several studies have shown that experts cluster items into meaningful units. Master chess players (Chase & Simon, 1973) and GO players (Reitman, 1976) clustered pieces into offensive and defensive configurations. These studies, plus studies from other domains, suggest that experts form abstract conceptual representations of problems, whereas

novices form representations based on surface elements of the problem.

The offensive and defensive systems of most sports are designed around specific concepts that increase the chances of scoring and decrease the chances of the opposing team scoring. Creating mismatches, isolating a player one-on-one, overloading a zone, and screening or picking are examples of such concepts. Many of these concepts transfer across sports; for example, the concepts just named are common to both basketball and football. We speculate that expert sport performers represent offensive and defensive plays as abstract concepts rather than details of who moves where. A common observation of beginners learning offensive plays in basketball is a tendency to focus on where to move rather than on the goal of the offense or the appropriate cues to use to recognize specific options of the offense.

Research has shown that expert basketball players use different visual cues to make decisions in solving basketball problems. Bard and Fleury (1976) had expert and novice basketball players view slides of offensive and defensive player positions. Subjects were asked to decide whether to shoot the ball, dribble, or pass to one of the other players. Expert players tended to concentrate visual fixation on a pair of offensive and defensive players, whereas novice players tended to ignore the defensive player.

3. *Experts have extraordinarily fast and accurate pattern recognition.* Three types of studies suggest that expert sport participants have superior pattern recognition capabilities. First, expert sport participants have been shown to exhibit superior recall of game-structured information. Chase and Simon (1973) found that when chess configurations represented natural configurations in actual chess games, master chess players recalled more chess piece positions than novice or intermediate chess players. No differences in recall performance existed when the chess pieces were presented in a random manner. Similar findings have been reported comparing basketball players and nonplayers (Allard, Graham, & Paarsalu, 1980) and field hockey players and nonplayers (Starkes & Deakin, 1984). These studies suggest that experts recognize patterns in stimuli, often offensive and defensive configurations, which aid in the encoding and retrieval processes necessary for recall.

A second type of study that indicates experts have superior pattern-recognition capabilities was conducted by Allard and Starkes (1980). After viewing slides of volleyball playing, in game and nongame situations, the volleyball players identified the presence of the ball much faster than nonplayers. However, there were no differences in accuracy in detecting the ball. Starkes and Deakin (1984) report similar differences in detection speed for field hockey players and nonplayers.

Experts have also been shown to identify movement patterns more rapidly than novices. Vickers (1986) presented a series of randomly ordered photographs of a gymnastics routine to elite, intermediate, and novice gymnasts. Subjects were asked to re-order the photographs in the proper sequence as quickly as possible. Elite gymnasts performed the task significantly faster and committed fewer errors than the intermediate gymnasts, who were faster and committed fewer errors than the novices. These findings suggest that expert sport participants can recognize movement patterns faster and with greater precision than novices.

4. *Experts may be slower than novices in the initial stages of problem solving.*
5. *Experts are sensitive to the task demands and social structure of the job situation.*
6. *Experts have been shown to be opportunistic planners.* Expert sport participants are likely to develop planning strategies for sport-specific situations. For example, skilled infielders in baseball must monitor the number of outs, positions of runners on base, and so forth. This information can be used to preplan the possible responses in game situations prior to initiation of game action. Infielders commonly either discuss or remind teammates of the most appropriate responses in given situations during the course of a game. Preplanning strategies reduce the number of choices that must be made (e.g., to which base to throw the ball) so that players need only respond to a given stimulus (e.g., ground ball). Initial attention can be focused on fielding the ball; time necessary for response selection is reduced. Thus, the time needed to execute the throw to the appropriate base is reduced. Frequently, beginning baseball players have not developed preplanning strategies. Common advice given by youth sport coaches in baseball is to know where you are going to throw the ball before it is hit.

The distinction between discrete sport and continuous sport is important. In discrete sport there is a pause between sequences of game actions (e.g., baseball, football). There are few breaks in the sequences of game actions in continuous sport (e.g., basketball, soccer, field hockey, hockey). Tennis and other racquet sports represent sport with characteristics of both discrete and continuous sport. Discrete sport allows time for planning responses before game actions occur (before the ball is hit in baseball). In racquet sports, the pause between sequences of continuous actions also allows for planning future strategies. A recent study (McPherson, 1987) suggests that advanced child tennis players are more likely than novice child tennis players to plan game strategies between points. Advanced child tennis players were more likely to verbalize specific tennis strategies, whereas novice child players did not verbalize future game strategies.

Monitoring game actions and planning can also occur in continuous sport. Monitoring player positions, offensive and defensive strategies, and positions of the ball occurs throughout the game. Planning future responses could occur during such breaks in the action as time-outs, the end of quarters (basketball), halftime, free throws (basketball), free kicks (soccer), or during discussions with teammates during actual game play.

7. *Experts show self-regulatory or meta-cognitive capabilities that are not present in less experienced learners.* Brown and DeLoache (1978) listed several basic skills involved in meta-cognition. These skills include predicting the consequences of an action or event, checking the results of one's own actions, monitoring one's ongoing activity, reality testing, and other behaviors for coordinating and controlling deliberate attempts to learn and solve problems. Many of these skills have been discussed in previous sections. For example, expert sport participants are likely to predict game events, monitor game conditions, preplan responses, and plan or develop strategies prior to and during game play.

8. *Expertise develops over long periods of time.* Expertise in sport takes considerable time to develop and is sport-specific. Much time and practice must take place to master the cognitive and motor skills in a given sport. Participants must devote a long period of time developing the knowledge of the specific sport, including knowledge of the rules, the goals and subgoals of the game, specific offensive and defensive patterns, and the appropriate perceptual cues that aid in anticipations during game play. The development of the procedural knowledge necessary to make correct decisions within the context of the game takes considerable time and long hours of practice. In addition, expertise in sport requires years of practice to master the motor skills involved.

9. *An expert's knowledge shows up in relation to the goal structure of the problem.* Chiesi, Spilich, and Voss (1979) and Spilich, Vesonder, Chiesi, and Voss (1979) reported a series of experiments that compared the processing of baseball-related text by subjects with high and low knowledge of baseball. The results of these experiments suggested that the goal structure of baseball plays a salient role in the organization and selective processing of baseball information. High-knowledge subjects generated more responses related to the major goals in baseball, monitored changes in game states and actions, restructured information in an effective manner, and selectively processed information in terms of the goal structure in baseball. These differences in the processing of information between high-knowledge subjects

and low-knowledge subjects were attributed to a hierarchical organization of baseball knowledge in terms of the goal structure of baseball.

10. *Expert sport participants possess a higher level of sport-specific motor skills than novices.* Much of the discussion in this chapter has been devoted to the development of cognitive skills present in expert sport participants. But expertise in sport also requires superior sport-specific motor skills. We do not mean to undervalue the importance of motor skill. Clearly, expert sport participants have greater skill than novices. However, experts who possess high levels of skill must also have the knowledge of how to use these skills in the context of specific sport situations. Thus, expertise in sport involves the development and interaction of cognitive skills and motor skills.

The Development of the Knowledge Base in Sport

Chi (1981), Chi and Rees (1983), and Anderson (1982) suggest that declarative knowledge must be developed first to provide a foundation for the development of procedural knowledge within a given knowledge domain. Procedural knowledge is developed as task-specific knowledge of how to perform given tasks within the knowledge domain. Declarative knowledge is used to form the condition side (if) and the action side (then do) of productions. This process is known as *knowledge compilation* (see Anderson, 1982 for more details). The last type of knowledge to develop is strategic knowledge. Strategic knowledge may be developed by generalizing specific productions for application in different types of tasks. This framework is useful in explaining why many attempts to train children in mnemonic strategies fail to transfer to different tasks. Children lack sufficient prerequisite declarative and procedural knowledge in the new knowledge domain to effectively use the mnemonic strategy.

Children often lack sport-specific declarative knowledge when they enter a specific youth sport program. Such knowledge includes the rules, the goals and subgoals of the game, and the offensive and defensive strategies. This knowledge is necessary to make appropriate decisions concerning what action to perform during the course of the game (procedural knowledge—under certain conditions, perform specific skills). The decision concerning what skill to execute and when to execute a skill is as important as the actual quality of the movement pattern used to execute the skill. Thus, cognitive (perception) and motor (action) skills are closely linked, with both skills necessary for skillful performance.

The first study to examine the relation of the knowledge base to sport performance in children was conducted by French and Thomas (1987).

The authors hypothesized that a foundation of sport-specific declarative knowledge is necessary to make appropriate decisions within the context of game play (procedural knowledge, or how to execute the actions in the context of the game). Furthermore, a foundation of sport-specific motor skills is necessary to execute sport skills effectively during game play.

In order to examine these relations, an observational instrument was developed to measure the quality of game decisions, the successful execution of motor skills during game play, and the success of maintaining control of the ball. French and Thomas (1987, Experiment 1) found child experts to score significantly better in measures of dribbling skill, shooting skill, and basketball knowledge. Child experts also exhibited a higher percentage of successful decisions made during game play, superior control of the basketball, and a higher percentage of successful execution of motor skills in game play. Furthermore, the children's ability to make successful decisions within the context of game play was related to their amount of basketball knowledge, whereas successful execution of motor skills during game play and control of the basketball were related to dribbling skill and shooting skill.

French and Thomas (1987, Experiment 2) measured 8- to 10-year-old expert and child novice basketball players on dribbling skill, shooting skill, basketball knowledge, and measures of game performance at the beginning and end of the season. Both child expert and novice players improved the quality of their decisions and control of the basketball during game play from pretest to posttest. Subjects also improved their scores on the basketball knowledge test. Dribbling skill, shooting skill, and motor execution of skills during game play did not improve. The scores of the basketball knowledge test remained significantly related to the quality of decisions made during game play at the end of the season.

The results of these two experiments indicate that the relation between cognition and motor skill plays a salient role in the development of skilled sport performance in young children. However, the development of cognitive skills progressed at a faster rate than the development of motor skills. Children were learning what to do in the context of the sport situation faster than they were learning the motor skills necessary to effectively carry out the actions.

Gender Differences in Expertise

Gender differences have been documented for various movement skills. Thomas and French (1985), in a large scale meta-analysis of motor performance, reported that males performed better (were more expert) than females in 17 of the 20 motor tasks they studied and females performed better than males in two of the motor tasks. There was no difference in one performance. However, they reported that the differences were age related in 12 of the 20 tasks; that is, the difference between male and female performance increased in some systematic fashion. Thomas and French suggested that, prior to puberty, only one task, throwing (distance and velocity), had differences large enough to be attributable to biological factors. The differences in the other tasks were small enough to be accounted for by the varying treatments and expectations of girls and boys by parents, teachers, coaches, and peers.

However, the throwing differences were large, present as early as 3 years of age, and difficult to change. A follow-up to Thomas and French by Nelson, Thomas, Nelson, and Abraham (1986) indicated that in 5-year-old children an adjustment for a combination of three biological variables (joint diameters, shoulder/hip ratio, and sum of skinfolds) increased girls' performance from 57% of boys' to 69%. Although this is not the major factor in gender differences in throwing, it is interesting to note that prior to puberty only 1 of 20 tasks differed enough to be considered to have a biological component.

If gender differences in motor performance prior to puberty are mainly environmentally induced, then practice and expectations are the likely causes. As more practice probably results in more sport-specific knowledge, a substantial part of better performance by males in sport settings is likely due to their increased knowledge base about the sport and use of the sport skills and to their higher skill level. Instructors and coaches of youth sport should consider this factor when coaching boys and girls. Part of the performance difference observed may be because girls have poorer skills than boys as a result of less opportunity and encouragement to practice, but performance differences may also be due to girls not knowing how to use the skills they have mastered.

The Development and Use
of Mnemonic Strategies and Working Memory

The preceding sections discussed two of the three types of knowledge: procedural and declarative. The third type, strategic knowledge, includes general strategies (control processes) such as rehearsal and encoding, and specific strategies used to solve a problem. Both types of strategies influence performance and learning. In addition, strategies are used more often and more effectively as age increases. Experience, expertise, or practice may also influence the use of strategies. Considerable research, using both verbal and motor paradigms, has produced valuable information about how children learn and remember, how learning and memory can be influenced, and several areas for future inquiry. Since 1970, developmental memory research has focused on three broad topics: information processing, metamemory, and memory strategies.

Information Processing

Early work focused on sensory and perceptual aspects of memory (Vernon, 1966; Vurpillot, 1974) and suggested that changes in the sensory components of the memory system do not account for the improvement in performance associated with increased age. A portion of the age-related motor performance decrement is probably a result of sensory or neural differences that cannot be altered; instead, activities must be adapted to accommodate those deficits. The sensitivity of the proprioceptive receptors, which detect movement, and the neurological system, which controls movement, might be considered "hardware" that matures and produces more efficient movement. Baseball is one sport that can be altered to accommodate the differences in sensitivity of the proprioceptive receptors and the neurological system: Young children play T-ball; children a bit more mature try to hit the slow pitches a coach feeds them; finally, older children play traditional baseball. As important to performance and as difficult to modify as those motor control variables are, the impact of memory differences is also great and may continue to influence performance even after the hardware has matured (as indicated by the novice-expert differences in mature performers and the differential use of strategies to aid performance described in the following section).

Each component and operation of the information processing system has been studied in both the verbal memory and motor research. The results of early studies in developmental verbal memory were considered weak because they relied on inference, while later studies allowed more direct observation of those processes and included manipulation of each process (Naus & Ornstein, 1983). Rather than focusing on a specific task or activity (e.g., a particular sport), this research focused on a component or operation of the information processing system. The studies used a wide variety of tasks and activities, yet the results were consistent. The major conclusion was that children are not miniature adults; children are developing physically, cognitively, and emotionally. The fact that adults process verbal and motor information more efficiently than children has been supported by numerous studies (e.g., Chi, 1976; Gallagher & Thomas, 1980; Thomas, Mitchell, & Solmon, 1979; Winther & Thomas, 1981). With increased age, children can process more information in the same time limits, or process the same information in a shorter time frame (Chi, 1976). Clearly then, shortening or lengthening the processing time will affect motor performance, particularly in younger children (Gallagher & Thomas, 1980). Speed of processing—from simple reaction time (Thomas, Gallagher, & Purvis, 1981) to processing feedback (Thomas, Mitchell, & Solmon, 1979) to decision making (Newell & Kennedy, 1978)—decreases as age increases through childhood (Chi & Gallagher, 1982).

   This decrement and the type of information children process can be observed in sport. For example, a young child playing T-ball will see the ball bouncing in his or her direction, chase it, catch it, then think, Now what? The child must pause to determine where to throw the ball, then plan and execute the actual movement. There are three separate operations, all of which demand time and processing. A more experienced (or expert) and/or older child begins to get into position as soon as the ball is hit. The catch and throw occur without any delay, almost as if they are a single movement. In the first instance, the child has attended to three separate acts, each cuing the next, each taking time. In the second instance, the situation has cued a response that included the acquisition of the ball, the choice of where to throw the ball, and the throw. What, then, causes the memory process of young children to be less efficient or to respond more slowly to their demands?

   In a series of experiments using two-dimensional arm movements, children's performance improved with age, due to both perceptual and memory factors (Thomas & Thomas, in press). Perception is the transformation of sensory information, which is dependent, in part, on related past experience. In a task where a movement was well learned, young children (5-year-olds) needed nearly 3 times as much error (lateral deviation at the end point of a movement) than adults to detect a difference between the well-learned movement and a foil. Whether this deficit was a result of experiential, neurological, or sensory deficits is unknown. In a situation where a child is expected to reproduce a movement—even a well-learned movement—he or she may think the movement has been effectively reproduced when in fact it has not. Adults are quite effective at detecting their errors, which perhaps allows them to correct their errors on succeeding trials. When the same task was used in a recognition memory paradigm, where each pair of movements were presented one time, the children made more errors than adults when the pairs of movement were close to their level of perceptual sensitivity, but performed like adults when the movements exceeded their perceptual sensitivity. A third experiment used the same movements, but this time in a recall paradigm using a task that demanded more from the memory system. The children's error increases were beyond the age-related perceptual differences. The results suggested that (a) in real-world settings age differences may be decreased by reducing the memory demands of the task, and (b) children should not be assumed to perceive the same level of information from a situation as an adult.

   Several aspects of movement information need processing, including the extent (distance), location, angle, acceleration, and velocity (speed) of the movement. Children are often not aware of these parameters and their role in motor performance. Children can, when cued to do so, use this information to improve their performance. For example, children can often learn to define the point in an overarm throw where acceleration occurs to produce a short or long throw. In general, young children are unaware that they must do anything to remember, while older children may select inappropriate ways to remember.

Two studies (Winther & Thomas, 1981; Gallagher & Thomas, 1984) demonstrate that manipulating either rehearsal strategies or labels (one form of children's encoding) for movement positions can enhance younger children's motor performance and depress that of older children and adults. These two studies support the production-mediation hypothesis (Flavell, 1971). This hypothesis indicates that children may or may not be capable of producing a desired cognitive strategy at a given age; however, using a strategy does not necessarily improve performance (mediation hypothesis). Five-year-old children can rehearse when cued to do so, but cannot produce a rehearsal strategy on their own (production deficiency). Generally, the spontaneous use of rehearsal as a memory strategy does not occur until about 6 to 8 years of age. If the quality of the rehearsal strategy is poor, or if the strategy is inappropriate, rehearsal may fail to improve performance (mediation deficiency). Between 7 and 11 years of age, a considerable increase occurs in the use and quality of rehearsal strategies. The child of 11 or 12 uses a strategy similar to that of an adult. Because the adult strategy improves performance, teaching this strategy to children should result in improved skill acquisition; for example, practicing fielding and throwing to a base rather than repetitively catching in isolation and then throwing in isolation.

Labeling is viewed as rehearsal for children under 5 years of age. With these children, and with adults to some extent, relevant labels will enhance memory for an item (Winther & Thomas, 1981). A labeling strategy could be applied to the glove position for a ground ball— "fingers on the ground"—or for a fly ball—"fingers to the sky."

Another important memory process that develops throughout childhood is organization of memory (a combination of grouping and recoding, Thomas, 1980). The placing together of independent units of incoming information as one unit is called *grouping*. For instance, adults will typically group a series of random numbers into groups of three for rehearsal and permanent storage (as part of the knowledge base). A young child will rehearse and store each number independently. Although memory span (sometimes used to measure working memory) may appear greater in adults, children's poorer performance is caused by inefficient use of the memory process of grouping and not by a deficit in memory capacity. Evidence indicates that remembering a series of movements is affected in the same way (Gallagher & Thomas, 1986).

Incoming stimuli can be manipulated to facilitate learning in young children by breaking movement sequences into logical units that can be rehearsed together. A coach might cue a certain strategy by reminding players that when the batter hits the ball they should make their throws to first base. Players would have rehearsed the angle and the catch-throw sequence together.

A second aspect of organization is *recoding*, which involves searching memory (knowledge base) for two or more independently stored pieces of information that could logically be put together. The two pieces of information are combined (recoded) in working memory and reentered into the knowledge base as a new unit of information. When needed, recoded information requires less space in working memory because it has become one unit instead of two. Grouping and recoding are two ways to reduce the demands on working memory. Recoding can combine two well-learned movements, such as catching and running, to create a new skill—the pass reception in football—or it can transform a concept or perception of an event into something new. For example, combining the current outcome of a contest with past outcomes involves recoding.

A series of studies by Gallagher and Thomas (1984, 1986) provides empirical support for this developmental trend. Children begin to use rehearsal strategies spontaneously at about age 7, with a rapid increase in both frequency and quality between ages 7 and 11. The use of organization in memory lags considerably behind rehearsal however. The test of utility for a strategy is whether it will transfer to similar situations, or even be generalized to appropriate but less similar situations. By 11 years of age, rehearsal transfers and is generalized to most situations, but organization of memory may not transfer.

Metamemory

Brown (1975) defined metamemory as the factors affecting the emergence of memory skills. These factors included knowing (the knowledge base), knowing how to know (memory strategies or control processes), and knowing about knowing (understanding one's memory). Unfortunately, there is virtually no research that deals specifically with metamemory using motor or sport tasks, perhaps as a result of the lack of correlation between metamemory and memory performance in the verbal literature (Kail, 1979; Wellman, 1977). The consensus is that although metamemory is an interesting concept, which obviously improves with age, it is not a superstructure controlling memory development, as once thought.

Memory Strategies

Naus and Ornstein (1983) differentiate between control processes and task-specific memory strategies that are under the deliberate control of the subject. One problem is that task-specific strategies are often confounded with control processes, especially rehearsal and encoding, and are therefore difficult to study. Children begin using task-specific strategies at about the same time they begin rehearsal, although they can employ a strategy much earlier if given one. Specific strategies may influence the selection of a movement, the storage of information about movement, or the perception of the movement situation. In a series of studies looking at the use of strategies for storing information about movements (Thomas, Thomas, Lee, Testerman, & Ashy, 1983), children were asked to remember how far they jogged. Young children did nothing special to help themselves remember and consequently did poorly on the recall task. Older children used a counting strategy. Although this same strategy was used by adults, the children were not as successful because they did not recognize the importance of keeping step size constant. One of the most interesting discoveries is that practice, experience, or intervention (cuing, in this instance) can eliminate the age differences! When young children were forced to use the adult strategy, their performance was similar to that of older children. The task of counting is used in several sport situations—counting strokes in swimming the backstroke, or counting steps in a pass pattern before turning to catch the ball in football. Adults typically have the most effective strategy readily available; by simply telling children how to solve the movement problem, their performance will improve.

Experience with the use of strategies in a sport-specific setting will probably not generalize to all settings, or even transfer to other sport settings. However, appropriate use of strategies enhances performance and separates experts from novices.

Automation of Performance

Automation implies reduction of the attention-demanding aspects of the movement. An automated movement does not rely heavily on the central capacity store, is thought to occur without conscious awareness (Posner & Snyder, 1975), and occurs with a high degree of resistance to suppression (Shiffrin & Schneider, 1977). Given the proper stimulus, an automatic process will engage and run itself off. Attempts to resist this processing will (to varying degrees) fail. For example, after a child has learned to walk over an obstacle in a familiar environment, he or she will maintain a high stepping pattern even when the obstacle is removed. Automatic processes also operate in parallel and are virtually unaffected by task load (Shiffrin & Schneider, 1977; Stelmach & Hughes, 1983). Eberts and Schneider (1980) have summarized the benefits of automatic processing as follows: (a) Fewer resources are required, (b) processing is faster, (c) the task is less susceptible to distraction, (d) performance is more accurate, and (e) the internal structures associated with the movements become more economical and efficient. Movement development researchers need to determine how individuals learn to automate a response (develop a motor program) and how they automate parameter selection. Stelmach and Larish (1980) add that the operational characteristics of the automatic state and the variables that influence the development of automation are also important factors.

Attention is important initially; however, given sufficient practice, reliance on attention diminishes. An important key is the context in which the skill is performed (Schneider & Shiffrin, 1977). Theoretically, stimuli in the environment activate certain codes from the knowledge base. Memory codes that share common features are activated, while memory codes that share fewer features are less affected. In reviewing the literature on development of skill memory, Chase and Ericsson (1982) suggest that attended information is automatically bound to current context. This provides for relatively fast and direct access to knowledge structures relevant to the task. Skilled individuals (i.e., experts) apparently are able to associate information to be remembered with the large knowledge base in the domain of their expertise and are able to index that information for speedy retrieval without much attentional demand. Additionally, practice storing and retrieving the information facilitates the speed of processing. Stelmach and Hughes (1983) suggest the ability to retrieve information efficiently might be due to the discovery of an optimum self-organizational strategy. A major point, then, is the contiguity of context and action (Stelmach & Larish, 1980). If this is indeed the case, the literature on contextual interference is important in the study of automation.

An alternative viewpoint to the development of automation has been proposed by Navon and Gopher (1979) and Fowler and Turvey (1978). They suggest that attention is not withdrawn from processing, but that there is a unique change in control of the movement. LaBerge (1975) indicates that automatization is the specialized process strengthened through practice rather than learning. According to Fowler and Turvey, automation is a control problem; the control becomes neurologically efficient and various body segments are linked together, thus reducing the degrees of freedom in the movement. The question, then, is whether automation occurs as a shift in attention, a change in control, or a combination of both.

Regardless of how it occurs, automation is important for two aspects of motor performance—action and strategy. Action automation frees the individual from consciously thinking, How do I perform this skill? or, How do I change the parameters to effectively respond to the environment? Attention is then redirected to strategy development.

In sport performance, the expert must be able to switch attention rapidly from the performance of the skill (movement) to the game context and back to the skill in order to determine the appropriate tactical strategy. Acquisition of a generalized motor program (automation) allows the player to switch attention from control of movements required in the skill to higher order structures. Practice (experience) is the principal means by which the games player learns to apportion his or her attention from the movement to the larger context in which that movement is being performed. Thus, the contextual information is used to modify the motor program controlling the movement. As a basketball player acquires the general program for dribbling a ball, he or she also acquires a facility for switching attention to the opposing players, using the information to modify the height, speed, and direction of the dribble.

Summary

In this paper we have attempted to demonstrate how the memory system may operate as children learn sport skills during childhood. In particular, we have focused on the development of domain-specific knowledge—in this instance the knowledge associated with specific sports—as well as the strategies that are learned across the childhood years. The interaction of the knowledge base (and its strategies) with the acquisition of specific sport skills as they are used during games and contests is the key to understanding children's sport performance.

In the introduction to this paper we suggested the value of the sport-specific model for studying skill acquisition. We also pointed out some of the shortcomings associated with previous research on motor skill acquisition. The next section provides additional justification for using a sport-specific model to study children's performance and learning of sport skills.

Development of a Sport-Specific Research Model

The use of a sport-specific research model offers both theoretical and applied benefits to the study of children's skill acquisition (Thomas, French, & Humphries, 1986). The complex sets of rules, strategies, and skills associated with each sport offers many opportunities to gain understanding about how competence is developed. In fact, Ornstein and Naus (1985) make this very point when they indicate the need to determine what children of various ages know about specific content domains. Further, the sport-specific rules, strategies, and skills (a specific content domain for each sport) are of great interest to children over many years—in some instances, over the life span. Thus, motivation, interest, and persistence are inherent in the sport. Data obtained from various sports can be compared and common features determined, resulting in substantial opportunities to infer to theories about acquisition of cognitive knowledge and strategies as well as to theories of motor skill acquisition and control.

Coaches, instructors, and performers also benefit in applied ways from a sport-specific research model. Much information is acquired about ways to structure practice; how knowledge can be organized for effective instruction; techniques for teaching sport-specific strategies; and rates at which skills, knowledge, and strategies are learned and how they interact. Thus, researchers using a sport-specific model are in position to contribute to both theory and application.

Expert-Novice Paradigm.   The use of the expert-novice paradigm is a good beginning point for sport-specific research. Understanding what expert players do differently from novice players offers potential ways to determine what should be learned. Of course, expertise may vary. For example, an unskilled 13-year-old may be an expert when compared to a novice 10-year-old, but not nearly as expert as a skilled 10-year-old. Thus, defining expertise is an essential feature of sport-specific research. It is also important to note that expertise and experience do not necessarily covary. A performer could have 10 years of experience but still be a poor player.

How Is Expertise Acquired?   Of course that is the essential question. To answer it requires following children over one or more seasons of sport participation. The researcher should evaluate changes in knowledge, strategy use, and skill, but much of the interest lies in evaluating game performance. What does the child do in competition that results in increased competence? What can the coach (instructor, parent) do to enhance expertise?

Studying Expertise

Studying expertise is not easy. The researcher (or research team) must possess a variety of skills. First, the researcher must have detailed knowledge about the sport; otherwise, he or she cannot hope to understand what constitutes expertise. Second, the researcher must be a test developer. He or she must develop (or select) tests of declarative knowledge about the sport, tests of procedural knowledge about game performance, and tests of the specific sport skills. Third, questionnaires are frequently needed to determine demographic and attitudinal data about children, coaches, and parents. Fourth, behavioral coding instruments must be developed for use in evaluating game performance. This involves establishing the validity and reliability of these instruments as well as of the coders and scorers. Further, the skills associated with videotaping performances are frequently needed in order to acquire good information. Finally, the researcher must understand both developmental and learning theory about knowledge, strategies, and skills for maximum gains from the investigations.

References

Adams, J.A. (1971). A closed-loop theory of motor learning. *Journal of Motor Behavior*, **3**, 111-149.

Adelson, B. (1984). When novices surpass experts: The difficulty of a task may increase with expertise. *Journal of Experimental Psychology: Learning, Memory, and Cognition*, **10**, 483-495.

Allard, F., Graham, S., & Paarsalu, M.E. (1980). Perception in sport: Basketball. *Journal of Sport Psychology*, **2**, 14-21.

Allard, F., & Starkes, J.L. (1980). Perception in sport: Volleyball. *Journal of Sport Psychology*, **2**, 22-23.

Anderson, J.R. (1982). Acquisition of cognitive skill. *Psychological Review*, **89**, 369-406.

Bard, C., & Fleury, M. (1976). Analysis of visual search activity during sport problem situations. *Journal of Human Movement Studies*, **3**, 214-222.

Berliner, D.C. (1986). In pursuit of the expert pedagogue. *Educational Researcher*, **15**(7), 5-13.

Brown, A.L. (1975). The development of memory: Knowing, knowing how to know and knowing about knowing. In H.W. Reese (Ed.), *Advances in child development and behavior* (Vol. 10, pp. 104-153). New York: Academic Press.

Brown, A.L., & DeLoache, J.S. (1978). Skills, plans, and self-regulation. In R.S. Siegler (Ed.), *Children's thinking: What develops?* (pp. 3-35). Hillsdale, NJ: Erlbaum.

Chase, W.G., & Ericsson, K.A. (1982). Skill and working memory. In J.R. Anderson (Ed.), *The psychology of learning and motivation* (Vol. 16, pp. 1-58). New York: Academic Press.

Chase, W.G., & Simon, H.A. (1973). Perception in chess. *Cognitive Psychology*, **4**, 55-81.

Chi, M.T.H. (1976). Short-term memory limitations in children: Capacity or processing deficits. *Memory and Cognition*, **4**, 559-572.

Chi, M.T.H. (1978). Knowledge structures and memory development. In R.S. Siegler (Ed.), *Children's thinking: What develops?* (pp. 73-105). Hillsdale, NJ: Erlbaum.

Chi, M.T.H. (1981). Knowledge development and memory performance. In M.P. Friedman, J.P. Das, & N. O'Connor (Eds), *Intelligence and learning* (pp. 221-229). New York: Plenum Press.

Chi, M.T.H., Feltovich, P.J., & Glaser, R. (1981). Categorization and representation of physics problems by experts and novices. *Cognitive Science*, **5**, 121-152.

Chi, M.T.H., & Gallagher, J.D. (1982). Speed of processing: A developmental source of limitation. *Topics in Learning & Learning Disabilities*, **2**, 23-32.

Chi, M.T.H., & Koeske, R.D. (1983). Network representation of a child's dinosaur knowledge. *Developmental Psychology*, **19**, 29-39.

Chi, M.T.H., & Rees, E.T. (1983). A learning framework for development. In M.T.H. Chi (Ed.), *Contributions to human development* (pp. 71-107). Basel: Karger.

Chiesi, H.L., Spilich, G.J., & Voss, J.F. (1979). Acquisition of domain related information in relation to high and low domain knowledge. *Journal of Verbal Learning and Verbal Behavior*, **18**, 257-273.

Eberts, R., & Schneider, W. (1980). *The automatic and controlled processing of temporal and spacial patterns* (Report No. 8003). Arlington, VA: Office of Naval Research.

Flavell, J.H. (1971). What is memory development the development of? *Human Development,* **14**, 225-286.

Fluery, M., Goulet, C., & Bard, C. (1986). *Eye fixation as visual indices of programming of service return in tennis.* Paper presented at the annual meeting of the North American Society for the Psychology of Sport and Physical Activity, Scottsdale, AZ.

Fowler, C.A., & Turvey, M.T. (1978). Skill acquisition: An event approach with special reference to searching for the optimum of a function of several variables. In G.E. Stelmach (Ed.), *Information processing in motor control and learning* (pp. 1-40). New York: Academic Press.

French, K.E., & Thomas, J.R. (1987). The relation of knowledge development to children's basketball performance. *Journal of Sport Psychology,* **9**, 15-32.

Gallagher, J.D., & Thomas, J.R. (1980). Effects of varying the post-KR interval upon children's motor performance. *Journal of Motor Behavior,* **12**, 41-46.

Gallagher, J.D., & Thomas, J.R. (1984). Rehearsal strategy effects on developmental differences for recall of a movement series. *Research Quarterly for Exercise and Sport,* **55**, 123-128.

Gallagher, J.D., & Thomas, J.R. (1986). Developmental effects of grouping and recoding on learning a movement series. *Research Quarterly for Exercise and Sport,* **57**, 117-127.

Jones, C.M., & Miles, T.R. (1978). Use of advanced cues in predicting the flight of a lawn tennis ball. *Journal of Human Movement Studies,* **4**, 231-235.

Kail, R.V. (1979). *The development of memory in children.* San Francisco: Freeman.

Kelso, J.A.S., & Clark, J.E. (Eds.). (1982). *The development of movement control and co-ordination.* New York: Wiley.

Kelso, J.A.S., Holt, K.G., Kugler, P.N., & Turvey, M.T. (1980). On the concept of coordinative structures in dissipative structures: II. Empirical lines of convergence. In G.E. Stelmach & J. Requin (Eds.), *Tutorials in motor behavior* (pp. 49-70). New York: North-Holland.

LaBerge, D. (1975). Acquisition of automatic processing in perceptual and associative learning. In P.M.A. Rabbitt & S. Dornic (Eds.), *Attention and performance V* (pp. 50-64). London: Academic Press.

Leavitt, J. (1979). Cognitive demands of skating and stickhandling in ice hockey. *Canadian Journal of Applied Sport Science,* **4**, 46-55.

Lindberg, M.A. (1980). Is the knowledge base development a necessary and sufficient condition for memory development? *Journal of Experimental Child Psychology, **30**, 401-410.

McPherson, S.L. (1987). *Development of children's expertise in tennis: Knowledge structure and sport performance.* Unpublished doctoral dissertation, Louisiana State University, Baton Rouge.

Murphy, G.L., & Wright, J.C. (1984). Changes in conceptual structure with expertise: Differences between real-world experts and novices. *Journal of Experimental Psychology: Learning, Memory, and Cognition, **10**, 144-155.

Naus, M.J., & Ornstein, P.A. (1983). Development of memory strategies: Analysis, questions, and issues. In M.T.H. Chi (Ed.), *Contributions to human development* (Vol. 9, pp. 1-30). Basel: Karger.

Navon, D., & Gopher, D. (1979). On the economy of the human-processing system. *Psychological Review, **86**, 214-255.

Nelson, J.K., Thomas, J.R., Nelson, K.R., & Abraham, P.C. (1986). Gender differences in children's throwing performance: Biology and environment. *Research Quarterly for Exercise and Sport, **57**, 280-287.

Newell, K.M., & Kennedy, J.A. (1978). Knowledge of results and children's motor learning. *Developmental Psychology, **14**, 531-536.

Ornstein, P.A., & Naus, M.J. (1984). *Effects of the knowledge base on children's processing.* Unpublished manuscript, University of North Carolina, Chapel Hill.

Ornstein, P.A., & Naus, M.J. (1985). Effects of the knowledge base on children's memory strategies. In H.W. Reese (Ed.), *Advances in child development and behavior* (pp. 113-148). New York: Academic Press.

Posner, M.I., & Snyder, C.R. (1975). Attention and cognition control. In R.L. Solson (Ed.), *Information processing and cognition* (pp. 55-86). Hillsdale, NJ: Erlbaum.

Reitman, J. (1976). Skilled perception in GO: Deducing memory structures from inter-response times. *Cognitive Psychology, **8**, 336-356.

Roberton, M.A. (1984). Changing motor patterns during childhood. In J.R. Thomas (Ed.), *Motor development during childhood and adolescence* (pp. 48-90). Minneapolis: Burgess.

Saltzman, E.L., & Kelso, J.A.S. (1983). Toward a dynamical account of motor memory and control. In R.A. Magill (Ed.), *Memory and control of action* (pp. 17-38). New York: North-Holland.

Schmidt, R.A. (1975). A schema theory of discrete motor skill learning. *Psychological Review, **82**, 225-260.

Schneider, W., & Shiffrin, R.M. (1977). Controlled and automatic human information processing: I. Detection, search, and attention. *Psychological Review, **84**, 1-66.

Shiffrin, R.M., & Schneider, W. (1977). Controlled and automatic human information processing: II. Perceptual learning, automatic attending, and a general theory. *Psychological Review*, **84**, 127-190.

Spilich, G.J., Vesonder, G.T., Chiesi, H.L., & Voss, J.F. (1979). Text processing of individuals with high and low domain knowledge. *Journal of Verbal Learning and Verbal Behavior*, **18**, 275-290.

Starkes, J.L. (1985). *The role of expertise in the use of advance visual cues for shot prediction*. A paper presented at the annual meeting of the North American Society for the Psychology of Sport and Physical Activity, Biloxi, MS.

Starkes, J.L., & Deakin, J. (1984). Perception in sport: A cognitive approach to skilled performance. In W.F. Straub & J.M. Williams (Eds.), *Cognitive sport psychology* (pp. 115-128). Lansing, NY: Sport Science Associates.

Stelmach, G.E., & Hughes, B. (1983). Does motor skill automation require a theory of attention? In R.A. Magill (Ed.), *Memory and control of action* (pp. 67-92). New York: North-Holland.

Stelmach, G.E., & Larish, D. (1980). A new perspective on motor skill automation. *Research Quarterly for Exercise and Sport*, **51**, 141-157.

Thomas, J.R. (1980). Acquisition of motor skills: Information processing differences between children and adults. *Research Quarterly for Exercise and Sport*, **51**, 158-173.

Thomas, J.R. (1984). Children's motor skill development. In J.R. Thomas (Ed.), *Motor development during childhood and adolescence* (pp. 91-104). Minneapolis: Burgess.

Thomas, J.R., & French, K.E. (1985). Gender differences across age in motor performance: A meta-analysis. *Psychological Bulletin*, **98**, 260-282.

Thomas, J.R., French, K.E., & Humphries, C.A. (1986). Knowledge development and sport skill performance: Directions for motor behavior research. *Journal of Sport Psychology*, **8**, 259-272.

Thomas, J.R., Gallagher, J.D., & Purvis, G.J. (1981). Reaction time and anticipation time: Effects of development. *Research Quarterly*, **48**, 592-597.

Thomas, J.R., Mitchell, B., & Solmon, M.A. (1979). Precision knowledge of results and motor performance: Relationship to age. *Research Quarterly*, **50**, 687-698.

Thomas, J.R., & Thomas, K.T. (in press). Perceptual development and its differential influence on limb positioning under two movement conditions in children. In J.E. Clark & J. Humphrey (Eds.), *Advances in motor development research* (Vol. 2). Baltimore: AMS Press.

Thomas, J.R., Thomas, K.T., Lee, A.M., Testerman, E., & Ashy, M. (1983). Age differences in use of strategy for recall of movement in a large scale environment. *Research Quarterly for Exercise and Sport,* **54**, 264-272.

Vernon, M.D. (1966). Perceptions in relation to cognition. In A.H. Kidd & J.L. Riviore (Eds.), *Perceptual development in children* (pp. 363-406). New York: International Universities Press.

Vickers, J.N. (1986). The resequencing task: Determining expert-novice differences in the organization of a movement sequence. *Research Quarterly for Exercise and Sport,* **57**, 260-264.

Vurpillot, E. (1974). The developmental emphasis. In E.C. Carterette & M.P. Friedman (Eds.), *Handbook of perception* (Vol. 1, pp. 363-373). New York: Academic Press.

Wellman, H.M. (1977). The early development of intentional memory behavior. *Human Development,* **20**, 86-101.

Winther, K.T., & Thomas, J.R. (1981). Developmental differences in children's labeling of movement. *Journal of Motor Behavior,* **13**, 77-90.

CHAPTER 15

Determinants and Consequences of Children's Competitive Stress

Michael W. Passer

The explosive growth of youth sport programs during the 1970s drew considerable attention to the issue of children's competitive stress. Instances of overzealous coaches and parents subjecting young athletes to extreme pressures to excel were reported periodically in the media. Social scientists and educators criticized youth sport for overemphasizing winning and expressed concern about youngsters' ability to cope with the psychological pressures of intense athletic competition (Brower, 1979; Ogilvie, 1979). By the turn of the decade, youth sport researchers, administrators, and coaches felt that learning more about competitive stress and helping children cope with stress were top priorities (Gould, 1982). Today, with youth sport participation at an all-time high in many countries, concern about reducing children's competitive stress and enhancing the general emotional quality of their athletic experience remains strong (Duda, 1985; Smoll & Smith, this volume; see Weiss & Gould, 1986).

This chapter examines the extent, determinants, and consequences of psychological stress among youth sport participants. Psychological stress can be viewed as a process that begins when a person encounters a situational demand. This *demand* might be a task, an opportunity, or something else requiring action or adjustment by the individual (Sarason, 1980). Next, the person appraises the situation and the personal resources available to meet the demand. Sometimes the person will judge the situation to be threatening in some way. According to Lazarus (1966), *threat* is "the condition of the person when confronted with a stimulus that he appraises as endangering important values and goals" (p. 28). For example, the person may judge the situational demand (e.g., performing well) to be important but either appraise personal resources to be inadequate ("I can't do it") or feel uncertain whether those resources are adequate ("I don't know if I can do it").

The perception of threat influences the next phase of the stress process, the person's emotional response. Unpleasant emotional states such as anxiety, anger, and guilt represent a major class of stress responses and have physiological and cognitive-attentional components. Thus, perceived threat may trigger physiological changes as well as self-preoccupational thoughts (e.g., worries, thoughts of helplessness) that divert the individuals's attention from the task at hand. The final stage of the stress process focuses on the behavioral, psychological, and health-related consequences of the person's emotional response. Within the realm of youth sport, for example, we could ask whether stress influences players' performance, their decision to participate or drop out, their feelings of satisfaction and enjoyment, and their susceptibility to illness and injury. In turn, these consequences can bring the stress process full cycle by modifying the initial situation, as happens when a player who performs poorly because of high anxiety is moved to a less demanding role or position.

Stress is not defined as any single component of this process, for it reflects the interaction of situational and personal factors. That is, stress connotes an unpleasant or aversive emotional state that arises from situational demands appraised as threatening. (For a more detailed discussion of the stress process, see Passer, 1982b.) This process-model provides a useful framework for examining stress in youth sport. First, the major situational demands encountered by players and their appraisal of these demands are examined. Next, research on youngsters' emotional responses to athletic competition are reviewed. The consequences of stress among youth sport participants are then addressed. The chapter concludes with a discussion of whether youth sport is too stressful and provides some suggestions for future research.

The Youth Sport Setting: Demands and Appraisal

Athletic competition provides youngsters with many challenges and opportunities that are important to them. Like other competitive activities, the most basic demands of sport focus on the demonstration, comparison, and evaluation of ability (Martens, 1975). How are these three demands appraised by children? First, sport involves the demonstration of athletic ability, which is a highly valued attribute among children and adolescents (Buchanan, Blankenbaker, & Cotten, 1976; Coleman, 1961; Duda, 1981). Second, the opportunity to compare their athletic ability with that of peers is important to children because it represents a primary means by which they gain information about their physical competence (Horn & Hasbrook, 1986; see Scanlan, this volume). During the elementary school years, children increasingly seek out competitive situations for their social comparison value; it is not by coincidence that youth sport participation increases significantly during this time (see Passer, this volume). Third, the youth sport setting typically involves pervasive social evaluation by adults and peers.

This is important not only because such evaluation is a major source of feedback to children about their ability (Horn & Hasbrook, 1986; see Scanlan, this volume), but also because it provides them a direct means for obtaining adult social approval (Roberts, 1986). In sum, the demands inherent in athletic competition—to demonstrate physical skill, to compare this skill against that of peers, and to obtain evaluation from others—are very important to youth sport participants.

These are not the only aspects of youth sport, however, that children perceive as important and which can therefore induce stress. For example, some children are more concerned with mastering skills and improving their own performance than with relative outcomes such as winning or losing (Roberts, 1986). Opportunities to learn and improve athletic skills are consistently reported by children as major reasons for participating in sport (see Gould & Horn, 1984; Passer, 1982a). Thus, such mastery-oriented children might find it particularly stressful to play for a coach who is a poor teacher or who places insufficient emphasis on skill instruction. The youth sport setting also involves many social demands; opportunities to be with friends, make new friends, and belong to a team are very important to many children (see Gould & Horn, 1984; Passer, 1982a). Therefore, peer conflict, low popularity, or the inability to be with friends because of sport involvement can all cause stress, even to the point that a few children will drop out of youth sport entirely (Gould, Feltz, Horn, & Weiss, 1982).

As illustrated, the potential sources of stress in youth sport are as varied as the goals of its participants. Realistically, such goals will not always be met by all children; in fact, sport competition typically is structured so that some goals and demands (e.g., winning a particular contest) *cannot* be satisfied by everyone. If we recall Lazarus's (1966) definition of threat (i.e., the perception that important goals are endangered), then it is clear that at such times the sport setting will be appraised as threatening. The key, then, is to determine the types of situations that induce the most stress and the types of children who find sport competition most stressful.

Emotional Responses to Competition

Although various emotional states can serve as indicants of stress, youth sport researchers have focused their attention on children's anxiety responses to competition. Some studies have obtained children's restrospective reports of how anxious they usually are or of what they typically worry about when they compete. Other researchers have measured youngsters' actual anxiety at specific points, such as right before, during, or after a game or match. *State anxiety* is the term used to represent this transitory, *right now* response to a particular situation; it involves feelings of apprehension and tension associated with physiological arousal (Spielberger, 1966).

Measuring Stress

Competitive state anxiety has most often been assessed by self-report inventories that ask children how nervous, jittery, worried, calm, etc., they are feeling at a certain moment. The *State Anxiety Inventory for Children* (Spielberger, 1973) and the children's version of the *Competitive State Anxiety Inventory* (Martens, Burton, Rivkin, & Simon, 1980) have been two of the most frequently employed scales. Both inventories treat state anxiety as a unidimensional construct; that is, a single overall anxiety score is obtained for each child. Recently, the *Competitive State Anxiety Inventory—2* (Martens, Burton, Vealey, Smith, & Bump, 1983) was developed to separately assess the cognitive (worry) and somatic (physiological arousal) components of state anxiety.

Physiological recordings represent a second method of measuring state anxiety and stress. Included in this category would be measures of cardiovascular responses (e.g., heart rate, skin temperature) and electrodermal activity (e.g., skin conductance level). Another technique used to assess anxiety is the observation of overt behaviors such as trembling, pacing, performance changes, avoidance and escape, and alterations in eating and sleeping patterns. Such behaviors are viewed here as consequences of stress and will be discussed later. For the moment, I will focus on research that has assessed the cognitive or physiological components of children's emotional responses to competition, beginning with studies that have examined what youngsters typically worry about when they compete.

Sources of Worry

Fear of failure is the predominant source of worry among young athletes, particularly with regard to concerns about the adequacy of personal performance. Recent studies of 13- to 19-year-old junior elite wrestlers (Gould, Horn, & Spreeman, 1983b) and 9- to 15-year-old elite long-distance runners (Feltz & Albrecht, 1986) found that, out of about 30 potential sources of stress, youngsters worried most frequently about performing up to their level of ability, improving on their last performance, participating in championship events, and not performing well. Between 53% and 42% of the wrestlers and 54% and 41% of the runners rated each of these factors as something they worried about frequently. Concerning nonelite athletes, Pierce (1980) asked 10- to 16-year-old participants in agency-sponsored basketball, gymnastics, and swimming to indicate what worried them the most during sport. Also polled were 11- to 17-year-old schoolchildren, most of whom were sport participants at the intramural, interscholastic, or agency level. Not playing well and making mistakes were by far their major worries, being chosen by 50% and 42% of the agency sport sample, and by 67% and 64% of the school sample, respectively.

Although Pierce (1980) found that only 7% of agency sport participants and 14% of schoolchildren chose "winning the game" as something they worried about "the most," studies assessing the *frequency* of youngsters' various worries consistently indicate that concern about losing is an important source of stress. Among junior elite athletes, 32% of runners and 44% of wrestlers worried frequently about losing, ranking just below several worries about personal performance (Feltz & Albrecht, 1986; Gould et al., 1983b). Similarly, Passer (1983) found that nonelite youth soccer participants worried almost as frequently about losing as they did about not playing well and making mistakes. Thus, worries about process (i.e., quality of performance) and outcome (i.e., losing) both contribute to fear of failure in young athletes.

Social evaluation from others is a significant but less major source of worry to most young athletes (Feltz & Albrecht, 1986; Gould et al., 1983b; Passer, 1983; Pierce, 1980). Unfortunately, no consistent findings have emerged in terms of whether children worry most about evaluation from parents, coaches, or teammates. Other relatively important worries are specific to certain types of sport. For example, whereas 43% of junior elite wrestlers reported worrying frequently about "making weight" (Gould et al., 1983b), 23% of agency basketball participants said they worried most about "being taken out of the game" (Pierce, 1980). Finally, Gould and others (1983b) found that relatively few wrestlers worried frequently about factors related to external control (e.g., having bad luck, being bothered by specators) and guilt (e.g., hurting an opponent).

Situational Determinants of Precompetition Stress

The type of sport in which the child is participating is a powerful situational determinant of precompetition stress. The most extensive comparison of youngsters' precompetition stress in different sports was conducted by Simon and Martens (1979), who administered the children's form of the *Competitive State Anxiety Inventory* (Martens et al., 1980) to 468 male youth sport participants within 10 minutes (and usually within 2 or 3 minutes) before the start of competition. The 9- to 14-year-old boys were drawn from the following sports: baseball, basketball, football, ice hockey, gymnastics, swimming, and wrestling. The findings, which controlled for the possibility that players in different sports might have different baseline levels of anxiety, indicated that participants in individual sports generally had higher state anxiety prior to competition than players in team sports. Wrestling and gymnastics were the two most anxiety-inducing sports, whereas football, hockey, and baseball were the least stressful. An overall comparison of contact (wrestling, football, hockey) versus noncontact (gymnastics, swimming, baseball, basketball) sports revealed no significant differences in pregame anxiety.

Griffin (1972) administered the *State Anxiety Inventory* (Spielberger, Gorsuch, & Lushene, 1970) to 682 female athletes within 1 hour prior to competition. The athletes were drawn from three age groups—12 to 13, 16 to 17, and 19 years and older. Gymnasts had the highest pre-competitive state anxiety, followed in rank order by participants in track and field, swimming, tennis, football, volleyball, basketball, and field hockey. Thus, Griffin's (1972) results are consistent with those of Simon and Martens (1979) in revealing that individual sports, which maximize the social comparison and evaluation of personal perfor-mance, generally elicit higher levels of precompetition anxiety than team sports.

The amount of time prior to competition is a second situational fac-tor that affects precompetition anxiety. Gould, Horn, and Spreeman (1983a) asked junior elite wrestlers to rate how anxious they typically were 1 week, 24 hours, 1 hour, and 2 minutes prior to competing. These retrospective reports indicated a steady increase in anxiety as the time of competition approached. Further research by Gould and his col-leagues (Gould, Petlichkoff, & Weinberg, 1984) on female high school volleyball players expanded on these findings in two important ways. First, actual state anxiety was measured 1 week, 48 hours, 24 hours, 2 hours, and 20 minutes prior to competition. Second, cognitive and somatic anxiety components were assessed separately by the *Competi-tive State Anxiety Inventory—2* (Martens et al., 1983). The findings revealed that cognitive anxiety remained very stable throughout the entire week and was higher than somatic anxiety. Somatic anxiety was fairly stable until it rose at the 2-hour mark, and then rose again at the 20-minute mark. Thus, only the somatic anxiety of young athletes seems to increase as competition nears, a finding consistent with other sport psychology research and work on test anxiety (see Gould et al., 1984).

The importance of the game or match is a third factor found to influ-ence precompetition stress. Lowe and McGrath (1971) directly assessed the effects of game criticality on the stress of 60 boys, 10 to 12 years of age, throughout an entire 18-game season of Little League baseball. Game criticality was objectively defined by a formula that took into account the ranking of the two teams within the league, the difference in their win-loss percentage, and the remaining number of games in the season. Stress was assessed by two physiological measures, pulse rate and respiration rate, which indicated that pregame arousal in-creased under conditions of higher game criticality. More recently, Gould and others (1983b) noted support for a relationship between stress and criticality in their finding that junior elite wrestlers rated "participating in championship meets" as a major source of worry. Feltz and Albrecht (1986) found that participating in championship events also was a major source of stress among junior elite runners. In sum, the criticality of the competition, the type of sport (individual or team), and the temporal countdown to competition have been found to influence young athletes' precompetition stress.

Situational Determinants of Stress During Competition

Lowe and McGrath's (1971) study of Little Leaguers also examined the effects of game and situation criticality on stress during competition. Situation criticality reflected the importance of the immediate situation within the game and took into account the difference in score between the two teams, the inning of play, the number of outs, and the number and location of any base runners. Because of practical constraints, pulse and respiration rates were recorded each time a player was in the dugout, waiting to go to the on-deck circle (i.e., the player was two turns from coming to bat). Greater game and situation criticality each produced higher arousal, with game criticality having the stronger effect.

Different tasks or roles within a sport may differ in importance or in how demanding they are to execute. Hanson (1967) used telemetry to monitor the heart rates of 10 male Little League baseball players, ages 9 to 12. Each player was observed for a single game, with recordings taken when the player was at bat, standing on base after a hit, sitting in the dugout after making an out, standing in the field, and sitting and standing at rest before and after the game. The most striking finding was the magnitude of response shown when players came to bat, where the average heart rate was 166 beats per minute (bpm) and the highest recorded rate was 204 bpm. In comparison, players' average heart rates were 110 bpm while standing before the game and 128 bpm while in the field. Batting, of course, is one of the most demanding and important activities in baseball, and Hanson (1967) concluded that the emotional stress of being at bat was high but short-lived. Interestingly, after the game most players reported that they did not feel particularly nervous while batting. One interpretation of this apparent inconsistency between players' self-reports and physiological responses is that the players refused to acknowledge their anxiousness (Brower, 1979). Another possibility, however, is that players were not feeling especially nervous and their arousal at bat primarily reflected some other emotional state, such as excitement or feeling psyched-up (see Passer, 1982b).

In contrast to the Lowe and McGrath (1971) study, in which trailing or leading was among several criteria used to judge situation criticality, several laboratory experiments have directly examined how children's stress is affected by being ahead or behind during competition. For example, Martens and Gill (1976) and Gill and Martens (1977) had children compete at a motor skills task over a series of trials, with the win-loss outcome of each trial controlled by the experimenters. State anxiety was measured during midcompetition by Spielberger's (1973)

State Anxiety Inventory for Children. The findings revealed that children who lost the early trials became more anxious than children who found themselves ahead. In sum, children's stress during competition has been linked to the criticality of the game, the criticality of the immediate situation within the game, the specific task or activity being performed, and to whether one is leading or trailing the opposition.

Situational Determinants of Postcompetition Stress

Most youth sport participants view winning as important (see Passer, 1982a); consequently, it is not surprising that children's postcompetition stress is strongly influenced by win-loss outcomes. Two studies by Scanlan and Passer (1978, 1979) illustrate this point. In the first study 191 boys, 11 and 12 years of age, were administered Spielberger's (1973) *State Anxiety Inventory for Children* 30 minutes before and immediately after youth soccer games. A preseason baseline measure was taken as a control factor. The second study involved 176 ten- to twelve-year-old girls and employed the same procedure. Both studies found that losing players had substantially higher postgame anxiety than winning players, and a direct comparison of players' pregame versus postgame anxiety indicated that losers' anxiety increased while winners' anxiety decreased. Losers were also less satisfied with their performance than winners and had less fun playing the game (Passer & Scanlan, 1980).

In a recent study by Scanlan and Lewthwaite (1984), prematch and postmatch anxiety of 76 junior wrestlers was measured for two consecutive tournament rounds by the children's form of the *Competitive Stress Anxiety Inventory* (Martens et al., 1980). The pretournament baseline anxiety of these 9- to 14-year-olds was recorded as a control factor. For both rounds, losers experienced greater postgame state anxiety than winners. Taken together, these three field studies demonstrate that win-loss outcomes influence postcompetition stress across both sexes in team and individual sports. Similar win-loss effects have been obtained in laboratory studies in which children's success-failure at motor skill tasks is experimentally manipulated (e.g., Gill & Martens, 1977; Martens & Gill, 1976).

Win-loss is not the only situational determinant of postcompetition stress. The closeness of the game also can affect players' anxiety. In their study of male soccer players, Scanlan and Passer (1978) classified games as either very close, close, or not close, based on the pattern of scoring and the final margin of victory. The closeness of the game did not influence the postgame anxiety of winners, suggesting that a victory by any margin was sufficient to minimize stress. Players who lost a very close game, however, had higher postgame anxiety than players who lost either a moderately close game or one that was not close. These latter two groups did not differ in postcompetition anxiety. Scanlan and Passer (1978) speculated that losers of very close games may have entertained hopes of a victory or tie right up to the end of the game; thus, the experience of losing would have been especially stressful when the final whistle sounded.

What about a tied outcome? The responses of male and female youth soccer participants (Passer & Scanlan, 1980; Scanlan & Passer, 1979) showed that players who had participated in a tie experienced a significant increase in pregame to postgame state anxiety; they had greater postcompetition anxiety than winners, but less than losers. Under some circumstances, however, such as playing a bitter rival and relinquishing the lead just before the game ended, a tie induced as much anxiety as a loss. Tying players were less satisfied with their performance and had less fun playing the game than winners, but their feelings were more positive than those of losers. Overall, tying appears to be an aversive outcome, not a neutral one.

Intrapersonal Factors Related to Competitive Stress

On the day of a game or match some children may experience high anxiety while others feel little to moderate stress. This raises the important question of whether intrapersonal factors can account for these individual differences and help predict children's state anxiety reactions to specific competitive situations. Martens (1977) proposes that competitive trait anxiety is an important mediator of stress responses to athletic competition. In contrast to state anxiety, which reflects a momentary response to a specific situation, *competitive trait anxiety* (CTA) represents a person's general tendency to appraise competitive sport situations as threatening and is thought to be a relatively stable personality disposition. CTA is measured by the *Sport Competition Anxiety Test*, which asks people to indicate how they *usually* feel (e.g., nervous, uneasy) when competing in sport and games (Martens, 1977).

Several field and laboratory studies have assessed children's CTA a few weeks or months prior to a specific competition and examined how well this disposition could predict their state anxiety responses to that competitive event (Gill & Martens, 1977; Martens & Gill, 1976; Scanlan & Lewthwaite, 1984; Scanlan & Passer, 1978, 1979). Overall, the results form an interesting pattern. Before competition, high-CTA children show greater state anxiety than low-CTA children. During competition, a similar but slightly weaker relationship is obtained, as ongoing success-failure outcomes begin to influence youngsters' anxiety. The relationship between CTA and state anxiety is weakest (and usually nonexistent) after the game or match is over; at that time, state anxiety is significantly affected by the final win-loss outcome. In sum, CTA helps predict children's pre- and midcompetition state anxiety.

Researchers have examined the relationship between competitive stress and two other dispositional factors—self-esteem and achievement orientation. Correlational analyses consistently indicate that children with low self-esteem are more anxious prior to competition than those with high self-esteem, but when multiple regression analyses are used to control for other factors this esteem-anxiety relationship either disappears or becomes quite weak (Scanlan & Lewthwaite, 1984; Scanlan & Passer, 1978, 1979). Mid- and postcompetition state anxiety do not appear to be related to self-esteem. Concerning achievement orientation, children who are motivated primarily by sport mastery (i.e., the desire to improve and do well personally) generally perceive less competitive stress than children who care most about winning and demonstrating greater skill than their peers (see Roberts, 1986). Mastery-oriented children do experience stress, however, when coaches or others criticize their effort and commitment.

Pre- and postcompetition stress also are related to several intrapersonal factors that do not represent personality dispositions. First, studies of male junior wrestlers (Scanlan & Lewthwaite, 1984) and male and female youth soccer players (Scanlan & Passer, 1978, 1979) indicate that before competition children with lower expectancies for success in the event have higher state anxiety than children with more positive performance expectancies. In individual sports, such as wrestling, success expectations obviously focus on personal performance. In team sports, such as soccer, expectancies concerning team performance are related more strongly and consistently to precompetition state anxiety than expectancies concerning the quality of personal performance (see Scanlan & Lewthwaite, 1984). Finally, Scanlan & Lewthwaite (1984) found that young wrestlers who worried more about failure and making mistakes and who felt greater parental pressure to wrestle (i.e., wrestling to please one's parents) exhibited higher state anxiety prior to the first of two consecutive tournament matches. In sum, intrapersonal factors that reflect perceived situational demands (e.g., parental pressure) and perceived response capabilities (e.g., performance expectancies) affect precompetitive stress.

Postcompetition state anxiety has consistently been related to players' postgame ratings of how much fun they had during the game. Although winning players generally have more fun than losing players (Passer & Scanlan, 1980), within each of these groups the level of fun experienced varies from player to player. For winners and losers, girls and boys who report having less fun during a game or match have greater postcompetition anxiety than children who report having more fun (Scanlan & Lewthwaite, 1984; Scanlan & Passer, 1978, 1979). This finding is important because it suggests that, even among losing players, stress might be reduced by making the process of competition as enjoyable as possible.

Gender, age, and amount of sport experience generally appear to be unrelated to children's acute competitive stress. Concerning gender, field studies of youth soccer players (Scanlan & Passer, 1978, 1979) and laboratory experiments (Gill & Martens, 1977; Martens & Gill, 1976) indicate that boys and girls exhibit similar levels of pre- and postcompetition state anxiety. With regard to age, Lowe and McGrath

(1971) found that 10- to 12-year-olds did not differ in their physiological arousal during baseball competition. Gould and others (1983a) asked junior elite wrestlers how anxious they usually became 1 week, 24 hours, 1 hour, and 2 minutes prior to competition. No significant differences were found in the ratings of younger (13- to 16-year-old) and older (17- to 19-year-old) wrestlers, nor in the ratings of less-experienced (1 to 5 years) and more-experienced (5 years or greater) wrestlers. Similarly, actual state anxiety measurements of female high school volleyball players, taken at 1 week, 48 hours, 24 hours, 2 hours, and 20 minutes prior to competition, revealed no differences in cognitive or somatic anxiety between experienced and inexperienced players (Gould et al., 1984).

Chronic Competitive Stress

Some children chronically experience competitive stress. Studies of youth soccer participants (Passer, 1983) and junior elite wrestlers (Gould et al., 1983b) indicate that these high-CTA youngsters have greater fears of failure and social evaluation than low-CTA youngsters. Passer's (1983) study of 10- to 15-year-old boys also found that high- and low-CTA children differed in their general expectations about the upcoming season. Although the groups had equal soccer ability according to the coach and self-ratings, high-CTA children still expected to play less well. High-CTA youngsters also expected to feel more upset and ashamed over poor play, which they felt would cause their parents and coaches to get mad or yell at them. Thus, high-CTA children's greater fears of failure and social evaluation may result in part from their relatively more threatening general expectations about the sport environment. In turn, these expectancies may stem from several developmental factors, including the child's history of competitive outcomes; the responses of parents, other adults, and peers to the child's performance; and the attributions made for that performance (see Passer, 1984).

Some cross-sectional data suggest that within the age range of about 9 to 17, schoolchildren and youth sport participants have slightly higher CTA scores, with this trend leveling off or reversing slightly by the late teens and early twenties. (Gould et al., 1983a; Martens, 1977; Passer, 1983). Additionally, some research has found that females have slightly higher CTA than males (Martens, 1977; see Passer, 1984), and that less-experienced young athletes have higher CTA than more-experienced young athletes (Gould et al., 1983a). These differences, although relatively small, are somewhat surprising given the previously discussed lack of age, gender, and experience differences in youngsters' state anxiety responses to competition.

Stress in Youth Sport Versus Other Achievement Activities

Do children find youth sport more stressful than other achievement activities? To examine this issue, Simon and Martens (1979) compared the precompetition state anxiety of 468 youth sport participants from several sports with the anxiety experienced by 281 other boys just prior to their participation in one of the following events: an interclass physical education softball game, a school test, a band group competition, or a band solo competition. Overall, team sports were found to be no more anxiety-inducing than a PE softball game, school test, or band group competition (see Figure 1). Individual sports, however, generally elicited more anxiety than a softball game or school test but did not differ significantly from band group competition. All sport was found to induce *less* anxiety than band solo competition. The fact that band solo competition proved to be the most stressful of the 11 activities, followed by wrestling and gymnastics, further attests to the greater potential of individual events to induce stress.

In an earlier study, Skubic (1955) assessed the galvanic skin response (GSR) of 9- to 15-year-old boys during youth league baseball games and physical education softball games. For both activities, GSR was measured immediately before, immediately after, and 90 minutes after competition. No significant differences occurred at any age level between players' precompetition GSR scores in league games and in PE class softball. Few differences were found when comparisons were made immediately after and 90 minutes after competition—when differences did occur it was the class softball competition, as often as not, that elicited greater arousal. These findings are consistent with those of Simon and Martens (1979) in suggesting that the degree of children's emotional reactivity to youth sport competition is similar to that experienced when participating in several other achievement or competitive activities.

Consequences of Stress

The deleterious effects of stress on behavior and health have been documented repeatedly in the general scientific literature (e.g., Dohrenwend & Dohrenwend, 1981; Sarason & Spielberger, 1980). A growing body of research indicates that competitive stress also produces its share of negative consequences.

Effects on Enjoyment and Participation

Numerous sources of stress can detract from youngsters' enjoyment of sport. Youngsters who play for relatively punitive or critical coaches perceive more pressure and negative responses from their mothers, feel that their parents and coaches are less satisfied with their overall sport performance, and view themselves as having less skill, express less enjoyment from their participation, and like their sport less (Scanlan & Lewthwaite, 1986; Smith, Smoll, & Curtis, 1978; Wankel & Kreisel, 1985). Ultimately, these stresses may decrease enjoyment so severely

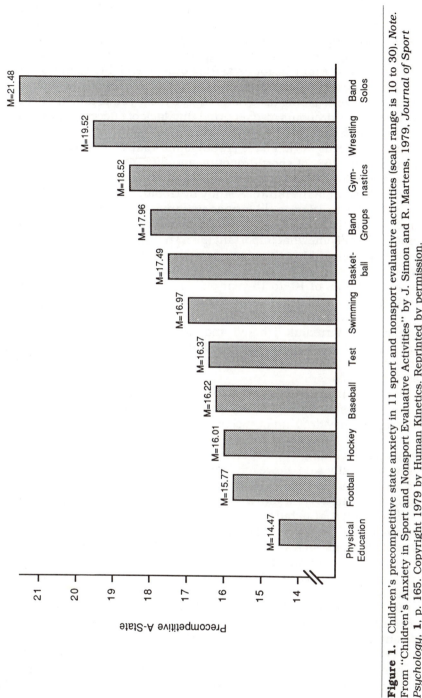

Figure 1. Children's precompetitive state anxiety in 11 sport and nonsport evaluative activities (scale range is 10 to 30). *Note.* From "Children's Anxiety in Sport and Nonsport Evaluative Activities" by J. Simon and R. Martens, 1979, *Journal of Sport Psychology,* **1,** p. 165. Copyright 1979 by Human Kinetics. Reprinted by permission.

that young athletes stop participating. Further, anticipated stresses may cause some children to avoid sport participation in the first place. Inceptive work by Orlick (see Orlick & Botterill, 1975) with 8- and 9-year-old nonparticipants and 7- to 19-year-old dropouts illustrated that (a) youngsters' self-reports suggested they avoided sport because of fears of failure and disapproval from others, and (b) negative factors related to the competitive emphasis of sport (e.g., overemphasis on winning, aversive coaching behaviors) caused most young athletes to quit. Most younger dropouts also reported that lack of success was a factor in their decision to quit.

In more recent work, Pierce (1980) found that 26% of agency sport participants, 26% of sport dropouts, and 32% of nonparticipants reported certain worries bothered them so much that they might not participate in sport in the future. A study by Gould, Feltz, Horn, and Weiss (1982) of 10- to 18-year-old former swimmers revealed that over half of the youngsters rated the pressure involved as either a very important (16%) or somewhat important (36%) reason for dropping out, and many rated not liking the coach as a very important (20%) or somewhat important (24%) factor. Pooley (cited in Gould & Horn, 1984) found that 33% of 10- to 15-year-old youth soccer dropouts reported quitting because of negative coaching behaviors and an overemphasis on competition. And, in a study of over 1,000 age-group swimmers, McPherson, Marteniuk, Tihanyi, and Clark (1980) found that too much pressure, conflict with coaches, and insufficient success were among the reasons swimmers reported for their teammates' discontinued participation.

Of course, many reasons given for dropping out do not overtly reflect competitive stress (see Gould & Horn, 1984). Most youngsters, for example, say they drop out of specific sport programs primarily because it is no longer fun, they have other interests, and are involved in other activities (including other sports). Such reasons are very general and psychologically safe, however. Why is participation for a given child no longer fun? Is it due in part to various stresses? In an intriguing study of 8- to 17-year-old wrestling dropouts, Burton and Martens (1986) found that nebulous factors such as "other things to do" and "stops being fun" were again top-ranked reasons for dropping out. Overall, reasons such as "doesn't like losing," "isn't showing improvement," and "too much pressure to win" were lower ranked. In contrast, a theoretically based comparison of dropouts' and participants' win-loss records, performance expectancies, attributions, and sport values led Burton and Martens (1986) to conclude that youngsters appeared to drop out when their perceived ability was threatened by consistent failure. Thus, the former wrestlers may have downplayed the importance of ability-related factors as causes of dropping out in order to minimize feelings of threat (Burtons & Martens, 1986).

In sum, competitive stress contributes significantly to the dropout rate in youth sport. Based on the preceding research and other studies on dropouts (see Gould & Horn, 1984), a very rough guess would be that such factors as competitive pressure, an overemphasis on winning, dislike of the coach due to negative behaviors (e.g., frequent criticism of players, pushing them too hard), and intense competition-related worries are major reasons that about 25% to 35% of young dropouts have left their sport program; for many other dropouts, such factors undoubtedly play a secondary role. Interestingly, young athletes who feel that winning is the most important aspect of sport (and who therefore may place themselves under added competitive stress) appear to derive less enjoyment from their participation and are more prone to drop out (Orlick & Botterill, 1975; Roberts, 1986; Robinson & Carron, 1982). Some studies indicate that younger participants are more likely to drop out because of an overemphasis on competition and other negative sport experiences than are older athletes, but this finding has not been consistent (see Gould et al., 1982, and Gould et al., 1984).

Effects on Performance

Two general methods have been used to examine how competitive stress influences young athletes' performance. In the first and more powerful approach, stress is assessed prior to or during competition and related to actual performance measures (e.g., getting a hit or making an out, win-loss, coaches' ratings). Unfortunately, such studies conducted with Little League baseball players (Lowe & McGrath, 1971), youth wrestlers (Scanlan, Lewthwaite, & Jackson, 1984), young golfers (Martens et al., 1983), and interscholastic basketball players (Klavora, 1978) simply have not yielded a consistent pattern of results.

The second approach is to have youngsters report how they feel their performance is typically affected by stress. Pierce (1980) found that 31% of agency sport participants and 42% of schoolchildren felt that various worries prevented them from playing their best when they competed in sport. In a study by Gould and others (1983a) of junior elite wrestlers, 12% reported that anxiety usually hurt their performance, 39% said it usually helped their performance, and 49% felt it sometimes helped and sometimes hurt. More recently, Feltz & Albrecht (1986) reported that 50% of junior elite runners felt that nervousness helped their performance. How accurate people are in detecting the true causal effects of stress on their performance is, of course, open to debate. Nevertheless, we can conclude that while some young athletes feel anxiety usually hurts their performance, far more feel that it usually helps or at least helps as much as it hurts.

Youth sport research has only begun to tap the complexities of the stress-performance relationship. On the stress side, for example, Martens and others (1983) propose that performance is affected primarily by cognitive rather than somatic anxiety. Despite some initial unsupportive findings (see Gould et al., 1983a), continued research with the *Competitive State Anxiety Inventory—2* will enable researchers to test this hypothesis more fully. On the performance side, studies using movement kinematics with children (Beuter & Duda, 1985) and electromyography with adults (Weinberg, 1978) have found that the patterning of movement is less efficient under higher stress. Beuter and Duda (1985) propose that, when feasible, the use of such process-oriented techniques may help pinpoint the mechanisms by which stress influences young athletes' performance. More generally, this research should serve as a needed reminder that discrete outcomes (e.g., making a shot, winning) are not the only way to judge the quality of performance.

Health-Related Effects

Case examples cited by clinical sport psychologists and the media suggest that severe competitive stress has significant adverse effects upon some children's physical and psychological well-being. Such effects are reported to include the development of chronic headaches, ulcers and other gastro-intestinal disorders, dermatological problems, eating disorders including anorexia and bulimia, hyperanxiety and panic attacks, heightened guilt feelings, depressive symptoms, obsessive thoughts, social withdrawal, family disruption, sibling conflicts, and traumatic effects on self-esteem (D. Coppell, personal communication, February 11, 1986; Ogilvie, 1979; Shelton, 1983). Unfortunately, I am not aware of any research documenting the prevalence of such conditions among youth sport participants. Such work should take a high priority. Some data exist, however, on the degree to which involvement in sport disrupts youngsters' sleeping and eating routines. Gould and others (1983a) found that 58% of junior elite wrestlers reported generally having "some" to "a lot" of difficulty sleeping the night before a match because of competitive anxiety. A remarkably similar figure was obtained in Skubic's (1956) earlier survey of Little and Middle League baseball players; 60% reported occasional or frequent sleep disruption the night before or after competition. Diminished appetite after losing a game was reported by 11% of players.

The most definitive data on sleep disruption are provided by the State of Michigan Youth Sports Study (1978). Of 1,118 male and female youth sport participants sampled from around the state, 21% indicated that there were times when they did not receive enough sleep because of their involvement in sport. Of the players experiencing sleep loss, 46% rated worrying about performance as a contributing factor and 25% indicated that being upset after losing was a cause. Other sources of sleep disruption were not directly related to competitive stress. These included the time of day at which games and practices were scheduled (46%), being too excited about winning (38%), and travel time (29%). Of course, time conflicts caused by games, practices, and travel can lead to various stress responses (e.g., guilt, frustration, anxiety), and sleep disruption may itself cause some players stress regardless of the initial cause. Another interesting finding was that a representative sample of children participating in recreational activities other than youth sport (e.g., music, drama, clubs) reported an even higher incidence (36%) of sleep loss. For these children, the two most prominent causes were the time of day at which the activity was scheduled (67%) and concern about performing well (50%). Overall, then, youngsters' sleep appears to be disrupted somewhat less by sport involvement than by other achievement activities; when sleep loss occurs, competitive stress is only one among several causes. It remains unclear, however, why the percentage of young athletes reporting sleep loss across these different studies is so variable (21% to 60%). Finally, Gould and others (1983a) recently found that high-CTA junior elite wrestlers reported considerably more frequent trouble falling asleep the night before competition than low-CTA wrestlers.

Injury is another potential negative consequence of athletic participation. Although most youth sport injuries are relatively minor, serious injuries due to accidents and overuse do occur and have been the subject of much concern (Kozar & Lord, this volume; see Weiss & Gould, 1986). Several studies have examined whether athletes who experience a high degree of "life stress" are at greater risk for subsequent athletic injury. Stressful sport experiences (e.g., troubles with the coach) contribute to athletes' life stress, as do numerous other stressful life events (e.g., moving, change of school). In the sole study of younger athletes, Coddington and Troxell (1980) found no relationship between overall life stress and injury rates among high school football players. However, a subgroup of life events reflecting *object loss* (the actual or threatened loss of someone close) was related to a higher risk of injury. In fact, athletes who suffered the actual loss of a parent were 5 times more likely to be injured than their teammates. Partial support for a relationship between object loss and injury has also been obtained among collegiate football players (Passer & Seese, 1983). Two other studies of collegiate football players (Bramwell, Masuda, Wagner, & Holmes, 1975; Cryan & Alles, 1983) have found a strong relationship between overall life stress and injury rates. Thus, while the specific results across these studies are not entirely consistent, each provides some evidence that stressful life events may enhance the risk of athletic injury. Further research with young athletes obviously is needed.

Is Youth Sport Too Stressful?

Studies examining youngsters' state anxiety before, during, or after competition have yielded valuable information about the types of situations that are most stressful and the types of children who experience the greatest stress, but such analyses do not in themselves determine whether that stress is excessive. For example, if we note that the mean state anxiety scores obtained in most studies generally fall in the low-to-moderate range (e.g., Scanlan & Passer, 1978, 1979; Simon & Martens, 1979), does this tell us that athletic competition is not too stressful? There are two difficulties with such an interpretation. First, mean scores do not reflect the extent of individual variability; most youngsters may experience low to moderate state anxiety, but others will be in the moderate-to-high range. How many children must fall in this range in order for sport to be considered excessively stressful? Second, children who experience the same operational level of stress (e.g., anxiety score or heart rate) may differ not only in how aversive they perceive that stress to be, but also in their behavioral response (e.g., performance impairment versus enhancement). Thus, even when viewed at the individual (rather than sport) level, there are simply no absolute standards by which to judge how great an anxiety test score or physiological response must be to indicate that a child is too psychologically stressed (Martens, 1978).

Similar interpretive problems arise if we examine research on players' worries. If junior elite wrestlers feel nervous in 66% of their matches, and if 44% worry frequently about losing (Gould et al., 1983a, 1983b), should we take this as evidence that these athletes are excessively stressed? Just how frequent, intense, and bothersome need these worries be before we accept them as indicants of overanxiety? If we turn next to the finding that youth sport generally induces no more stress than music competition, school tests, and physical education ball games, do we conclude at last that youth sport is not too stressful? Or, might we ask whether all of these achievement activities generate too much stress? Focusing on the consequences of stress, we can note that for some youngsters competitive stress impairs performance, disrupts sleep, reduces the enjoyment of sport, and/or leads to dropping out. For at least a few young athletes, competitive stress appears to produce or exacerbate serious medical or psychological conditions. But, again, how chronic or severe must such stress effects be in order to constitute a problem for a given child? And, on an aggregate level, how many children must experience such consequences in order to render an overall judgment that youth sport is too stressful?

A related issue is whether stress is necessarily bad. Often, stress appears to have no consequences beyond the immediate unpleasantness associated with the person's emotional state. Stress can also have beneficial consequences. Many youngsters thrive on the challenge and pressures of competition. Anxiety is viewed by more young athletes as a performance enhancer than as an inhibitor. Exposure to stressful events may also help people deal more efficiently with such situations in the future, provided, as Sarason (1980) notes, that effective coping responses have been learned. These remarks are not meant to imply that making youngsters feel anxious is a desirable way to facilitate performance (i.e., there are more positive ways to generate performance-enhancing arousal), nor do they suggest that exposure to competitive stress will, in fact, produce any long-term benefits. Rather, these comments are intended solely to illustrate the complexity of judging whether youth sport is too stressful.

Several investigators (e.g., Martens, 1978; Seefeldt & Gould, 1980) have suggested that the problem of competitive stress in youth sport has been overemphasized. The present review supports this conclusion to an extent. Some critics portray youth sport as an atypically stressful achievement activity and/or contend that the majority of participants suffer significant deleterious effects from competitive stress. It is equally clear, however, that competitive stress is a moderate to serious problem for a significant number of children and adolescents. Even if only 10% of the over 25 million young athletes in the United States and Canada (see Weiss & Gould, 1986) repeatedly experience adverse effects from competitive stress, we would be dealing with several million youngsters in North America alone. In this context, stress in youth sport is an issue that cannot be emphasized enough.

Future Directions

Although many issues are in need of further exploration, I will mention only a few here. More attention must be given to the health-related effects of competitive stress. In particular, we need to document the incidence and prevalence of various physical and psychological problems among youth sport participants and assess whether they are caused by sport-related stresses, including coach, parent, and peer conflicts. A related point is that research has only begun to examine how young athletes' stress is related to their perceptions of coach and parent behaviors (Passer, 1983; Scanlan & Lewthwaite, 1984). Further, although behavioral observations have documented the effects of specific coaching behaviors on children's sport-related attitudes (e.g., Smith, Smoll, & Curtis, 1978), I am aware of no research linking actual coach or parent behaviors to players' competitive state or trait anxiety.

Increased use of the *Competitive State Anxiety Inventory—2* (Martens et al., 1983) should provide a fuller understanding of the cognitive and somatic components of youngsters' competitive stress. In contrast, the current measure of CTA (i.e., the *Sport Competition Anxiety Test*, Martens, 1977) is unidimensional. Although the concept of multidimensional trait anxiety has received some attention in the sport psychology literature (e.g., Endler, 1978; Sonstroem, 1984), a good multidimensional sport-specific inventory to assess CTA needs to be developed. Along these lines, more attention should be given to examining the etiology of CTA, particularly since chronically stressed young athletes may incur more negative consequences from sport involvement than children who experience only occasional stress.

Finally, as stress occurs when important goals are threatened, our understanding of stress in youth sport should be enhanced by taking into account each child's motives for participation (Passer, 1982a).

Work relating children's perception of stress to their achievement orientation (see Roberts, 1986) illustrates this approach. Future research should explore how the wide range of children's participation motives influences not only their competitive stress, but also the other stresses they may encounter in the youth sport setting (e.g., social stress).

Summary

Athletic competition presents children with numerous demands that are important to them. The potential for stress exists in youth sport because players may doubt their capability to meet these demands or may receive feedback that, in fact, these demands have not been met. Fear of failure is the primary source of worry for most young athletes; fear of social evaluation is also an important factor. Precompetition stress is influenced by a variety of situational and intrapersonal factors including the type of sport (individual/team), the criticality of the game or match, the passage of time as competition approaches, expectations about the quality of personal and team performance, perceived parental pressure to compete, and competitive trait anxiety. Stress during competition is affected by trailing or leading the opponent, the criticality of the game and particular situation within the game, the specific activity or role being performed, and competitive trait anxiety. Postcompetition stress is influenced by winning or losing and, regardless of outcome, is related to players' perceptions of how much fun they had. Children's competitive stress is also related to their general achievement orientation in sport. Finally, youngsters who experience chronic competitive stress have more negative general expectations about the sport environment than their peers.

A significant number of young athletes experience adverse effects from competitive stress, including loss of sleep, performance impairment, and decreased enjoyment of their athletic experience. A few children appear to suffer from health-related problems that may be caused by various stresses stemming from their involvement in sport. And, perhaps about a third of the youngsters who drop out of sport do so because of stresses related to competition. Yet, the level of stress elicited by youth sport is similar to that found in other achievement activities in which children participate. Further, the percentage of youth sport participants experiencing stress-related problems does not appear to be greater than that found among children engaged in other recreational activities. Whether these findings are viewed as cause for optimism or pessimism about the state of youth sport is a matter of personal judgment. What is certain, however, is that our knowledge about psychological stress in youth sport has expanded considerably in recent years and that many exciting avenues for research still lie ahead.

References

Beuter, A., & Duda, J.L. (1985). Analysis of the arousal/motor performance relationship in children using movement kinematics. *Journal of Sport Psychology*, **7**, 229-243.

Bramwell, S.T., Masuda, M., Wagner, N.N., & Holmes, T.H. (1975). Psychological factors in athletic injuries: Development and application of the Social and Athletic Readjustment Rating Scale (SARRS). *Journal of Human Stress*, **1**(2), 6-20.

Brower, J.J. (1979). The professionalization of organized youth sport: Social psychological impacts and outcomes. *Annals of the American Academy of Political and Social Science*, **445**, 39-46.

Buchanan, H.T., Blankenbaker, J., & Cotten, D. (1976). Academic and athletic ability as popularity factors in elementary school children. *Research Quarterly*, **3**, 320-325.

Burton, D., & Martens, R. (1986). Pinned by their own goals: An exploratory investigation into why kids drop out of wrestling. *Journal of Sport Psychology*, **8**, 183-195.

Coddington, R.D., & Troxell, J.R. (1980). The effect of emotional factors on football injury rates: A pilot study. *Journal of Human Stress*, **6**(4), 3-5.

Coleman, J.S. (1961). Athletics in high school. *Annals of the American Academy of Political and Social Science*, **338**, 33-43.

Cryan, P.D., & Alles, W.F. (1983). The relationship between stress and college football injuries. *Journal of Sports Medicine and Physical Fitness*, **23**, 52-58.

Dohrenwend, B.S., & Dohrenwend, B.P. (Eds.). (1981). *Stressful life events and their contexts*. New York: Prodist.

Duda, J.L. (1981). *A cross-cultural analysis of achievement motivation in sport and the classroom*. Unpublished doctoral dissertation, University of Illinois, Urbana-Champaign.

Duda, J.L. (1985). Consider the children: Meeting participants' goals in youth sport. *Journal of Physical Education, Recreation and Dance*, **21**(8), 55-56.

Endler, N.S. (1978). The interaction model of anxiety: Some possible implications. In D.M. Landers & R.W. Christina (Eds.), *Psychology of motor behavior and sport—1977* (pp. 332-351). Champaign, IL: Human Kinetics.

Feltz, D.L., & Albrecht, R.R. (1986). Psychological implications of competitive running. In M.R. Weiss & D. Gould (Eds.), *Sport for children and youths* (pp. 225-230). Champaign, IL: Human Kinetics.

Gill, D.L., & Martens, R. (1977). The role of task type and success-failure in group competition. *International Journal of Sport Psychology*, **8**, 160-177.

Gould, D. (1982). Sport psychology in the 1980's: Status, direction and challenge in youth sport research. *Journal of Sport Psychology*, **4**, 203-218.

Gould, D., Feltz, D., Horn, T., & Weiss, M. (1982). Reasons for discontinuing involvement in competitive youth swimming. *Journal of Sport Behavior*, **5**, 155-165.

Gould, D., & Horn, T. (1984). Participation motivation in young athletes. In J.M. Silva, III & R.S. Weinberg (Eds.), *Psychological foundations of sport* (pp. 359-370). Champaign, IL: Human Kinetics.

Gould, D., Horn, T., & Spreeman, J. (1983a). Competitive anxiety in junior elite wrestlers. *Journal of Sport Psychology*, **5**, 58-71.

Gould, D., Horn, T., & Spreeman, J. (1983b). Sources of stress in junior elite wrestlers. *Journal of Sport Psychology*, **5**, 159-171.

Gould, D., Petlichkoff, L., & Weinberg, R.S. (1984). Antecedents of, temporal changes in, and relationships between CSAI-2 subcomponents. *Journal of Sport Psychology*, **6**, 289-304.

Griffin, M.R. (1972, Spring). An analysis of state and trait anxiety experienced in sports competition at different age levels. *Foil*, pp. 58-64.

Hanson, D.L. (1967). Cardiac response to participation in Little League baseball competition as determined by telemetry. *Research Quarterly*, **38**, 384-388.

Horn, T.S., & Hasbrook, C. (1986). Informational components influencing children's perception of their physical competence. In M.R. Weiss & D. Gould (Eds.), *Sport for children and youths* (pp. 81-88). Champaign, IL: Human Kinetics.

Klavora, P. (1978). An attempt to derive inverted-U curves based on the relationship between anxiety and athletic performance. In D.L. Landers & R.W. Christina (Eds.), *Psychology of motor behavior and sport—1977* (pp. 369-377). Champaign, IL: Human Kinetics.

Kozar, B., & Lord, R.H. (1988). Overuse injuries in young athletes: A "growing" problem. In F.L. Smoll, R.A. Magill, & M.J. Ash (Eds), *Children in sport* (3rd ed., pp. 119-129). Champaign, IL: Human Kinetics.

Lazarus, R.S. (1966). *Psychological stress and the coping process*. New York: McGraw-Hill.

Lowe, R., & McGrath, J.E. (1971). *Stress, arousal and performance: Some findings calling for a new theory* (Report No. AF 1161-67). Washington, DC: Air Force Office of Strategic Research.

Martens, R. (1975). *Social psychology and physical activity.* New York: Harper & Row.

Martens, R. (1977). *Sport Competition Anxiety Test.* Champaign, IL: Human Kinetics.

Martens, R. (1978). *Joy and sadness in children's sports.* Champaign, IL: Human Kinetics.

Martens, R., Burton, D., Rivkin, F., & Simon, J. (1980). Reliability and validity of the Competitive State Anxiety Inventory (CSAI). In C.H. Nadeau, W.R. Halliwell, K.M. Newell, & G.C. Roberts (Eds.), *Psychology of motor behavior and sport—1979* (pp. 1-99). Champaign, IL: Human Kinetics.

Martens, R., Burton, D., Vealey, R., Smith, D., & Bump, L. (1983). *The development of the Competitive State Anxiety Inventory—2 (CSAI—2).* Unpublished manuscript.

Martens, R., & Gill, D.L. (1976). State anxiety among successful and unsuccessful competitors who differ in competitive trait anxiety. *Research Quarterly,* **47**, 698-708.

McPherson, B., Marteniuk, R., Tihanyi, J., & Clark, W. (1980). The social system of age group swimmers: The perception of swimmers, parents and coaches. *Canadian Journal of Applied Sport Sciences,* **4**, 142-145.

Ogilvie, B. (1979). The child athlete: Psychological implications of participation in sport. *Annals of the American Academy of Political and Social Science,* **445**, 47-58.

Orlick, T., & Botterill, C. (1975). *Every kid can win.* Chicago: Nelson-Hall.

Passer, M.W. (1982a). Children in sport: Participation motives and psychological stress. *Quest,* **33**, 231-244.

Passer, M.W. (1982b). Psychological stress in youth sports. In R.A. Magill, M.J. Ash, & F.L. Smoll (Eds.), *Children in sport* (2nd ed., pp. 153-177). Champaign, IL: Human Kinetics.

Passer, M.W. (1983). Fear of failure, fear of evaluation, perceived competence, and self-esteem in competitive-trait-anxious children. *Journal of Sport Psychology,* **5**, 172-188.

Passer, M.W. (1984). Competitive trait anxiety in children and adolescents: Mediating cognitions, developmental antecedents, and consequences. In J.M. Silva, III & R.S. Weinberg (Eds.), *Psychological foundations of sport* (pp. 130-144). Champaign, IL: Human Kinetics.

Passer, M.W. (1988). Psychological issues in determining children's age-readiness for competition. In F.L. Smoll, R.A. Magill, & M.J. Ash (Eds.), *Children in sport* (3rd ed., pp. 67-77). Champaign, IL: Human Kinetics.

Passer, M.W., & Scanlan, T.K. (1980). The impact of game outcome on the postcompetition affect and performance evaluations of young athletes. In C.H. Nadeau, W.R. Halliwell, K.M. Newell, & G.C. Roberts (Eds.), *Psychology of motor behavior and sport—1979* (pp. 100-111). Champaign, IL: Human Kinetics.

Passer, M.W., & Seese, M.D. (1983). Life stress and athletic injury: Examination of positive versus negative events and three moderator variables. *Journal of Human Stress, 9*(4), 11-16.

Pierce, W.J. (1980). *Psychological perspectives of youth sport participants and nonparticipants.* Unpublished doctoral dissertation, Virginia Polytechnic Institute and State University, Blacksburg.

Roberts, G.C. (1986). The perception of stress: A potential source and its development. In M.R. Weiss & D. Gould (Eds.), *Sport for children and youths* (pp. 119-126). Champaign, IL: Human Kinetics.

Robinson, T.T., & Carron, A.V. (1982). Personal and situational factors associated with dropping out versus maintaining participation in competitive sport. *Journal of Sport Psychology, 4*, 364-378.

Sarason, I.G. (1980). Life stress, self-preoccupation and social supports. In I.G. Sarason & C.D. Spielberger (Eds.), *Stress and anxiety* (Vol. 7, pp. 73-92). Washington, DC: Hemisphere.

Sarason, I.G., & Spielberger, C.D. (Eds.). (1980). *Stress and anxiety* (Vol. 7). Washington, DC: Hemisphere.

Scanlan, T.K. (1988). Social evaluation and the competition process: A developmental perspective. In F.L. Smoll, R.A. Magill, & M.J. Ash (Eds.), *Children in sport* (3rd ed., pp. 135-148). Champaign, IL: Human Kinetics.

Scanlan, T.K., & Lewthwaite, R. (1984). Social psychological aspects of competition for male youth sport participants: I. Predictors of competitive stress. *Journal of Sport Psychology, 6*, 208-226.

Scanlan, T.K., & Lewthwaite, R. (1986). Social psychological aspects of competition for male youth sport participants: IV. Predictors of enjoyment. *Journal of Sport Psychology, 8*, 25-35.

Scanlan, T.K., Lewthwaite, R., & Jackson, B.L. (1984). Social psychological aspects of competition for male youth sport participants: II. Predictors of performance outcomes. *Journal of Sport Psychology, 6*, 422-429.

Scanlan, T.K., & Passer, M.W. (1978). Factors related to competitive stress among male youth sport participants. *Medicine and Science in Sports, 10*, 103-108.

Scanlan, T.K., & Passer, M.W. (1979). Sources of competitive stress in young female athletes. *Journal of Sport Psychology, 1*, 151-159.

Seefeldt, V., & Gould D. (1980). *Physical and psychological effects of athletic competition on children and youth.* East Lansing: Michigan State University. (ERIC Document Reproduction Service No. ED 180 997)

Shelton, D. (1983, February 20). Pressure: Athletic competition can be a vicious pressure cooker . . . and many simply boil over. *Journal-American*, pp. C1, C4.

Simon, J.A., & Martens, R. (1979). Children's anxiety in sport and non-sport evaluative activities. *Journal of Sport Psychology*, **1**, 160-169.

Skubic, E. (1955). Emotional responses of boys to Little League and Middle League competitive baseball. *Research Quarterly*, **26**, 342-352.

Skubic, E. (1956). Studies of Little League and Middle League baseball. *Research Quarterly*, **27**, 97-110.

Smith, R.E., Smoll, F.L., & Curtis, B. (1978). Coaching behaviors in Little League baseball. In F.L. Smoll & R.E. Smith (Eds.), *Psychological perspectives in youth sport* (pp. 173-201). Washington, DC: Hemisphere.

Smoll, F.L., & Smith, R.E. (1988). Reducing stress in youth sport: Theory and application. In F.L. Smoll, R.A. Magill, & M.J. Ash (Eds.), *Children in sport* (3rd ed., pp. 229-249). Champaign, IL: Human Kinetics.

Sonstroem, R.J. (1984). An overview of anxiety in sport. In J.M. Silva, III & R.S. Weinberg (Eds.), *Psychological foundations of sport* (pp. 104-117). Champaign, IL: Human Kinetics.

Spielberger, C.D. (Ed.). (1966). *Anxiety and behavior*. New York: Academic Press.

Spielberger, C.D. (1973). *Preliminary test manual for the State-Trait Anxiety Inventory for Children*. Palo Alto, CA: Consulting Psychologists.

Spielberger, C.D., Gorsuch, R.L., & Lushene, R.E. (1970). *Manual for the State-Trait Anxiety Inventory*. Palo Alto, CA: Consulting Psychologists.

State of Michigan (1978). *Joint legislative study on youth sports programs: Phase II, agency sponsored sports*. East Lansing: Author.

Wankel, L.M., & Kreisel, P.S.J. (1985). Factors underlying enjoyment of youth sports: Sport and age group comparisons. *Journal of Sport Psychology*, **7**, 51-64.

Weinberg, R.S. (1978). The effects of success and failure on the patterning of neuromuscular energy. *Journal of Motor Behavior*, **10**, 53-61.

Weiss, M.R., & Gould, D. (Eds.). (1986). *Sport for children and youths*. Champaign, IL: Human Kinetics.

CHAPTER 16

Reducing Stress in Youth Sport: Theory and Application[1]

Frank L. Smoll
Ronald E. Smith

Potential sources of stress in the lives of children are many and varied. Within the realm of athletics, a degree of stress is as much a part of the competitive process as striving for victory. Perhaps because of the commonly held belief that the sport setting is highly stressful for many children, youth sport authorities have been concerned with understanding the nature of stress, its antecedents, and its consequences. In fact, the results of a brief questionnaire administered to sport psychologists and to nonschool youth sport coaches and administrators indicated that "competitive stress placed on youth athletes" and "helping young athletes cope with competitive stress" were among the five topics rated most important for study (Gould, 1982). In view of this, it is not surprising that competitive anxiety in youth athletics has been the focus of increasing empirical attention (see Passer, this volume).

The amount of stress the child experiences is a joint function of environmental demands and the coping skills possessed by the child. Such skills are, in turn, developed by dealing successfully with challenging situations. One of the benefits of youth sport is that it provides a setting in which effective coping skills can be acquired. These personal resources can be used to deal more adaptively not only with competitive stress, but with other stressful life events as well. Moreover, the developmental period spanned by youth sport programs constitutes an ideal time for the acquisition of stress-coping skills.

In spite of the many problems associated with highly structured sport for children, our position is that the youth sport setting can foster the psychological growth of the child. However, in view of the negative consequences of stress, development of intervention strategies to minimize sources of undue stress in the athletic environment is definitely warranted, as is the development of training programs designed to help young athletes acquire more effective coping skills. We believe that the

[1]Preparation of this chapter was facilitated by grant 86-1066-86 from the William T. Grant Foundation.

sport psychologist can influence the facilitation of the stress reduction process (R.E. Smith & Smoll, 1978). Whether attention is focused on the determinants of stress or on the methods for alleviating it, the presence of a conceptual model can enhance progress at both theoretical and applied levels. The initial focus of this chapter is a conceptual model of stress that can serve to guide research. After discussing the components of the model and the relationships among its various elements, we will explore some of the model's implications for designing stress reduction intervention programs for young athletes.

A Theoretical Model of Stress

Anyone who has sat in a dentist's waiting room, taken a surprise quiz in school, or encountered a traffic jam on the way to an important appointment is familiar with stress. People typically use the word *stress* in two different but related ways. First, we use the term to refer to situations that tax the physical and/or psychological capabilities of the individual (R.S. Lazarus & Folkman, 1984). For example, running a race against a superior opponent or, for some, listening to Howard Cosell could be considered *stressors*. The focus here is on the balance between the demands of the situation and on the personal and social resources of the person to cope with these demands. Such situations are likely labeled *stressful* when their demands test or exceed the resources of a person.

The second use of the word *stress* refers to a person's cognitive, emotional, and behavioral responses to situational demands. For example, "I have a meeting with my boss, and I feel nervous and uptight about it." Clearly, these two uses of the word are not synonymous, as people may vary considerably in how stressful they find the same situation to be. After describing the stress model, our discussion of ways of reducing stress in youth sport will include approaches designed to reduce situational stress as well as ways to help individuals develop more effective coping skills.

Figure 1 contains a conceptual model of stress that takes both the situation and the individual's reactions into account. The model emphasizes relations among the situation, the individual's cognitive appraisal of various aspects of the situation, physiological arousal responses, and behavioral attempts to cope with the situation. Each of these components is, in turn, influenced by personality and motivational variables.

The Situational Component

The first component of the model, the *situation*, involves interactions between environmental demands and personal or environmental resources. Whenever a young athlete encounters a demand, resources are mobilized to meet it. When demands and resources are relatively

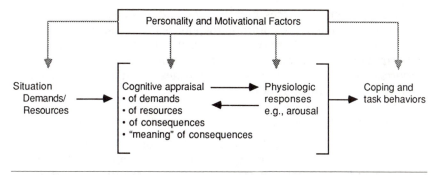

Figure 1. A conceptual model of stress showing hypothesized relationships among situational, cognitive, physiological, and behavioral components. Motivational and personality variables are assumed to affect and interact with each of the components. *Note.* From "A Component Analysis of Athletic Stress" by R.E. Smith. In *Sport for Children and Youths* (p. 108) by M.R. Weiss and D. Gould (Eds.), 1986, Champaign, IL: Human Kinetics. Copyright 1986 by Human Kinetics Publishers. Reprinted by permission.

balanced, stress is minimal. When demands slightly exceed resources, the situation is likely to be viewed as challenging. But, when a significant imbalance occurs because of increased demands or decreases in resources for meeting them, the situation is likely to cause stress.

Ordinarily we think of emotional responses as being stimulated by an *external* situation. In the youth sport setting, many external demands may be stressful, including abusive behaviors of coaches, a critical group of teammates, facing a strong opponent in an important contest, closeness of the score, and so on. Other situational demands actually have an *internal* locus of causation, resulting from personality or motivational factors. Internal demands include desired goals, personal standards of performance relating to values or commitments, or even unconscious motives or conflicts. Memories of past situations and anticipations of future consequences may interact with the current external situation to affect its psychological meaning and its effect on the young athlete.

A variety of personality and motivational variables play an important role in determining which of the complex environmental demands will be most salient or demanding. For example, a need for competence, mastery, affiliation, or power can each cause the athlete to focus on and respond to particular aspects of the sport environment. Similarly, different types of resources (e.g., physical skills, social skills, or social support within the environment) may differ in their relative importance to individual athletes. Therefore, in any analysis of situational stress, it is important to take into account the specific demands, resources, and imbalances that are of concern to the individual athlete.

Stress is usually thought to occur in "overload" situations, where demands greatly exceed resources. Conversely psychological stress can

also result when resources greatly exceed demands. Boredom, stag-
nation, and staleness are common responses to such situations. A condition of "underload" may also take a toll on a young athlete's
performance, commitment, and enjoyment. Thus, both over- and
undertaxing situations have been hypothesized to cause athletes to
burn out (R.E. Smith, 1986b).

The Cognitive Component

The second component of the stress model, *cognitive appraisal*, plays
a central role in understanding stress. People generally view their emo-
tions as triggered directly by situational demands. But, in most cases,
situations exert their effects on emotionality through the intervening
influence of thoughts. Through their own thought processes, people
create the psychological reality to which they respond. Thus, the intensity of emotional responses is a function of what people tell themselves about a situation, the situation's meaning, and their ability to
cope with the demands of the situation.

As specified in the model, the active process of cognitive appraisal
includes perceptions of several elements. People not only appraise the
demands of the situation, they also appraise the nature and adequacy
of their coping resources. This appraisal is not always accurate. For
example, a young athlete low in self-confidence may perceive a greater
discrepancy between demands and resources than is actually present.
In essence, the perception of balance and imbalance, rather than the
objective situation, determines whether or not the young athlete is
stressed. The degree of emotion experienced also plays a part. Here
again, individual difference variables, such as self-efficacy and competitive trait anxiety, can play a vital role (Passer, 1984).

In addition to mentally evaluating demands and resources, people
appraise the possible consequences of failure to meet the demands. A
situation is likely to be perceived as stressful if a perceived imbalance
between demands and resources threatens harm or the loss of desired
goals (R.S. Lazarus & Folkman, 1984). Here again, an individual's appraisal process may not be accurate. An athlete who exaggerates the
consequences of failing to successfully deal with demands may experience unnecessary stress.

The final aspect of the appraisal process is the personal meaning
attributed to the consequences. These meanings derive from personal
beliefs, one's self-concept, and conditions of self-worth. The central role
of irrational assumptions and beliefs in psychological distress are well
documented (Ellis, 1962). Clearly, athletes who believe their basic self-
worth is defined by athletic success will attribute different meaning
to athletic outcomes than will athletes whose self-worth is more
securely and realistically anchored. Unfortunately, many young athletes are victimized by irrational beliefs concerning the meaning and
importance of success and approval of others; such beliefs predispose
them to inappropriate or excessive stress reactions.

The Physiological Component

The third component of the model is comprised of *physiological responses*. Bodily responses (e.g., increased heart rate, irregular respiration) are reciprocally linked to cognitive appraisal and thus constitute another aspect of the mediational portion of the stress process. When appraisal indicates the existence of threat or danger, physiological arousal occurs as part of the mobilization of resources to deal with the situation. Arousal, in turn, provides feedback concerning intensity of the emotion being experienced. Arousal feedback thus contributes to the ongoing process of appraisal and reappraisal. For example, a young athlete who becomes aware of an increasing level of arousal may appraise the situation as more threatening than one who experiences low arousal in the same situation. This threat appraisal may, in turn, generate even more emotional arousal. Conversely, a young athlete who experiences low arousal in a potentially stressful situation is likely to appraise the situation as less threatening or as one with which he or she can cope successfully.

The Behavioral Component

The fourth component of the model consists of *output behaviors* that occur in response to the situation. These include task-oriented, social, and coping behaviors. Rather than being directly affected by the demands of the situation, instrumental behaviors, as the model emphasizes, are mediated by cognitive appraisal processes and by the nature and intensity of physiological responses that may occur. Furthermore, the adequacy or success of these coping behaviors affects the balance between demands and resources, as well as the ongoing appraisal process. Thus, each of the components of the model interacts with all the others; changes in one component can ultimately affect all the others.

Stress Reduction Strategies

The conceptual model just presented has clear implications for stress reduction in youth sport. Consideration will now be given to how intervention might be directed at each of the four components of the model.

Situational Component

The most practical and economical approach to solving stress-related problems involves utilization of measures at the situational level to dramatically alter the situation's capacity to generate stress. Reduction of situational sources of stress will be considered relative to (a) changes in certain features of the sport itself, (b) the role of coaches in creating a psychologically healthy athletic environment, and (c) the role of parents in combating competitive stress.

Modification of the Sport.   The organization and administration of a sport program can be the focus of environmental change aimed at eliminating potential sources of stress. As it is well known that children greatly vary in physical and psychological maturation, diverse programs should be offered to provide for varied levels of athletic skill and competitive intensity. With adult counseling and guidance, youngsters could then participate in selecting the level at which they will play.

Other methods of matching children to the appropriate level of competition can serve to combat stress associated with inequity of competition and risk of injury. Some youth leagues utilize various homogeneous grouping procedures that allow children to compete against others of their own ability and size. Examples of homogeneous grouping procedures include (a) keeping the age range as narrow as possible (i.e., leagues for 9- and 10-year-olds and 11- and 12-year-olds, rather than 9- to 12-year-olds), (b) using measures of height and weight in conjunction with chronological age for grouping purposes, and (c) using sport skills tests to group children (Martens & Seefeldt, 1979).

Organizational modification might also involve attempts to minimize situational demands that many youngsters find stressful. For example, to eliminate the stress-related emphasis on winning, some programs do not keep game scores, league standings, or individual performance statistics.

A more direct approach to change at the situational level involves modification of the sport itself. The purpose here is to decrease performance demands on growing children, thereby maximizing their chances of success and enjoyment. For example, Potter (1986) identified four categories in which sports are modified in the Eugene (Oregon) Sports Program: equipment, dimensions of the playing area, length of the contest, and rule changes. Examples of equipment changes include reduced ball size, lowered hoops in basketball, and lowered nets in volleyball. In addition to reducing the overall dimensions of the playing area, appropriate scaling modifications are applied to restraining lines for particular skills—such as serving in volleyball, and shooting free throws in basketball. The length of the contest for all sports is shortened until at least the middle-school grades. Finally, specific rule changes are implemented to reduce demands on players. Examples include no press defense in basketball, no fumble recovery in football (i.e., ball is dead), and no stealing in baseball and softball.

The kinds of modifications described above are highly desirable improvements. However, given that youth sport administrators and parents are often reluctant to implement change, it is important that reasonable proposals for adaptation be supported with factual information. Haywood (1986) emphasized that the rationale for a suggested modification should be based on (a) growth and developmental status of child athletes, (b) biomechanics of young athletes' skill performance, and/or (c) systematically obtained empirical evidence substantiating the benefits of the modification. For example, research has shown that the use of a smaller basketball results in better ball-handling skills and slightly better shooting for 9- to 13-year-old children (Haywood, 1978).

Coaching Roles and Relationships.   Youth coaches typically have a major controlling influence on the athletic environment. The manner in which coaches structure the athletic situation, the goal priorities they establish, and the ways in which they relate to athletes are primary determinants of the outcomes of sport participation (Martens, 1978; Seefeldt & Gould, 1980; R.E. Smith, Smoll, Hunt, Curtis, & Coppel, 1979; Smoll, Smith, Curtis, & Hunt, 1978). In their analyses of competitive stress in children, Passer (1984), Roberts (1986), and Scanlan (1986) identified coaches as having a profound influence in shaping athletes' perceptions of achievement demands and capabilities. Thus, interaction with coaches can be a major source of stress for young athletes. It follows, then, that measures designed to assist coaches in creating a less stressful and more enjoyable athletic atmosphere should ultimately have a positive impact on youth sport programs.

Clearly, stressors do not affect all people in the same way: Some people are highly susceptible; others are quite resilient. In an attempt to understand the bases for such variability in response to stress, researchers have examined a number of situational factors. Observations in a variety of settings have highlighted the importance of social attachments in facilitating adaptation and in helping people to confront stressors successfully. Sarason (1980) has defined *social support* as the existence or availability of "people on whom we can rely, people who let us know that they care about, value, and love us" (p. 84). A number of studies have shown that individuals who have high levels of social support in their lives are far more resistant to health-threatening stressors (Cohen & McKay, 1984; Dohrenwend & Dohrenwend, 1981; Heller & Swindle, 1983; Sarason & Sarason, 1985).

In sport, most social support comes from relationships with coaches and teammates. We might expect that increasing the level of social support within the athletic environment, by training coaches to relate more effectively to athletes and to develop team cohesion, would serve as a buffer against the effects of stress. We have developed an effective and economical intervention called *Coach Effectiveness Training* (CET), which provides instruction for coaches in creating a more positive interpersonal environment for athletes.

CET was developed on the basis of a large-scale research project on coaching behaviors and their effects on young athletes. In the first phase of the project, a behavioral assessment system was developed to permit direct observation and coding of coaches' behavior (R.E. Smith, Smoll, & Hunt, 1977). The *Coaching Behavior Assessment System* (CBAS) comprises 12 behavioral categories divided into two major classes: reactive (elicited) and spontaneous (emitted) behaviors. The reactive behaviors are responses to either desirable performance or effort (reinforcement, nonreinforcement), mistakes and errors (mistake-contingent encouragement, mistake-contingent technical instruction, punishment, punitive technical instruction, ignoring mistakes), or athletes' misbehaviors (keeping control). The spontaneous behaviors include general technical instruction, general encouragement, organization, and general communication. The CBAS was developed on the basis of extensive naturalistic observation of coaches and provides a means of directly assessing behaviors relating to social support, such as reinforcement, encouragement, and technical instruction, as well as nonsupportive behaviors, such as punishment. Subsequent use of the system has proven very satisfactory in observing and coding coaching behaviors in a variety of sports. The system is sufficiently comprehensive to incorporate the vast majority of coaching behaviors, individual differences in behavior patterns can be discerned, and interrater reliabilities in the mid-.90s can be obtained in field settings (Horn, 1985; Rejeski, Darracott, & Hutslar, 1979; R.E. Smith, Zane, Smoll, & Coppel, 1983).

Following development of the CBAS, a study was conducted to establish relationships between coaches' behaviors and the attitudes and reactions that they ultimately evoke in their athletes. Fifty-one male Little League baseball coaches were observed during a total of 202 complete games. A behavioral profile was established for each coach based on an average of 1,122 of his behaviors. After the season, 542 players were interviewed and administered attitude and personality measures in their homes. Among the most important scales were measures of the degree of enjoyment experienced by players during the season, their liking for the coach and their teammates, their recall and perception of the coach's behaviors, and their levels of general and athletic self-esteem. These outcome measures were related to observed and player-perceived coaching behaviors, and the obtained relationships were used as the foundation for a set of behavioral guidelines that are the core of CET (R.E. Smith, Smoll, & Curtis, 1979).

The series of behavioral guidelines (i.e., coaching's dos and don'ts) presented in CET are based on a positive-versus-negative approach to influencing behavior (Smoll & Smith, 1979). The positive approach uses reinforcement and encouragement to strengthen desirable behaviors and to motivate athletes to perform these behaviors. The negative approach uses various forms of punishment to eliminate undesirable behaviors. The guidelines recommend the liberal use of positive reinforcement for effort as well as performance, the giving of encouragement after mistakes, and the giving of technical instruction in an encouraging and supportive fashion. For example, when technical instruction is given after a mistake, the guidelines recommend that the coach first attempt to compliment the athlete for something done correctly during the performance sequence. Then the corrective instruction should be given, with the coach focusing on the positive things that will happen in the future if the instruction is followed, rather than on the negative consequences of the mistake. The use of punitive behaviors and criticism is discouraged. Positive reinforcement is also recommended as a means of strengthening mutual encouragement and social support among teammates and of establishing compliance with team rules. The ultimate goal of the guidelines is to increase the desire of young athletes to learn and give maximum effort, while reducing the stress engendered by fear of failure. Use of the positive approach tends to enhance positive coach-athlete and athlete-athlete relationships.

Another aspect of CET designed to reduce stress is the conception of success or *winning* as giving maximum effort. To assist coaches in placing winning in a *healthy* perspective, a four-part philosophy is taught in CET (Smoll & Smith, 1981):

1. *Winning isn't everything, nor is it the only thing.* Young athletes cannot possibly learn from winning and losing if they think that the only objective is to beat their opponents. Although winning is an important goal, it is *not* the most important objective.

2. *Failure is not the same thing as losing.* It is important that athletes do not view losing as a sign of failure or as a threat to their personal value.

3. *Success is not synonymous with winning.* Neither success nor failure need depend on the outcome of a contest or a win-loss record. Winning and losing pertain to the outcome of a contest, whereas success and failure do not.

4. *Children should be taught that success is found in striving for victory (i.e., success is related to effort).* Youngsters should be taught that they are never "losers" if they give maximum effort. A major source of athletic stress is fear of failure; knowing that making a mistake or losing a game while giving maximum effort is acceptable to the coach should remove an important source of pressure from the child.

In what ways does this philosophy combat athletic stress? With respect to Point 1, given that sport is heavily achievement-oriented, seeking victory is encouraged. However, this philosophy attempts to reduce the ultimate importance of winning relative to other prized participation motives (e.g., skill and fitness development, affiliation with teammates and friends). In particular, *fun* is highlighted as the paramount objective. Research indicates that boys and girls who report having less fun during a sporting event experience greater postcompetition stress than children who had more fun. It is important to note that the inverse relationship between fun and stress was independent of victory or defeat. Therefore, it is not simply the case that winners have more fun than losers (Scanlan & Lewthwaite, 1984; Scanlan & Passer, 1978, 1979).

Points 2 and 3 of the philosophy of winning promote separation of the athlete's feelings of self-worth from the game outcome. This orientation is supported by Gallwey and Kriegel (1977), who emphasized that "the key to overcoming fear of failure is breaking one's attachment to results" (p. 85).

Finally, in Point 4, young athletes are encouraged to attribute their failures to an unstable, controllable factor (i.e., lack of effort) instead of to lack of ability. Dweck's (1975) attributional retraining program involved nothing more complicated than explicitly attributing failure to a lack of effort and encouraging subjects to try harder. Children who received direct instruction in how to interpret the causes of their failures showed improved performance (in a math problem-solving task) and were better able to cope with failure. Within the realm of sport, one might expect this approach to lessen the negative effects of failure, thereby reducing stress for athletes.

CET also includes instructions for coaches on how to organize and conduct a sport orientation meeting with parents (Smoll, 1986). Some purposes of the meeting are to inform parents about their responsibilities for contributing to the success of the sport program and to guide them toward working cooperatively and productively with the coach. Establishing coach-parent rapport might serve to eliminate conflicts that constitute another potential source of environmental stress for young athletes.

In the second phase of our research project, we attempted to modify coaching behaviors and evaluated the success of the CET intervention program. Thirty-one Little League baseball coaches were randomly assigned to either an experimental or a no-treatment control group. The techniques employed in the training program were designed to make coaches more aware of their behaviors, to create appropriate expectancies concerning the likely consequences of various coaching behaviors, and to develop or enhance their ability to perform desirable behaviors effectively. The program included verbal and written presentation of specific behavioral guidelines, the use of modeling by the trainers to demonstrate how to carry out the guidelines, training in self-monitoring to increase awareness of their behavior patterns, and guidelines to obtain feedback on their behavior and its consequences (Smoll & Smith, 1980).

The effects of the training program were assessed by essentially repeating the procedures of the first phase. Coaches in the experimental and control groups were observed during four randomly chosen games in the course of the season by trained observers who were blind to the experimental procedure. Behavioral profiles were generated for each coach. At the end of the season, 325 players who had played for the coaches were interviewed and tested to obtain player outcome measures.

The results of the experiment indicated that the training program had strong effects on the behavior patterns of the coaches and on the experiences of the athletes. On both observed behaviors and player perceptions of coaching behaviors the trained coaches differed from the controls in a manner consistent with the behavioral guidelines. The trained coaches gave more reinforcement in response to good effort and performance and responded to mistakes with more encouragement and technical instruction and with fewer punitive responses. As the two groups of coaches had not differed on these behavioral categories the previous season, the results suggest that the training program had salutary effects on their coaching conduct.

These behavioral differences were reflected in youngsters' responses to their athletic experience as well. Despite the fact that the mean win-loss records of the two groups of coaches did not differ, trained coaches were better liked by players and were rated as better teachers. Also, athletes on the trained coaches' teams liked one another more, indicating that the coaches' efforts to increase team cohesion and social support had been successful. Overall, athletes who played for the trained coaches reported more enjoyment of the activity. Finally, youngsters who played for the trained coaches exhibited a significant increase in self-esteem over a 1-year period, whereas those who played for untrained coaches exhibited no change in self-esteem (R.E. Smith, Smoll, & Curtis, 1979). It should be noted that self-esteem is among several personality variables that have been shown to influence the relationship between stressful life events and their effects. Specifically, stressful events appear to have more deleterious effects on those who are low in self-esteem, whereas high self-esteem individuals are more capable of weathering stressful events (Cooley & Keesey, 1981; Rutter, 1983). Considering the evidence, it appears that coaches can be trained to relate more effectively to young athletes, to create a more supportive athletic environment, and to enhance athletes' feelings of self-worth—all of which ultimately serve to decrease athletic stress.

Parent Roles and Responsibilities. Although coaches have the most direct contact with children within the sport environment, parents also play an important role. The literature on sport socialization confirms that parents are instrumental in determining children's sport involvement (see Lewko & Greendorfer, this volume; McPherson & Brown, this volume). Moreover, the negative impact that parents can have on young athletes is all too obvious. Some parents assume an extremely active role in their children's sport involvement, and, in some instances, their influence constitutes an important source of stress (see Passer, 1984; Scanlan, 1986).

Because of the harmful consequences caused by overzealous and unknowing adults, some youth leagues have banned parents from attending games in order to reduce the stress placed on young athletes and officials (Martens, 1978). We view this as an unfortunate example of situational change, as parents can strongly and positively affect the quality of their children's sport experience. More desirable and constructive efforts are reflected in an increasing number of publications concerning parent responsibilities toward youth sport participation (e.g., Ferrell, Glashagel, & Johnson, 1978; Martens, 1980; Thomas, 1977, Vandeweghe, 1979). With specific reference to stress, *Kidsports* (N.J. Smith, Smith, & Smoll, 1983) attempts to guide and educate parents about the nature and consequences of athletic stress. This volume provides information on how parents might teach their children how to use stress management relaxation skills and how to prevent the development of fear of failure.

In view of the growing concern for providing volunteer coaches with youth sport training, it is surprising that there has been no attempt to systematically develop and assess the effects of a sport-oriented educational program for parents. Many of the principles and guidelines contained in CET would assist parents in facilitating their children's personal growth through athletics. For example, the conception of success or winning as giving maximum effort is as relevant for parents as it is for coaches. Indeed, the notion may be more important for parents to grasp because they can apply it to areas of the child's life outside athletics. The basic principles contained in the positive approach to social influence also apply to parents. By encouraging youngsters to do as well as they are currently able, by reinforcing effort as well as outcome, and by avoiding the use of criticism and punishment, parents might help foster the development of positive motivation to achieve and help prevent fear of failure.

Cognitive and Physiological Components

In youth sport, there is an inevitable "athletic triangle" consisting of coach, parent, and child athlete. We have discussed some guidelines and procedures that are useful in working with coaches and parents to reduce situational stress and to enhance the athletic environment for children. The third point in the athletic triangle that may be the focus of intervention is the child athlete. Given that the amount of stress experienced is a joint function of the intensity of environmental stressors and the way the individual appraises and copes with them, it follows that actively assisting youngsters in developing coping skills can increase their ability to deal effectively with athletic stress. Reduction of stress at the cognitive and physiological levels is the focus of stress management programs that seek to teach specific physiological and cognitive coping skills.

Training programs in stress management behaviors have promising applications with child athletes for several reasons. First, it is highly desirable to acquire adaptive coping responses prior to the turbulent years of adolescence. Second, unlike many adults, children have not generally developed maladaptive coping strategies that are deeply ingrained and therefore difficult to change. Third, the athletic arena requires child athletes to cope with stress-evoking situations on a regular and fairly predictable basis, thereby providing many opportunities to practice and strengthen coping skills in situations that are unlikely to exceed the children's adaptive ability. Finally, developing a range of highly generalizable coping skills should enhance children's ability to handle stress both in athletics and in other aspects of their lives.

Stress Management Training (SMT), developed by R.E. Smith (1980), consists of a number of clinical treatment techniques combined into an educational program for self-control of emotion. SMT was originally developed for individual and group psychotherapy clinical populations. The program components have been adapted and combined to form a training package that has been used successfully with a variety of populations, including preadolescent, college, and professional athletes (R.E. Smith, 1984), problem drinkers (Rohsenow, Smith, & Johnson, 1985), and medical students (Holtsworth-Munroe, Munroe, & Smith, 1985).

When presented to athletes, the SMT program is labeled *mental toughness training*, the latter being defined as the ability to control emotional responses that might interfere with performance and to focus attention on the task at hand. Ordinarily, the training involves six 1-hour group training sessions held twice a week, a series of specific homework assignments geared to self-monitoring, and the development and rehearsal of coping skills. The steps through which SMT proceeds are presented in Table 1.

The training program provides for the learning of an *integrated coping-response* having physiological-somatic and cognitive components and for the rehearsal of these stress-reducing skills under conditions of high affective arousal. Note that the goal of SMT is not to eliminate emotional arousal. Some degree of arousal enhances athletic

Table 1   Steps Through Which the Cognitive-Affective Stress Management Training Program Proceeds

Step	Action
1	Orientation and relaxation training. The nature of emotion and stress is discussed as is the nature of coping with stress. Training is begun in deep muscular relaxation, which serves as a physical coping response.
2	Continuation of relaxation training and discussion of the role of mental processes in coping with stress.
3	Practice in the use of relaxation to control emotional responses induced during the session through imagining of stressful situations. Development of mental coping responses.
4	Practice in using relaxation and stress-reducing mental statements to control emotional reactions induced through imagination.
5	Continued practice in use of coping mechanisms with emphasis on development of the end product of the program: the integrated coping response.
6	Training in the use of a meditation technique having stress-reducing properties.

performance. Rather, the goal of the training is to give young athletes greater control over emotional responses, enabling them to reduce or prevent high and aversive levels of arousal that interfere with performance and enjoyment. For the purpose of presenting a descriptive overview of the program, SMT can be divided into three major phases: (a) pretraining assessment and conceptualization, (b) skill acquisition, and (c) skill rehearsal.

Pretraining Assessment and Conceptualization Phase.   When SMT is administered to child athletes, the initial phase is devoted to assessing the nature of stress responses, the circumstances under which stress occurs, and the effects of stress on performance and other behaviors. The children are introduced to a simplified version of our conceptual model of stress to help them understand their problematic stress responses and are provided with a rationale for the training program. As Meichenbaum (1977) has emphasized, the initial conceptualization of the problem is of crucial importance in obtaining commitment to a training program. It is suggested that the difference between high- and low-stress athletes is that the latter have been fortunate in having previous life experiences that enable them to learn the kinds of coping skills to be taught in the program.

During the conceptualization phase and throughout training, it is stressed that SMT is not psychotherapy, but an educational program. A second point emphasized is that SMT is a program in *self-control*, and coping abilities that result from the program are a function of how much effort the individual devotes to their acquisition.

Skill-Acquisition Phase.   The goal of this phase is the development of an integrated coping response having relaxation and cognitive elements. This phase involves (a) the learning of voluntary muscle relaxation skills, and (b) an analysis of thought processes and the replacement of stress-eliciting ideas and self-statements with specific cognitions designed to reduce stress.

A variant of progressive muscle relaxation (Jacobson, 1938) and deep breathing are taught as methods of lowering physiological arousal. The written training exercises are presented elsewhere (N.J. Smith et al., 1983, pp. 144-148). As training proceeds, the children are taught to breathe slowly and deeply and to emit the mental command *relax* while they exhale and voluntarily relax their muscles. The mental command is repeatedly paired with the relaxation that occurs with exhalation; with time, the command becomes a cue for inducing relaxation, as well as an important component of the integrated coping response that will be learned. Because it is incompatible with physiological arousal, the relaxation response, once mastered, is a highly effective means of reducing or preventing the stress responses.

Training in cognitive coping skills is carried out concurrently with relaxation training. With the aid of the trainer, two related procedures are used. In cognitive restructuring (Goldfried & Davison, 1976;

A. Lazarus, 1972), the child is assisted in identifying and altering irrational beliefs that cause the competitive situation to be appraised as threatening. Dysfunctional stress-producing ideas (e.g., "It would be awful if I failed or if someone disapproved of me.") are rationally analyzed, challenged, and replaced with self-statements that are both rationally sound and likely to reduce or prevent a stress response (e.g., "All I can do is give 100%. No one can do more."). The same philosophy of winning (giving maximum effort) stressed in working with coaches and parents is emphasized in helping children develop a way of appraising athletic achievement less likely to generate stress than the belief that not winning is the same as failing.

In self-instructional training (Meichenbaum, 1977), the focus is on helping children develop and use specific task-relevant self-commands that can be employed in relevant situations (e.g., "Don't get shook up. Just think about what you have to do."). For many children who are not psychologically minded enough to profit from extensive cognitive restructuring, self-instructional training proves to be far more helpful. But in most instances, both approaches are used in the development of cognitive coping skills.

Eventually, the physiological and cognitive coping responses are combined into an integrated coping response that ties both into the breathing cycle. As children inhale, they emit an antistress self-statement. At the peak of inhalation, they mentally say the word *so*; then, as they slowly exhale, they mentally instruct themselves to *relax* and deepen muscular relaxation. Thus, both classes of coping responses are integrated into the breathing cycle.

Skill-Rehearsal Phase.   Stress-coping skills are no different than any other kind of skill. In order to be most effective, they must be rehearsed and practiced under conditions that approximate the real-life situations in which they will eventually be employed. A skill-rehearsal phase is therefore an integral part of the stress management program.

In SMT, a variant of a psychotherapeutic procedure known as *induced affect* is used. Children are asked to imagine as vividly as possible stressful athletic situations. They are then asked to focus on the feeling that the imagined situation elicits. The trainer suggests that when focused upon, the feeling becomes increasingly stronger. When a heightened state of arousal is produced, the child is asked to "turn it off" with the relaxation-coping skill. In a later rehearsal, antistress self-statements alone are used. Finally, the integrated coping response is used.

After the skill rehearsal phase is completed, the SMT program ends with training in Benson's (1976) meditation procedure. The meditation technique cannot ordinarily be used in stressful athletic situations, but it is a general relaxation and tension-reduction technique that can be used in situations that do not require the athlete to perform. Many athletes find it useful in reducing pre-event stress.

Behavioral Component

At the behavioral level, it is intuitively obvious, as well as theoretically sound (Roberts, 1986), that increasing the young athlete's physical prowess can make athletic demands easier to cope with. It follows that training to improve sport skills should be one way to reduce competitive stress, as youngsters' anxiety reactions are derived in part from perceived deficits in ability. Specifically, feelings of insecurity and heightened anxiety might arise because of an athlete's perceived lack of skill to cope with a situation. Support for this assumption is provided by research indicating that all-star athletes had significantly lower competitive trait anxiety scores than playing substitutes (T. Smith, 1983). Also, Gould, Horn, and Spreeman (1983) reported that wrestlers with low competitive trait anxiety (CTA) rated themselves higher in ability than did high-CTA wrestlers. On the other hand, other investigators have reported that self-perceived and actual ability of high-CTA children is just as great as that of low-CTA youngsters (Magill & Ash, 1979; Passer, 1983; Passer & Scanlan, 1980). Thus, research is equivocal as to whether high-CTA youngsters experience competitive stress because of lack of athletic skill.

For some youngsters, increasing their level of skill may serve to reduce the perceived imbalance between athletic demands and resources; for others, skill improvement may not be sufficient to reduce anxiety. For the latter, assistance in changing excessively high performance standards or distorted fears of the consequences of possible failure may be required. Well-informed and sensitive coaches and parents can play a major role in helping the young athlete develop healthy attitudes and values concerning sport participation—which can help enhance the child's adjustment in other areas of life as well.

Summary

This chapter has presented a theoretical framework for understanding the stress process. The conceptual model of stress specifies relationships among situational, cognitive, physiological, and behavioral factors. Each of these basic components of the model is assumed to be influenced by personality and motivational variables. At the situational level, stress involves the balance/imbalance between situational demands and the resources available to deal with them. However, these situational factors affect the person primarily through the intervening influence of cognitive processes. Among the most important of these processes are appraisal of (a) the situational demands, (b) available personal and social resources, (c) the possible consequences of failure to meet the demands, and (d) the perceived meaning of the consequences. A reciprocal relationship exists between cognitive and physiological processes; the nature of the appraisals influences the level of physiological arousal that is likely to occur, and arousal, in turn, influences the ongoing appraisal process through physiological feedback mechanisms. Finally, the behavioral component of the model includes the person's learned behavior tendencies, task-relevant skills, and social skills. Personality and motivational individual difference variables are important, as they influence the kinds of situations to which people expose themselves, how they appraise themselves and the situations, how they react physiologically, and how they customarily respond at the behavioral level.

The model not only provides a conceptual framework for guiding stress research, but also suggests foci for intervention strategies designed to reduce stress in youth sport. In this chapter, consideration has been given to intervention directed at each of the model's components. Specifically, measures may be instituted that decrease situational demands associated with the nature of the sport, coaching roles and relationships, and parental roles and responsibilities. At the levels of cognitive appraisal and physiological arousal, intervention attempts involve implementation of stress management programs that are directed at distortions in the cognitive appraisal process and at helping athletes acquire greater control over the physiological arousal response through training in self-control relaxation techniques. Stress reduction at the behavioral level has been explored with respect to increasing young athletes' level of physical skill. It is our hope that in addition to developing and applying intervention strategies based on sound theory and research results, youth sport researchers and practitioners will work cooperatively to assess the short- and long-term effects of such efforts.

References

Benson, H. (1976). *The relaxation response.* New York: Avon.

Cohen, S., & McKay, G. (1984). Interpersonal relationships as buffers of the impact of psychological stress on health. In A. Baum, J.E. Singer, & S.E. Taylor (Eds.), *Handbook of psychology and health* (Vol. 4, pp. 253-268). Hillsdale, NJ: Erlbaum.

Cooley, E.J., & Keesey, J.C. (1981). Moderator variables in life stress and illness relationship. *Journal of Human Stress,* **7**, 35-40.

Dohrenwend, B.S., & Dohrenwend, B.P. (1981). Life stress and illness: Formulation of the issues. In B.S. Dohrenwend & B.P. Dohrenwend (Eds.), *Stressful life events and their contexts* (pp. 1-27). New York: Prodist.

Dweck, C.S. (1975). The role of expectations and attributions in the alleviation of learned helplessness. *Journal of Personality and Social Psychology,* **31**, 674-685.

Ellis, A. (1962). *Reason and emotion in psychotherapy.* New York: Lyle Stuart.

246 Smoll and Smith

Ferrell, J., Glashagel, J., & Johnson, M. (1978). *A family approach to youth sports*. La Grange, IL: Youth Sports Press.

Gallwey, W.R., & Kriegel, R. (1977, November). Fear of skiing. *Psychology Today*, pp. 78-85.

Goldfried, M.R., & Davison, G. (1976). *Clinical behavior therapy*. New York: Holt, Rinehart, & Winston.

Gould, D. (1982). Sport psychology in the 1980s: Status, direction, and challenge in youth sports research. *Journal of Sport Psychology*, **4**, 203-218.

Gould, D., Horn, T., & Spreeman, J. (1983). Competitive anxiety in junior elite wrestlers. *Journal of Sport Psychology*, **5**, 58-71.

Haywood, K.M. (1978). *Children's basketball performance with regulation and junior-sized basketballs*. St. Louis: University of Missouri-St. Louis. (ERIC Document Reproduction Service No. ED 164 452)

Haywood, K.M. (1986). Modification in youth sport: A rationale and some examples in youth basketball. In M.R. Weiss & D. Gould (Eds.), *Sport for children and youths* (pp. 179-185). Champaign, IL: Human Kinetics.

Heller, K., & Swindle, R.W. (1983). Social networks, perceived social support, and coping with stress. In R.D. Felner, L.A. Jason, J.N. Moritsugu, & S.S. Farber (Eds.), *Preventive psychology: Theory, research, and practice* (pp. 87-103). Elmsford, NY: Pergamon.

Holtzworth-Munroe, A., Munroe, M., & Smith, R.E. (1985). Effects of a stress-management training program on first- and second-year medical students. *Journal of Medical Education*, **60**, 417-419.

Horn, T.S. (1985). Coaches' feedback and changes in children's perceptions of their physical competence. *Journal of Educational Psychology*, **77**, 174-186.

Jacobson, E. (1938). *Progressive relaxation*. Chicago: University of Chicago Press.

Lazarus, A. (1972). *Behavior therapy and beyond*. New York: McGraw-Hill.

Lazarus, R.S., & Folkman, S. (1984). *Stress, appraisal, and coping*. New York: Springer.

Lewko, J.H., & Greendorfer, S.L. (1988). Family influences in sport socialization of children and adolescents. In F.L. Smoll, R.A. Magill, & M.J. Ash (Eds.), *Children in sport* (3rd ed., pp. 287-300). Champaign, IL: Human Kinetics.

Magill, R.A., & Ash, M.J. (1979). Academic, psycho-social, and motor characteristics of participants and nonparticipants in children's sport. *Research Quarterly*, **50**, 230-240.

Martens, R. (1978). *Joy and sadness in children's sports.* Champaign, IL: Human Kinetics.

Martens, R. (1980). *Parent guide to kids wrestling.* Champaign, IL: Human Kinetics.

Martens, R., & Seefeldt, V. (1979). *Guidelines for children's sports.* Washington, DC: American Alliance for Health, Physical Education, Recreation and Dance.

McPherson, B.D., & Brown, B.A. (1988). The structure, processes, and consequences of sport for children. In F.L. Smoll, R.A. Magill, & M.J. Ash (Eds.), *Children in sport* (3rd ed., pp. 265-286). Champaign, IL: Human Kinetics.

Meichenbaum, D. (1977). *Cognitive-behavior modification.* New York: Plenum.

Passer, M.W. (1983). Fear of failure, fear of evaluation, perceived competence, and self-esteem in competitive-trait-anxious children. *Journal of Sport Psychology, 5,* 172-188.

Passer, M.W. (1984). Competitive trait anxiety in children and adolescents: Mediating cognitions, developmental antecedents and consequences. In J.M. Silva, III & R.S. Weinberg (Eds.), *Psychological foundations of sport* (pp. 130-144). Champaign, IL: Human Kinetics.

Passer, M.W. (1988). Determinants and consequences of children's competitive stress. In F.L. Smoll, R.A. Magill, & M.J. Ash (Eds.), *Children in sport* (3rd ed., pp. 203-227). Champaign, IL: Human Kinetics.

Passer, M.W., & Scanlan, T.K. (1980, May). *A sociometric analysis of popularity and leadership status among players on youth soccer teams.* Paper presented at the meeting of the North American Society for the Psychology of Sport and Physical Activity, Boulder, CO.

Potter, M. (1986). Game modifications for youth sport: A practitioner's view. In M.R. Weiss & D. Gould (Eds.), *Sport for children and youths* (pp. 205-208). Champaign, IL: Human Kinetics.

Rejeski, W., Darracott, C., & Hutslar, S. (1979). Pygmalion in youth sports: A field study. *Journal of Sport Psychology, 1,* 311-319.

Roberts, G.C. (1986). The perception of stress: A potential source and its development. In M.R. Weiss & D. Gould (Eds.), *Sport for children and youths* (pp. 119-126). Champaign, IL: Human Kinetics.

Rohsenow, D.J., Smith, R.E., & Johnson, S. (1985). Stress management training as a prevention program for heavy social drinkers: Cognitions, affect, drinking, and individual differences. *Addictive Behaviors, 10,* 45-54.

Rutter, M. (1983). Stress, coping, and development. In N. Garmezy & M. Rutter (Eds.), *Stress, coping, and development in children* (pp. 1-41). New York: McGraw-Hill.

Sarason, I.G. (1980). Life stress, self-preoccupation, and social supports. In I.G. Sarason & C.D. Spielberger (Eds.), *Stress and anxiety* (Vol. 7, pp. 73-92). Washington, DC: Hemisphere.

Sarason, I.G., & Sarason, B.R. (Eds.). (1985). *Social support: Theory, research and applications*. Boston: Nijhoff.

Scanlan, T.K. (1986). Competitive stress in children. In M.R. Weiss & D. Gould (Eds.), *Sport for children and youths* (pp. 113-118). Champaign, IL: Human Kinetics.

Scanlan, T.K. & Lewthwaite, R. (1984). Social psychological aspects of competition for male youth sport participants: I. Predictors of competitive stress. *Journal of Sport Psychology*, **6**, 208-226.

Scanlan, T.K., & Passer, M.W. (1978). Factors related to competitive stress among male youth sports participants. *Medicine and Science in Sports*, **10**, 103-108.

Scanlan, T.K., & Passer, M.W. (1979). Sources of competitive stress in young female athletes. *Journal of Sport Psychology*, **1**, 151-159.

Seefeldt, V., & Gould, D. (1980). *Physical and psychological effects of athletic competition on children and youth* (Report No. SP 015398). Washington, DC: ERIC Clearinghouse on Teacher Education.

Smith, N.J., Smith, R.E., & Smoll, F.L. (1983). Athletic stress: Developing coping skills through sport. In *Kidsports: A survival guide for parents* (pp. 132-148). Reading, MA: Addison-Wesley.

Smith, R.E. (1980). A cognitive-affective approach to stress management training for athletes. In C.H. Nadeau, W.R. Halliwell, K.M. Newell, & G.C. Roberts (Eds.), *Psychology of motor behavior and sport—1979* (pp. 54-72). Champaign, IL: Human Kinetics.

Smith, R.E. (1984). Theoretical and treatment approaches to anxiety reduction. In J.M. Silva, III & R.S. Weinberg (Eds.), *Psychological foundations of sport* (pp. 157-170). Champaign, IL: Human Kinetics.

Smith, R.E. (1986a). A component analysis of athletic stress. In M.R. Weiss & D. Gould (Eds.), *Sport for children and youths* (pp. 107-111). Champaign, IL: Human Kinetics.

Smith, R.E. (1986b). Toward a cognitive-affective model of athletic burnout. *Journal of Sport Psychology*, **8**, 36-50.

Smith, R.E., & Smoll, F.L. (1978). Sport and the child: Conceptual and research perspectives. In F.L. Smoll & R.E. Smith (Eds.), *Psychological perspectives in youth sports* (pp. 3-13). Washington, DC: Hemisphere.

Smith, R.E., Smoll, F.L., & Curtis, B. (1979). Coach effectiveness training: A cognitive-behavioral approach to enhancing relationship skills in youth sport coaches. *Journal of Sport Psychology*, **1**, 59-75.

Smith, R.E., Smoll, F.L., & Hunt, E. (1977). A system for the behavioral assessment of athletic coaches. *Research Quarterly*, **48**, 401-407.

Smith, R.E., Smoll, F.L., Hunt, E., Curtis, B., & Coppel, D.B. (1979). Psychology and the bad news bears. In G.C. Roberts & K.M. Newell (Eds.), *Psychology of motor behavior and sport—1978* (pp. 109-130). Champaign, IL: Human Kinetics.

Smith, R.E., Zane, N.W.S., Smoll, F.L., & Coppel, D. (1983). Behavioral assessment in youth sports: Coaching behaviors and children's attitudes. *Medicine and Science in Sports and Exercise*, **15**, 208-214.

Smith, T. (1983). Competitive trait anxiety in youth sport: Differences according to age, sex, race, and playing status. *Perceptual and Motor Skills*, **57**, 1235-1238.

Smoll, F.L. (1986). Coach-parent relationships: Enhancing the quality of the athlete's sport experience. In J.M. Williams (Ed.), *Applied sport psychology: Personal growth to peak performance* (pp. 47-58). Palo Alto, CA: Mayfield.

Smoll, F.L., & Smith, R.E. (1979). *Improving relationship skills in youth sport coaches*. East Lansing: Michigan Institute for the Study of Youth Sports.

Smoll, F.L., & Smith, R.E. (1980). Psychologically-oriented coach training programs: Design, implementation, and assessment. In C.H. Nadeau, W.R. Halliwell, K.M. Newell, & G.C. Roberts (Eds.), *Psychology of motor behavior and sport—1979* (pp. 112-129). Champaign, IL: Human Kinetics.

Smoll, F.L., & Smith, R.E. (1981). Developing a healthy philosophy of winning in youth sports. In V. Seefeldt, F.L. Smoll, R.E. Smith, & D. Gould (Eds.), *A winning philosophy for youth sports programs* (pp. 17-24). East Lansing: Michigan Institute for the Study of Youth Sports.

Smoll, F.L., Smith, R.E., Curtis, B., & Hunt, E. (1978). Toward a mediational model of coach-player relationships. *Research Quarterly*, **49**, 528-541.

Thomas, J.R. (Ed.). (1977). *Youth sports guide for coaches and parents*. Washington, DC: American Alliance for Health, Physical Education and Recreation.

Vandeweghe, E. (1979). *Growing with sport: A parents' guide to the child athlete*. Englewood Cliffs, NJ: Prentice-Hall.

CHAPTER 17

Children's Sport and the Development of Social Behaviors

Ana M. Estrada
Donna M. Gelfand
Donald P. Hartmann

With as many as 20 million children now involved in organized sport in the United States (Martens, this volume), the influence of sport on children has become an important issue. The rapid expansion of youth programs in the recent past has stimulated increasing recognition that the competitive sport environment may have a major impact on development (Scanlan, this volume). Sport psychologists (e.g., May, 1986) have recently emphasized the need to understand the complex social interactions inherent in children's athletic competition. Unfortunately, the few studies addressing the psychosocial nature of children's development through sport have lacked an integrative theoretical base (Weiss & Bredemeier, 1983). Thus, it is a scattered literature we report here.

This chapter focuses on the development of children's sport-related social behaviors, and employs Bandura's cognitive social learning model (Bandura, 1977, 1982, 1986) as a conceptual approach. *Cognitive social learning theory* describes how behavioral repertoires derive from imitation of and reinforcement by significant role models. The environment of competitive sport represents one context in which social learning takes place. For example, the social interactions inherent in team sport provide opportunities for appropriate competition, learning the social skills of cooperation, and experiencing camaraderie (Feltz, 1986). Other researchers have stressed the sometimes adverse effects of aggressive responses learned from participation in certain sports (Heyman, 1986). Unfortunately, because of the widespread portrayal and acceptance of violence in sport, many athletes may come to feel that blatantly aggressive acts will not only be tolerated, but may be viewed favorably by their coach, teammates, and spectators. As a result, young athletes may perpetuate, and even escalate, the present climate of violence found in sport-related activities. Thus, participation in sport can affect children positively or negatively, depending on the social learning experiences they undergo. Social learning principles can be applied in sport *context* to optimize the results of children's participation. Our recommendations for children's sport focus on the potential contribution of parents, coaches, and peers in promoting children's social development.

Socialization Factors

Bandura's theory outlines the influence of two powerful learning mechanisms: imitation (observational learning) and reinforcement. Bandura (1986) argues that observation or vicarious experience can produce the same learning as direct experience. A major function of modeling is to transmit information to observers on how responses can be combined into new patterns. From observing others one forms an idea of how behaviors are performed, and on later occasions this coded information serves as a guide for action. This response information can be conveyed by physical demonstration, pictorial representation, or verbal description. A great deal of children's social behavior is acquired by the imitation of such models as parents, other significant adults (e.g., coaches), peers, and the media. We later discuss their impact upon children's social behavior.

Social behaviors are shaped not only by observation but also by experiencing rewarding and punishing events. According to Bandura, human behavior is susceptible to external reinforcement from others and the environment, and to self-administered reinforcement as well. Regardless of its form, reinforcement serves informational and motivational functions, informing people that their behavior is correct and stimulating them to continue to behave in the same manner in order to obtain further reinforcement. For example, if a child is reinforced by peers for aggressive behavior, he or she learns that aggression works and will likely act aggressively whenever it serves his or her needs. In contrast, team members who receive direction and praise from their coach for cooperative, rule-governed behavior can be expected to act in a generally well-behaved manner. Various socializing agents in addition to peers and coaches contribute to the acquisition of aggressive behavior patterns. Aggressive behavior is shaped by reinforcement from and imitation of family members and sources in the community (e.g., approving TV commentators). Let's consider the actions and effects of each of these sources.

Family and Peer Effects

Many prosocial and aggressive behaviors develop at an early age. The family initiates the socialization process for children, as parents are intimately and continuously involved with child management and typically provide the child with his or her first exposure to rules and role requirements. Psychologists increasingly recognize the reciprocal influences that the child, parents, and siblings exert on each other during interaction. Patterson (1982) views the family as a system of interacting members who develop characteristic patterns of behavior in the process of learning to respond to one another. He and his colleagues have identified a particular *coercive pattern* that serves to elicit, maintain, and even increase aggression in all family members. Basically, in coercion, an aversive social interchange develops, continues, and escalates in intensity until one person gives in. At this point, the aggressor withdraws, thereby breaking the cycle of aversive interchanges. Consequently, the person who forces another member of the family to capitulate has been reinforced for highly aggressive behavior by successfully terminating the aversive interaction. Through this coercive interaction, children can learn quickly to become initiators as well as victims of aggression. Additionally, both parents and children learn to use highly punitive strategies to suppress another's high-intensity aggressive behavior.

In welcome contrast, the positive effect of socially appropriate modeling on children's prosocial acts has also been demonstrated. A number of laboratory experiments of sharing and helping have produced stable modeling effects on children's behavior from several days to several months after exposure to a prosocial adult model (e.g., Yarrow, Scott, & Waxler, 1973). In fact, research has provided evidence of durable (e.g., Rushton, 1975) and generalized modeling effects (e.g., Yarrow et al., 1973), affecting children's helpfulness on various measures taken some time after exposure to generous models.

Families undoubtedly influence young children's levels of aggression, but children's peers play a crucial role in the later development, maintenance, and modification of aggressive behavior. Peers serve as reinforcing agents, elicitors of aggression, targets of hostility, and social models. As in family interactions, aggressive acts between peers are also reciprocally determined. Each member of a peer dyad reciprocally controls the level of aggression of the other partner, in part through social modeling (e.g., Hicks, 1968). The role of peers as reinforcing agents for aggression has also been shown in laboratory studies (Hartup, 1964) and other studies using trained confederates in naturalistic observations of peer interactions (Charlesworth & Hartup, 1967). As cognitive social learning theory predicts, antisocial aggressive behaviors can be learned and modified though modeling and reinforcement in various social contexts.

Similarly, prosocial behaviors are sensitive to peer reinforcement and modeling effects. Peer modeling has been found to influence sharing rates (e.g., Canale, 1977), and peer models can induce behavior that is either consonant with or counter to a prohibition (Slaby & Parke, 1971). Taken together, these studies suggest that peer interactions are important predictors of children's aggressive and prosocial behaviors through the social learning processes of reinforcement and modeling.

Media Effects

Finally, media presentations can affect the development and maintenance of children's social behavior. The consensus among most researchers and the conclusions of a 1982 report by a panel of the National Institute of Mental Health are that viewing televised violence increases children's and teenagers' aggression (Pearl, Bouthilet, & Lazar, 1982). This well-established effect has been demonstrated in the laboratory (e.g., Hartmann, 1969) as well as in field studies (e.g., Steuer, Applefield, & Smith, 1971). Similarly, several studies have examined the effects of viewing television programs with prosocial (helpful and cooperative) content upon the children's social behavior. Friedrich and Stein (1973) found that prosocial television programs were more likely to have positive effects on child viewers' behavior when other aspects of the environment supported the cooperative message. Children whose prosocial interactions increased after viewing had not only watched the programs but had been helped to rehearse the program themes through verbal labeling or role-playing.

D. Roberts and Bachen (1981) reviewed the social effects of mass media on children and concluded that newscasts are a major source of children's knowledge beginning in early elementary school years. These authors argue that such televised and printed news reports are important socializing influences in defining normative, sanctioned, and punished forms of behavior. A source of concern in sport broadcasts is the commentators' tendency to highlight, condone, and make light of athletes' aggression and unsportsmanlike tactics. Cognitive social learning theory would suggest that the broadcasting of admiring and approving remarks concerning hockey players and other athletes' engaging in ugly brawls has socially damaging effects. Indeed, for behavior that is usually prohibited, such as fighting, the enactment in the mere absence of disapproval increases the likelihood that the behavior will be engaged in by child viewers (Bandura, Ross, & Ross, 1963).

Recommendations

Thus far we have identified a variety of socializing agents in the child's environment, including family, peers, and the communications media. It has generally been assumed that these different agents exert fairly independent influences in altering children's social behaviors. On the contrary, there is increasing recognition of the interdependence of socializing agents in influencing social behaviors (Parke & Slaby, 1983). For example, families provide the initial context for children's socialization, and they also influence their children's peer relationships. This idea was supported long ago in a study of adolescent aggression reported by Bandura and Walters (1959). These researchers found that the parents of aggressive boys were more inclined to actively encourage and condone aggression directed toward siblings and peers than were parents of nonaggressive boys. The influence of parents and families on children is immense and extends to school and sport contexts.

Cognitive social learning theory argues that social behaviors are modeled in the social environment. Competitive sport represents a context in which observational learning and reinforcement operate to influence children's social behavior patterns. The following recommendations are based on Bandura's (1977, 1982, 1986) cognitive social learning theory and will focus on the potential contribution of participants in the competitive sport context—parents, coaches, and peers—in promoting children's social development:

- Understand antisocial aggressive children.
- Provide appropriate models.
- Promote positive peer interactions.
- Involve the parents.
- Employ superordinate goals.
- Emphasize playing for fun.
- Provide opportunities for goals.

Understand Antisocial Aggressive Children

In addition to their socialization histories, other characteristics of aggressive children may make these children more difficult to handle (Patterson, 1982). Aggressive children seek to maximize short-term social payoffs and ignore long-term costs making frequent use of coercion to gain their ends. For example, such a child might knock down a classmate and take his or her belongings without reflecting on the likelihood of retribution. Additionally, antisocial children have skill deficits in the areas of work, peer relations, and academic achievement (Achenbach & Edelbrock, 1981). There are a variety of effective treatments for antisocial aggression, ranging from controlling and modifying aggression to increasing impulse control and promoting acceptable social behavior. Adults who operate youth sport programs should be aware of the needs and problems of the young athletes and understand when to refer them for psychological assistance if needed.

Provide Appropriate Models

Coaches hold considerable social power over their athletes and frequently serve as role models (Bird & Cripe, 1985). Harris (1983) points out that children typically adopt the social behavior and attitudes of their coach. Therefore, coaches should exhibit and reinforce the same appropriate sport conduct they would like to see in their players and spectators.

Coaching methods comprised of the systematic use of reasonable verbal instructions, reinforcement, and modeling have been used in fostering children's acquisition of social skills (Asher & Renshaw, 1981), as well as the correct execution of complex sport skills (Rush & Ayllon, 1984). These programs de-emphasize the competitive aspects of sport, increase recognition for participation, effort, and improvement, and downplay the importance of winning. The focus is on skill acquisition and recreation rather than on contest outcome. This orientation is appropriate for most children enrolled in athletic programs. In rewarding children, verbal and physical praise and feedback are more effective and meaningful than tangible trophies and rewards (Harter, 1981). Also, rewards should be based on the particular performer's achievements as compared with past experience rather than on comparisons made between or among the players (G.C. Roberts, 1984). Rewarding children in a way that will give them information about their personal competencies may make the reward more meaningful. Such rewarding is consistent with everyday social interactions, in which they typically receive praise and attention rather than tangible rewards.

Promote Positive Peer Interactions

Peers provide a very potent source of observational learning in sport. The peer group offers opportunities for youths to occupy a variety of social status positions and to try out various behavioral styles. For example, teammates may demonstrate appropriate sport behaviors (e.g., leadership, cooperation) and effective coping strategies for dealing with success (e.g., congratulating teammates, praising skill acquisition) and failure (e.g., responding to criticism, impulse control). According to Bandura's observational learning principles, peers can serve as effective social models in teaching appropriate social behavior to socially isolated and unskilled children. For example, socially isolated fifth graders were successfully taught a variety of friendship initiation skills by their peers, including: (a) greeting others, (b) asking for and giving information, (c) extending inclusion in an activity, and (d) employing coping strategies, such as using self-instructions to cope with rejection (Zander, 1984). By systematically applying simple reinforcement principles, peers can help children to control negative and aggressive behaviors and increase positive social behaviors (Dougherty & Fowler, 1983). These methods could be structured easily into youth sport programs.

Involve the Parents

Parents serve as powerful socializing forces in shaping children's social behavior through everyday caretaking and disciplinary actions. Several naturalistic and experimental studies demonstrate that the mere presence of parents or other adult models can affect children's social behaviors (Radke-Yarrow, Zahn-Waxler, & Chapman, 1983). Parents should recognize and act upon their potential influence on children's social behaviors. Martens (1978) suggests a variety of sport-related roles and responsibilities that parents should fulfill. For example, parents can reinforce the coaches' and teams' sportsmanlike conduct as well as display appropriate social behavior themselves.

Additionally, parents can indirectly influence their child's aggressive or prosocial behavior by organizing and arranging the home environment to structure and limit the child's activities (Parke & Slaby, 1983). Adults can directly influence children's understanding and expression of aggression by evaluating and interpreting televised violence. For example, evidence exists that coviewing a violent television program with an adult who systematically makes neutral or disapproving comments about the observed violence can successfully reduce a child's subsequent aggressive behaviors (Grusec, 1973). This tactic is particularly relevant given the sensationalism that some sportscasters and commentators give to unauthorized fighting and other rule infractions among well-known college and professional athletes. Another reasonable strategy is to increase the child's exposure to prosocial television programs that stress themes of positive and socially valued interaction. Slaby and Quarfoth (1980) found increases in a wide range of children's prosocial behaviors (e.g., helping, sharing, cooperation) following presentations of socially harmonious programs. Taken together, this research suggests that parents should be selective about their youngsters' television viewing and actively participate as their children watch prosocial and aggressive programs. In sum, we have listed a variety of ways parents contribute significantly to their children's sport socialization. Parents can teach, encourage, and enforce the enactment of social roles, thereby facilitating the learning of appropriate role behavior in sport.

Employ Superordinate Goals

Providing a structure that unites individuals from different and sometimes hostile groups to achieve overriding goals may reduce hostilities and support more cooperative and positive interactions. The research summarized by Sherif (1966) indicates that involvement in superordinate goals, such as repairing the league's playing field, reduces conflict and hostility between rival teams within the league. This exercise requires mutual efforts of both teams, increasing the communication and trust between the groups. Additionally, all participants benefit from the completed task.

A similar strategy may be used to foster cooperative behavior among parents or spectators who place an excessive emphasis on winning. For example, parents and spectators from different teams could work together to plan a fund-raising drive to benefit the entire league. Such a drive would be a unique opportunity for children to observe and learn appropriate prosocial behaviors from their parents in the context of sport and simultaneously benefit from the overall goal (financial support).

Emphasize Playing for Fun

Children consistently report they participate in sport for the fun of it (Gill, Gross, & Huddleston, 1983). We strongly believe that youth sport programs should provide an enjoyable experience for participants, both in the short term and in the future. Children should be encouraged to take up a variety of recreational sports, such as skiing, golf, tennis, swimming, and windsurfing, that can be developed and used in later years and that do not typically produce stressful competition or combative reactions among parents and other spectators.

Provide Opportunities for Girls

With the advent of Title IX, the fields of sport and recreation have an obligation, like the government and the schools, to provide equal opportunity for both sexes (Bammel & Bammel, 1982). The pervasive sex difference in athletic abilities and accomplishments by the end of adolescence is largely the result of social and cultural attitudes toward sport. Historically, females have been neither encouraged nor expected to excel in physical feats. Sex differences in athletic prowess were assumed to be physiological in nature. Males were believed to be stronger, faster, and naturally better athletes than females. However, today's highly trained female athlete is not much different from her male counterpart; often she is leaner, faster, and stronger than the average male (Wilmore, 1982). Hall and Lee (1984) found that with equal opportunity to learn skills and become physically fit, fourth and fifth grade girls matched the level of physical performance of their boy peers. Therefore, it is sensible to develop physical fitness and athletic skills in children of both sexes. There are several potential benefits of sport for girls. For example, sport involvement provides children with sex role models and may help prepare them for a society in which sex roles are becoming less restrictive. Sport offers children the opportunity to develop both physically and psychologically, so parents and coaches should encourage girls to participate fully in youth sport.

Summary and Conclusions

This chapter has portrayed athletics as one of many interacting contexts in which socialization takes place. Using Bandura's cognitive social learning model, we have highlighted the socialization processes and agents that shape the behaviors of children involved in sport programs. Coaches, parents, and other young athletes serve as influential models for sport skills and comportment. They also selectively reinforce children for their performances and for their sportsmanship or antisocial, unsanctioned aggression. Additionally, television coverage of sport events can heighten children's competitiveness and suggest that any effective tactic is acceptable, however unsportsmanlike.

Possible remedies for an overemphasis on winning at all costs and for illegally hurting opponents include identifying and referring for treatment any young participants who cannot manage the competitive situation. Also, coaches should recognize their potent function as role models and should attempt to counteract unhealthy, overly competitive attitudes. Parents and other adults also should be involved to help young athletes socially and competitively. In sum, youth sport is a natural and effective medium for promoting psychosocial and physical competence in children of both sexes. Given the widespread involvement of youngsters in recreation and sport programs, this is clearly a context that deserves further research study. We encourage coaches, parents, and others to provide multiple opportunities for skill acquisition and to eliminate or reduce factors that enhance aggression in youth sport programs.

References

Achenbach, T.M., & Edelbrock, C.S. (1981). Behavioral problems and competencies reported by parents of normal and disturbed children aged 4 through 16. *Monographs of the Society for Research in Child Development*, **46** (Serial No. 188).

Asher, S., & Renshaw, P. (1981). Children without friends: Social knowledge and social skill training. In S.R. Asher & J.M. Gottman (Eds.), *The development of children's friendships* (pp. 273-296). New York: Cambridge University Press.

Bammel, G., & Bammel, L.L. (1982). *Leisure and human behavior*. Dubuque, IA: Brown.

Bandura, A. (1977). *Aggression: A social learning analysis*. Englewood Cliffs, NJ: Prentice-Hall.

Bandura, A. (1982). Self-efficacy mechanism in human agency. *American Psychologist*, **37**, 122-147.

Bandura, A. (1986). *Social foundations of thought and action: A social cognitive theory*. Englewood Cliffs, NJ: Prentice-Hall.

Bandura, A., Ross, D., & Ross, S.A. (1963). Imitation of film-mediated aggressive models. *Journal of Abnormal and Social Psychology*, **66**, 3-11.

Bandura, A., & Walters, R.H. (1959). *Adolescent aggression*. New York: Ronald Press.

Bird, A.M., & Cripe, B.K. (1985). *Psychology and sport behavior*. St. Louis, MO: Times Mirror/Mosby College.

Canale, J.R. (1977). The effect of modeling and length of ownership on sharing behavior of children. *Social Behavior and Personality*, **5**, 187-191.

Charlesworth, R. & Hartup, W.W. (1967). Positive social reinforcement in the nursery school peer group. *Child Development*, **38**, 993-1002.

Dougherty, B.S., & Fowler, S.A. (1983, December). *The use of peer monitors to reduce aggressive behavior during recess*. Paper presented at the annual meeting of the Association for the Advancement of Behavior Therapy, Washington, DC.

Feltz, D.L. (1986). The relevance of youth sports for clinical child psychology. *The Clinical Psychologist*, **39**, 74-77.

Friedrich, L.K., & Stein, A.H. (1973). Aggressive and prosocial television programs and the natural behavior of preschool children. *Monographs of the Society for Research in Child Development*, **38** (4, Serial No. 151).

Gill, D.L., Gross, J.B., & Huddleston, S. (1983). Participation motivation in youth sports. *International Journal of Sports Psychology*, **14**, 1-14.

Grusec, J.E. (1973). Effects of co-observer evaluations on imitation: A developmental study. *Developmental Psychology*, **8**, 141.

Hall, E.G., & Lee, A.M. (1984). Sex differences in motor performance of young children: Fact or fiction? *Sex Roles*, **10**, 217-230.

Harris, J.C. (1983). Intepreting youth baseball: Players' understandings of attention, winning, and playing the game. *Research Quarterly for Exercise and Sport*, **54**, 330-339.

Harter, S. (1981). The development of competence motivation in the mastery of cognitive and physical skills: Is there still a place for joy? In G.C. Roberts & D.M. Landers (Eds.), *Psychology of motor behavior and sport* (pp. 3-29). Champaign IL: Human Kinetics.

Hartmann, D.P. (1969). Influence of symbolically modelled instrumental aggression and pain cues on aggressive behavior. *Journal of Personality and Social Psychology*, **11**, 280-288.

Hartup, W.W. (1964). Friendship status and the effectiveness of peers as reinforcing agents. *Journal of Experimental Child Psychology*, **1**, 154-162.

Heyman, S.R. (1986). Psychological problem patterns found with athletes. *The Clinical Psychologist*, **39**, 68-71.

Hicks, D.J. (1968). Effects of co-observer's sanctions and adult presence on imitative aggression. *Child Development*, **39**, 303-309.

Martens, R. (1978). *Joy and sadness in children's sports*. Champaign, IL: Human Kinetics.

Martens, R. (1988). Youth sport in the USA. In F.L. Smoll, R.A. Magill, & M.J. Ash (Eds.), *Children in sport* (3rd ed., pp. 17-23). Champaign, IL: Human Kinetics.

May, J.R. (1986). Sport psychology: Should psychologists become involved? *The Clinical Psychologist*, **39**, 77-81.

Parke, R.D., & Slaby, R.G. (1983). The development of aggression. In P.H. Mussen (Ed.), *Handbook of child psychology* (Vol. 4, pp. 597-641). New York: Wiley.

Patterson, G.R. (1982). *Coercive family processes*. Eugene, OR: Castilia Press.

Pearl, D., Bouthilet, L., & Lazar, J. (Eds.). (1982). *Television and behavior: Ten years of scientific progress and implications for the eighties* (Vols. 1 & 2). Washington, DC: U.S. Government Printing Office.

Radke-Yarrow, M., Zahn-Waxler, C., & Chapman, M. (1983). Children's prosocial dispositions and behavior. In P.H. Mussen (Ed.), *Handbook of child psychology* (Vol. 4, pp. 469-545). New York: Wiley.

Roberts, D., & Bachen, C. (1981). Mass communication effects. In M.R. Rosenzweig & L.W. Porter (Eds.), *Annual review of psychology* (Vol. 32, pp. 307-356). Palo Alto, CA: Annual Reviews.

Roberts, G.C. (1984). Toward a new theory of motivation in sport: The role of perceived ability. In J.M. Silva, III & R.S. Weinberg (Eds.), *Psychological foundations in sport* (pp. 214-228). Champaign, IL: Human Kinetics.

Rush, D.B., & Ayllon, T. (1984). Peer behavioral coaching: Soccer. *Journal of Sport Psychology*, **6**, 325-334.

Rushton, J.P. (1975). Generosity in children: Immediate and long-term effects of modeling, preaching, and moral judgment. *Journal of Personality and Social Psychology*, **31**, 459-466.

Scanlan, T.K. (1988). Social evaluation and the competition process: A developmental perspective. In F.L. Smoll, R.A. Magill, & M.J. Ash (Eds.), *Children in sport* (3rd ed., pp. 135-148). Champaign, IL: Human Kinetics.

Sherif, M. (1966). *In common predicament*. New York: Houghton-Mifflin.

Slaby, R.G., & Parke, R.D. (1971). Effect on resistance to deviation of observing a model's affective reaction to response consequences. *Developmental Psychology*, **5**, 40-47.

Slaby, R.G., & Quarfoth, G.R. (1980). Effects of television on the developing child. In B.W. Camp (Ed.), *Advances in behavioral pediatrics* (Vol. 1, pp. 62-87). Greenwich, CT: JAI Press.

Steuer, F.B., Applefield, J.M., & Smith, R. (1971). Televised aggression and the interpersonal aggression of preschool children. *Journal of Experimental Child Psychology*, **11**, 442-447.

Weiss, M.R., & Bredemeier, B.J. (1983). Developmental sport psychology: A theoretical perspective for studying children in sport. *Journal of Sport Psychology*, **5**, 216-230

Wilmore, J.H. (1982). The female athlete. In R.A. Magill, M.J. Ash, & F.L. Smoll (Eds.), *Children in sport* (2nd ed., pp. 106-117). Champaign, IL: Human Kinetics.

Yarrow, M.R., Scott, P.M., & Waxler, C.Z. (1973). Learning consideration for others. *Developmental Psychology*, **8**, 240-260.

Zander, T.A. (1984, April). *Group social skills training for children: A comparison of two coaching programs*. Paper presented at the annual meeting of the Western Psychological Association, Los Angeles.

SECTION 5

Social Processes

A sociological perspective on children's involvement in sport provides a level of explanation not possible from physiological and psychological viewpoints. For example, two children with similar physical and psychological characteristics often become involved in different sports. In this section, we find that social parameters might underlie this variance in participation. The three chapters presented here discuss a broad range of social factors that influence not only children's initial entry into sport but also decisions about staying involved. Moreover, consideration is given to a sociological perspective on the effects of youth sport participation.

As a general overview of the sociological orientation, the chapter by Barry D. McPherson and Barbara A. Brown increases our understanding of (a) how and why children get involved in sport, and (b) some of the consequences of this involvement. Their approach is to first describe the social structure of youth sport and then to discuss key factors in the social milieu that influence the decision to become involved in organized sport. Then, they consider some of the positive and negative aspects associated with youth sport participation. A unique part of this chapter is a discussion of some of the modifications in rules and structure of youth sport that have been attempted or suggested.

The final two chapters in this section focus more specifically on the influence of the family, peers, school, and coaches on youth sport participants. John H. Lewko and Susan L. Greendorfer organize chapter 19 around four major issues concerning the effects of these groups on sport socialization. First, they discuss the joint effects of parents and peers as social systems that influence children's decisions to become involved in sport. Second, the question of whether parents or siblings are more influential is addressed. Third, research is reviewed concerning the hypothesized role of the father as the most significant figure in socializing children into sport. Fourth, the potential influence of the school (i.e., teachers, coaches) is discussed. The chapter concludes by identifying important points for consideration in developing a comprehensive theory of sport socialization.

A major concern related to children's involvement in many sports is the effect of the violent behavior that seems to be so prevalent in these sports. In chapter 20, Michael D. Smith discusses violence from a sociological viewpoint as it applies to ice hockey, one of the world's most popular sports. He examines the ways in which parents, coaches, and teammates exert their influence on violent behavior by youth sport participants. A particularly interesting aspect of this chapter is the discussion of attitudes about violence in hockey and how these attitudes relate to the incidence and tolerance of violent behavior in hockey.

CHAPTER 18

The Structure, Processes, and Consequences of Sport for Children

Barry D. McPherson
Barbara A. Brown

For over 20 years there has been increasing interest[1] and concern about the involvement of children in highly competitive sport programs. In general, much of this interest has focused on the psychological aspects of participation (Iso-Ahola & Hatfield, 1986; Weiss & Gould, 1986), with little research directed toward issues of sociological concern. Much of the variation in involvement and subsequent success in sport is accounted for by the social milieu in which one is socialized as a child. Thus, ascribed social categories and cultural and ethnic values, norms, and ideologies must be considered in any attempt to explain how children become involved in competitive sport, and why the resulting social problems accrue in contemporary North American sport.

The purpose of this chapter is to (a) describe the social structure of the child's sport milieu; (b) discuss the key factors in the social milieu influencing the child to become involved in sport; (c) identify and discuss the consequences of being involved, including some social problems unique to a sport milieu where adults intrude and dominate; (d) report some of the alternative policies, rules, and structures that have been attempted in youth sport; and (e) suggest some future research directions for those interested in studying this phenomenon from a sociological perspective.

The Social Structure of Youth Sport

Sport does not occur in a social vacuum. Rather, the meaning and form of sport, and specifically the sports that are valued and considered important, vary across and within cultures. Popular sports may reflect and reinforce larger societal values and historical traditions of success

---

[1]A search in February 1988 of the Specialized Information Retrieval and Library Service (SIRLS) in the Faculty of Human Kinetics and Leisure Studies at the University of Waterloo generated a printout containing 1194 citations pertaining to the child or adolescent and sport.

within a specific country, region, community, or school. Therefore, it is important to understand and appreciate the cultural importance of sport in a given society, or in a given region or community. Where sport, or a specific sport, is highly valued it will be perceived by adults as an interest or activity that *must* be learned and consumed by children in order to inculcate the prevailing value and status systems. Similarly, children may perceive that participation in a given sport is highly valued and rewarded and, without questioning this importance, will seek to become involved in the sport.

Involvement in sport, as in all other forms of social behavior, is often determined by the social structure of the environment in which the social interaction occurs. Thus, in order to better understand why and how the child becomes involved in a competitive sport environment, we must recognize that sport is but one of many systems in which the child interacts. Figure 1 illustrates the various social systems to which a child may be exposed. Within each of these systems a set of values and social norms influences the attitudes and behavioral patterns that may be exhibited, the positive sanctions that reward normative behavior, and the negative sanctions that discourage behavior that deviates from what is considered socially acceptable or desirable.

Figure 1. Significant others in the social systems in which a child may interact. *Note.* From "The Child in Competitive Sport: Influence of the Social Milieu" by B.D. McPherson. In *Children in Sport* (2nd ed., p. 249) by R.A. Magill, M.J. Ash, and F.L. Smoll (Eds.), 1982, Champaign, IL: Human Kinetics. Copyright 1982 by Richard A. Magill, Michael J. Ash, and Frank L. Smoll. Reprinted by permission.

To summarize, social support or pressures within a variety of social systems provide children with values and norms that suggest which social roles they should play, who they should interact with, and how they should interact. Because this social support is usually provided by adults, the child's sport milieu often consists of values, norms, and expectations that are more appropriate for an adult milieu rather than a child milieu (Coakley, 1980). The result is a social environment in which there may be incongruence between the externally induced values and norms—as reflected in the demands or expectations of parents, teachers, and coaches—and the expectations, abilities, and desires of the child—as reflected by his or her level of physical and social maturation.

Becoming Involved in Sport

The Process of Socialization

A major factor influencing the type and amount of involvement in youth sport is the process of *socialization*. This process largely accounts for why children who are structurally and physiologically similar do or do not become involved in sport and attain, or fail to attain, success in sport.

Socialization is a process whereby individuals learn skills, traits, values, attitudes, norms, and knowledge associated with the performance of present or anticipated social roles. There are two categories of social learning: socialization *into* social roles and socialization *via* social roles. In the first category, individuals are socialized, formally and informally, into specific sport roles such as that of athlete and sport consumer. Socialization via the occupancy of sport roles refers to the learning of more general attitudes, values, skills, and dispositions (e.g., sportsmanship, teamwork, discipline, and aggressiveness) that are thought to be acquired while playing a specific sport role, such as the Little League athlete.

The topic of socialization has generated a great deal of research interest over the years, including within the sociology of sport[2] (Coakley, 1986a; McPherson, 1986). Although several theoretical approaches have been utilized, the social learning orientations have been the most productive in terms of both theoretical development and empirical findings, especially when linked with role theory and reference group theory (McPherson, 1981). In this approach it is argued that social learning occurs via imitation and modeling of significant others found within one or more social systems to which the individual is exposed. While it is generally agreed that most learning occurs very early

---

[2]A search in February 1988 of the SIRLS file generated 630 citations pertaining to socialization and sport.

in life, the process actually continues throughout the life cycle. However, it appears that most of the process of learning sport roles occurs during childhood and early adolescence. The three main elements of the socialization process include socializing agents, or sources of social support, who serve as role models; various social environments (e.g., the home, school, class, gymnasium, neighborhood), which provide the opportunity and encouragement for activity; and role learners, who possess a wide variety of ascribed and achieved personal attributes (e.g., personality traits, attitudes, motivation, values, motor ability, race, ethnicity, gender).

The process is influenced further by a number of social categories, most of which are ascribed rather than achieved. These include social class background, ethnicity, race, religion, gender, place and type of residence, and age. Based on these ascribed attributes, rights and opportunities in a variety of social situations are allocated. Thus, social categories often influence our life chances, including whether we have access to specific sport opportunities or sport organizations. Interestingly, most of these attributes are based within the family of origin but remain influential throughout the life cycle in other social systems. A form of double jeopardy often emerges if individuals are situated in two or more of these categories (e.g., a lower-class black female). Faced with such a situation, individuals may be more severely discriminated against, and the possibility of their becoming involved in sport may be considerably reduced or eliminated.

The importance of *class* background as it relates to opportunity set and success in sport has been noted in a number of countries (Loy, McPherson, & Kenyon, 1978). While many of these studies are concerned with the class background of successful athletes, the research literature does suggest that involvement in sport as a child is influenced by the social class of the parents. That is, each child does not have an equal opportunity to become interested in or to develop his or her inherent potential in a specific sport. Moreover, a recent study (Hasbrook, 1986) suggests that the influence of class background on participation in youth sport is more important for females. Specifically, Hasbrook found that young females from lower-class backgrounds participated in sport to a lesser degree than those from an upper-class background.

Social categories such as *ethnicity, race,* and *religion* also influence the socialization process by virtue of the opportunity set that members of certain groups can provide, and by the prevailing behaviors, values, attitudes, and norms that are found within specific subcultures. Thus, if individuals are members of a particular ethnic, religious, or racial group, they often experience different opportunities, norms, and values from those of mainstream society. These differences have an impact on the socialization process, including the learning of sport roles. For example, studies have reported that blacks are underrepresented at certain playing positions and in certain sports, thereby suggesting that through the socialization process they do not receive an opportunity or encouragement to occupy certain sport roles. Similarly, young children socialized within a particular ethnic community may be strongly discouraged from participating in sport for cultural, religious, or socioeconomic reasons.

Based on an increasing body of research literature, we know that there are *sex* differences in the socialization process that result in disproportionately fewer females than males engaging in sport. These differences seem to occur because there are cultural prescriptions for "appropriate" activity for males and females, and sport, traditionally, has been more closely associated with the male role. As a result, socialization processes, beginning in early infancy, have encouraged sport participation among males while directing females away from sport. If girls are to overcome these stereotypic socializing influences, they must be exposed to several sources of positive influence, especially within the family and peer group (see Lewko and Greendorfer, this volume).

Closely related to gender is the social category of *age*. There are age-related norms, unique to particular cultures or subcultures, that influence the learning and enactment of appropriate or inappropriate behavior at particular stages in the life cycle. Whereas a female may be permitted to participate in sport and physical activities during early childhood, she may begin to receive negative sanctions if she continues this type of behavior into adolescence.

Similarly, much of youth sport is structured according to chronological age, with little concern for variation in physical size, ability, or level of maturation. Hence, especially among late-maturing, preadolescent males, potential athletes are rejected by the competitive system because they are perceived to be too small. By the time these individuals pass through puberty and perhaps catch up in size, they have either lost interest in the sport or fallen far behind in skill development.

A final social category that influences the socialization process is the *geographical* area where an individual spends the first 10 to 15 years of life. It is this location within the country and within a specific community that often dictates the opportunity set and sport values that are available in the formative sport years. Furthermore, living in a rural or urban environment, in an apartment or a house, in the suburbs or the urban core often determines the set of opportunities available. Rooney (1974) indicated that there is considerable geographical variability in the production of athletes within each sport. While these findings relate to the effects of geographical location on the propensity to become an elite athlete, children born and raised in a particular geographic location, regardless of their natural ability for a particular sport, may never be exposed to a social milieu that fosters maximum development of their talents in a specific sport. Moreover, in some areas of a country, particularly the West in Canada and the United States, people consistently report higher levels of physical activity during their leisure time (Curtis & McPherson, 1987). That is, there are regional differences in the importance of physical activity during leisure. Hence, opportunities to participate in youth sport may be influenced by these related lifestyle variations in values, beliefs, and opportunities.

Socialization Into Competitive Sport Roles

Most of our knowledge about the processes whereby children become involved in competitive sport roles is derived from retrospective studies of elite athletes. This research has identified the importance of a number of socializing influences, including the availability of opportunities and the influence of role models found among family members and the peer group, in the community and school, and through the mass media. Overall, this research suggests that although there are a number of common elements in the process, socialization into specific sport roles varies according to the sport, the components of the role being learned, the stage in the life cycle, and the sociodemographic characteristics of the role aspirant.

One consistent finding that emerges from the literature is that a positive relationship exists between the amount and type of social support received and the degree and type of participation in sport. That is, those individuals who receive positive reinforcement for sport participation are more likely to become and to remain involved in sport than those who receive neutral or negative messages concerning their interest or participation.

The family has been found to exert the earliest and most persistent influence on the sport involvement of the child, especially for sports like figure skating, tennis, golf, squash, and skiing. Several authors have found that the socializing influence of the family with regard to sport involvement begins when the child is in early infancy. Such influence is reflected in the play behaviors that are encouraged and rewarded and in the toys that are selected by the parents. Both conscious and unconscious parental actions are believed to influence later involvement in sport. Moreover, differences observed in parental treatment of male and female infants and young children have been associated with the greater likelihood that sport will become part of the social repertoire of males rather than females as they mature (Boutilier & San Giovanni, 1983). Specifically, family members provide social support for the sport role in a variety of ways, including creating a positive value climate for participation, giving encouragement for involvement, making participation opportunities available to their children, and acting as active sport models themselves.

Several studies have found that those who achieve elite status in sport often began their participation as early as 5 or 6 years of age and that their initial interest in sport was generated within the family (Sage, 1980; Weiss & Knoppers, 1982). Among family members, parents appear to be more influential than older siblings, and fathers are generally more influential than mothers. Although early studies suggested that female role models within the family were essential if girls were to be socialized in primary sport roles (Loy et al., 1978), more recent evidence indicates that female role models are not essential for young girls to become involved in competitive sport. Rather, the relative importance of the mother or the father may vary by social class and race (Greendorfer, 1983).

Recent research has also explored the extent to which the family socialization process is reciprocal. Clearly, parents influence the sport behavior of their children; but it has also been found that youngsters who become involved in sport, regardless of the extent of family influence, subsequently socialize their parents into greater knowledge about, and perhaps participation in, both primary (i.e., participant) and secondary (e.g., coach, administrator) sport roles (Hasbrook, 1982; Seip, 1987).

As a child enters adolescence, the influence of the family appears to decline. At this stage the child's peer group and significant others within such institutions as school and community sport groups become more influential. The provision of sport opportunities through the educational system still appears to be considerably greater for boys (Greendorfer, 1983).

Several studies have documented the more important role played by the school system and by teachers and coaches in encouraging and reinforcing male sport participation in comparison to that of females (McPherson, 1981). However, a recent study suggests that social change may be occurring in this respect. Higginson (1985) found that teachers and coaches were identified as the significant others providing the most important socializing influence on sport involvement for girls over 13 years of age. This finding suggests that as sport becomes more acceptable as an activity for adolescent females, the school may provide more opportunities and encouragement for female competitive sport experiences. Moreover, the study points to the need to examine socialization influences at different stages of the life cycle for both males and females.

The availability of sport opportunities also influences the likelihood that a child will become involved in sport. Regional and neighborhood location (e.g., urban vs. rural; suburban vs. inner city), often reflecting social class differences, influences the types of opportunities available to potential young athletes. Given the costs involved in many sports, it is not surprising that many youth participants are drawn from the more privileged sectors of society. Similarly, the range of available opportunities for participation are usually greater in urban than rural areas, particularly for individual sports like swimming, tennis, or figure skating, which require specialized coaching or expensive facilities.

Parents, peers, teachers, and coaches can influence not only whether the sport role is adopted initially, but also the ways in which the role is enacted. For example, Vaz (1982) argues that through formal and informal socialization mechanisms, young athletes are socialized into normative institutionalized forms of conduct, such as aggressive checking and fighting in hockey, or hard hitting in football. Similarly, professional and elite amateur athletes also function as significant role models for the behavior and attitudes of young athletes, particularly males. These models are readily visible through the media. For example, Smith (1983) reviewed several studies examining the relationship between hero selection and violence in hockey. He concluded that the viewing of aggressive models appeared to influence the behavior of young athletes. Similarly, he argued that the coverage of sport in both the electronic and print media can convey ideas to young athletes about what constitutes acceptable and expected behavior in specific sport contexts.

In summary, the processes leading children into competitive sport roles begin early in life. Children who become involved in sport are likely to have been exposed to a positive value climate and to have received positive sanctions for participation from a number of significant others, of which the family, peer group, teachers, and coaches appear to be most influential. Athletes who achieve elite status generally become interested and involved in sport at an early age and participate, usually with a great deal of success, in a number of sports before they begin to specialize in a particular sport during adolescence. They receive continuous positive reinforcement from significant others for their involvement. In addition, such factors as social class, race, gender, stage in the life cycle, and type of sport greatly influence whether the sport role socialization process is initiated. These factors are also influential in determining whether the process continues into early adulthood or is terminated at some point during the childhood or adolescent years.

Consequences of Being Involved in Youth Sport

Having become socialized into competitive sport roles, children find themselves in a social milieu that has the potential to enhance or inhibit their personal growth. In this section, some of the negative outcomes of being involved in highly competitive sport programs are discussed.

Socialization via Sport

In order to legitimate the initiation or continuation of youth sport programs, educators and community volunteers have frequently argued that there are many beneficial outcomes that result from participation in sport and physical activity. These outcomes include the development of individual traits and skills (personality, cooperation, creativity, need achievement, independence, self-esteem, emotional dispositions, aggressiveness, citizenship, etc.), learning about the environment, and learning to interact with the environment (e.g., survival of the fittest). Frequently it is argued that these social skills and knowledges can be learned only by participating in sport—hence, the phrase *socialization via sport.*

It is beyond the scope of this paper to review the literature on this subject. However, it can be concluded that little empirical evidence exists to substantiate the many claims that have been made for the contribution of sport, physical education, and physical activity to the learning of larger societal skills and values. As Loy and Ingham (1973) concluded:

> Socialization via play, games and sport is a complex process having both manifest and latent functions, and involving functional and dysfunctional, intended and unintended consequences. Since research on the topic is limited, one must regard with caution many present empirical findings and most tentative, theoretical interpretations of these findings. (p. 298)

In the following subsections, two issues pertaining to socialization via sport are briefly discussed.

Sport Participation and Achievement Values. It has frequently been alleged that involvement in competitive sport can lead to the acquisition or strengthening of achievement values that are highly valued in a society. This argument often implies that sport is the only activity that can facilitate the learning of achievement values. However, these achievement values may be learned prior to involvement in sport and may be necessary prerequisites for success. The evidence to date is inconclusive, and two competing explanations may be offered to account for differences in achievement values at different levels of competition. First, individuals may be socialized into these values while participating at a certain competitive level; second, individuals may be selected into, or place themselves into, different levels of competition or involvement because their personal achievement values are suited to the perceived values in a given sport milieu.

The Dysfunctional Outcomes of Socialization. In contrast to the frequently cited positive and functional learnings that are hypothesized to be derived from involvement in competitive sport, some scholars have argued that games and sport are essentially useless and perhaps deleterious for society. Soule (1966) noted that many consider the frivolity of games damaging, as adult life requires the performance of many serious and unpleasant duties, whereas play and games overemphasize pleasure-seeking pursuits. Similarly, Aries (1962) stated that tennis, bowling, and the like are essentially quasi-criminal activities, no less serious in their deleterious social effects than drunkenness or prostitution. Bend (1971) identified a number of dysfunctional effects of sport, including the intrusion of adult expectations on the play of children, an overinvolvement in one activity rather than the involvement in a number of leisure pursuits, pressure from parents to participate and achieve, and the emergence of deviant normative patterns such as the *win at all costs* philosophy and the unethical practices of coaches and athletes.

As further evidence of the potential dysfunctional outcomes of involvement in competitive sport, Bredemeier, Weiss, Shields, and Cooper (1986) concluded that "involvement in sports characterized by a relatively high degree of physical contact may be developmentally counterproductive for most preadolescent children" (p. 316). Specifically, they found that boys participating in high-contact sports and girls participating in medium-contact sports exhibited less mature moral reasoning and greater tendencies to aggress in both sport and everyday life. Some passages by Voigt (1974) provide observational data that competitive sport programs contribute little to the socialization process, and may, in fact, be detrimental to the individual:

> A player berating his own teammate underscores the seamy side of little league baseball. I personally felt the ugly emotion of hate, a surge of uncontrollable rage tempting me to lash out at my players and my gloating rivals . . . It is this kind of emotional reaction that is so often cited in the charges against the character-building claims of little league baseball . . . I now confess that my Brockton team experience affords no evidence that any of these character-building virtues gets into my players. (pp. 40-41)

> As for sportsmanship, it was lacking from the start . . . The plumbers suffered the most, being treated by the regulars as incompetents, which says little for baseball's claim for inculcating brotherhood or community solidarity.

> Nor did parents set examples . . . parents of rivals constantly hassled us . . . at home, our supporters returned rivals the same kind of treatment. That our parents gave a bit less . . . owed simply to . . . our big leads and heavy hitting . . . If there is a point in all of this, I think it demonstrates the fact that in baseball, sportsmanship and good character go mostly to the winners and regular players and only slightly to benchwarmers. (p. 42)

> I conclude that little league baseball is no shaper of lofty values or ethics. Rather it merely provides one setting for the playing out of norms and values already embedded in our culture. (p. 42)

To date, there is little empirical support for the many beliefs and hypotheses concerning the positive or negative outcomes for character and personality development that are alleged to be derived from involvement in competitive sport.

Social Problems in the Child's Sport Milieu

Although social problems involving children, such as delinquency, poverty, and drug addition, have been identified and studied, it is only in recent years that conditions inherent in the sport milieu have become intolerable and classified as social problems. Most of this attention has consisted of anecdotal accounts by journalists, field observations, and conceptual analyses of particular sports. Little concrete evidence is presently available to assist us in understanding why the inherent problems occur and how they might be alleviated. For example, the following headlines, while isolated and perhaps atypical, do suggest that there is a problem in children's sport that must be faced and solved. Furthermore, these situations must be eliminated because the more frequently they appear in the popular press, the more likely government officials, educators, and taxpayers will question whether funds should be allocated for building or renovating sport facilities and for supporting the volunteer work of minor sport organizations. The headlines have included these:

- Bloodshed, Brutality: That's Hockey
- Referee Files Charge Against Fan
- Parents, Pressure and the (Hockey) Puck
- Unhealthy Climate in Minor Hockey
- Little League: Good or Bad?
- It's Fun for Adults, Heartbreak for Kids
- Ban Parents from Sport Events
- Taking the Fun Out of a Game
- Don't Let Your Son Play Smallfry Football
- Little League Filled with 'Little' Adults
- Manager Assaults Umpire with Bat

The following topics are being discussed more frequently by journalists and scholars, thereby creating an increased awareness of the problems. However, there is still little understanding as to how or why the problems develop, or how they can be controlled or eliminated.

Social Mobility. For years educators and journalists have argued that sport provides an avenue for upward social mobility. Unfortunately, because of methodological and conceptual weaknesses, little empirical support exists for this hypothesis. For example, the absence of longitudinal studies or studies using subjects matched on education or on the original socioeconomic status level of parents have made it impossible to determine whether mobility occurred because of sport success or because most members of a particular cohort improved their socioeconomic status over time. Although studies have indicated that some athletes, in certain sports, come from lower-class backgrounds, attend a college, and subsequently achieve success in high-level amateur or professional sport, only a few research studies have shown the level of social status held by these athletes 10 to 15 years after their college or professional career is completed (Howell, Miracle, & Rees, 1984; Picou, McCarter, & Howell, 1985). To show that the predicted or hypothesized level of occupational attainment is seldom attained, Ralbovsky (1974) interviewed the members of a world champion Little League team 20 years later. Of the players on that team, none became a major league star or a senator, as was predicted the year they became champions. As Gruneau (1975) notes:

> Mobility through sport for both the lowest classes and status groups may in fact stop at the comfortable level of middle class athlete. In this sense, the structure of rewards is not so much a ladder on which individuals may continue to climb but rather a tree wherein a specified limb spells the absolute extent of upward travel. (p. 167)

Unrealistic Career Aspirations. Closely related to the question of mobility is the effect that participation in sport has on career aspirations. Too many young athletes are pushed into sport and encouraged to achieve excellence because of the remote possibility that this might lead to an attractive career with high levels of prestige and income. Often this push comes from parents and coaches who seek vicarious gratification and success through children's achievements. Child athletes must be informed about the realistic chances of achieving a career in professional sport. For example, there are approximately 300,000 boys playing organized minor hockey in Canada, but there are only 300-500 positions available in the major and minor professional leagues. Moreover, unlike 10 years ago, professional hockey players are no longer recruited exclusively from Canada. Thus, the chance of making a team in professional hockey is not very high. Because similar ratios exist for other professional sports, coaches and parents should not provide excessive encouragement for children to aspire to this type of career. Instead, young children should be encouraged to achieve in both the educational and the sport domain. As Conacher (1971) noted, "with an education, sport will always be a thing of choice, rather than a necessity" (p. 20).

Adult Domination. For a variety of reasons, adults organize and ultimately dominate the child's sport milieu. Strong empirical evidence is lacking, but the following list includes some of the hypothesized reasons for adult control:

- To receive gratification and prestige in the sport milieu by becoming emotionally involved in children's play.
- To vicariously experience success that is unavailable to them in the adult world.

- To facilitate the attainment of career aspirations they may hold for their child in college, professional, or elite amateur sport.
- To protect their child from some of the practices and values that may be forced on the child by a coach whose philosophy is to win at all costs.

As a result of this adult control, which was not present years ago, the levels of aspiration and the degree of commitment and involvement held by the young athlete are frequently unrealistic. This is often reflected in the norms and goals that young athletes are forced to adhere to and strive for (e.g., win at all costs, play with pain, only a winner can be proud, etc.). For example, Brower (1973) observed that boys playing adult-organized baseball were like pawns in a chess game: Adults called the shots and the kids got in line and did what they were told. He further stated that what appears to be fun for adults is often heartbreak for some of the players. He concluded that he has seen boys playing unorganized baseball without adult supervision and noted how much spontaneous fun they were having—something he did not see when adults were in charge.

More recently, this theme of adult domination has been extended to a concern with the potential for child abuse in sport. This potential abuse, which is often unconscious and sometimes self-induced by the child, is more likely to occur in highly intensive training programs such as swimming, gymnastics, track and field, and figure skating. In these competitive activities the participants may be engaged in two workouts per day, amounting to 20 to 30 hours of work per week. These athletes have been labeled as *child athletic workers* (Cantelon, 1981) who become victims of the "lost childhood" or "lost adolescence" syndrome[3] (Donnelly & Sargent, 1986). Grupe (1985) identifies a number of problems emanating from the type of sport environment where child athletes

- "are not allowed to be children,
- are abandoned by adults when they retire from competition,
- lose important social contacts and experiences while growing up,
- are subject to excessive psychological and physiological stress,
- are victims of a disrupted family life,
- face the risk of an endangered intellectual development, and
- may become lost within the sport context and detached from the larger society." (pp. 10-11)

Socially Induced Aggression. The appearance of aggression in sport settings appears to be socially induced and learned via the socialization process (Smith, this volume). Through exposure to role models and

---

[3]Postman (1982) introduced this concept of a disappearing childhood.

reference groups, an individual observes aggressive behavior or is explicitly taught to be aggressive in certain sport situations. For example, Smith (1971) suggests that within some sporting social systems there are

> values which legitimize aggression, norms which provide rules for the conduct of aggression, and mechanisms by which individuals are mobilized into aggressive roles. The techniques of violence may be socially learned, legitimized, and reinforced by various types of reference groups. (p. 25)

Vaz (1982) also suggests that physically aggressive behavior is normative, institutionalized behavior learned during the formal and informal socialization process of young hockey players. In a participant observation study of boys 8 to 20 years of age engaged in amateur hockey, Vaz observed that illegal tactics are both encouraged and taught, that rough play and physically aggressive performance are strongly encouraged, and that sometimes players are taught the techniques of fighting. Faulkner (1975), in a case study of a minor league professional hockey team, found that players consider violent behavior (e.g., fighting) a personal and occupational resource used for achieving and maintaining mastery over opponents and for attaining positive evaluations from their work peers. These are the role models that children imitate! Such perceived legitimacy of rule violation is generally thought to occur only in male sport. However, more recently, females with sport experience tended also to rate perceived rule violations as legitimate, especially if they had been participants in "collision" sports or in a combination of sports (Silva, 1983).

How can some of this aggressive behavior in children's sport be eliminated, or at least controlled? First, role models exhibiting violent forms of behavior should be eliminated as often as possible. Hence, children will have few opportunities to imitate such behavior and will consequently be less likely to learn and employ these deviant behavior patterns. For deviant role models to disappear, rule changes in the form of severe negative sanctions must be initiated. Other ways to reduce violent behavior include (a) changing the behavioral norms that coaches require their players to meet, and (b) understanding players, so that when signs of frustration appear the player can be removed from potentially aggressive or violent situations. Finally, coaches should deemphasize the importance of aggression and violence in order to win games.

Controlling aggressive behavior in sport is difficult for one individual to accomplish alone; sport associations must arrive at a common philosophy as to how the game should be played with respect to the amount of physical contact, aggression, or violence they are willing to tolerate in their particular sport milieu. Meetings between coaches, officials, parents, and players are necessary to arrive at a consensus concerning normative behavior. Otherwise, such change will never occur unless *all* individuals involved in the sport are in agreement, which rarely is the case. Arriving at a consensus is especially important when individuals are attempting to change a behavioral pattern that already exists, particularly at the professional level. For the change to be successful it must be uniform and involve consistent reinforcement from all significant others (e.g., coaches, parents, and officials) to whom the child is exposed.

Withdrawal From Youth Sport.   Although millions of children are involved in youth sport at any one time, the retention rate appears to be quite low. That is, many children withdraw from sport involvement, often before reaching their performance potential or peak enjoyment level. The existence and magnitude of this withdrawal pattern has been documented extensively for a variety of sports and for both males and females.

The major question that has been addressed is, Why do children withdraw from participation in organized youth sport? Critics of youth sport have pointed to negative elements within the sport environment as being responsible. Several studies have found a relationship between withdrawal from organized sport and such factors as the emphasis on competition, the pressure to win in youth sport, the lack of fun, the lack of success, a dislike of practices, a lack of skill development, or conflict or dissatisfaction with the coach (Fry, McClements, & Sefton, 1981; McPherson, Marteniuk, Tihanyi, & Clark, 1980). Martens (1980), summarizing the reasons children quit competitive sport, identified these important factors in the withdrawal decision: (a) not getting to play, (b) receiving negative reinforcement (i.e., criticism), (c) mismatching of athletes in terms of physical maturity, (d) psychological pressure as a result of the emphasis on competition and performance, (e) continuous failure, and (f) too much organization.

In addition to the negative aspects of the sport environment often introduced by adults, negative self-perceptions of the child athlete must also be studied. Young athletes with self-induced or externally induced low perceptions of their abilities are more likely to withdraw from sport participation than children with higher levels of perceived competence (Roberts, 1984). Similarly, Butcher (1985) notes that for some levels of participation, nonparticipant adolescent girls had lower levels of satisfaction with their sport ability than did participants.

Recognizing the diversity of participation motives, researchers have examined the influence of a much broader range of variables on adherence to and withdrawal from organized sport. The results of these studies suggest that children who withdraw from participation in competitive sport have different socialization experiences than those who maintain their involvement. Moreover, it has been found that a variety of factors interact to influence the decision to withdraw and that not all factors involved are related to the pressures and philosophy of the program.

A major factor influencing withdrawal is a conflict of interests. That is, young athletes, faced with opportunities to participate in a variety of social activities, are often forced into making choices between sport and nonsport alternatives (Brown, 1985).

Another factor that discriminates between those who maintain their involvement in sport and those who withdraw is the degree of social support received from significant others for the sport role. The results of several studies suggest that nonadherers and nonparticipants receive less social support for their participation in sport than do those who stay involved (Brown, 1985; Butcher, 1985). Moreover, Brown (1985) found that nonadherers also received more encouragement to partici- pate in nonsport activities. Other variables found to be associated with withdrawal from participation include having a job, loss of interest in sport, the time commitment required by the sport, the withdrawal of friends, the expense of participation, and the extent to which personal identity ceases to be associated with the sport role. The importance and presence of one or more of these factors vary across different sports and different levels of competition (Brown, 1986).

In summary, a number of interacting factors within and outside the sport milieu appear to influence the timing and process of withdrawal from competitive sport by young athletes. What remains unclear is what precisely initiates the process, why it is initiated at a specific point in time, and whether those who withdraw from a particular sport role or a specific sport are withdrawing from sport completely or forever. Moreover, although withdrawal from sport has been seen as a social problem by those involved in sport, it may be that withdrawal from sport roles is a natural occurrence for young people as they experiment with various roles and activities during adolescence. The process of withdrawal from sport may be no different or no more problematic than that observed when highly committed participants withdraw from such other forms of social participation as music, art, and dance. A compari- son of the process and outcome of withdrawal from high levels of involvement in sport and nonsport activities is a needed research direction.

Toward Social Change: Alternative Policies, Rules, and Structures

Given the number and severity of problems, isolated though they may be, it is not surprising that educators, politicians, recreation person- nel, and parents have sought to initiate social changes in the competi- tive sport milieu for youth. These changes have involved introducing alternative models, a new structure, or new rules to existing youth sport programs. Also, educational programs for administrators, coaches, and parents have been developed that seek to change attitudes and pro- vide guidelines for appropriate behavior in the child's sport milieu. It is hoped that these measures, briefly described below, will reduce the pressures on children and reduce the level of ego involvement on the part of coaches and parents.

Alternative Structures, Rules, and Models

Many of the problems in youth sport have arisen because the organizational structure was established by adults. Initially, these adults had honest intentions to provide nothing more than an enjoyable competitive opportunity for children. Unfortunately, at some point the end (i.e., winning, success, the prestige of the adults) became more important than the means, and the children were largely forgotten in their own play world. The situation has led to a loss of enjoyment and self-esteem and an increase in the pressure placed on children to achieve adult expectations. One outcome has been the high withdrawal rate mentioned previously. A more viable and satisfactory solution to the stresses of youth sport has been the introduction of structural or rule changes that maximize skill development, promote safety, and enhance enjoyment, thereby keeping children involved in youth sport (Pooley, 1986; Weiss & Gould, 1986). These changes include

- providing unstructured leagues, where standings and scoring records are not kept and there are no play-offs;
- organizing instructional programs with games of minimal organization rather than organized games;
- decreasing the number of players on a team and having more teams;
- reducing the size of the equipment and playing area (e.g., using smaller, lighter balls in soccer, football, and basketball; lowering the height of the net in volleyball or basketball);
- allowing no body contact in such sports as hockey and football;
- playing cooperative games rather than competitive games;
- eliminating all-star competitions and competitive traveling teams; and
- eliminating the offside rule in soccer and hockey—a complex rule for beginners to comprehend.

Many of these changes were initiated by a concern with the level of readiness of children for competitive sport experiences. Hence, researchers have examined the question of psychological, physiological, and social readiness for competition (Coakley, 1986b; Passer, 1986; Sharkey, 1986). These scholars agree that competition in sport should be delayed until psychological, physical, and social maturity are attained, whereby the child can understand the meaning of competition and the demands of competitive relationships. For most, competition, as implied in the professional sport model, will not be understood until the early teens. Coakley (1986b) recommends that children not be involved in competition before 8 years of age; that between 8 and 12 years of age some, but not all, rules, strategies, and competitive relationships can be introduced; and, that only during the teenage years should youth begin to engage in full-scale competitive settings similar to college or professional sport.

Educational and Training Programs

In order to better prepare the volunteer coach, official, or administrator, and to educate the parents as to their role in youth sport, educators and government officials have prepared a number of printed and audiovisual materials. Some of these have been prepared by adults who have had years of practical experience in youth sport and wish to share their knowledge and philosophy. Others are based on the increasing amount of research on youth sport. The following list contains some examples of such educational packages:

- Sport Canada Development Model (Valeriote, 1986)
- *Fair Play Codes for Children in Sport* (National Task Force on Children's Play, 1979)
- Model instructional programs, practice and drill manuals, and instructional films for specific sports
- Booklets and posters to educate parents as to their responsibilities and role in youth sport
- University courses on youth sport for majors in physical education and recreation

While many materials have been produced, we do not know to what extent these materials have been distributed, read, understood, and assimilated. Nor do we have enough research information to know if the material that is produced is valid. Hence, there is an urgent need for further high-quality basic, applied, and program evaluation research on youth sport, especially from an interdisciplinary perspective.

Future Research Directions

As noted throughout this chapter, there is an urgent need to understand the processes and problems inherent in competitive sport programs for children. We really do not know very much about how or why children become socialized into competitive sport programs, why they continue to be involved, or how and why they become desocialized (i.e., withdraw). Furthermore, as educators, researchers, and parents, we now know that many of the more serious problems in children's sport lie outside the educational setting. Therefore, more efforts should be directed toward understanding and enhancing the social milieu of community sport programs. More specifically, an urgent need exists for greater understanding of the interpersonal dynamics within the "Little League Triangle"—that is, the coach-parent-child triad.

Methodologically, national rather than local studies must be initiated. If this is not possible, then studies should be replicated in a variety of communities, both within a society and cross-nationally, in order to control for historical and environmental effects. To date, most evidence is anecdotal. Consequently, greater efforts should be directed toward initiating field studies that employ such methods as interviews, questionnaires, and both obtrusive and unobtrusive participant observation. Further efforts should include both male and female athletes and should control for social class, age, and level of competition. In addition, more studies should survey the child athlete and not seek only the opinions of coaches or parents. Finally, the initiation of longitudinal studies might eliminate some of the problems inherent in the retrospective type of research that has been most common to date (e.g., reliance on recall, failure to survey athletes who have already withdrawn, lack of control for maturation and playing experience).

References

Aries, P. (1962). *Centuries of childhood*. New York: Vintage Books.

Bend, E. (1971, August). *Some potential dysfunctional effects of sport upon socialization*. Paper presented at the Third International Symposium on the Sociology of Sport, Waterloo, Ontario.

Boutilier, M., & San Giovanni, L. (1983). *The sporting woman*. Champaign, IL: Human Kinetics.

Bredemeier, B., Weiss, M., Shields, D., & Cooper, B. (1986). The relationship of sport involvement with children's moral reasoning and aggression tendencies. *Journal of Sport Psychology*, **8**, 304-318.

Brower, J. (1973). *Little leagues mostly for parents*. Unpublished manuscript, California State University, Fullerton.

Brown, B. (1985). Factors influencing the process of withdrawal by female adolescents from the role of competitive age group swimmer. *Sociology of Sport Journal*, **2**, 111-129.

Brown, B. (1986, October). *Factors related to adherence to and withdrawal from physical activity among female adolescents*. Paper presented at the annual meeting of the North American Society for the Sociology of Sport, Las Vegas, NV.

Butcher, J. (1985). Longitudinal analysis of adolescent girls' participation in physical activity. *Sociology of Sport Journal*, **2**, 130-143.

Cantelon, H. (1981). High performance sport and the child athlete: Learning to labour. In A. Ingham & E. Broom (Eds.), *Career patterns and career contingencies in sport* (pp. 258-286). Vancouver: University of British Columbia.

Coakley, J. (1980). Play, games and sport: Developmental implications for young people. *Journal of Sport Behavior*, **3**, 99-118.

Coakley, J. (1986a). Socialization and youth sports. In C. Rees & A. Miracle (Eds.), *Sport and social theory* (pp. 135-143). Champaign, IL: Human Kinetics.

Coakley, J. (1986b). A sociological perspective. In M.R. Weiss & D. Gould (Eds.), *Sport for children and youths* (pp. 59-63). Champaign, IL: Human Kinetics.

Conacher, B. (1971). *Hockey in Canada: The way it is.* Richmond Hill, Ontario: Gateway Press.

Curtis, J., & McPherson, B. (1987). Regional differences in the leisure physical activity of Canadians: Testing some alternative interpretations. *Sociology of Sport Journal, 4,* 363-375.

Donnelly, P., & Sargent, L. (1986, October). *Adolescents and athletic labour: A preliminary study of elite Canadian athletes.* Paper presented at the annual meeting of the North American Society for the Sociology of Sport, Las Vegas, NV.

Faulkner, R. (1975). Coming of age in organizations: The comparative study and career contingencies of musicians and hockey players. In D. Ball & J. Loy (Eds.), *Sport and social order* (pp. 521-558). Reading, MA: Addison-Wesley.

Fry, D.A.P., McClements, J.D., & Sefton, J.M. (1981). *A report on participation in the Saskatoon Hockey Association.* Saskatoon, Saskatchewan: Saskatoon Hockey Association.

Greendorfer, S. (1983). Shaping the female: The impact of the family. In M. Boutilier & L. San Giovanni (Eds.), *The sporting woman* (pp. 135-155). Champaign, IL: Human Kinetics.

Gruneau, R. (1975). Sport, social differentiation and social equality. In D. Ball & J. Loy (Eds.), *Sport and social order* (pp. 117-184). Reading, MA: Addison-Wesley.

Grupe, O. (1985). Top level sports for children from an educational viewpoint. *International Journal of Physical Education, 22,* 9-16.

Hasbrook, C.A. (1982). The theoretical notion of reciprocity and childhood socialization into sport. In A.D. Dunleavy, A.W. Miracle, & C.R. Rees (Eds.), *Studies in the sociology of sport* (pp. 139-151). Fort Worth: Texas Christian University Press.

Hasbrook, C. (1986). The sport participation—social class relationship: Some recent youth sport participation data. *Sociology of Sport Journal, 3,* 154-159.

Higginson, D. (1985). The influence of socializing agents in the female sport-participation process. *Adolescence, 20,* 73-82.

Howell, F., Miracle, A., & Rees, C. (1984). Do high school athletics pay?: The effects of varsity participation on socioeconomic attainment. *Sociology of Sport Journal, 1,* 15-25.

Iso-Ahola, E.S., & Hatfield, B. (1986). The social psychology of youth sports. In E.S. Iso-Ahola & B. Hatfield (Eds.), *Psychology of sports: A social psychological perspective* (pp. 85-106). Dubuque, IA: Brown.

Lewko, J.H., & Greendorfer, S.L. (1988). Family influences in sport socialization of children and adolescents. In F.L. Smoll, R.A. Magill, & M.J. Ash (Eds.), *Children in sport* (3rd ed., pp. 287-300). Champaign, IL: Human Kinetics.

Loy, J.W., & Ingham, A. (1973). Play, games, and sport in the psychosocial development of children and youth. In G. Rarick (Ed.), *Physical activity: Human growth and development* (pp. 257-302). New York: Academic Press.

Loy, J.W., McPherson, B.D., & Kenyon, G.S. (1978). *Sport and social systems*. Reading, MA: Addison-Wesley.

Martens, R. (1980). The uniqueness of the young athlete: Psychologic considerations. *American Journal of Sports Medicine*, **8**, 382-385.

McPherson, B. (1981). Socialization theory and research: Toward a "new wave" of scholarly inquiry in a sport context. In C. Rees and A. Miracle (Eds.), *Sport and social theory* (pp. 111-134). Champaign, IL: Human Kinetics.

McPherson, B. (1982). The child in competitive sport: Influence of the social milieu. In R.A. Magill, M.J. Ash, & F.L. Smoll (Eds.), *Children in sport* (2nd ed., pp. 247-278). Champaign, IL: Human Kinetics.

McPherson, B. (1986). Socialization into and through sport. In G. Luschen & G. Sage (Eds.), *Handbook of social science of sport* (pp. 246-273). Champaign, IL: Stipes.

McPherson, B., Marteniuk, R., Tihanyi, J., & Clark, W. (1980). The social system of age group swimming: The perceptions of swimmers. *Canadian Journal of Applied Sport Sciences*, **5**, 142-145.

National Task Force on Children's Play. (1979). *Fair play codes for children in sport*. Ottawa, Ontario: Council on Children and Youth.

Passer, M.W. (1986). A psychological perspective. In M.R. Weiss & D. Gould (Eds.), *Sport for children and youths* (pp. 55-58). Champaign, IL: Human Kinetics.

Picou, S., McCarter, A., & Howell, F. (1985). Do high school athletics pay? Some further evidence. *Sociology of Sport*, **2**, 72-76.

Pooley, J. (1986). A level above competition: An inclusive model for youth sport. In M.R. Weiss & D. Gould (Eds.), *Sport for children and youths* (pp. 187-193). Champaign, IL: Human Kinetics.

Postman, N. (1982). *The disappearance of childhood*. New York: Delcorte.

Ralbovsky, M. (1974). *Destiny's darlings*. New York: Hawthorne.

Roberts, G.C. (1984). Toward a new theory of motivation in sport: The role of perceived ability. In J.M. Silva, III & R.S. Weinberg (Eds.), *Psychological foundations of sport* (pp. 214-228). Champaign, IL: Human Kinetics.

Rooney, J. (1974). *The geography of American sport*. Reading, MA: Addison-Wesley.

Sage, G.H. (1980). Parental influence and socialization into sport for male and female intercollegiate athletes. *Journal of Sport and Social Issues*, **4**, 1-13.

Seip, R. (1987). *The socialization of youth sport coaches*. Unpublished master's thesis, University of Western Ontario, London, Ontario.

Sharkey, B.J. (1986). A physiological perspective. In M.R. Weiss & D. Gould (Eds.), *Sport for children and youths* (pp. 51-54). Champaign, IL: Human Kinetics.

Silva, J.M., III (1983). The perceived legitimacy of rule violating behavior in sport. *Journal of Sport Psychology*, **5**, 438-448.

Smith, M.D. (1971). Aggression in sport: Toward a role approach. *Canadian Association of Health, Physical Education and Recreation Journal*, **37**, 22-25.

Smith, M.D. (1983). *Violence and sport*. Toronto, Ontario: Butterworths.

Smith, M.D. (1988). Interpersonal sources of violence in hockey: The influence of parents, coaches, and teammates. In F.L. Smoll, R.A. Magill, & M.J. Ash (Eds.), *Children in sport* (3rd ed., pp. 301-316). Champaign, IL: Human Kinetics.

Soule, G.H. (1966). *Time for living*. New York: Viking Press.

Valeriote, T. (1986). The development model in Canadian sport. In M.R. Weiss & D. Gould (Eds.), *Sport for children and youths* (pp. 201-204). Champaign, IL: Human Kinetics.

Vaz, E.W. (1982). *The professionalization of young hockey players*. Lincoln: University of Nebraska Press.

Voigt, D. (1974). *A little league journal*. Bowling Green, OH: Bowling Green University Press.

Weiss, M.R., & Gould, D. (Eds.). (1986). *Sport for children and youths*. Champaign, IL: Human Kinetics.

Weiss, M.R., & Knoppers, A. (1982). The influence of socializing agents on female collegiate volleyball players. *Journal of Sport Psychology*, **4**, 267-279.

CHAPTER 19

Family Influences in Sport Socialization of Children and Adolescents

John H. Lewko
Susan L. Greendorfer

Several years ago we attempted to review the existing literature pertaining to children in sport in order to understand the underlying mechanisms and social processes that determine sport involvement. Given the paucity of research on children in sport at that time and noting the research bias toward only male participation, our initial chapter relied on the pertinent literature in child development that related to sex differences, socialization, play behavior, sex roles, and behavior of significant others (Lewko & Greendorfer, 1977). When asked to update the references for this volume, we accepted the challenge to revise, expecting to cite the substantial changes and inroads that have been made relative to the topic of sex differences in general and sport socialization in particular. Unfortunately, we were struck by the fact that despite the amount of accumulated research pertaining to each domain area discussed in the initial review, relatively little has been found to substantially alter the content or trends identified in that summary of sex differences.

For example, although considerably more research exists on the topics of differential expectations and treatment, adult-infant interaction, early toddler-infant-childhood play styles, and game and toy selection and preference as aspects of gender schema, most findings reveal the continued prevalence of (a) either gender labeling (Weinraub, Clemens, Sockloff, Ethridge, Gracely, & Myers, 1984) or sex-typing and continuity in choice of children's toys (Eisenberg, Wolchick, Hernandez, & Pasternack, 1985; Lloyd & Smith, 1985); (b) differential parental treatment and play interactions with sons and daughters (Power, 1985; Power & Parke, 1983, 1986; Williams, Goodman, & Green, 1985); (c) differential teacher behaviors toward the play of boys and girls (Fagot, 1984; Oettingen, 1985; A.B. Smith, 1985); and (d) more vigorous play, higher amounts of rough and tumble play, and greater motor activity among boys (DiPietro, 1981; Eaton & Enns, 1986; Eaton & Keats, 1982; Fagot & Leinback, 1983; Liss, 1983; Lloyd & Smith,

1985)—all of which suggests gender differences in socialization outcomes relative to orientation, predisposition, selection and preference
for specific play, physical activity, or sport experiences. Although we
still feel that the issue of gender difference is worthy of conceptual and
empirical attention (cf. Greendorfer & Brundage, 1987), in light of the
fact that findings from this more recent research do not differ significantly or suggest different trends from those cited in our first review,
we have chosen to limit our attention in this chapter to only that
research which pertains to sport socialization.

Socialization and Sport

Although large numbers of children and adolescents continue to engage in various types and levels of sport and physical activities, we are
still relatively uninformed as to the forces that shape their involvement.
The family and the peer group are recognized as essential in the socialization process, yet our understanding of the processes inherent in this
assumption has not been greatly enhanced since the days of Cooley
(Baumrind, 1980; Cooley, 1909). Given the current state of socialization research in general, it is not surprising to find that we are only
now beginning to unravel the processes by which individuals become
active participants in sport and physical activities.

As previously indicated, our first review on family influences and sex
differences in children's sport socialization noted several emergent
trends in the socialization of children into sport (Lewko & Greendorfer,
1977). These trends were based on relatively liberal generalizations
from a sparse data base, which, although intuitively appealing, remained open to verification. Therefore, the purpose of this chapter is
to examine the sport socialization research that has emerged since our
initial review in order to determine what progress has been made in
clarifying the process by which children become active participants
in sport and physical activity. The reader should be forewarned that
the extant research in this area is fragmented and not overly abundant.
In order to render the information more meaningful, four trends, identified in our earlier review, will serve as our organizational framework:

- The family was emerging as more influential than peers or school.
- Parents were more influential than siblings.
- The father was the most significant other, regardless of sex of the
  child.
- The school was a more influential social system for boys than for
  girls.

Family, Peer, and School Influences

The largest number of sport socialization studies has focused on a comparison of some combination of three sets of variables—family, peer,

and school—typically using the social role/social systems approach (Loy, McPherson, & Kenyon, 1978). Apart from any methodological concerns, these studies reflect considerable variability in sample selection, thereby limiting the generalizability of the findings. Of particular concern is the tendency to focus on the adolescent age range and virtually ignore the early and middle childhood years. Therefore, we examined the literature for patterns that might shed light on the three variables we just mentioned and ignored specific variations within individual studies.

Across the studies examining the three variables, the family and peer group are clearly more influential than the school. However, the balance of influence shifts between childhood and adolescence and between sexes. A number of the studies (Ebihara, Ikeda, & Myiashita, 1983; Greendorfer & Ewing, 1981; Higginson, 1985; Patriksson, 1981; Yamaguchi, 1984) focusing on socialization during childhood have called into question our earlier assumption that the family was prepotent in children's sport socialization. What appears to be the case is the emergence of a combination of family and peer influences. For example, in a study of 9- to 12-year-old black and white children, Greendorfer and Ewing (1981) found differential patterns of influence based on race and sex. Peers and fathers were important influences in socializing white males into sport, while peers alone were influential for black males. For white females, mothers and teachers emerged as important, while for black females it was teachers and sisters.

In a retrospective study involving Japanese adolescents and English- and French-speaking adolescents from Canada, Yamaguchi (1984) reported that peers, not parents, were important influences in female sport involvement across the three cultures. However, parents emerged as important for the English and French males. In another retrospective study, involving Swedish adolescents, Patriksson (1981) found that fathers were perceived as important in influencing the primary and secondary sport involvement of both males and females from 7 to 12 years of age. The father's influence emerged in the form of a passive, yet positive, role model generally supporting his son's or daughter's sport interest. Higginson (1985) also reported that parents were selected as important influences by young female athletes (under 13 years) who were attending the Empire State Games in New York.

The study by Ebihara, Ikeda, and Myiashita (1983) is worth noting because it is one of the few investigations that included children younger than 9 years of age. Although the study was based entirely on a Japanese population and was more concerned with examining birth-order effects and sport socialization, the pattern of findings is of interest. The researchers found a very strong peer effect for both boys and girls. While the configurations of significant other influences varied somewhat, depending upon the birth-order category or sex of respondent, it was generally found that friends of the same sex exerted a strong influence on the sport socialization of both males and females.

For the males, the father also emerged as a very important referent. With respect to the females, father influence was less pronounced than the influence of sisters or brothers.

The final study focusing on the childhood period of sport involvement was conducted in Israel and involved the mothers of three groups of young (12-13 years) gifted athletes and a control group of generally active children. Melnick, Dunkelman, & Mashiach (1981) reported that parents of the athletically gifted children provided a significantly different home environment for their children than did the control parents. Specifically, the parents of the gifted children held significantly higher expectations and aspirations regarding their child's performance and offered more encouragement for participation.

Generally speaking, parents and peers apparently both hold the potential for influencing a child's sport involvement. While previous research on the sport socialization process has focused on identifying the most influential significant other, the current research suggests that a more fruitful approach would be to examine the parent-peer dialectic (see Youniss, 1978). Effective socialization of children is clearly an interactive and reciprocal process involving multiple inputs (see Bronfenbrenner, 1979; Hasbrook, 1982) that should be reflected in future research on childhood sport socialization.

A limited number of studies have also examined sport socialization in adolescence (Brown, 1985; Butcher, 1983, 1985; Higginson, 1985; McElroy & Kirkendall, 1980; Patriksson, 1981; Schellenberger, 1981; M.D. Smith, 1979; Yamaguchi, 1984). The general trend of these studies has been to reinforce the importance of the peer group during the adolescent age span. In this vein, Yamaguchi (1984) reported that parental influence on English-speaking males decreased from childhood to adolescence, while remaining strong for French-speaking adolescents. The females from all three cultural groups reported that parental influence was negligible but that peer influence on sport involvement was very important. Patriksson (1981) reported that peers of the same sex exerted a major influence in the sport involvement of Swedish adolescents by functioning as active role models.

Running counter to the peer findings is the study by McElroy and Kirkendall (1980), which involved a large sample of males and females between the ages of 10 and 18 years who were involved in the National Youth Sports Program. In response to a forced-choice question concerning which person seemed to show the most interest in their sport participation, both males and females selected parents above friends or teacher/coach. The males selected father and mother, whereas the females selected mother and father. In her cross-sectional and longitudinal studies of young females in grades 6 to 10, Butcher (1983, 1985) also found that fathers' and mothers' socializing influences contributed to initial and continued involvement in community-organized activities such as sport lessons and leagues. However, she also reported that the socializing influences of the significant others declined between grades 6 and 10. Adding a third dimension to the peer and the family influence studies are the data reported by M.D. Smith (1979), which involved males and females, 12 to 19 years of age, who were attending a sport training camp. The females selected teacher/coach, followed by female friends, as most responsible for their first becoming interested in the particular sport that brought them to the training camp. Males also chose teacher/coach first, followed by their peers. In a study of female athletes, Higginson (1985) found that the teacher/coach influence emerges during adolescence—the same period that parental influence is decreasing. This particular pattern supports earlier research on female sport socialization by Greendorfer (1977), who found that while peers and parents strongly influence childhood sport involvement, peers and teachers/coaches are the most influential on adolescents.

Evidently, the research on adolescent sport socialization is no clearer than the research on the childhood period. While the adolescent studies are somewhat contradictory, the emergent role of the peer group is quite evident. Once again, the question is not so much, Which significant other is more influential? but, Which factors interact to influence sport involvement? A study by Brown (1985) provides an example of the extent to which family and peer variables combine to influence the sport experience. In her study of female swimmers' withdrawal from competitive activity, Brown found significant changes in social support from both the family and peer group, which included the girl's boyfriend, male and female teammates, and female friends outside of swimming. In fact, the desire to spend more time with friends was one of the most important reasons for withdrawing from swimming. A second illustration of this joint effect can be found in the study by Patriksson (1981). In an effort to capture the potential combined influence of parents and peers, Patriksson constructed two extreme groups—positive and negative parent-peer environments toward sport—from his data. Not surprisingly, both males and females from positive parent-peer environments took part in sport more frequently than males and females from negative parent-peer environments (males, 63% vs. 35%; females, 45% vs. 10%). These trends are consistent with recent research on parent-adolescent relationships, wherein the peer group assumes a critical role in numerous facets of the adolescent's social experiences (Youniss & Smollar, 1985).

In summary, the recent research on family, peer, and school effects on sport socialization of children and adolescents provides the basis for rejecting the view that the family is the most influential social system. Sufficient evidence is now available to accord the peer group a more prominent role in the socialization process, particularly during adolescence. In spite of the increased volume of research in this area, the factors that contribute most to the early involvement of children in sport have not been addressed, leaving unanswered the general question of how family, peers, and school shape children's socialization into sport.

Parents and Siblings as Socializing Agents

The second hypothesis put forth in our earlier review suggested that parents were more influential than siblings in socializing children into sport. Given the impoverished state of sibling research in general, it was not surprising to find very few studies that examined these variables directly in relation to sport socialization. In a study of males and females between the ages of 9 and 12, Lewko and Ewing (1980) examined the differential effects of father, mother, brother, and sister on sport involvement. By sex, the subjects were divided into high- and low-involved groups. Fathers emerged as most influential for the high-involved boys, whereas mother, father, brother, and sister discriminated between high- and low-involved girls. According to this evidence, siblings do not appear to play a major role in sport socialization of males; rather, they appear to reinforce the parental input to female sport socialization. This pattern is supported by Patriksson's (1981) study of adolescents in which older brothers and sisters were reported as being of no importance for primary and secondary involvement of both males and females at 7 to 12 years (retrospective) or at 16 years, which was the current age of the sample.

Findings from a study on Japanese elementary school children (Ebihara, Ikeda, & Myiashita, 1983) also support this pattern of parent versus sibling influence. Ebihara, Ikeda, and Myiashita report that, for males, the father was the most significant socializing agent in general, with older siblings emerging as important for the youngest child. For the females, both father and mother were important socializing influences, as were siblings. This study, although conducted on a sample from another culture, supports the Lewko and Ewing (1980) findings, particularly with respect to the young females. In order for young girls to become highly involved in sport, a broad base of significant other support must be present.

The question of whether parents or siblings are more influential in the sport socialization process remains unanswered. Perhaps the focus should be shifted away from attempting to assign primary influence to one group in favor of concentrating on determining the relative influence of each group. We must not lose sight of the fact that social relationships of children and adults are different. The ability of siblings to exert influence on the social environment apart from their parents is quite circumscribed, as they are virtually subordinate to the power of adults (Youniss, 1978). Consequently, their influence over younger siblings will be monitored and defined in part by their parents.

Father as the Most Influential Sport Socializer

To this point in our review, a number of studies have suggested that the sport socialization process is complex and interactive. These studies have enabled us to clarify the role of the father in the sport socialization process, an important finding because our previous review argued quite strongly that the father was a central figure, due in part to what was known about his role in the process of gender role socialization. In that review we noted that fathers appeared to play a major role in sex-typing of activities and in gender role socialization because they were more strict in their differentiation of sex roles and more rigid in their reinforcement of sex-appropriate behavior, particularly for males. We hypothesized that fathers were perhaps the most influential figure in the sport-socialization process.

The studies reported by Butcher (1983, 1985), Greendorfer and Ewing (1981), Lewko and Ewing (1980), McElroy and Kirkendall (1980), Patriksson (1981), Sage (1980), and M.D. Smith (1979) all provide relevant information on the issue of paternal influence. Across all of the studies, the father does not emerge consistently as the most significant socializer for both males and females. The situation is perhaps best illustrated in the Lewko and Ewing (1980) study in which high- and low-sport-involved males and females were studied. While the father was the most influential factor in discriminating high- and low-involved boys, he shared the load with mother and siblings in the case of the high-involved girls. While Sage (1980), in a retrospective study of college athletes, has reported that both parents were viewed as very influential by both sexes, M.D. Smith (1979), in his study of adolescent athletes, reported that parents were not seen as important in male or females athletes becoming interested in their chosen sport.

One of the difficulties in resolving the paternal supremacy issue rests with the marked variability in the studies that have incorporated the father as a sport socializer. Not all studies have employed the same number of significant others. In addition, there has been significant variability in the stimulus questions used in the studies to determine significant other influences. Compounding this are the differences in sample frames that have employed different age ranges, cultures, and levels of sport involvement. These criticisms could be raised in each of the major sections addressed in this chapter. Aside from design features, however, one important factor that can weigh heavily in father influence is social-class background. Unfortunately, few studies have considered this important structural variable. Moreover, few studies have reported socioeconomic background of subjects in order to make appropriate comparisons (see Greendorfer and Ewing, 1981).

Finally, there is the distinct possibility that the influence exerted by the father during the child's early development (0-5 years) could be significantly modified once the child has made the initial transition to school and becomes part of a wider social network. Certainly the recent research on social development of children (see Youniss, 1978) would lend support to this argument. In fact, by the age of 6, children are engaging in a broad range of relationships, all of which require careful negotiation and which contribute to the child's evolving social fluency. While the father may exert considerable influence, the child now has recourse to a range of social relationships that will shape his or her development.

School as More Influential for Boys Than Girls

In the earlier section on family, peer, and school influences, the limited research on school effects led us to conclude that the school or teachers/coaches were not very influential in the sport socialization of children or adolescents. Although the strongest evidence supporting this position can be found in a study by Yamaguchi (1984), who reported that school factors were of no significance for English-speaking males and females or for French-speaking males, this position is tempered by two studies on female athletes. In one retrospective study of intercollegiate athletes, Greendorfer (1977) found that teachers/coaches were significant predictors of adolescent participation only. In a second retrospective study focusing only on elite level volleyball players, Weiss and Knoppers (1982) found that parents, peers, and physical education teachers, collectively, had significant influence on sport involvement, but only during childhood. Despite the fact that different periods of influence were identified, both studies suggest some school influence on the socialization process, though the nature or degree of impact might be minimal.

Results from the Greendorfer and Ewing (1981) study on childhood sport socialization also demonstrated school influence, as teachers emerged as important for both black and white females. Teachers were also influential for both males and females in the study by Ebihara and others (1983), although not very strongly. A study by M.D. Smith (1979) on sport camp participants provides the strongest support for the influence of teachers: Both male and female adolescents reported that their teacher/coach was the most influential individual in their becoming interested in a specific sport. While these studies serve to keep the school influence as an issue to be resolved, a more sophisticated approach to the potential influence of the school in sport socialization will have to emerge in order to guide the research process. The current literature does not reflect the existence of such a conceptual framework at this time.

In Search of a New Model for Sport Socialization

The current literature focusing on child and adolescent socialization into sport demonstrates that we have not yet arrived at a clear understanding of how individuals become involved in sport. The considerable amount of information generated around the topic does not appear to be ordered or systematic. Recently, Theberge (1984) has called for the development of a more adequate theory of sport participation. Our review leads us to agree that one is needed. While it is beyond the scope of the current chapter to undertake such a task, several points are worthy of comment in assisting others in questioning their assumptions regarding the sport socialization process.

One of the critical gaps in the childhood sport socialization literature that has emerged from our review is the virtual absence of research on younger children. The early childhood years are acknowledged as a critical period for shaping children's orientations to the world; yet, the majority of the sport socialization research has focused on pre-adolescence and beyond. One might argue that in most cases what is being investigated is not the socialization into sport but rather the social influences that maintain children in sport once they have become actively involved. In a study of 9- to 12-year-old children who had been classified as highly or lowly involved in physical activities (Lewko & Ewing, 1980), the high-low pattern was found to have been set by age 9. If in fact the initial entry into sport is shaped much prior to preadolescence, then our attention must focus directly on that time period. We should not rely on what would now appear to be retrospective data from older children and adolescents.

In focusing on the earlier age range we draw attention to the potential effects of childhood sport involvement on the family system. While it is acknowledged that sport involvement carries with it a realignment of family functioning, we do not know how such changes affect the sport-involved child or the other children in the family (Berlage, 1982). Given the recent advances in conceptualizing the family as a system, examining the sport socialization process within this framework would be fruitful.

Reviewing the literature, it becomes apparent that socialization into sport has been viewed somewhat differently by various authors. Differences were particularly evident in the use of elite-level athletes as a primary source of information on the socialization process. What we appear to have in the literature is a mixture of facts pertaining to the influence of significant others on children and adolescents at various levels of accomplishment, ranging from nonparticipants to elite athletes. From our reading of the literature, at least three distinct features of the process are being confounded: (a) factors that affect initial involvement, (b) factors that maintain involvement once committed, and (c) factors that shape the pursuit of excellence. Although all three aspects are subject to influence from significant others and can be generally categorized as socialization, we feel that some conceptual reformulation is necessary. First of all, socialization can be viewed along a temporal (or horizontal) continuum: (a) introduction or initiation into sport; (b) maintenance, persistence, or continuation of involvement; and (c) role withdrawal or desocialization (i.e., retirement, dropping out, or temporarily leaving sport). These stages could be adapted to an age continuum as well— one that begins at early childhood, includes adolescence, and, feasibly, extends to old age. The mastery or skill factor, which encompasses pursuit of excellence, adds a second dimension (perhaps a vertical continuum) that is conceptually and operationally separated from the first; still, its levels become an important consideration when examining the temporal features of the sport socialization process.

Such a framework would alter our approaches, definitions, and problem focus, and, we hope, would facilitate our understanding of how significant others influence the sport socialization process at varying degrees of skill during different stages of the life cycle. We would then have the beginning of a conceptual framework toward which various theoretical positions could be applied. Hypotheses could specifically address the *nature* of the influence of significant others during various phases of the process. For example, such a perspective would allow us to understand more clearly how interactive and reciprocal effects (Hasbrook, 1982, in press; Snyder & Purdy, 1982) influence any stage of the process, whether it be initiation into sport or desocialization (Brown, 1985). These conceptual issues also have implications for research design. Additionally, to gain more in-depth understanding, methodological approaches other than survey instruments would be needed. Because socialization is a dynamic and interactive process, it is important that several aspects of the play, game, or sport *experience* itself be understood. To this end we suggest the use of more qualitative approaches, such as observation and interviews. In addition to these considerations, we feel that longitudinal studies would enable us to better understand the consequences of antecedent influences— not only those related to sport socialization, but also those that impinge upon early childhood and gender role socialization.

This plea for a developmental approach is supported not only by our previous literature review on family influence and sex differences (Lewko & Greendorfer, 1977), but also by an emergent theme from the research findings cited in the present review. Findings from several studies indicate that sport socialization research can no longer trivialize the prominent role that the peer group plays in the sport experience of children and adolescents. This position is reinforced by early developmentalists such as Sullivan (1953) and Piaget (1965), who, joined more recently by Damon (1977) and Youniss (1978), emphasized that peers play a central role in social development. As already suggested, researchers interested in sport socialization, whether considering initiation into or enhancement of performance, have given only fleeting attention to peer-group influence and social development in general as important components of the sport experience. Our review suggests that the traditional controversy, which maintained that the peer group displaces the influence of parents, can now be laid to rest. Researchers now accept the joint effects that social systems, family, and peers have on the process (Youniss & Smollar, 1985). Moreover, given the heterogeneous and complex nature of peer relations (cf. Oden, Herzberger, Mangione, & Wheeler, 1984), peer influence must be more carefully differentiated and identified if we are to truly understand the nature of influence by significant others in sport involvement. One example illustrating our point comes from Brown's (1985) finding that the peer group was an extremely powerful influence in the decision of female swimmers to withdraw from sport. Of particular interest, Brown found a cross-sex relationship, suggesting that more attention should be devoted to this aspect of peer constellations in future research.

We began this review by acknowledging the centrality of family and peers in the sport socialization of children. While the existing research appears to have raised more questions than were answered, it does demonstrate the need for gaining a better understanding of social development in general and locating sport socialization within such a framework or context. Both the family and peer group represent complex sets of social relations that serve to facilitate or impede general child development. The task for the future is for researchers to understand how such social-psychological forces affect the child's entry into, persistence in, and/or withdrawal from physical activity and sport and shape his or her desire to excel.

References

Baumrind, D. (1980). New directions in socialization research. *American Psychologist*, **35**(7), 639-652.

Berlage, G.I. (1982). Children's sports and the family. *Arena Review*, **6**(1), 43-47.

Bronfenbrenner, U. (1979). *The ecology of human development: Experiments by nature and design*. Cambridge, MA: Harvard University Press.

Brown, B.A. (1985). Factors influencing the process of withdrawal by female adolescents from the role of competitive age group swimmers. *Sociology of Sport Journal*, **2**, 111-129.

Butcher, J. (1983). Socialization of adolescent girls into physical activity. *Adolescence*, **18**(72), 753-766.

Butcher, J. (1985). Longitudinal analysis of adolescent girls' participation in physical activity. *Sociology of Sport Journal*, **2**, 130-143.

Cooley, C.H. (1909). *Social organization*. New York: Scribner.

Damon, W. (1977). *The social world of the child*. San Francisco: Jossey-Bass.

DiPietro, J.A. (1981). Rough and tumble play: A function of gender. *Developmental Psychology*, **17**, 50-58.

Eaton, W.O., & Enns, L.R. (1986). Sex differences in human motor activity level. *Psychological Bulletin*, **100**, 19-28.

Eaton, W.O., & Keats, J.G. (1982). Peer presence, stress and sex difference in the motor activity levels of preschoolers. *Developmental
Psychology*, **18**, 534-540.

Ebihara, O., Ikeda, M., & Myiashita, M. (1983). Birth order and children's socialization into sport. *International Review of Sport
Sociology*, **18**(1), 69-88.

Eisenberg, N., Wolchick, S.A., Hernandez, R., & Pasternack, J.F. (1985).
Parental socialization of young children's play: A short-term longitudinal study. *Child Development*, **56**, 1506-1513.

Fagot, B.I. (1984). Teacher and peer reactions to boys' and girls' play
styles. *Sex Roles*, **11**, 691-702.

Fagot, B.I., & Leinback, M.D. (1983). Play styles in early childhood:
Social consequences for boys and girls. In M. Liss (Ed.), *Social and
cognitive skills* (pp. 93-116). New York: Academic Press.

Greendorfer, S.L. (1977). Role of socializing agents in female sport
involvement. *Research Quarterly*, **48**, 304-310.

Greendorfer, S.L., & Brundage, C.L. (1987). Sex difference in children's motor skills: Toward a cross-disciplinary perspective. In M.
Adrian (Ed.), *Medicine and sport science: Sportswomen* (Vol. 24,
pp. 125-137). Basel: Karger.

Greendorfer, S.L., & Ewing, M.E. (1981). Race and gender differences
in children's socialization into sport. *Research Quarterly for Exercise and Sport*, **52**(3), 301-310.

Hasbrook, C.A. (1982). The theoretical notion of reciprocity and child-
hood socialization into sport. In A.D. Dunleavy, A.W. Miracle, &
C.R. Rees (Eds.), *Studies in the sociology of sport* (pp. 139-151).
Fort Worth: Texas Christian University Press.

Hasbrook, C.A. (in press). Reciprocity and childhood socialization into
sport. In J.H. Humphrey & L. VanderVelden (Eds.), *Current selected research in the psychology and sociology of sport*. New
York: AMS Press.

Higginson, D.C. (1985). The influence of socializing agents in the
female sport-participation process. *Adolescence*, **20**(77), 73-82.

Lewko, J.H., & Ewing, M.E. (1980). Sex differences and parental influence in sport involvement of children. *Journal of Sport Psychology*, **2**, 62-68.

Lewko, J.H., & Greendorfer, S.L. (1977). Family influence and sex
differences in children's socialization into sport: A review. In D.M.
Landers & R.W. Christina (Eds.), *Psychology of motor behavior and
sport* (pp. 434-447). Champaign, IL: Human Kinetics.

Liss, M. (1983). Learning gender-related skills through play. In M. Liss
(Ed.), *Social and cognitive skills* (pp. 147-166). New York: Academic Press.

Lloyd, B., & Smith, C. (1985). The social representation of gender and young children's play. *British Journal of Developmental Psychology*, **3**, 65-73.

Loy, J.W., McPherson, B.D., & Kenyon, G.S. (1978). *Sport and social systems*. Reading, MA: Addison-Wesley.

McElroy, M.A., & Kirkendall, D.R. (1980). Significant others and professionalized sport attitudes. *Research Quarterly for Exercise and Sport*, **51**, 645-653.

Melnick, M.J., Dunkelman, N., & Mashiach, A. (1981). Familial factors of sports giftedness among young Israeli athletes. *Journal of Sport Behavior*, **4**, 82-94.

Oden, S., Herzberger, S.D., Mangione, P.L., & Wheeler, V.A. (1984). Children's peer relationships: An examination of social processes. In J.C. Masters & K. Yarkin-Levin (Eds.), *Boundary areas in social and developmental psychology* (pp. 132-160). New York: Academic Press.

Oettingen, G. (1985). The influence of the kindergarten teacher on sex difference in behavior. *International Journal of Behavioral Development*, **8**, 3-13.

Patriksson, G. (1981). Socialization to sports involvement. *Scandinavian Journal of the Sports Sciences*, **3**(1), 27-32.

Piaget, J. (1965). *The moral judgment of the child*. New York: Free Press.

Power, T.G. (1985). Mother-and-father-infant play: A developmental analysis. *Child Development*, **56**, 1514-1524.

Power, T.G., & Parke, R.D. (1983). Patterns of mother and father play with their 8-month-old infants: A multiple analysis approach. *Infant Behavior and Development*, **6**, 453-459.

Power, T.G., & Parke, R.D. (1986). Patterns of early socialization: Mother- and father-infant interactions in the home. *International Journal of Behavioral Development*, **9**, 331-341.

Sage, G.H. (1980). Parental influence and socialization into sport for male and female intercollegiate athletes. *Journal of Sport and Social Issues*, **4**(2), 1-13.

Schellenberger, B. (1981). The significance of social relations in sport activity. *International Review of Sport Sociology*, **16**(2), 69-76.

Smith, A.B. (1985). Teacher modeling and sex-typed play preferences. *New Zealand Journal of Educational Studies*, **20**, 39-47.

Smith, M.D. (1979). Getting involved in sport: Sex differences. *International Review of Sport Sociology*, **14**(2), 93-99.

Snyder, E.E., & Purdy, D.A. (1982). Socialization into sport: Parent and child reverse and reciprocal effects. *Research Quarterly for Exercise and Sport*, **53**, 263-266.

Sullivan, H.S. (1953). *The interpersonal theory of psychiatry*. New York: W.W. Norton.

Theberge, N. (1984). On the need for a more adequate theory of sport participation. *Sociology of Sport Journal*, **1**, 26-35.

Weinraub, M., Clemens, L.P., Sockloff, A., Ethridge, T., Gracely, E., & Myers, B. (1984). The development of sex role stereotypes in the third year: Relationships to gender labeling, gender identity, sex-typed toy preference and family characteristics. *Child Development*, **55**, 1493-1503.

Weiss, M.R., & Knoppers, A. (1982). The influence of socializing agents on female collegiate volleyball players. *Journal of Sport Psychology*, **4**, 267-279.

Williams, K., Goodman, M., & Green, R. (1985). Parent-child factors in gender role socialization in girls. *Journal of the American Academy of Child Psychiatry*, **26**, 720-731.

Yamaguchi, Y. (1984). A comparative study of adolescent socialization into sport: The case of Japan and Canada. *International Review of Sociology of Sport*, **19**(1), 63-81.

Youniss, J. (1978). The nature of social development: A conceptual discussion of cognition. In H. McGurk (Ed.), *Issues in childhood social development* (pp. 203-227). London: Methuen.

Youniss, J., & Smollar, J. (1985). *Adolescent relations with mothers, fathers and friends*. Chicago: University of Chicago Press.

CHAPTER 20

Interpersonal Sources of Violence in Hockey: The Influence of Parents, Coaches, and Teammates

Michael D. Smith

Research indicates that parents, coaches, and teammates provide youth hockey players with a guide to action by advocating norms of conduct, usually through expressions of approval and disapproval, and that players' perceptions of these others' approval or disapproval of violence influences players' own behavior. This chapter is an examination of the way in which and the extent to which parents, coaches, and teammates exert their influence.

Parents

To understand parents' feelings about their children's participation in hockey violence, one must first grasp the extent and nature of parent involvement in youth hockey. To start with, parents' sheer physical presence is overwhelming. Some 60,000 boys play so-called competitive minor hockey in Ontario. Eighty percent of their parents attend at least three-quarters of their boys' games (McPherson & Davidson, 1980). In Toronto, 61% of players' fathers attend their sons' games at least once a week, and 75% attend at least two or three games a month. Nineteen percent of these fathers watch their sons practice at least once a week, 27% at least two or three times a month (Smith, 1979).

Field observations of minor hockey help convey something about the intensity of parents' involvement.[1] Typically, minor hockey families arrive at the arena anywhere from 1 hour to a half hour before a game. While the players dress, parents stand in the lobby talking, usually about hockey. Some parents wear such team paraphernalia as jackets, scarves, hats, or buttons. During the game, parents of players on the same team sit together, sometimes behind their sons' bench, distinctly separate from opposing parents. As the action unfolds on the ice, the

---

[1]Unless otherwise indicated, all field observations and quotes are from the author's own field studies and interviews.

bodies in the stands strain, faces contort, parents jump to their feet. Organized cheering and spontaneous bursts of applause are frequent. Immersion in the game is total and attuned principally to the performance of one's own offspring. Booing and catcalls are sometimes directed at opposing players, frequently at the referees. Occasionally, groups of rival parents engage in unfriendly verbal exchanges; fights are not unknown. The rougher the game, the greater the likelihood of this sort of misbehavior. Consider a typical example (most of these field observations were conducted prior to 1980 when minor hockey leagues in Canada began banning body contact for youngsters 12 and under):

It took me about 30 seconds after entering the arena to realize that the game in progress was "getting out of hand." The play on the ice between the Don Mills and Red Wing Pee Wee teams was exceptionally rough, with a lot of heavy body checks and a great deal of pushing and shoving. Even more noticeable was the behavior of the fans. Apparently the Don Mills parents felt that the referee was "shafting" them, and they were very vocal in their criticisms. There were standard comments such as "C'mon ref, there's two teams on the ice, why don't you take a look?" and the old standby, "How much did the Red Wings pay you to throw this one?" to mention only a few.

Naturally these attacks did not go unnoticed by the Red Wing parents who were sitting about 50 feet from the Don Mills group. The Red Wing fans felt that every call was justified and that the Don Mills parents were "poor sports." This led to numerous verbal exchanges between the groups, like this one:

RED WING FAN: "Why don't you stop crying, your kids deserve everything they're getting."

DON MILLS FAN: "Sit down and shut up, you idiot."

SAME RED WING FAN: "Do you want to step outside and make me, big mouth?"

DON MILLS FAN: "I wouldn't waste my time."

In the eyes of parents and others, the *sine qua non* of hockey is hustling. Hockey parents want to see their kids hustle—and in hockey, hustling includes hitting. Among hockey parents, hitting, or "taking the body," usually elicits shouts of approval; it is regarded as a sign of desire and gameness. A conversation between two fathers at a Pee Wee game went as follows: "Stick checks, never body checks," exclaimed the first father, disgustedly. Then, yelling, "Take the body, for Chrissakes!" Father two: "Boy, little Ian isn't afraid to hit." In addition, verbal encouragement of legal hitting often extends to the encouragement of semilegal acts, sometimes even to fighting and more extreme behaviors.

Fisticuffs appear to be character-building in the eyes of some parents who see hockey as a training ground for life. One father, an official in a youth hockey organization, put it this way: "It's a violent society, eh? This is a tough society we're in. I put my own kid in hockey so he would learn to take his lumps." He said he saw "nothing wrong with taking off the gloves" and that "the day they turn hockey into a namby-pamby game for sissies is the day I get out." Picture this arena lobby scene after an Atom game featuring a multiplayer "semifight" ("real" fighting starts around age 14): When two of the 10-year-old combatants approached a group of parents, one father, smiling, said, "Looks like we've got a couple of scrappers." Approving chuckles were heard all around.

How widespread is parents' approval of violence? Six hundred four randomly selected Toronto players were asked if they thought their father and mother would approve of a minor hockey player punching another player in four situations: (a) if ridiculed, (b) if threatened, (c) if shoved, or (d) if punched by the other player. Indexes of Parents' Approval of Hockey Fighting were constructed by summing the *yes* responses to these items. Table 1 shows variations in players' scores on these indexes by age and level of competition (house league or recreational versus competitive).

Table 1   Hockey Players' Perceptions of Their Parents' Approval of Hockey Fighting by Age and Level of Competition (in Percent)[1]

	Fathers' approval			Mothers' approval		
	Low	Medium	High[2]	Low	Medium	High
Age						
12-13 (N = 166)	77	20	3	89	8	3
14-15 (N = 196)	66	25	9	85	12	3
16-17 (N = 130)	47	31	22	81	14	5
18-21 (N = 112)	40	19	41	75	18	7
Level of competition						
House league						
(N = 330)	76	18	6	94	6	0
Competitive						
(N = 274)	41	31	29	71	21	8
All players						
(N = 604)	60	24	16	83	13	4

[1]Adapted from Smith (1979, p. 113).

[2]Low = approval in no situations; medium = approval in one or two situations; high = approval in three or four situations.

The majority of fathers (60%) rank low on the Fathers' Approval Index, which is to say these fathers would not, in the eyes of their offspring, approve of a player punching another player in any of the situations presented. But approval increases sharply with age and level of competition. In the older-age and competitive rows, the majority of fathers fall into the medium- (one or two situations) and high- (three or four situations) approval categories. Forty-one percent of the 18- to 21-year-olds felt their fathers would approve of fighting in at least three of the situations, compared to only 3% of the 12- to 13-year-olds; 29% of the fathers of competitive-level players were seen as high approvers, compared to 6% of the house-league fathers. Mothers consistently were perceived as less approving than fathers; still, 25% and 29% in the 18- to 21-year-old and competitive rows are in the medium- and high-approval categories combined.

A massive public opinion poll conducted for the Ontario Hockey Council by McPherson and Davidson (1980) suggests that the above perceptions approximate parents' own expressed attitudes about violence in minor hockey. In 1979, 78,000 questionnaires were mailed to the parents of all competitive-level players in the province. Over 31,000 parents responded, a return rate of 40%, remarkably high for a survey of this kind. Table 2 shows responses to several of the questionnaire items relevant to violence. The proportion of *no* and *OK*

Table 2   Hockey Parents' Attitudes About Violence in "Competitive" Minor Hockey (in Percent)[1]

Item	Response		
	Yes	No	No response
Would you support a rule preventing body-checking for Pee Wee and under players?	54	30	16
Do you think there is too much violence in your child's league?	42	55	3
	OK as is	Needs improvement	No response
Do you think enforcement of the rules relating to the use of hockey sticks is OK as is or needs improvement?	32	66	2
Do you think enforcement of the rules relating to fighting is OK as is or needs improvement?	36	62	2

[1]Adapted from McPherson and Davidson (1980, pp. 69, 71).

as is responses corroborates in a rough way the medium- and high-approval data in the competitive row of Table 1.

Levels of and variations in parents' approval of fighting and other acts of violence are of considerable interest. But can it be demonstrated that parents' approval has an impact on players' attitudes and behavior? Yes. Vaz (1982), in his study of over 1,900 youth hockey players in Waterloo, Ontario, showed that fathers' sanctions for a variety of assaultive acts in hockey are statistically related to their sons' attitudes regarding the same acts. Smith (1979), in his Toronto survey, found a substantial correlation between players' scores on the foregoing Parents' Approval Index and number of (self-reported) hockey fights. The more approval for violence, the more violence.

Coaches

Hockey coaches, like hockey fathers, encourage physically aggressive play, including fighting and other assaultive acts, both for what it symbolizes (gameness and strong character) and for its utility in winning games and enhancing players' occupational careers. Because coaches' own careers—or at least their self-images—in most professionalized minor hockey leagues depend to some degree on producing winning teams and upwardly mobile individual performers, coaches tend to choose players on the basis of size and toughness, among other attributes. Almost from the start, big kids who can handle the heavy going are selected over smaller, less aggressive, though sometimes more skilled, performers. By age 13 or 14, a boy's willingness and ability to hit are highly important in determining his upward mobility, as the following pregame pep talk suggests. This coach did not conceal his irritation at the team's recent poor performances.

> I hope you guys realize if you don't start playing better hockey you've probably reached the end of the line at this level. From here on things are a lot tougher. I was talking to Metcalfe [the Bantam coach] and he said that right now he figures there are only two guys on this club who can make it in Bantam. He saw the way you guys were pushed around by Nats the other night and said there was no way that kind of stuff goes in Bantam. You realize that there are only four guys from that club moving up next year and probably a couple of guys will get cut. So at most there are only likely to be six openings, and that's not counting anyone he recruits. You can see that if you hope to move on next year, you've got to start showing some hustle. Teams have just been walking by our defense all year without being touched. We've gotta start knocking them on their cans. Guys know they don't have to keep their heads up when they come into our end!

Legal hitting almost always leads to the penalty-getting kind, for the line between the two is often fine. Coaches do not approve of penalties

per se, of course, but accept a certain number as an inevitable consequence of spirited, aggressive play. Then there is the "good" penalty.
"You should have tripped him," a house-league coach admonished a
wide-eyed boy of 8. "Never let a guy go around you." Many hockey
coaches also expect players to fight in self-defense and to retaliate
against flagrant fouls. A Junior A hockey coach, once an NHL professional, put it this way:

> It's important to be tough. I don't think it's all that important that
> you have to go out and knock somebody right off, but I believe it's
> important to be tough because if trouble comes you have to stand
> up. That's what they taught us in the old days. Take the man out
> clean, but if he raises his stick and goes at you be ready for him.
> Stand up to it and be counted.

Some coaches communicate their attitudes regarding violence as
much by what they do as by what they say. Incidents like the following are not uncommon. As the buzzer sounded to end a penalty-filled
Pee Wee game, one boy appeared to spear another in the stomach. The
coaches began shouting at one another as the teams left the ice:

> COACH A: What the hell's the matter with you guys? You beat us
> five-nothing and now you want to take one of our players out for
> the season.

> COACH B: Ah, shut up and go home you goddam crybaby.

> Coaches and players filed together down a corridor toward the
> dressing rooms.

> COACH A (to the player who was speared): You have my permis-
> sion to go and punch the shit out of that son-of-a-bitch (indicating
> the other player).

> The first player threw down his stick and gloves, charged his oppo-
> nent, and began pummeling him from behind. Surprised, the latter
> went down, his assailant on top, punching. Coach B attempted to
> pull him off. Coach A pushed Coach B. A short, shoving match en-
> sued, which was finally broken up by bystanders.

Some youth hockey organizations have reputations for sponsoring
excessively rough or "dirty" teams. There is at least one of these teams
in every age division, almost always accompanied by a coach of matching notoriety. Opposing coaches make special preparations for games
against such teams. "C'mon now guys," one exhorted, "we need a win
tonight. We played well on Tuesday. Let's keep it up. Now these guys
are gonna be hitting, so we've got to stay cool. We can't afford stupid
penalties." Indeed, this particular game was very rough. Penalties were
numerous. The other coach directed a tirade at the referee and at his
own players. "If you're going to hit him after the whistle make it a *good*

one." After the game, a boy who had played for this coach the year before explained: "He's mental. He's always yelling and screaming at guys. He used to try and make me do 50 push-ups after games. No one else, just me. The guys on the team are just as crazy as he is."

More than a few minor hockey coaches tolerate, even nurture, "goons" or "enforcers," some of them as young as 13 or 14. Consider "The Animal," as one 14-year-old was known by players and coaches in a Toronto league. When opposing coaches prepared for games against "The Animal's" team they always made special plans to handle him. A coach explained his plan to his team in a pregame talk that went as follows:

Look, if this character starts anything, take him out early. We can't have him charging around hammering people. Somebody's going to have to straighten him out. Just remember, get the gloves off and do it in a fair fight. If you shake him up early he can't keep it up. Besides, it's best to take the penalties early in the game before we get too tired to kill them effectively.

The Flyers jumped to a 3-0 lead before the St. Mikes coach decided to play "The Animal." As soon as he came over the boards he ran at Johnson (the Flyers' captain) and wrestled him to the ice. They fought and each player got 5 minutes. When he came back on "The Animal" ran at another guy, but he was ready for him and decked him with an elbow. He got 2 minutes for elbowing, but it was worth it. He said after that "The Animal" was like a piece of jello. In fact, he hardly got on the rest of the game.

In Junior professional ranks, employing one or more "enforcers" on a team is standard practice. The following is an excerpt from an interview with a 19-year-old Junior A player:

Q: So you think Ron [the enforcer] was brought on the team for that purpose?

A: Well definitely. You can even hear him [the coach] you know. Bill [the coach] would say, "Ron, go out and get that guy." He'd tell him, and I didn't like that, you know, "go out and get that guy," because half the time I knew the guy he was going to get. I've played in this league so long, I've got some pretty good friends in there. What are you going to do?

Such coaches appear to have much the same attitude toward violence as their counterparts in professional hockey. But the professional coach must concern himself more with the ultimate business of hockey: winning games and filling seats. To produce a team that can do this, certain player types are required, among them tough, combative "grinders" who can win the physical battles for the puck and fight if necessary, which inevitably it is. Also needed is at least one "tough guy," "bad guy," "policeman," "enforcer," "animal," "goon," "cement head," "hit man," "designated fighter," or "role-player" (these roles are not exactly the same). An NHL player, one of 60 interviewed by Smith (1983), explains further:

> Every team picks up their tough guys. In our case we never got a guy who just fought. Nobody on our team has been sent out just to fight. We've always had, like, Jim Schoenfeld, who was, like, our tough guy, but he always played 30, 40 minutes a game, so he had to do his job the way it should be done. He's tough, but he also plays a lot. There are other teams, of course, who have guys just to fight. They send them out to play about 10 minutes a game, and their only job is to stir up trouble, start fights, and get the good guys off the ice.

Most of these professionals saw the coach as trying to do a difficult job and as having to cope with the caprices of owners and general managers in the process. Coaches, players point out, do not expect all players to be fighters, or even highly physically aggressive, if it is not their "nature," especially if the players are small and possess compensatory skills.

> Like, we had guys that were expected to be like a policeman, you know. Straighten a guy out once in a while. That's what they were getting paid for. They [coach and general manger] knew this guy wasn't a 20-goal scorer, so they didn't expect it. By the same token if you were a 20- or 25-goal scorer and you weren't a rough guy, they didn't expect you to run into the corner and jump on somebody and get into a big fight, because they weren't paying you to fight. They were paying you to score goals. So, you know, I think it was more or less the individual.

Coaches have minimum requirements, however. You must help a teammate in trouble, and you must not let opponents' attempts at intimidation affect your performance.

How widespread is hockey coaches' approval of rough play? Almost all of 83 high school players interviewed by Smith (1975) stated that their coaches would approve (most of them "strongly") of "hard but legal body-checking." Over half of the more than 1,900 boys surveyed by Vaz (1982) reported that their coaches regularly emphasized "playing rough and being aggressive." When asked, What are the three most important qualities a coach looks for in selecting players for all-star teams? 62% of the oldest boys (aged 15 and 16) included, out of nine possible response choices, "being aggressive at all times"; 56% included "physical size and strength"; 25% included "guts and courage." (More than half these boys were house-leaguers, and their responses probably pulled these percentages down.)

**Table 3   Hockey Players' Perceptions of Their Coaches'
Approval of Hockey Fighting by Age and Level of Competition
(in Percent)[1]**

		Coaches approval	
	Low	Medium	High[2]
Age			
12-13 (N = 166)	74	17	9
14-15 (N = 196)	59	30	11
16-17 (N = 130)	39	36	25
18-21 (N = 112)	25	23	52
Level of competition			
House league			
(N = 330)	70	22	8
Competitive			
(N = 274)	32	32	36
All players			
(N = 604)	53	26	21

[1]Adapted from Smith (1979, p. 113).

[2]Low = approval in no situations; medium = approval in one or two situations;
high = approval in three or four situations.

Such findings are not surprising; much of what is called *aggressive*
play is sanctioned by the official rules of the game. What of officially
illegal violence? Table 3 reveals that Toronto minor hockey players see
coaches as somewhat more approving of fighting than fathers, yet only
21% of all coaches come under the high-approval heading. Again, this
overall figure obscures differences in age and level of competition. Over
50% of the 18- to 21-year-olds and 36% of the competitive-level players
saw their coaches as high approvers.

Players' perceptions of coaches' sanctions for assaultive play do seem
to have an impact on players' attitudes and conduct at all levels of
hockey. Vaz (1982) reports statistically significant associations in all
age divisions between players' perceptions of how much their coaches
emphasized "playing rough and being aggressive" and players' approval of "taking out an opposing player any way you can in order to
save a goal even though you risk injuring the opposing player." Smith
(1979) has demonstrated statistically that the more coaches approve
of fighting, the more players fight, and the more major penalties they
receive.

Teammates

The importance of peer approval in understanding violence in gangs,
prisons, violent subcultures of all sorts, and among boys and men in

general has long been recognized. Respect is what counts. You get it by demonstrating physical courage, gameness, recklessness sometimes, disdain for injury, and a willingness to fight if necessary. You lose it by revealing a lack of "heart" or "guts," by "chickening out."

Quantitative data on hockey players' violence approval—their own and their perceptions of their teammates'—are shown in Table 4. These data indicate that amateur hockey players perceive their teammates as considerably more approving of fighting than their coaches and parents. Sixty-four percent of the respondents viewed other team members as approving of fighting in at least three of the four situations presented. Comparisons with players' own attitudes, however, reveals an anomaly described by Matza (1964) in his research on delinquency. It is apparent in Table 4 that individual violence approval is extensive, but not as extensive as that which individuals attribute to teammates collectively. It seems what individuals say and do about violence in the presence of peers is one thing, but their private attitudes are another. This results in a shared misunderstanding in which individuals think others value violence more than they actually do.

To what extent would players privately *prefer* less fighting and other sorts of illegal rough play? The foregoing players were asked, Would you like to see more, about the same, or less fistfighting in your games? Forty-five percent said less. When asked, Would you like to see more, about the same, or less illegal stickwork in your games? 82% said less. How many players quit hockey because of violence? This question has yet to be adequately answered, but more than a few have done so, one suspects.

Closer inspection of the data in Table 4 shows that the gap in violence approval between individuals and teammates closes with age, as does the gap in violence approval between house-league and competitive-level players. Probably selection and socialization processes jointly account for this. As the less pro-violent get older, they quit hockey at increasingly faster rates than the more pro-violent. In fact, the general dropout rate is precipitous after age 12. Further, as the less pro-violent who stay in hockey are socialized into the culture of the game with age, and in competitive-level as opposed to house-league competition, they bring their attitudes increasingly into line with the attitudes they impute to their peers.

Among the less than half of one percent of organized hockey participants who in any given year reach the game's zenith, there is even more unanimity. Smith's (1979, 1983) NHL interviewees were asked how their teammates react to someone who does not fight when challenged. About half were unequivocal: "I'd rather see a guy fight and lose than turn his cheek and not fight at all, and I think a lot of the players are like that. You pretty well realize that you have to fight, otherwise the guys look down on you." The nonfighter is seen as untrustworthy and, therefore, a threat to group solidarity. "You get a couple of guys trying to beat you up, you know he's not going to be

Table 4   Hockey Players' Approval of Hockey Fighting and Perceptions of Teammates' Approval of Hockey Fighting by Age and Level of Competition (in Percent)[1]

	Players' approval			Teammates' approval		
	Low	Medium	High[2]	Low	Medium	High
Age						
12-13 (N = 166)	54	25	21	23	23	54
14-15 (N = 196)	37	39	24	11	27	61
16-17 (N = 130)	13	49	38	4	26	70
18-21 (N = 112)	17	24	59	9	13	78
Level of competition						
House league (N = 330)	48	28	24	16	25	59
Competitive (N = 274)	15	42	43	8	21	71
All players (N = 604)	33	34	33	13	23	64

[1]Adapted from Smith (1979, p. 113).

[2]Low = approval in no situations; medium = approval in one or two situations; high = approval in three or four situations.

there to help you out. That's a big thing. You don't look at these guys with much respect, really." Being able to depend on colleagues, on the other hand, helps in coping with the uncertainty inherent in a dangerous work environment. This kind of trust is the basis of peer respect in high-risk occupations and environments everywhere.

The other half of the NHL interviewees stated, contrary to Faulkner's (1974) findings on minor league hockey professionals, that fighting per se is not required ("some guys are fighters, some aren't"), but a player must at least be willing to grapple with a man in a melee to prevent ganging up and be tough enough to withstand opponents' attempts at coercion (cf. Colburn, 1985). As noted earlier, these are also coaches' minimum requirements for players.

As for those whose role it is to start fights, the professionals talk about two main types: the "policeman" and the "goon." Both are supposed to (a) protect weaker teammates, (b) put heart into their team by drubbing an opponent, and (c) intimidate opposing players. But they go about their tasks differently.

The "cement head" or "goon" does not adhere to the informal rules of fighting (he wields his stick indiscriminately, attacks from behind, etc.) and is thus feared and disliked for his unpredictability and potential to injure (albeit more so by opponents than teammates, who stand to benefit by the havoc he wreaks). "There are crazy people in this game," complained one player, "Why should I get my head whacked by some cement head? A guy whose job is to go out and hit people with a stick! It's crazy! I worry about that."

The "policeman" can be divided into two subtypes. Both stick basically to the rules of fighting; both are respected, even admired, by other players. The first looks for fights with anyone, anytime—he never avoids a potentially faster gun. The second fights infrequently, but his menacing reputation acts to deter those who might think of challenging him or one of his teammates.

> Like Bob Kelly, he doesn't get into a lot of fights but everybody knows he can so he keeps the teams balanced. He doesn't have to go out and fight all the time. Then another guy like Maloney, when he was with LA, everybody knew he was tough. It's like, you know, you're sitting in a store, and a policeman is watching you. Just because he's there doesn't mean he has to grab you by the neck. But because he's there, you're not going to try stealing that magazine.

Hockey players approve of violence, it seems, to the extent that it brings respect and works as a game tactic and career booster. Separable analytically, these uses merge empirically, each reinforcing the other. Though the latter becomes increasingly salient as players learn the occupational culture, the former remains important. Professional hockey players—grown men—cling to rituals of fighting (even when it is counterproductive in terms of winning) that most males leave behind in the schoolyard.

Summary

To sum up, parents, coaches, and teammates are important reference groups when it comes to explaining hockey violence. Qualitative and quantitative data indicate that for hockey parents, coaches, and teammates violence both expresses strong character and helps win hockey games, the former at almost all levels of competition, the latter increasingly as players move up through the system. Do players' perceptions of these others' attitudes regarding violence have an impact on players' behavior? The evidence indicates they do.

References

Colburn, K., Jr. (1985). Honor, ritual, and violence in ice hockey. *Canadian Journal of Sociology*, **10**, 153-171.

Faulkner, R.R. (1974). Making violence by doing work: Selves, situations and the world of professional hockey. *Sociology of Work and Occupations*, **1**, 288-312.

Matza, D. (1964). *Delinquency and drift*. New York: Wiley.

McPherson, B.D., & Davidson, L. (1980). *Minor hockey in Ontario: Toward a positive learning environment for children in the 1980s.* Toronto: Ontario Government Book Store.

Smith, M.D. (1975). The legitimation of violence: Hockey players' perceptions of their reference groups' sanctions for assault. *Canadian Review of Sociology and Anthropology,* **12**, 72-80.

Smith, M.D. (1979). Towards an explanation of hockey violence. *Canadian Journal of Sociology,* **4**, 105-124.

Smith, M.D. (1983). *Violence and sport.* Toronto, Ontario: Butterworths.

Vaz, E.W. (1982). *The professionalization of young hockey players.* Lincoln: University of Nebraska Press.

SECTION 6

Future Directions

The opening section of this book presented a historical look at the development of organized youth sport in America and a view of its current status. In the sections that followed, youth sport was considered from a variety of perspectives. The main thrust was to synthesize information about the readiness of children to participate, the effects of being involved in youth sport, and how to deal with problems related to participation in youth sport. One of the common conclusions was that we do not know enough about the youth sport phenomenon, either in terms of the appropriate role youth sport should have in society or in terms of understanding what we should about the participants. These concerns are the focus of the concluding section, the ultimate goal of which is to promote change so that youth sport will fulfill its potential as a valuable developmental experience.

In chapter 21, Daniel Gould looks at the future from the perspective of sport-psychology research. If we are going to know what we should about the psychological effects of being a participant in youth sport, or if we are going to know how we should effectively deal with the psychological issues related to being a youth sport participant, we clearly need more research-based information to give us direction in these areas of concern. The approach taken by Gould to address this need is to first consider what has characterized the past research that has given us the most useful or meaningful information. From this base, he develops what future sport-psychology research should be like if it is to provide significant information about youth sport. He argues that the key is to choose the right questions to investigate and to engage in the type of research that provides meaningful answers to these questions.

A different focus on the future is provided by Vern Seefeldt in the final chapter. Rather than being concerned with where future research should go, he presents what is needed in youth sport if the widespread negative image of youth sport is to be changed. His approach to the problem is to identify individuals whom he sees as "agents of reform" and to indicate what these leaders need to do to bring about change. Seefeldt then predicts what the future holds for youth sport. His prophecies emanate from consideration of several variables that will most likely influence modifications in youth sport. The result is a chapter that provides a stimulating basis for discussion about what lies ahead for youth sport and why these changes will occur.

CHAPTER 21

Sport Psychology: Future Directions in Youth Sport Research[1]

Daniel Gould

Historical research by Berryman (this volume) has shown that competitive athletic programs for children have existed in North America since the early 1920s. Although these programs have a long heritage, their period of greatest growth has occurred within the last 2 decades. Today, it is estimated that 16 to 20 million children between the ages of 6 and 16 years participate in a wide variety of organized sport programs (Martens, 1978, 1986). Not only is participation in these programs enormously popular, but the participants are intensely involved. Gould and Martens (1979), for example, found that, on the average, young athletes participate in these programs 12 hours a week during an 18-week season. Clearly, the youth sport setting involves a large proportion of the population and constitutes an important part of children's lives.

Historically, sport psychologists have paid only scant attention to the study of youth sport. Recently, however, the topic has drawn considerable psychological interest. Unfortunately, increased empirical efforts in the area will not necessarily guarantee beneficial results of either a theoretical or an applied nature. To adequately examine psychological aspects of youth sport participation, long-range, systematic, well-conducted research programs will be needed. Before such projects can be initiated, however, it will be necessary to examine the existing literature and determine current lines of research that have provided the greatest empirical and applied benefits. Thus, the purpose of the present paper is to examine key lines of past youth sport research, identify critical research questions, outline appropriate theoretical and methodological approaches, and suggest future research directions.

---

[1]This is an abridged and updated version of a manuscript by Gould (1982) titled "Sport Psychology in the 1980's: Status, Direction and Challenge in Youth Sports Research" that appeared in the *Journal of Sport Psychology*, **4**, 203-218.

Meaningful Lines of Youth Sport Research

In recent years, the number of youth sport psychological studies has greatly increased, as evidenced by the large number of review articles summarizing existing research and outlining practical implications for coaches, parents, and administrators (e.g., Gerson, 1977; Roberts, 1980; Thomas, 1978). The majority of implications made in these reviews were based on research from the parent discipline of psychology and not from sport-psychology research. Consequently, one finds oneself asking why many of the sport psychological studies are telling us so little about youth sport! Although there are a number of reasons why the youth sport research has provided little practical information (e.g., scant amount of research, infancy of the field), one of the primary reasons stems from the questions being asked. Many times we do not ask the most appropriate questions. To identify the most important research questions we need to more closely examine the objectives of our research.

Three of the various objectives the sport psychologist may have for studying youth sport seem most prevalent. These include the following reasons:

- To *provide psychological information that will help those involved in youth sport provide its young participants with positive and productive experiences.* Specifically, the methods of the behavioral sciences could be used to identify and evaluate behavioral guidelines and strategies that adult leaders could use to more effectively communicate with, reinforce, and instruct young athletes. Providing this type of information is important because most nonschool youth sport coaches have little formal coaching education and develop coaching guidelines based on experiences of trial and error or through the modeling of college and professional coaches, who work with vastly different populations.
- To *test existing psychological theory in a sport setting.* Theory is the ultimate goal of science, and psychologists (Bronfenbrenner, 1977) and sport psychologists (Smith & Smoll, 1978) alike have emphasized the need for the behavioral scientist to test existing psychological theory in complex and diverse social settings. The youth sport domain provides a readily accessible, naturalistic field setting where this can be accomplished.
- To *develop new theory.* Although it is extremely important to test existing theory, a number of investigators (Martens, 1979, 1987; Siedentop, 1980) have suggested that existing psychological theory will not have all the answers for the sport psychologist. New theories that account for multivariate, highly complex athletic settings must be identified and tested. The youth sport setting is ideal for this purpose.

Given these objectives for conducting youth sport research, the body of knowledge in the area was examined.[2] Key studies were identified based on two criteria: (a) their practical significance and (b) their contribution to the development or extension of psychological theory. Characteristics of these studies were also identified. The two key lines of research identified were the coaching effectiveness research of Smith, Smoll, and their associates and the anxiety studies of young athletes conducted by Scanlan and her associates.

Coaching Effectiveness Research

The coaching effectiveness research of Smith, Smoll, and their associates (Curtis, Smith, & Smoll, 1979; Smith, Smoll, & Curtis, 1978, 1979; Smith, Smoll, & Hunt, 1977; Smith, Smoll, Hunt, Curtis, & Coppel, 1979; Smoll, Smith, Curtis, & Hunt, 1978) can be categorized into three distinct phases. First, a Coaching Behavior Assessment System (CBAS) was developed over several years. This observational system consisted of behavioral categories derived from social learning theory and assessed individual differences in behavioral profiles of coaches. Both reactive and spontaneous coaching behaviors were assessed and included behaviors such as positive reinforcement, non-reinforcement, mistake-contingent encouragement, mistake-contingent technical instruction, punishment, punitive technical instruction, ignoring mistakes, keeping control behaviors, general technical instruction, general encouragement, organization, and general communication. The CBAS inventory was found to be a highly reliable and valid assessment instrument.

In a second phase of the project, the relationship between coaching behaviors of Little League baseball coaches as assessed by the CBAS instrument ($N = 51$), and player perceptions ($N = 542$) of coaching behaviors, attitudes, and self-esteem were examined. It was found that coaches who were rated more positively by the children gave more technical instruction compared to general encouragement, gave more reinforcement and mistake contingent feedback, and engaged in more behaviors associated with keeping control. Negatively evaluated coaches generally were more punitive and gave more punitive technical instruction. Finally, children who played for the positively evaluated coaches had higher general and athletic self-concepts.

Because the results of this second phase were descriptive and no causal inferences could be made, a third phase was conducted. In this

---

[2]Due to space limitations it is not possible to include a comprehensive review of the psychological investigations conducted in the youth sport area. Therefore, the interested reader is referred to related reviews (Gould & Seefeldt, 1981; Seefeldt & Gould, 1980) and upon request from the author, may receive a detailed listing of the references reviewed.

phase, 34 Little League baseball coaches were randomly assigned to either an experimental group that received training in a positive approach to coaching (e.g., were given behavioral guidelines derived in the previous phase that emphasized the desirability of reinforcement, encouragement, and technical instruction) or to a control condition in which they coached as they normally would. The intervention program received by the experimental group of coaches consisted of a 2-hour coaching clinic, self-assessment of coaching behaviors, and observer feedback concerning emitted coaching behaviors. Dependent variables observed included coaching behaviors, self-perceived coaching behaviors, player perceptions of coaching behaviors, as well as attitudinal and self-esteem measures of 325 of their players. Findings revealed that the behavioral profiles of the experimental coaches differed from the control coaches in the expected direction. Moreover, the children who played for the experimental coaches, as compared to children who played for the control coaches, demonstrated greater enjoyment, a greater desire to play, rated their coaches as more knowledgeable, and rated their team higher in attraction. Thus, this three-phase project added significantly to our understanding of the influence that coaching behaviors have on the affective reactions of young athletes.

Competitive Anxiety Research

In the second important line of research, Scanlan and Passer (1978a, 1978b, 1979), Passer and Scanlan (1980), and Scanlan and Lewthwaite (1984) examined the relationships between competitive trait anxiety, self-esteem, team performance expectancies, personal performance expectancies, worries about failure, worries about adult expectations and social evaluation, parental pressure to participate, game or match outcome, perceived fun, and pre- and post-contest state anxiety in youth sport participants. In all, a series of three interrelated field studies were conducted using a similar methodological format. Competitive stress or state anxiety was assessed just prior to and immediately following competition and was correlated to various individual difference factors (e.g., trait anxiety, self-esteem, worries about adult expectations) taken well before the contests. In the first investigation, male youth soccer players, ages 10 to 12 years, were used as subjects (Scanlan & Passer, 1978b). The second investigation replicated and extended the first by employing female youth soccer players of the same age (Scanlan & Passer, 1979). Finally, the latest study in the series (Scanlan & Lewthwaite, 1984) extended the results of the soccer studies to the sport of wrestling, examining male youth wrestlers, ages 10 to 14.

Overall, the findings of these studies have shown that sport competition is perceived as anxiety-producing by *some* children in *some* situations. In particular, the findings

demonstrate that competitive trait anxiety, performance expectancies pertinent to the particular sport context, victory versus defeat and its varying degrees, and the amount of fun experienced while competing are strong and consistent predictors of competitive stress for both genders across diverse sport contexts. Self-esteem also was found to be a significant, although relatively weak predictor of stress for boys and girls in the soccer studies and was significantly correlated with but not predictive of stress in wrestling. . . . Finally, the latest study in this series (Scanlan & Lewthwaite, 1984) has identified several new factors associated with stress that focus on children's characteristic prematch thoughts and worries, as well as their perceptions of the significant adults in their lives. (Scanlan, 1986, p. 117)

Lessons To Be Learned

Both of these comprehensive research projects, as well as other lines of research that have proven to be fruitful in the area of youth sport, are characterized by several features. First and foremost, they asked important questions of practical concern for youth sport personnel. Second, these studies integrated previous research and directly tested theory or attempted to generate new theory to explain the relationships between variables. Third, both lines of research were methodologically sound. They examined more than a few isolated teams (entire leagues), were multivariate in nature, and involved more than one assessment. Finally, both projects were part of a systematic series of studies, not isolated, single studies. The research of Smith, Smoll, and associates, for instance, was conducted in three distinct phases (Phase 1—development of assessment instruments; Phase 2—descriptive hypothesis generating research; Phase 3—hypothesis testing experimental research) and provides a good model for future researchers to follow. Similarly, the competitive-stress investigations of Scanlan and her associates were part of a series of field studies, but the researchers also tested theoretical principles derived from a line of laboratory research on competitive anxiety in a field setting. Moreover, three studies were conducted, which allowed the investigators to replicate and extend their findings to young female athletes and across sports.

In contrast, a review of the literature reveals that youth sport studies that did not have the same impact as the work of Scanlan and her colleagues and Smith, Smoll, and their associates did not reflect many of these characteristics. Investigations with less impact, for example, did not ask questions of practical importance, were often methodologically weak, and were not multivariate in their approach. Moreover, these investigations typically were not part of a systematic series of studies, nor did they integrate previous research into the design.

Conducting Youth Sport Research That Counts

Boring (1963), eminent historian of psychology, wrote that "one finds that he [or she] needs to know about the past, not in order to predict the future, but rather in order to understand the present" (p. 89). Thus, historically examining the youth sport literature will not let us predict what the future will bring. However, understanding the past research may help us design studies that have a higher probability of having greater impact and may help make our research efforts more fruitful and economical. If we agree with some recently presented positions in the field (Martens, 1979; Siedentop 1980; Smith & Smoll, 1978) and assume that one of the sport psychologist's major objectives is to conduct socially significant research that will make meaningful contributions to those involved in sport, then we must address three issues:

- What questions should we ask if we are to have the greatest impact in providing information that ensures productive and healthful programs for children?
- What types of research settings are needed if answers to these questions are to be derived?
- What methodological approaches should be employed if valid and reliable answers are to be provided to these questions?

What Questions Should We Ask?

Do we ask important questions? Does our research really make a difference? All too often the answer to these questions has been *no*. Locke (1969), for example, has indicated that

> if you wiped out the last 50 years of research in physics or chemistry or medicine, life in our world would instantly change. If you wiped out the last 50 years of research in physical education would physical education and physical educators continue to function as usual? The answer is usually an emphatic "yes." (p. 6)

Psychologists like Bronfenbrenner (1977) and, more recently, sport scientists like Martens (1979, 1987) and Siedentop (1980) have suggested that the time has come for sport psychologists to spend less time in their laboratories and more time on the playing fields, in the gymnasiums, and in natatoriums. In essence, we must establish ecological validity for our theories (Bronfenbrenner, 1977). Siedentop (1980) warns that all too often, applied research has been thought of as only extending laboratory research to practical settings. Behaviorists like Baer, Wolf, and Risely (1968), however, suggest that "the label applied is not determined by the research procedures used but by the interest which society shows in the problems being studied" (p. 12). Thus, if the sport psychologist conducting youth sport research is to have practical impact, then questions of practical importance must be identified.

To identify these issues, a content analysis of the practical and empirical youth sport literature was conducted by the author and topics of psychological significance in youth sport were identified. A brief questionnaire was then formulated and administered to 23 sport psychologists working in youth sport throughout North America, as well as to 33 nonschool youth sport coaches and administrators. The results of this survey revealed that "reasons why young athletes stop participating," "competitive stress placed on young athletes," "helping young athletes cope with competitive stress," "effects of competition on the psychological health and development of children," "skills for enhancing communication with young athletes," "strategies for developing self-confidence," "why young athletes participate in sport," "effects of winning and losing on young athletes," "what young athletes like and dislike about sport," and "effects of parent-child relationships on sport involvement and success" were the topics rated as most important by the combined sample. Moreover, no differences were found between the groups on their ratings of the 10 topics ranked as most important for study.[3]

These findings identify a number of sport psychological topics of practical significance for the youth sport researcher. However, asking questions of a practical significance does not mean the abandonment of theory, be it the testing of existing theory in youth sport field settings or the development of a new theory. Theory is the major goal of science, whether it be of basic or applied nature (Kerlinger, 1973). Moreover, it has often been said that if one is interested in practical implications, there is nothing more practical than a good theory. The previously mentioned work of Scanlan and her associates, as well as that of Simon and Martens (1979), are excellent examples of research that test existing theory in youth sport settings while addressing practical problems.

It is also important to recognize that applying existing theory to sport can advance knowledge in sport psychology only so far. The sport psychologist must not only test existing theory, but must also develop new sport-specific theories that better explain the complex interaction of personal and environmental variables in the naturalistic youth sport field setting (Martens, 1979, 1987; Siedentop, 1980; Smith & Smoll, 1978; Thomas, 1980). The need to test existing theory and to develop new theory is of paramount importance because we are sometimes blinded by the *zeitgeist* in which we work. For example, the research on attributions in the youth sport setting has primarily consisted of an extension of laboratory research findings to naturalistic environments. Although these findings are important in that they further verify previous research, the scientist must not be blinded by the theory's assumptions and limitations.

One might ask, Are the four basic attributions found in the laboratory appropriate for sport settings? Some research (Roberts & Pascuzzi,

---

[3]A more detailed presentation and explanation of the results of this survey can be found in the original unabridged form of this review (Gould, 1982).

1979) indicates that alone they may not be. Why has the critical link between attributions and performance or participation in youth sport not been assessed? Similarly, the feasibility of identifying learned-helpless young athletes and modifying their helpless states through attributional retraining has not been examined. Finally, the effects of extrinsic rewards on the young athlete's intrinsic motivation have not been examined in the field, although the author and a number of other reviewers have based practical implications on laboratory research within the attributional framework. In essence, whether we are testing existing theory and/or developing new theory, from time to time we must be able to step back and examine whether the *zeitgeist* or paradigm in which we are working is blinding us—preventing us from testing basic assumptions or asking theoretically important, but forgotten questions.

When testing existing theory and developing new theory, the youth sport researcher must also remember that the young athlete is not a miniature adult. Too often we erroneously assume that psychological processes and theories that have been based on research with adults automatically transfer to younger age groups. M.R. Weiss and Bredemeier (1983), however, have presented convincing evidence that shows that psychological processes systematically vary with age or the developmental level of the child. Thus, when testing existing theory and developing new sport-specific theories in youth sport, developmental factors must be considered.

The present review of the existing youth sport research showed that the areas that have provided the most impact are ones where the investigators pursued a series of interrelated questions. Thus, in planning youth sport research, it may be more fruitful for investigators to think in terms of lines of research, focusing on a number of interrelated questions and subquestions rather than on single, isolated questions. It may be fruitful to adopt elements of the method of strong inference developed by Platt (1964). That is, we should conduct lines of research in a logical fashion by attempting to devise and test alternative hypotheses, critically examining the results of previous studies and formulating questions in future investigations that will eliminate rival hypotheses.

A good example of this approach in the youth sport research is the work of Smith and Smoll and their associates. As already mentioned, this series of investigations was carried out in three phases. Phase 1 focused on the question of whether coaching behaviors could be reliably and validly assessed. After this was established, the question of what relationship exists between coaching behaviors and player attitudes was explored. The authors did not stop here, however. When stable relationships were found between coaching behaviors and player attitudes, the next interrelated question was posed. Can coaching behaviors be changed, and will these changes result in changes in attitudes on the part of players? This question was answered in Phase 3. Although no further investigations were conducted, strong inference would suggest that the next logical question would focus on what specifically caused the changes in coaching behaviors and player attitudes. Were the results of Phase 3 due to a placebo effect associated with the training program? Were they caused by the 2-hour coaching clinic, the self-assessment procedures employed, or the feedback given to the coaches about their actual behavior?

Although the strong inference process has much to offer the youth sport researcher, its limitations also must be recognized. Hafner and Presswood (1965), for example, suggest that the notion of strong inference is idealistic because alternative hypotheses do not always appear. Moreover, if we encounter an occasional mistake in observation, the idea that a systematic series of interrelated questions results in valid answers to a problem may be false. We may be systematically pursuing subquestions in the wrong direction. Similarly, Feltz (in press) convincingly argues that the strong inference notion that science can only advance by disproofs is faulty. In contrast, she contends that the sport-psychology researcher must employ a planned critical multiplism approach, where a series of investigations are planned using multiple ways to formulate research questions, measure variables, design investigations, analyze results, and interpret findings. Consequently, sport psychologists conducting youth sport research must simultaneously consider sets of contending theoretical ideas, design and evaluate experiments with the greatest care, use multiple methods, replicate results, and view results from a single investigation with great care.

What Types of Research Settings Are Needed?

In preparing this manuscript a number of papers on the philosophy of science (Boring, 1955, 1963; Bronowski, 1973; Hafner & Presswood, 1965; Kuhn, 1970; Platt, 1964), the future direction of social psychology (Gergen, 1973; Helmreich, 1975; McGuire, 1973; Schlenkar, 1974), and direction of the research in sport psychology (Martens, 1979, 1987; Siedentop, 1980; Smith & Smoll, 1978; Thomas, 1980) were reviewed. One common theme in all of these papers was that we should beware of those who employ one method or instrument, either experimental or theoretical. If the state of knowledge in a field is to be advanced, diverse methods must be employed. Descriptive studies, evaluation research, and systems approach research are all types of research that are applicable in the psychological study of youth sport.

Descriptive Research. In the early 1970s, if a particular sport psychological investigation was not theoretical, highly controlled, and conducted in the laboratory, it was more than likely not highly evaluated. Times have changed and we have come a long way since them. More and more field research is being conducted, and we now encourage new and different approaches to the field. We are still not completely open-minded, however. For example, the utility of descriptive research needs to be recognized and more highly supported, especially in the area of youth sport. Although theory is our ultimate goal, we must recognize that youth sports are conducted in a highly complex physical and social environment. We know little about this environment; some feel it cannot be explained with existing laboratory-generated theories (Martens, 1979, 1987; Siedentop, 1980; Smith & Smoll, 1978). Thus, descriptive research could play an important role in helping us understand this complex setting and, in so doing, provide us with the groundwork needed for the development of new theory.

Descriptive research could also be extremely useful in answering practical problems. At the Michigan Youth Sports Institute, for example, a 3-year descriptive study of the children's sport scene was conducted (Universities Study Committee, 1976, 1978a, 1978b). A descriptive study was selected because little was known about children's sport in Michigan. The number of participants involved; participation patterns; player attitudes toward sport, coaching, and officiating; and parental attitudes toward a variety of issues had never been extensively examined. The results of these investigations have provided a wealth of data. For example, it was found that children's sport participation steadily increased up to the ages of 12, 13, and 14, after which it markedly declined, with approximately 35% of the children discontinuing participation at this time. Information also was obtained on the reasons for children's involvement and discontinuation of participation. These findings have provided the staff of the Youth Sports Institute with valuable athletic motivation information to convey to youth sport coaches.

Descriptive research can also be extremely useful in solving controversial youth sport issues. Critics of youth sport, for example, suggest that coaches' overemphasis on winning places children under too much stress, that adult leaders demonstrate unsportsmanlike behavior, and that parents often stifle fun in children's sport programs. The sport psychologist could develop behavioral observation systems for assessing behaviors like these and examine the relationships between these factors.

Finally, descriptive research does not have to be atheoretical. Descriptive methods could be used to provide support for theoretical formulations. For example, Bandura (1977) suggests that performance accomplishments are one primary means of influencing an individual's self-efficacy. If so, one would expect changes in a young athlete's athletic efficacy to be associated with various performance accomplishments over the course of a season. Similarly, changes in Harter's (1981) perceived competence scale scores could be examined over the course of several seasons, and relationships between competence and various environmental factors (coaching behavior assessments, success) could be made.

Evaluation Research.   Edward Suchman (1967) indicates that "evaluation research is a specific form of applied research whose primary goal is not the discovery of knowledge but rather a testing of the application of knowledge" (p. 75). Evaluation research includes the process of determining the value or amount of success in achieving some predetermined program objective or objectives (C.H. Weiss, 1972). In essence, evaluation research involves the careful planning of specific program objectives, the identification of criteria to measure the success of these objectives, determination and exploration of the degree of success, and recommendations for further program activity.

Although little has been conducted by sport psychologists, evaluation research holds great promise for those interested in youth sport. A number of sport psychologists, for example, have been involved in making sport psychological presentations in clinics and workshops held for youth coaches. Although it is easy for us to assume that we are contributing to the betterment of children's sport by conducting these programs, little empirical evidence exists to support this assumption. Do youth coaches conduct themselves in a more sportsmanlike manner after receiving information on the psychology of sportsmanship? If so, do these behaviors affect the young athlete's sportsmanship attitudes and behaviors? Evaluation research could be used to answer these and related questions.

Evaluation research could also be used to provide information that could assist program administrations in ending controversies in children's sport. Martens, Rivkin, and Bump (1984) and Spieth (1977), for instance, compared the amount of activity youngsters experience in traditional versus nontraditional baseball leagues. Specifically, in both studies it was found that young athletes who played in a nontraditional league where their own coach pitched to them had more swings at pitches, made more contact with the ball, and had more balls hit to them in the field than children who played in traditional leagues. Similarly, Corbin and Laurie (1980) used evaluation research to assess the effects of rule changes in children's baseball on parental attitudes toward those rule changes. Specifically, it was found that parents generally supported program changes designed to reduce competition and focus attention on fun and skill development. These initial efforts demonstrate the practical implications that youth sport evaluation research can have.

Systems Approach Research.   A third type of research that could be useful to the sport psychologist conducting youth sport research is systems approach research. Smith and Smoll (1978) indicate that because the youth sport setting involves the extensive interplay of a variety of social systems and subsystems, to fully understand the setting one must examine the various systems. Specifically, in the systems approach, the investigator (a) identifies all social systems and subsystems, (b) focuses on system change and factors related to change, (c) develops a model that describes causal patterns between systems and factors affecting systems, and (d) manipulates model elements to test their predicted effect on the system. This model would be especially appropriate in studying socialization into and through sport. Systems such as the child, teammates, and parents could be identified and observed simultaneously and longitudinally. Relationships between systems could be examined, models developed, and predictions of the model tested.

What Methodological Approach Should Be Employed?

The sport psychologist can pose the appropriate and socially relevant questions and conduct research in the most appropriate setting to answer these questions, but unless good methodological procedures are utilized all of his or her efforts are in vain. What is the best methodological format to follow when conducting naturalistic research in field settings? There is no one *best* method. The problem at hand determines which methods are most appropriate. For example, when conducting research in an underdeveloped area (e.g., sportsmanship development in youth athletes), noncausal survey techniques may be the most appropriate methods to employ. In essence, the primary purpose of this type of investigation would be the description of the phenomenon of concern and the identification of variables that covary with it. After a number of noncausal relationships are established, however, the manipulation of various independent variables thought to influence the behavior of concern may be in order (e.g., coaching strategies designed to develop sportsmanship), or statistical techniques such as structural or path analyses may be employed, which will allow one to test theoretically derived paths or relationships between variables.

It is becoming more apparent, however, that the same procedures that have guided both social psychologists in general and sport psychologists in particular are not always appropriate for field settings (Martens, 1979, 1987). Because we are investigating a complex phenomenon where a large number of internal and external factors are affecting the populations we sample, the traditional methodology of linear causation and convenient ANOVA categories are often inappropriate. For instance, in studying the effects of coaching behaviors on the attitudinal development of young athletes, isolating and assessing the effects of one particular coaching behavior (e.g., positive reinforcement) on attitudinal development will not be enough. Numbers of behaviors (e.g., positive reinforcement, punishment, technical instructions) of coaches and other role models (e.g., parents, peers) will need to be assessed in a variety of settings (games and practices) across time. Consequently, the sport psychologist interested in providing valid answers to many of the questions posed in this manuscript must consider multivariate longitudinal designs, use regression analyses that look at all subjects—not just dichotomized or trichotomized groups, and employ a wide range of quantitative and qualitative assessment procedures. In addition, answers to many of the complex questions involving children in sport do not reside in the psychological domain alone. Instead, they are influenced by the complex interplay of psychological, physiological, and kinesiological factors. Thus, team research of a multidisciplinary nature is also needed.

A final methodological issue that cannot be ignored focuses on sampling concerns. Too often, youth sport researchers select the most convenient sample of young athletes for their investigations rather than choosing the most appropriate sample available for answering the questions posed. For example, Feltz and Ewing (in press) have indicated that many of the controversies surrounding sport competition for children are most prominent at the elite levels of involvement. They indicate, however, that few investigators have examined critical issues, such as burnout and excessive competitive stress, with samples of elite young athletes. Similarly, in a follow-up investigation to the previously discussed work of Smith, Smoll, and their colleagues, Horn (1985) has found that behaviors emitted by youth sport coaches differ depending on the sampling context; that is, whether coaching behaviors were observed in practices or competitions. These sampling context findings are of critical importance, as it was previously assumed that the pattern of observed coaching behaviors was similar across both practices and competitions. Hence, sport psychologists conducting youth sport research must pay particular attention to sampling issues and the effects of these issues on both their findings and their interpretation of findings.

A Final Comment

Social philosopher Herbert Marcuse (1964) has indicated that many times societal issues and problems remain unanswered, but not because those in the society are incapable of answering them. On the contrary, answers to these problems could be successfully achieved if the societal members only took the time to ask the appropriate questions. In many ways, the sport psychologist interested in studying youth sport is in a similar situation. We are in an emerging area and have the opportunity before us to conduct research that can have a tremendous impact on the estimated 16 to 20 million children involved in youth sport. However, to conduct research that will have this practical significance, we need to stop, step back, and examine the major practical and theoretical issues in the field. In addition, we must expand our horizons by employing varied methodologies, research settings, and paradigmatic approaches to the field.

References

Baer, B., Wolf, M., & Risely, T. (1968). Current dimensions of applied behavior analysis. *Journal of Applied Behavior Analysis*, **1**, 91-97.

Bandura, A. (1977). Self-efficacy: Toward a unifying theory of behavioral change. *Psychological Review*, **84**, 191-215.

Berryman, J.W. (1988) The rise of highly organized sports for preadolescent boys. In F.L. Smoll, R.A. Magill, & M.J. Ash (Eds.), *Children in sport* (3rd ed., pp. 3-16). Champaign, IL: Human Kinetics.

Boring, E.G. (1955). Dual role of the zeitgeist in scientific creativity. *Scientific Monthly*, **80**, 101-106.

Boring, E.G. (1963). Science and the meaning of its history. In R.I. Watson & D.T. Campbell (Eds.), *History, psychology and science: Selected papers* (pp. 87-91). New York: Wiley.

Bronfenbrenner, U. (1977). Toward an experimental ecology of human development. *American Psychologist*, **32**, 513-531.

Bronowski, J. (1973). *The ascent of man*. Boston: Little, Brown.

Corbin, C.B., & Laurie, D.R. (1980, May). *Parental attitudes concerning modifications in baseball for young children*. Paper presented at the North American Society for Psychology of Sport and Physical Activity Conference, Boulder, CO.

Curtis, B., Smith, R.E., & Smoll, F.L. (1979). Scrutinizing the skipper: A study of leadership behaviors in the dugout. *Journal of Applied Psychology*, **64**, 391-400.

Feltz, D. (in press). Future directions in theoretical research in sport psychology: From applied psychology toward sport science. In J. Skinner (Ed.), *Future directions in exercise and sport research*. Champaign, IL: Human Kinetics.

Feltz, D.L., & Ewing, M.E. (1987). Psychological characteristics of elite young athletes. *Medicine and Science in Sport and Exercise*, **19**(5), S98-S105.

Gergen, K.J. (1973). Social psychology as history. *Journal of Personality and Social Psychology*, **26**, 309-320.

Gerson, R. (1977). Redesigning athletic competition for children. *Motor Skills: Theory into Practice*, **2**, 3-14.

Gould, D. (1982). Sport psychology in the 1980's: Status, direction and challenge in youth sports research. *Journal of Sport Psychology*, **4**, 203-218.

Gould, D., & Martens, R. (1979). Attitudes of volunteer coaches toward significant youth sport issues. *Research Quarterly*, **50**, 369-380.

Gould, D., & Seefeldt, V. (1981). Youth sports research and practice: A selected bibliography. *Physical Educator*, (Suppl.).

Hafner, E.M., & Presswood, S. (1965). Strong inference and weak interactions. *Science*, **149**, 503-510.

Harter, S. (1981). The development of competence motivation in the mastery of cognitive and physical skills: Is there a place for joy?

In G.C. Roberts & D.M. Landers (Eds.), *Psychology of motor behavior and sport—1980* (pp. 3-29). Champaign, IL: Human Kinetics.

Helmreich, R. (1975). Applied social psychology: The unfulfilled promise. *Personality and Social Psychology Bulletin*, **1**, 548-560.

Horn, T.S. (1985). Coaches' feedback and changes in children's perceptions of their physical competence. *Journal of Educational Psychology*, **77**, 174-186.

Kerlinger, F.N. (1973). *Foundations of behavioral research*. New York: Holt, Rinehart, & Winston.

Kuhn, T.S. (1970). *The structure of scientific revolutions*. Chicago: University of Chicago Press.

Locke, L.F. (1969). *Research in physical education*. New York: Teachers College Press.

Marcuse, H. (1964). *One-dimensional man*. Boston: Beacon.

Martens, R. (1978). *Joy and sadness in children's sports*. Champaign, IL: Human Kinetics.

Martens, R. (1979). About smocks and jocks. *Journal of Sport Psychology*, **1**, 94-99.

Martens, R. (1986). Youth sport in the USA. In M.R. Weiss & D. Gould (Eds.), *Sport for children and youths: 1984 Olympic Scientific Congress Proceedings* (Vol. 10, pp. 27-33). Champaign, IL: Human Kinetics.

Martens, R. (1987). Science, knowledge and sport psychology. *The Sport Psychologist*, **1**, 29-55.

Martens, R., Rivkin, F., & Bump, L.A. (1984). A field study of traditional and nontraditional children's baseball. *Research Quarterly for Exercise and Sport*, **55**, 351-355.

McGuire, W.J. (1973). The yin and yang of progress in social psychology: Seven koans. *Journal of Personality and Social Psychology*, **26**, 446-456.

Passer, M.W., & Scanlan, T.K. (1980). The impact of game outcome on the post competition affect and performance evaluations of young athletes. In C.H. Nadeau, W.R. Halliwell, K.M. Newell, & G.C. Roberts (Eds.), *Psychology of sport and motor behavior—1979* (pp. 100-111). Champaign, IL: Human Kinetics.

Platt, J.R. (1964). Strong inference. *Science*, **146**, 347-352.

Roberts, G.C. (1980). Childen in competition: A theoretical perspective and recommendations for practice. *Motor Skills: Theory into Practice*, **4**, 37-50.

Roberts, G.C., & Pascuzzi, D. (1979). Causal attributions in sport: Some theoretical implications. *Journal of Sport Psychology*, **1**, 203-211.

Scanlan, T.K. (1986). Competitive stress in children. In M.R. Weiss & D. Gould (Eds.), *Sport for children and youths: 1984 Olympic Scientific Congress Proceedings* (Vol. 10, pp. 113-118). Champaign, IL: Human Kinetics.

Scanlan, T.K., & Lewthwaite, R. (1984). Social psychological aspects of competition for male youth sport participants: I. Predictors of competitive stress. *Journal of Sport Psychology*, **6**, 208-226.

Scanlan, T.K., & Passer, M.W. (1978a). Anxiety inducing factors in competitive youth sports. In F.L. Smoll & R.E. Smith (Eds.), *Psychological perspectives in youth sports* (pp. 107-122). Washington, DC: Hemisphere.

Scanlan, T.K., & Passer, M.W. (1978b). Factors related to competitive stress among male youth sports participants. *Medicine and Science in Sports*, **10**, 103-108.

Scanlan, T.K., & Passer, M.W. (1979). Sources of competitive stress in young female athletes. *Journal of Sport Psychology*, **1**, 151-159.

Schlenkar, B.R. (1974). Social psychology and science. *Journal of Personality and Social Psychology*, **29**, 1-15.

Seefeldt, V., & Gould, D. (1980). *The physical and psychological effects of youth sports competition.* Washington, DC: Eric Clearinghouse on Teacher Education.

Siedentop, D. (1980). Two cheers for Rainer. *Journal of Sport Psychology*, **2**, 2-4.

Simon, J.A., & Martens, R. (1979). Children's anxiety in sport and nonsport evaluative activities. *Journal of Sport Psychology*, **1**, 160-169.

Smith, R.E., & Smoll, F. L. (1978). Sport and the child's conceptual and research perspectives. In F.L. Smoll & R.E. Smith (Eds.), *Psychological perspectives in youth sports* (pp. 3-13). Washington, DC: Hemisphere.

Smith, R.E., Smoll, F.L., & Curtis, B. (1978). Coaching behaviors in Little League baseball. In F.L. Smoll & R.E. Smith (Eds.), *Psychological perspectives in youth sports* (pp. 173-201). Washington, DC: Hemisphere.

Smith, R.E., Smoll, F.L., & Curtis, B. (1979). Coach effectiveness training: A cognitive-behavioral approach to enhancing relationship skills in youth sport coaches. *Journal of Sport Psychology*, **1**, 59-75.

Smith, R.E., Smoll, F.L., & Hunt, E. (1977). A system for the behavioral assessment of athletic coaches. *Research Quarterly*, **48**, 401-407.

Smith, R.E., Smoll, F.L., Hunt, E., Curtis, B., & Coppel, D.B. (1979). Psychology and the bad news bears. In G.C. Roberts & K.M. Newell (Eds.), *Psychology of motor behavior and sport—1978* (pp. 109-130). Champaign, IL: Human Kinetics.

Smoll, F.L., Smith, R.E., Curtis, B., & Hunt, E. (1978). Toward a mediational model of coach-player relationships. *Research Quarterly*, **49**, 528-541.

Spieth, W.R. (1977). Investigation of two pitching conditions as determinants for developing fundamental skills of baseball. *Research Quarterly*, **48**, 408-412.

Suchman, E.A. (1967). *Evaluation research: Principles and practice in public service and social action programs*. New York: Russell Sage Foundation.

Thomas, J.R. (1978). Attribution theory and motivation through reward: Practical implications for children's sports. In R.A. Magill, M.J. Ash, & F.L. Smoll (Eds.), *Children in sport: A contemporary anthology* (pp. 149-157). Champaign, IL: Human Kinetics.

Thomas, J.R. (1980). Half a cheer for Rainer and Daryl. *Journal of Sport Psychology*, **2**, 266-267.

Universities Study Committee. (1976). *Joint legislative study on youth sports programs: Agency sponsored sports—Phase I report*. Lansing: State of Michigan.

Universities Study Committee. (1978a). *Joint legislative study on youth sports programs: Agency sponsored sports—Phase II report*. Lansing: State of Michigan.

Universities Study Committee. (1978b). *Joint legislative study on youth sports program: Agency sponsored sports—Phase III report*. Lansing: State of Michigan.

Weiss, C.H. (1972). *Evaluative research: Methods of assessing program effectiveness*. Englewood Cliffs, NJ: Prentice-Hall.

Weiss, M.R., & Bredemeier, B.J. (1983). Developmental sport psychology: A theoretical perspective for studying children in sport. *Journal of Sport Psychology*, **5**, 216-230.

CHAPTER 22

The Future of Youth Sport in America

Vern Seefeldt

The need for change in the image of youth sport and, concurrently, the manner in which programs are implemented has been suggested by both its supporters and detractors. Prominent issues, such as the exclusion of unskilled athletes, exploitation of children for personal and commercial gain, and an undue emphasis on winning at the expense of other values, have consistently kept the proponents of youth sport in a defensive position. Whether the changes are imminent and already under way or are merely wishful thinking and impossible to achieve depends upon one's point of view. The continuing popularity of organized athletics for children implies that a significant number of adults believe that the inherent benefits of sport participation outweigh the potential detrimental effects. Those who enroll their children in competitive athletic programs either agree with the current philosophy and operation of the program or have sufficient confidence in the sponsors to assume that the required changes will take place as soon as the conflict between tradition and new information can be resolved.

Whether the promoters of children's sport deserve the annual vote of confidence they receive from millions of parents who enroll their children in competitive athletics is an issue that has aroused considerable controversy. The persistent attention to youth sport by the media has stimulated the scientific community to begin investigating the benefits and consequences of children's involvement in sport. Subject-matter specialists in sports medicine, sport psychology, sport sociology, sport physiology, and biomechanics now consider children to be legitimate subjects in their investigations. (For comprehensive reviews of research pertaining to children in athletic competition, see Albinson & Andrew, 1976; Haubenstricker, 1976; Micheli, 1984; Rarick, 1973; Seefeldt & Gould, 1980; Shephard, 1982; Smith, 1979; Smoll & Smith, 1978; and Weiss & Gould, 1986.)

The welcome attention of scientists to the problems of youth sport is destined to bring with it two important outcomes that have been missing in its turbulent history: (a) An interdisciplinary account of what happens to children as a result of their athletic participation will gradually emerge, and (b) suggestions for modifying the conditions that are currently not in the best interest of children will be incorporated into the rules and policies of the various sponsoring agencies. Proponents of youth sport have reason to believe that future changes in the structure and conditions under which competition takes place will be based on more abundant and valid information.

History of Youth Sport

Children's sport programs that are supervised by adults have been immersed in controversy almost from their modest beginning on the playgrounds of New York City at the turn of the century. Berryman (this volume) chronicled the growth of sport for children from the time sport emerged as an after-school recreational activity to the highly competitive *win at all costs* situations that resulted in their condemnation by public school educators after an existence of barely 30 years. Berryman's review reveals several important historical facts: (a) that youth sport was an outgrowth of the regular public school curriculum; (b) that sport was initiated as a diversionary activity to meet the perceived competitive needs of boys; and (c) that certain sports became highly competitive in a matter of years, even when they were under the auspices of public school personnel.

The withdrawal of support for competitive athletics by public school educators in the 1930s has had a lasting influence on youth sport programs. The elimination of athletic competition from many elementary school programs coincided with an increase in the number of physical education and intramural programs. The new school-based programs were to emphasize the acquisition of skills for all children, in lieu of specialized attention for a few highly skilled athletes. However, withdrawal of public school sponsorship of youth sport prompted a number of family-oriented agencies such as the YMCA, YWCA, and the Police Athletic League to offer competitive athletics in private facilities. These offerings became more numerous and diverse as additional agencies, created for the sole purpose of offering sport competition for children, were established.

The creation of nonschool agencies to teach sport skills to children brought about a paradox that has persisted to the present day. Schools that employed personnel educated to teach motor skills and to serve as coaches were offering limited opportunities for children to learn the sports of their culture, while nonschool agencies were spending substantially greater amounts of time teaching sport skills to children— but under the direction of administrators and coaches who were generally not well qualified to conduct the programs.

The indifference of public school personnel to the agency-sponsored sport programs that sprang up as replacements for elementary school athletic programs frequently led to animosity and hostility between the two groups. This unfriendly attitude prevailed throughout the 1950s and 1960s, fueled periodically by policy statements from the American Medical Association and the National Education Association, which opposed highly organized sport activities for children before the ninth grade. However, the number of programs and participants in youth sport continued to grow, unmindful of the unsolicited advice that was directed at them by physicians and educators. Ironically, children's athletics seemed to grow in direct proportion to the criticisms leveled against them.

By 1970 the opportunities for regional and national competition in children's athletics had expanded to include virtually every sport in which competition was available at the adult level. National ownership of programs also seemed to increase the intensity of competition to the point where even the agencies who proclaimed a philosophy of "everyone plays" contradicted their mottos by supporting national tournaments in which the elimination of all teams except the eventual victor was a foregone conclusion. Children also became involved in sport at younger ages. Data from the *Joint Legislative Study on Youth Sports,* Phase II (1978) indicated a modal age of 8 for boys and girls (see Table 1) as the time when competition in a specific sport began, with many children already competing at 4 or 5 years of age.

Evidence of a changing attitude about youth sport by physicians, educators, and administrators began to emerge in the 1970s. The culmination of this conciliatory position occurred at a meeting sponsored

Table 1   Percentages Reflecting Ages When Children First Enrolled in an Organized Sport[1]

Chronological age	Boys	Cumulative total	Girls	Cumulative total
Before age 3	4	—	2	—
3	3	7	3	5
4	6	13	6	11
5	13	26	9	20
6	10	36	10	30
7	16	52	11	41
8	17	69	15	56
9	13	82	12	68
10	9	91	14	82
11	4	95	8	90
12	3	98	6	96
13	1	99	2	98
14	1	100	2	100

[1]From *Joint Legislative Study on Youth Sports: Phase II* (1978). Copyright 1978 by the Michigan State University Youth Sports Institute. Reprinted by permission.

by the National Association for Sport and Physical Education in Washington, DC (R. Merrick, personal communication, November 5, 1976) in 1977. Two documents, *Youth Sports Guide for Coaches and Parents* (Thomas, 1977) and *Guidelines for Children's Sports* (Martens & Seefeldt, 1979), summarize the content of the historic meeting between two groups: those who formerly opposed children's sport and representatives from the nonschool sport agencies. In essence, the two groups agreed to recognize that athletic competition for children had become an enduring part of our culture. The conditions under which healthful competition should occur were described in a "Bill of Rights for Young Athletes" (Martens & Seefeldt, 1979). A significant change in the attitudes that physicians and educators held about youth sport was now a matter of record. Instead of their previous disapproval of athletic competition for children, its former antagonists and protagonists now agreed to work together for more desirable conditions under which competition could take place.

Agents of Reform

Changes in youth sport primarily depend upon the degree to which the attitudes of its adult leaders can be modified. These modifications receive their impetus from the leadership available at the institutions where teachers, recreation directors, sport managers, and coaches receive their formal education. This section identifies four categories of agents who are primarily responsible for the education and experiences of individuals who control youth sport in the United States. These four categories include administrators and professors from institutions of higher learning, directors of recreation, administrators of single-sport agencies, and public school physical education teachers and coaches.

Educators and Administrators in Higher Education

The attitudes and values concerning sport competition that are supported and advanced by coaches, teachers, and recreation directors are likely to have been influenced by their former instructors. To the degree that curricula reflect the importance of subject matter, as determined by faculty in colleges and universities, one is compelled to conclude that the management of youth sport holds a relatively low priority in the minds of those who prepare professional workers in recreation, athletics, and physical education. Few courses in the curricula of students who choose these areas of concentration are devoted specifically to the problems and proposed solutions of age-group athletic competition. In situations where the topic is included in course offerings, it receives the superficial treatment reserved for unimportant content. This direct or subtle omission of information about youth sport in the undergraduate preparation of students, who will eventually be responsible for guiding the athletic activities of children, is an inexcusable form of negligence on the part of those in leadership positions.

In addition to providing current information about children's athletic competition, administrators and faculty members in higher education can influence the attention directed at youth sport by: (a) providing students with practical day-to-day experiences in planning, conducting, and evaluating sport programs, and (b) encouraging students to become involved in basic and field-based research involving young athletes. The placement of students as interns into programs that are conducted according to an acceptable philosophy, with sound operating procedures, is an irreplaceable educational experience. Placing students into situations where they can be closely supervised as they learn their profession is a model that has been used successfully for decades. There is every indication that this model would serve an equally useful purpose in the education of coaches and directors of youth sport programs.

Research pertaining to the problems in youth sport has not kept pace with the phenomenal increase of participation in such programs. However, scientists who had previously concentrated on adults are now attempting to learn more about the effects of athletic participation on youthful competitors. As the intensity and duration of training programs for children increase, we are likely to learn that children encounter problems of a physiological and psychological nature similar to those observed for decades in adult competitors. Scientists, when working in the area of childhood, face the additional problems of defining intervening variables and their influence on an immature system. Educators should apprise their students of the potential problems that exist in children's sport and, whenever possible, enlist their assistance in conducting research that seeks basic and practical solutions to these problems.

Directors of Recreational Programs

Directors of recreation are essential agents in any attempt to change youth sport because they have a direct involvement with the coaches and officials who actually conduct the practices and contests. Although sport-specific agencies with regional or national affiliations conduct many programs at the local level, the vast majority of youth sport programs exist under the auspices of the local recreation department (*Joint Legislative Study on Youth Sports: Phase I*, 1976). Programs that are controlled under a national affiliation are often dependent upon local facilities for their implementation. Therefore, the philosophy and operational procedures promoted by the local recreation directors have a possibility of pervading all youth sports, even when the programs are not initiated or maintained by the Recreation Department.

Frequently, recreation directors have been accused of acting as "activity brokers" by relinquishing their responsibility for youth sports to the first agency or service club that requests permission to sponsor the programs (Greenslit, 1981). The criticism that recreation directors are more concerned about the number who participate than the quality of their participation may be unfair, but criticism seems appropriate when recreation directors permit other agencies to conduct programs on municipal properties even when the philosophies of the two groups are incompatible.

Desirable changes in youth sport depend upon recreation directors acknowledging that athletic competition involving children is here to stay, that it has potentially beneficial and detrimental effects, and that the potential for beneficial results can be increased by strong leadership within the local recreation program. The abdication of responsibility for youth sport programs to other agencies by recreation directors will usually generate more problems than it solves.

Managers of Single-Sport Agencies

Single-sport agencies are defined here as organizations that promote and sponsor competition in a specific sport for children of designated age ranges. Examples of single-sport agencies are Little League Baseball, Pop Warner Football, Amateur Hockey Association of the United States, and the American Youth Soccer Organization. Single-sport agencies have been instrumental in elevating certain sports for children to their present level of popularity and deserve much of the credit for the uniformity of rules and playing conditions throughout the nation. However, they have also received much of the criticism for practices that some adults consider to be unacceptable for children.

Single-sport agencies receive credit for the standard rules and modifications that distinguish children's sport from the sport of their adult prototypes. They have also been responsible for developing the concept of adult volunteer leadership that permits these programs to operate at low overhead costs to local communities. Credited to single-sport agencies by their detractors is their desire to maintain complete control over programs, to impose a set of inflexible playing conditions on local programs, and to extract membership fees in exchange for providing little more than playing rules and a tournament structure. The intensity associated with interleague, regional, and national competition is also attributed to sponsors of nationally affiliated programs.

If single-sport agencies are to maintain their roles as leaders in the organization and promotion of sport for children, they must adjust more readily to suggestions for change from research workers, educators, and local coaches and administrators. The current inflexibility of rules and the lack of local control will become increasingly intolerable to adult leaders in local programs as they become more knowledgeable about the content and structure of desirable youth programs. A philosophy that places the single-sport agency in a role that facilitates the leadership of local communities in sport-program management is likely to find greater acceptability at the local level in the future.

Public School Personnel

The concessions that educators made in the last decade to the involvement of children in athletic competition (Martens & Seefeldt, 1979) were based on the assumption that great changes would occur in what was regarded as current operating procedure in organized sport programs. Implicit in these changes was the important role that physical education teachers, coaches, and public school administrators would have in bringing about the cooperation between personnel in the public school and the youth agencies. The two groups must continue to negotiate such differences as overlap in seasons, eligibility of participants, frequency and intensity of competition, age when competition should begin, and the emphasis to be placed on the athlete's skill acquisition versus winning as the primary criterion for success. There are indications that some resolution to these problems has occurred, but changes have been slower than anticipated.

Much of the control over athletic facilities and the expertise for teaching and managing sport programs currently lies with the coaches and administrators of the public schools. Consequently, it appears that they are also in a position to make the greatest contribution to the youth sport movement. The "Bill of Rights for Young Athletes" argues distinctly that such contribution is possible without compromising the principles upon which physical education, interscholastic athletics, and youth sport programs are based. Agency-sponsored youth sport programs can no longer be viewed as an undesirable substitute for physical education programs or as farm systems for the athletic program. If the emphasis in youth sport programs is on maximum participation and skill acquisition for all individuals, there is no need to fear that overexposure and exploitation will occur in agency-sponsored sport or that children's participation in them will be detrimental to their welfare.

Projections for the Future of Youth Sport

Predictions may reflect both optimism and pessimism. The following projections for changes in youth sport are overwhelmingly optimistic. This does not imply, however, that youth sport is in a position where any change would be an improvement. The optimism is generated by the emerging information from the scientific community and the widespread desire of individuals currently involved in youth sport to provide the best experiences for children. These predictions resulted from speculation about the influence on youth sport by variables such as population migration, energy costs, structure of the family, attitudes toward persons with handicapping conditions, and childbearing practices of the various racial and ethnic groups. The following variables will be instrumental in determining the direction of youth sport programs in the next decade.

Scientific Inquiry

The influence of science on youth sport eclipses the importance of any other variable because of our depressed status of knowledge concerning the development of children involved in intensive physical activity. Currently, our training programs for children are modeled after those of adults, but without the associated experimental evidence to support them. Our knowledge about adults in stressful situations is relatively sophisticated because of the research that has been conducted during the past 2 decades. However, the influence of competitive stress on children has just begun to be the focus of scientific inquiry (see Boileau, 1984; Gould, 1984; Passer, this volume; Smith, 1983; Smoll & Smith, this volume). Consequently, the changes that have been made in children's sport programs are those that have been suggested on the basis of experience. Additional changes await the research evidence from a multidisciplinary scientific community.

Two issues are paramount in athletic competition for children: (a) the influence of physical stress on biological structure and function and (b) the psychological consequences and benefits of highly competitive situations. Many questions have been raised: How much physical and psychological stress is essential for optimum development and at what point does it become excessive? At what age should athletic competition begin? At what ages and in what sports can boys and girls compete on an equal basis on the same teams? What are the immediate and latent consequences of specific physically and emotionally stressful activities? Answers to such questions are just beginning to appear in the scientific literature. Leaders in youth sport must communicate their concerns to the scientific community, who must then conduct the kinds of research that will lead to solutions that can be incorporated into defensible practices.

Formal Education and Certification of Volunteer Coaches

The availability of new information about children in sport will be interpreted and passed on to volunteer coaches at a more rapid rate. Establishment of numerous organizations that have as their purpose the education of volunteer coaches (Vogel, 1982) will expedite the flow of materials in a form that hitherto has been inaccessible to them. As managers of sport programs become aware of the information available to coaches, they will provide inducements for their coaches to become involved in programs that lead to certification. Minimum knowledge and competency in various subject matter areas will be identified. Credits or equivalent competencies acquired by volunteer coaches will be transferrable across state and regional boundaries, similar to the transfer of certification in the Red Cross Lifesaving Program.

Local Ownership of Programs

As local managers become more knowledgeable about conducting sport programs for children, they will rely more on their own abilities to make sound decisions and depend less upon regionally or nationally based agencies for guidance. To compete with locally controlled programs, nationally based agencies will have to restore a greater share of the funds that they currently extract from communities through increased services for coaches and administrators. Providing educational programs for coaches, conducting research, and furnishing inducements such as insurance, certification, and newsletters are examples of ways a portion of the membership fees could be returned to communities. Greater representation in decisions that affect local programs and increased flexibility of rules to ensure greater participation are additional concessions that nationally affiliated programs will have to make.

Greater Reliance on Municipal Sport Programs

Reduction of federal and state revenues to finance public school operations will influence the number of sport programs available to elementary, middle school, and high school students. When sport programs are eliminated in the public schools, the burden of providing comparable opportunities is usually shifted to community recreation departments and service-oriented agencies. Of these two groups, the service-oriented agencies will be in the most advantageous position to provide temporary relief for curtailed school athletic programs because their present operating procedure already includes fund-raising and fees as means of acquiring revenue. Unless municipal recreation directors procure funds from extramural sources, they, too, will face many of the same budgetary problems as the public schools.

Municipal recreation programs will not only receive more frequent demands for competitive programs from displaced public school athletes, but their adult clients will demand more time and space as well. Parents are having fewer children and having them at a later age, thus freeing adults for their own recreational pursuits. The provisions of athletic programs for women in high schools and colleges will result in greater numbers who seek single-gender athletic experiences beyond their formal education. The demands for coeducational sport programs are also likely to increase as more women become involved in physical activities. Increased longevity has resulted in an additional generation of older, healthier adults competing for the facilities and personnel of local recreation departments.

Increased Role for Volunteers

The financial constraints and the increased demand for services that will cause municipal recreation departments to seek even more volunteer assistance for professional staff members will bring a series of problems, foremost of which will be the need for programs to educate the volunteers. Sport programs that depend on volunteers, whether locally controlled or offered by national sports governing bodies, will gradually demand certain levels of competence from their coaches and officials. The threat of lawsuits resulting from injuries, both physical and psychological, will force sponsoring agencies to require certain levels of competence that can most easily be assessed or certified through a formal instructional program.

Coaching as a Male-Dominated Profession

A unique problem arises when youth sport programs are conducted by volunteers. Today many children are being raised in single-parent homes, most frequently by the mother (Masnick & Bane, 1980). However, with the exception of gymnastics, swimming, and figure skating, most of the youth sport coaches are males (see Table 2, *Joint Legislative Study on Youth Sports: Phase III*, 1978).

The lack of females as youth sport coaches may be associated with the lower participation rates and higher attrition rates of girls, but extenuating circumstances most likely account for the disparity. Convincing a single-parent female, who also works full time, that she should devote several evenings a week, plus weekends, to attend coaching workshops and to coach her child's athletic team may challenge the persuasive powers of any recreation director. The later age of child-bearing also reduces the number of years a parent may be willing to assist as a volunteer coach, official, or administrator in a youth sport program.

Changes in Activity Patterns

The trend for adults to engage in activities that offer personal autonomy and less regimentation will also be evident in children's sport. Due to

Table 2   Who Coaches Michigan's Children in Non-School Sports?[1]

Sport	% of male coaches	% of female coaches
Baseball	96	4
Softball	42	48
Basketball	72	28
Tackle football	100	0
Flag football	100	0
Gymnastics	33	67
Ice hockey	99	1
Figure skating	22	78
Soccer	93	7
Tennis	74	26
Track/field	94	6
Wrestling	98	2

[1]From *Joint Legislative Study on Youth Sports: Phase III* (1978). Copyright 1978 by the Michigan State University Youth Sports Institute. Reprinted by permission.

a prevailing philosophy that emphasizes personal needs, the shift to local ownership and control by recreation departments will bring a greater emphasis on personal growth and participation, with less emphasis on the philosophy to win at all costs. Goals of sport programs will be readjusted to incorporate the qualities of social development, fun, skill acquisition, and personal fitness that have historically been a part of children's motivation for participation but have not always been evident in the conditions imposed on them by adults.

Sports that permit the attainment of personal goals and individual styles of play will become more popular, while those that require a high degree of regimentation will decrease in popularity. Racial and ethnic preferences will also determine the popularity of certain sports. An increasing proportion of black and Hispanic children and a decreasing proportion of white children suggests that sports that are part of the culture of minority groups, such as soccer, softball, and basketball, will have an increase in the proportion of child participants, while football, ice hockey, wrestling, and swimming will decrease in popularity. Due to a temporary decrease in the number of children eligible for memberships, the absolute number of youth sport competitors will stabilize through the remainder of this decade before increasing during the 1990s, when an increase in school-aged children is anticipated. Marten's (1986) projection of youth sport participation from 1977 to 1984 is shown in Table 3.

Integration of Mentally and Physically Handicapped Children

Despite the mandates of PL 94-142, Education for All Handicapped Children Act, and PL 93-112, Section 504 of the Rehabilitation Act, there is little evidence that attempts to incorporate handicapped persons into youth sport programs have been successful. Recent inquiries to representatives of six nationally affiliated sports governing bodies confirmed that all of these organizations welcome handicapped persons into their competitive programs. However, only one of the programs had special provisions in its rules to accommodate such individuals, and only one provided incentives and encouragement for the enrollment of special populations.

The positive attitude of program leaders from national sports governing bodies indicates that the merger of sport programs for handicapped and able-bodied individuals is possible, but progress in this area will be slow. Modification of rules involving equipment, playing conditions, eligibility, and skill requirements must occur prior to such a merger. Although the long-standing image that sport is reserved for the able-bodied will be difficult to overcome, the remainder of the 20th century will result in a gradual blending of available facilities and programs to accommodate more handicapped children and youths.

Table 3 Estimated Participation Patterns in Non-School Sports (1977-1984), for Children Aged 6-18 Years (in Millions)[1]

Sport	Boys 1977	Boys 1984	Girls 1977	Girls 1984	Combined 1977	Combined 1984	Percent gain-loss boys	Percent gain-loss girls
Baseball	4.20	3.91	0.79	0.62	4.99	4.53	-7	-12
Softball	1.97	2.10	2.41	2.62	4.38	4.72	+6	+9
Swimming	1.71	1.85	1.91	2.08	3.62	3.93	+8	+9
Bowling	2.07	2.07	1.51	1.50	3.58	3.57	0	-1
Basketball	2.13	2.13	1.22	1.22	3.35	3.35	0	0
Football (tackle)	1.56	1.16	0.29	0.10	1.85	1.26	-26	-66
Tennis	0.88	1.35	0.95	1.24	1.83	2.59	+53	+30
Gymnastics	0.59	0.75	1.17	1.50	1.76	2.25	+27	+28
Football (flag)	1.11	1.20	0.36	0.45	1.47	1.65	+8	+25
Track & field	0.76	1.00	0.54	0.75	1.30	1.75	+32	+39
Soccer	0.72	2.20	0.52	1.70	1.24	3.90	+305	+327
Wrestling	—	0.25	—	0.00	—	0.25	—	—
Other	1.24	1.00	0.79	0.80	2.03	1.80	-19	+1
Totals	18.94	20.97	12.46	14.58	30.41	35.55		
Percent by sex	62%	59%	38%	41%				

[1]From "Youth Sport in the USA" by R. Martens. In Sport for Children and Youths (p. 28) by M.R. Weiss and D. Gould (Eds.), 1986, Champaign, IL: Human Kinetics. Copyright 1986 by Human Kinetics. Adapted by permission.

Summary

Youth sport programs are at a place in their natural history where change is imminent. Plagued by controversies brought on by rapid growth and lack of a firm knowledge base, proponents of youth sport have frequently been defensive in their reactions to criticism rather than proactive in seeking solutions to problems. Four categories of adult leaders have been identified as the primary agents of change in youth sport. Variables likely to influence the impending changes are (a) the availability of scientific information about the effects of stressful competition on children and (b) the proliferation of educational programs for volunteer coaches. Additional changes will include a greater emphasis on athletic programs offered by recreation departments, a greater dependence upon volunteer workers to conduct the programs, and the integration of individuals with handicapping conditions into programs that have previously been reserved for able-bodied competitors.

References

Albinson, J., & Andrew, G. (Eds.). (1976). *Child in sport and physical activity.* Baltimore: University Park Press.

Berryman, J.W. (1988). The rise of highly organized sports for preadolescent boys. In F.L. Smoll, R.A. Magill, & M.J. Ash (Eds.), *Children in sport* (3rd ed., pp. 3-16). Champaign, IL: Human Kinetics.

Boileau, R. (1984). *Advances in pediatric sport science.* Champaign, IL: Human Kinetics.

Gould, D. (1984). Psychological development in children's sport. In J. Thomas (Ed.), *Motor development during childhood and adolescence* (pp. 212-236). Minneapolis: Burgess.

Greenslit, J. (1981, April). *Youth sports programs: Whose responsibility?* Paper presented at the Second Annual Youth Sports Forum, East Lansing, MI.

Haubenstricker, J. (1976). Stress hazards of competitive athletics. *Osteopathic Annals,* **5**, 16-31.

Joint legislative study on youth sports: Phase I. (1976). East Lansing: Michigan State University Institute for the Study of Youth Sports.

Joint legislative study on youth sports: Phase II. (1978). East Lansing: Michigan State University Institute for the Study of Youth Sports.

Joint legislative study on youth sports: Phase III. (1978). East Lansing: Michigan State University Institute for the Study of Youth Sports.

Martens, R. (1986). Youth sport in the USA. In M.R. Weiss & D. Gould (Eds.), *Sport for children and youths* (pp. 27-34). Champaign, IL Human Kinetics.

Martens, R., & Seefeldt, V. (1979). *Guidelines for children's sports.* Reston, VA: American Alliance for Health, Physical Education, Recreation and Dance.

Masnick, G., & Bane, M. (1980). *The nation's families: 1960-1990.* Cambridge, MA: MIT-Harvard Joint Center for Urban Studies.

Micheli, L. (1984). *Pediatric and adolescent sports medicine.* Boston: Little, Brown.

Passer, M.W. (1988). Determinants and consequences of children's competitive stress. In F.L. Smoll, R.A. Magill, & M.J. Ash (Eds.), *Children in sport* (3rd ed., pp. 203-227). Champaign, IL: Human Kinetics.

Rarick, G.L. (1973). Competitive sports in early childhood and early adolescence. In G.L. Rarick (Ed.), *Physical activity: Human growth and development* (pp. 364-386). New York: Academic Press.

Seefeldt, V., & Gould, D. (1980). *Physical and psychological effects of athletic competition on children and youth.* Washington, DC: ERIC Clearinghouse on Teacher Education.

Shephard, R. (1982). *Physical activity and growth.* Chicago: Yearbook Medical Publishers.

Smith, N. (Ed.). (1979). *Sports medicine for children and youth.* Columbus, OH: Ross Laboratories.

Smith, N. (Ed.). (1983). *Sports medicine: Health care for young athletes.* Evanston, IL: American Academy of Pediatrics.

Smoll, F.L., & Smith, R.E. (Eds.). (1978). *Psychological perspectives in youth sports.* Washington, DC: Hemisphere.

Smoll, F.L., & Smith, R.E. (1988). Reducing stress in youth sport: Theory and application. In F.L. Smoll, R.A. Magill, & M.J. Ash (Eds.), *Children in sport* (3rd ed., pp. 229-249). Champaign, IL: Human Kinetics.

Thomas, J.R. (Ed.). (1977). *Youth sports guide for coaches and parents.* Washington, DC: American Alliance for Health, Physical Education, Recreation and Dance.

Vogel, P. (1982). Evaluation of current national youth sports coaching programs. In R. Cox (Ed.), *Educating youth sport coaches: Solutions to a national dilemma* (pp. 97-119). Reston, VA: American Alliance for Health, Physical Education, Recreation and Dance.

Weiss, M.R., & Gould, D. (Eds.). (1986). *Sport for children and youths.* Champaign, IL: Human Kinetics.